ROCK'N'ROLL BABYLON

Gary Herman

Plexus, London

Text copyright © 1982, 1994, by Gary Herman;
copyright © 2002 by Plexus Publishing Limited
Published by Plexus Publishing Limited
55a Clapham Common Southside
London, SW4 9BX
www.plexusbooks.com

British Library Cataloguing-in-Publication Data

Herman, Gary, 1948-
    Rock 'n' roll Babylon. - 3rd ed.
    1.Rock musicians - History 2.Rock musicians - Biography
    I.Title
    782.4'2'166'0922

ISBN 0 85965 318 8

Printed in Spain

Cover design by Phil Gambrill

CONTENTS

To absent friends

'We are all in the gutter, but some of us are
looking at the stars.' *Oscar Wilde*

'If you're looking for trouble, you've come to the
right place.' *Elvis Presley*

PREFACE

I should make it clear from the outset that I love rock'n'roll. It has, at various times in my life, thrilled me, consoled me, saddened me and gladdened me. It has always, and in both senses, moved me. And, like most of the children of my generation, rock'n'roll stars have seemed to me friends, idols and infiltrators in the camp of an enemy dedicated to the ruthless pursuit of wealth, the promotion of a hypocritical morality and the suppression of youthful energies.

It is difficult to see these stars as traitors – harder still to understand that they may have become the enemy. Yet the rock business is a hard-nosed commercial world, with time for idealism and radical visions only if they sell. The stars – our stars? – can't escape it. They are prey to all the vices that a society obsessed with money and power has cultivated for centuries. Maybe they've been the enemy all along.

That doesn't diminish the music, but it does make rock stars fascinating case studies in the effects of success and failure. This is the subject of this book -- the perennially absorbing topic of how the rich and famous occupy their time, translated to a context in which wealth and fame have never been simply seen as unequivocally desirable goals for individuals to pursue.

The book is a product of the post-punk age, for it was the punks who – however naïvely or disingenuously – most precisely focused attention on the lumbering and indifferent dinosaur that rock had become. Babylon, it should be remembered, was the capital of a vast and profligate empire. In the rock world, its citizens may start from humble beginnings, but soon they are ushered into lush hanging gardens where there are no dreams of democracy or change, only dreams of power, wealth and the perfect tan. Rod Stewart's former manager once described the singer as 'a growth industry'. Mick Jagger talked about going into politics but not having 'the right wife'. Gregg Allman hobnobbed with Jimmy Carter and earned with Cher the coveted title of 'the Richard Burton and Elizabeth Taylor of rock'n'roll'. And the Beach Boys played at Ronald Reagan's presidential inauguration.

These are among the survivors. But one way or another the rock world eats its own young. Perhaps life would be better if it didn't or if we could, at least, believe that it didn't. Then again, perhaps the music would be less exciting, the art less moving, if it was rendered safe or its audience simple-minded. I don't know, but for those who care to speculate, I wrote this book.

A great deal has happened since it was first written, and it seemed appropriate to update it – but while much has happened, little may have changed. The bizarre world of rock'n'roll retains just as strong a hold over the imagination now as it ever did – and new generations of fans seem just as fascinated by the heroines and heroes of their parents' time as they are by the performers of today. It would appear that the music itself is the source of this fascination, while the stories of degradation, depravity and occasional redemption that litter the biographies of performers are of interest only to the degree that they touch the music, help to illuminate it, or enhance its enjoyment. Ironically, the surprising longevity of much of the rock'n'roll repertoire should undermine any arrogance or tendency to hubris felt by rock performers – the lesson, should it need repeating, is simple: it's what's in the groove that counts.

Gary Herman

THE PROMISED LAND

It was a warm and wet June weekend in 1967. The place was Monterey in northern California. The occasion – the rock culture's first international festival, a musical celebration of the youthful optimism embodied in rock'n'roll. By subsequent standards, the Monterey Pop Festival was a smallish and fairly sedate affair. Although the total attendance was estimated at between 30,000 and 100,000 people, only about 8,000 were allowed into the seated arena at any one time during the five concerts that made up the two and a half day event. Many of the performers were locally based and quite a few were all but unknown.

Despite the same lack of adequate facilities that was to plague future festivals, plentiful and often free supplies of grass, LSD and other hallucinogens, a visible police presence and an entrance fee to the arena of between $3.00 and $6.50, there were no riots, no appeals to stoned insurrection and few hassles. Good vibes were the order of the day – so much so that, by the time the second concert began on Saturday morning, one third of the police present had been sent home. A banner across the stage read 'Music, Love and Flowers' – a slogan which seemed, at the time, both reasonable and radical. Later it would look merely naïve.

The Monterey festival encapsulated all that is good and bad about the phenomenon of rock music. On the one hand, it embraced the dreams and aspirations of the 'class of '67'; on the other hand, it was planned on strict commercial principles. As so often before and since, the performers were floundering in the middle; torn between their sympathy with the hopes of their fans and their desire to fulfil them, and their own sometimes shamefaced eagerness for adulation and the undoubted attractions which only money can buy. Monterey was the microcosm of rock'n'roll Babylon: a signpost to the promised land which was really an open prison.

San Francisco, Monterey's nearest big city, was exploding with new ideas about how to live. The fragrance of liberation hung in the air, like an ether haze waiting to be ignited by the sparks that flew when radical student politics met the uncomplicated hedonism of rock'n'roll. The Beatles' *Sergeant Pepper* album had been released a few weeks before the festival into a world pregnant with possibilities. The Free Speech Movement based on the University of California's Berkeley campus was throwing down challenges to adult authoritarianism. The streets were alive with the look, smell, sound, taste and feel of 'mind-expanding'

drugs, new music, experimental arts and sexual adventures and, through 1966 and early 1967, the astronauts of inner space had danced to the music of pied piper bands like Jefferson Airplane, the Grateful Dead and Country Joe and the Fish at festivals and 'be-ins' all round the Bay.

These happenings had promised much. They had been free and fun. Performers mingled with audiences; politicos and weirdos rubbed comradely shoulders (and – why not? – other parts of their bodies); everybody turned on together. Rock'n'roll had always seemed more important than its detractors could give it credit for, except negatively by condemning it. Youth was beginning to show the sour establishment just how important it was, in social, even world terms, not just as entertainment. White and black, woman and man, gay and straight, worker and student, even (to a lesser extent) young and old were all washing their newly radicalized souls in the revitalizing flood of music. People everywhere seemed to be talking about the 'Summer of Love'. It looked like a tidal wave was truly about to sweep away the old order – and Monterey, it was hoped, would be its frothy, bubbling crest.

Monterey had been planned to feature a wider range and a greater quantity of music than ever before – almost the whole spectrum of pop from supper-club soul to body-shaking boogie, taking in folk, folk-rock, acid-rock, electric blues and even the classical Indian ragas of sitar-playing Ravi Shankar. However it is more significant, though less recognizable at the time, to realize that Monterey had been specifically planned as a media event. The Beatles' former publicist, Derek Taylor, had been hired almost at the outset. Any journalist who asked (and many who did not) got free tickets – some 1,200 in all. The concerts were to be recorded and ABC TV was sold the film and TV rights for some $300,000. People would certainly hear about Monterey, even if only from the pages of a magazine. TV, radio, cinema and record – every angle was covered. Massive publicity would announce to the world at large that Monterey was ushering in the long-awaited Age of Freedom, heralded back in the fifties when Elvis Presley first put on his blue suede shoes.

For a dozen years or more, rock'n'roll had travelled its fitful journey, offering moments of exultation in a joyless world trapped in its cycles of paranoid politics and economic fatalism. Elvis had been a revelation of youthful energy and sexual power. The Beatles were

7

an inspiration, Bob Dylan an education. They and their followers brought pleasure and purpose to a dry and dying world. Parents, the authorities, the establishment did not like it. They tried to put it down, stop the kids from listening, keep them away from parties and dances and 'dangerous' films. But the stars were in the sky for everyone to see. They played the music of resistance. If adult society threatened the world with nuclear weapons of mass destruction, youth had a weapon of mass liberation in rock'n'roll. The young could retaliate – and someday perhaps they could win. If any day looked a likely candidate for the start of the victorious final campaign, it was the first day of the Monterey Festival.

Things were never that simple, of course. The growth of a mass market for a kind of rock'n'roll that was seen as artistically important and socially valid meant that *big* business took over and performers found themselves removed from the crucial close contact with audiences. Finding themselves in a sort of creative vacuum they inevitably fell back on the company of other performers, the rich and the famous. Their friends became the friends of stars, their pastimes the pastimes of stars. Their lives were lived in the glare of spotlights, the confinement of backstage dressing-rooms and the luxury of limousines and expensive hotel rooms. Their fans might have seen them as leaders, but then – as now – it was a hollow sort of leadership. Open to the temptations of fame, wealth, and a life-style of unprecedented hedonism, rock stars have always been liable to turn into monsters – caricatures of their former golden youth, leftovers after rock'n'roll's banquet has passed them by, happy to sink into easy dissipation or simply unable to carry the weight of a generation's dreams.

Years after Monterey, it is easy to see its two opposing aspects. At the time few people recognized the dark face of rock'n'roll lurking around the stage area, roped and cordoned off from the audience. This was the Machiavellian face of hustling and profiteering, the bloated face of grotesque excesses and gross indulgence, the haggard face of failure and recrimination.

Maybe it was because of the sunshine and the amazing light shows that it could not be seen at the time. Or maybe it was the dope, or the raw, energetic sound of rock, inhabiting the narrow margin between chaos and order. The people on stage played the songs of social revolution and personal liberation. They were taking risks with their music as they were with their lives, but they were risks the audience understood and shared. Challenge was in the air. 'This is the love crowd, right?' asked Otis Redding from the stage, and the answer came, 'Yeah!' How could manipulation ever become a dirty word?

As one of the few black performers at the festival, Otis seemed to cement a greater unity than anybody else at Monterey. His performance brought Rolling Stone Brian Jones to the verge of tears, and had one Los Angeles record executive on his feet shouting, 'Heavy!' But it was hard to say if that unity had any

8

substance. Other black performers invited to Monterey were probably accurate in describing it as 'Whitey's festival', and it's worth noting that the 'Summer of Love' also experienced the worst black riots in contemporary American history.

All the same, rock stars never seemed so close to their audience as at Monterey. To bridge the gap between star and fan is one of rock'n'roll's most cherished dreams. The ligger, the lookalike, the groupie and the hanger-on all pursue that dream. So, frequently, do rock journalists (often accused of being musicians *manqués*). Even the rock'n'roll business establishment is fleshed out with fans who have found a respectable niche for their obsession. Finally, rock stars themselves do not escape the obsession. Few, if any, become rock'n'rollers for the uncomplicated love of money. Most start as fans, attracted by rock'n'roll's other magic ingredients: glamour, adulation, fame or the sheer joy of music-making. Many remain fans, idolizing greater or earlier talents than themselves. Some are even obsessed with their own star-images and forever try to blot out the ordinariness of their off-stage, off-record characters or to reproduce and sustain the sense of a performance's power and magical spontaneity through drugs, drink, frequent and fleeting sexual encounters or the cultivation of manic and egotistical behaviour. The rock'n'roll fan and the rock'n'roll star hold up mirrors to each other's world. Each can recognize themselves or friends or lovers in the mirror but neither can cross through the looking-glass.

Occasionally, the music succeeds in bringing star and fan close. Those are the moments when great rock'n'roll is created. They are moments when star and fan face each other across a narrow divide in their common interest – moments of self-immersion in the great Leviathan of rock'n'roll. Each such moment is a kind of suicide – sometimes bizarrely re-run in actual acts of self-destruction or in that curious conspiracy of need which makes stars the easy targets of angry or disappointed fans and which brought John Lennon face-to-face with his murderer: worshipper and idol finally united in the act of mutual self-destruction.

There is no doubt that Monterey witnessed some great rock'n'roll that summer of '67. Janis Joplin sang her heart out, stomping the stage with her feet as though kicking at a coffin lid. The Who, cuban-heeled English dandies at their most petulant, ended their set with a mind-boggling assault on the senses – a crescendo of feedback, a crazed attack on drums and speaker cabinets, a barrage of smoke-bombs. Pete Townshend rammed the neck of his guitar into a speaker-grille, rasped the fretboard with his microphone stand and hammered the instrument viciously on the stage until the neck snapped and splintered. A pall of smoke hung over the group as Keith Moon smashed into his drums. In a final gesture of gratuitous violence, he kicked the lot over and the group walked off. Jimi Hendrix, half black American and half Red Indian, 'fucked' his guitar, stroked it as though it was his own

member and, finally, set light to it – all the while squeezing pure rock'n'roll from it. And there was Otis Redding, his voice pleading and demanding in the same moment, expressing all the pain and anger of black America in a single song. 'We all love each other, right? Let me hear you say "Yeah"!'

'Yeah.'

But if the Festival was a celebration of the coming-of-age of rock'n'roll's guiltless trip through the wonderland of fun, it was also a prime-time star vehicle, as calculated a piece of exploitation as we are ever likely to see. Monterey was a showcase for new talent, a cattle-market with musicians as the beef. For the record executives in the audience (and there were plenty), considerations of profit far outweighed feelings of love – or, rather, they were the same thing. CBS's Clive Davis later recalled seeing Janis Joplin for the first time. 'I had to go after her,' he said. The festival was quickly followed by a spate of record deals, profitable releases and successful tours, and the chief beneficiary of all the good vibes was the music industry.

Don't get it wrong. Right from the start, rock'n'roll has been a heady mix of commerce and creativity. Rock'n'roll is a twentieth-century phenomenon – a modern folk music serving a community of young people with only their youth and their access to the mass media to tie them together. Without the media rock'n'roll music could not exist – and to be involved in the media so far is to be involved in commerce.

The rock'n'roll star system – designed to keep one name in the public eye and ear, to encourage identification and to promote record and concert-ticket sales – is commerce with a vengeance. The music becomes a commodity, the star little more than a super-salesperson. Even life-styles are sold – blue-jeans, punk chic, long hair, short hair, booze, guitar-strings – promoted through posters, the rock and pop press, TV, the cinema and radio. The star becomes a merchandizing trade-mark, the key to a vast revenue above and beyond that provided by the music alone. Stars are valuable items to be manipulated and yet cossetted. Their whims must be catered to – be they eggs benedict with brown sauce; a champagne supper in every dressing-room; an endless stream of groupies, heroin, cocaine, or all three; chauffeur-driven limousines; parties resembling bacchanalian orgies; or just an ever-present bottle of beer sitting on an amplifier at each gig. Stars must be protected from the press and over-zealous fans, they must be sheltered from the problems of everyday life – for as long, that is, as they keep packing houses, selling records and shifting merchandize. On this side of the rock'n'roll balance sheet, every star has a cash value which can be haggled over in courts of law and revalued in stock markets. Even being close to a star is worth money to the scandal-hungry popular press. The multi-billion dollar music industry happily dispenses with the reality which underpins star images and, in the end, the cash value is sometimes all that is left to mark the passing of a rock'n'roller. Time and again it has been demonstrated that stars like Buddy Holly, Otis Redding, Jim Morrison, Jimi Hendrix and Elvis Presley can be worth more dead than alive.

Inevitably, a life as carefully priced and as lovingly tended as a rock star's can seem a little distorted at times. For the stars themselves there is a further twist. Rock'n'roll feeds off risk. It is a music that takes chances with everything mundane and predictable. When stardom reaches the mundane and predictable heights of heaven and creative risks are no longer an option under your contract, it is all too easy to play with the self-destructive excitement of drugs or drink or fast cars or guns. The isolation of super-stardom, surrounded by a wall of paid protectors and cash-on-the-nail admirers, can be a powerful invitation to paranoia. And if extreme success seems like a recipe for disaster, think what unexpected decline could make with the same ingredients.

So, as a piece of rock'n'roll exploitation, Monterey was nothing peculiar. Most would-be stars are, in any case, quite willingly exploited in the first place. But from Presley to the Pistols, the lesson has been the same: willing as you may be, exploitation can seriously damage your health. If there is no rock life after forty, the business must take at least as much blame as the rock star's own relentless drive for pleasure. For most people, the pursuit of happiness is a leisurely jog through life with an occasional sprint (if they are allowed to enter the race at all). For rock stars, it has become a sort of Indianapolis 500 on a track fenced and policed by the business. There is no way off except along the track itself. Hardly surprising that the casualty rate sometimes seems staggering. If you do it in the road, you must expect to get run over.

What was unusual about Monterey was just how eager people were to ignore the obvious signs of exploitation and then just how quickly and completely their innocent beliefs were shattered. Monterey was a kind of self-delusion, a con-trick with willing victims, carried out by people who seemed to believe the lies they told.

The Festival was originally conceived by a Los Angeles booking-agent called Ben Shapiro and a promoter from the same city named Alan Pariser. These two originally planned a simple, profit-making venture utilizing the undeniable talents of Derek Taylor to gain maximum media exposure. They went to see John Phillips, leader of the very successful Mamas and the Papas and author of the Summer of Love's big international hit – a timeless ditty which went 'If you're going to San Francisco, be sure to wear some flowers in your hair'. Phillips (and Paul Simon, who was present at the meeting) agreed to perform only if the Festival was organized on a non-profit making basis. Derek Taylor favoured this proposition and Shapiro and Pariser followed suit. Phillips brought in his manager and producer, Lou Adler, and a 'board of governors' was put together including such musical luminaries as Mick Jagger, Paul McCartney, Brian Wilson and Smokey Robinson.

Shapiro and Adler fell out – Shapiro suspecting Adler of 'a lust for contracts and prestige' (in critic Robert Christgau's words). Shapiro was eased out and

11

a press statement appeared in the American entertainment trade paper, *Variety*, to the effect that Shapiro's ideas were 'not compatible with the original festival concept' but that he had left 'amicably to press on with many movie commitments'.

The calculated hustling began. Derek Taylor announced that the Festival's profits would be donated to San Francisco's hippy relief agency, the Diggers, who gave aid and assistance to the hundreds of young people who daily arrived in the city without food, work or money. It was a piece of office gossip that Taylor presented as fact. The Monterey town council believed it and began to have visions of thousands of starving hippies arriving on their doorsteps with nowhere to stay, incited by drugs and music to 'lewd and violent behaviour'. The Festival organizers hurriedly assured the council that 'the profits will not go to a hippy organization', and that 'we have omitted acts that draw the real young kids, and our publicity has solicited family groups'. 'We haven't invited the sort of groups that inspire acting up on the part of the audience,' said Phillips. 'If that happens, we'll pull them off the stage.' The city fathers were appeased.

The Diggers and a number of groups however were not. Bands had been asked to play for expenses only, but an initial investment of $50,000 had been well covered by ABC TV's $300,000 rights payment. With an expected attendance far in excess of the arena's capacity of 7,500 seats, Adler was planning to charge one dollar admission to the Festival site's unseated surroundings. The Grateful Dead's manager and several other music people from San Francisco planned to counter with a completely free 'anti-festival'. Groups dropped out for various reasons – the Beach Boys could not see themselves in this 'hippy community'; the Young Rascals subsequently talked of Monterey as representing 'a clique among music people'. Everybody wanted to know where the money would go and what, exactly, the Festival was all about. Only the organizers knew for sure – which is why they invited the press and record company executives in such great numbers.

Not surprisingly, the Mamas and Papas topped the bill. Another of Adler's acts, Johnny Rivers, was also featured. Adler himself, who had previously sold his Dunhill record label for nearly $3 million to ABC (who had also bought the Monterey film rights), landed a distribution deal after the Festival for his new label, Ode, with CBS. As Adler later recalled, Clive Davis – soon to be head of CBS Records – 'had gone to the . . . Festival where he saw something happening, and he knew that I had put it on'. Deal followed deal and San Francisco was soon rocketed into the big time under the careful guidance of the LA record industry establishment. Most of the direct profits from Monterey (some $200,000) were donated to a variety of charities, chosen by the festival's directors. These included the Sam Cooke Memorial Scholarship established by Atlantic Records' Jerry Wexler, the Monterey Symphony Orchestra, a fund to buy guitars for Harlem's black kids and the LA Free Medical Clinic. But the fate of the money itself was less important than Monterey's promotional worth.

Months after the Mamas and Papas had closed the show, 'a bad taste remains', wrote critic Michael Lydon some time later. Especially bitter was the fate of many of the stars who had first shone so brightly at Monterey. By the onset of the seventies, Janis Joplin was dead, officially though somewhat mysteriously, from an overdose of heroin probably compounded by an alcohol habit of staggering proportions. Jimi Hendrix was dead, too, having apparently choked on his own vomit after taking an excessive number of sleeping pills. Otis Redding had been killed in a plane crash. Canned Heat's Al Wilson had died from a drug overdose, effectively putting to an end a group career that had blossomed after Monterey. Brian Jones had died from drowning.

There have been further tragedies, great and small. Mama Cass Elliott met an untimely death, as did the Grateful Dead's Ron 'Pigpen' McKernan and the Who's Keith Moon. The list is still growing. There have been drug busts, bouts of alcoholism, bizarre reformations, absurd obsessions. Rock has flirted with the occult, with mysticism, with straight-forward religions, with curious science fiction fantasies, with politics. Veins were awash with heroin, cocaine, methedrine, quaaludes (mandrax); Jack Daniels, Remy Martin, neat vodka; uppers, downers and in-betweeners; anything, it seemed, to unlock the walls of the prison. They had thought the promised land was outside the walls, but they were still – are still – captives in Babylon. For many the only possible gesture of rebellion left after all the groupies had gone home, after all the permutations had been tried twice, after all the damage done in all the wild hotel parties had been paid for, after they had consumed so much alcohol they could consume no more, after the strongest drugs had worn off, after the weirdest visions had all faded . . . was self-destruction, final and complete.

Many stars made legends at Monterey have survived, of course, to live in some sort of elegant ease – but there are no longer any risks involved for them, no sense of urgency, nothing of what once made their music so important. They become preening peacocks, sucking up to the social register, or filled with a dull religiosity that denies the sense of sin that once liberated them, or retired major-generals endlessly refighting the old youth culture campaigns in their heads. Even then, they may meet their nemesis as John Lennon met Mark Chapman – a fan filled with the knowledge of betrayal but desperate to identify, crucifier and crucified. It is of course unfair, but there is no such thing as safe retirement for a rock'n'roll star. The rock star's tragedy is that he or she is forced to live a disorienting series of magic moments, draining every last drop from short-lived success, inhabiting a timeless world in which a list of venues takes the place of a calendar, one darkened studio or concert hall is much like another and Saturday night is a working day.

CRASH LANDING IN TEENAGE HEAVEN

Rock'n'roll is an itinerant phenomenon. It leaps fences and challenges boundaries. In the frightened fifties, when the world seemed to have frozen into the power blocs of a cold war, such casual disregard as rock'n'roll showed for the barriers and conventions of race, geography, sex and age was terrifying to both the masters and slaves of the established order. Fifties rock'n'roll – with its rebel images, its heady mixture of sentimentality and angst and its disobedience to the rules of melody and rhythm and decent performance – helped create a sense of community between the disparate groups of teenagers who discovered in the music the symbols of their darkest dreams. No wonder rock'n'roll was condemned as 'lewd' and 'lascivious' by the self-appointed guardians of morality.

Of course, in many ways rock'n'roll was not an unmixed blessing. It confirmed and deepened shameful divisions between men and women. If it led to progress and liberation, it also created stars whose very success has been an object lesson in reaction and repression. And the very fact of stardom resulted in enormous wastage of resources – not just in material things but also and most often tragically in terms of human life and freedom.

Two deaths, in 1953 and 1954, were auguries for rock'n'roll's notorious profligacy in matters of life and talent. On 1st January, 1953, Hank Williams, the country and western star whose career had burnt brilliantly for a brief four years before being doused by the vast quantities of alcohol he consumed, died in the back of a car while being driven to a show by an off-duty taxi driver. Williams' death from heart failure was brought on by drink and the drugs he obtained illegally from a quack doctor. He had drunk heavily while still a teenager but touring and the isolation of fame combined to deepen his familiar depressions. His sizeable ego, which may well have been necessary to his success as a performer, did not help and he relied increasingly on booze to keep him going. His performances suffered, his marriage fell apart and he started taking pills to wake himself up and more to get himself to sleep. He was 29 when he died, and had done more than anyone else to justify country music's description as 'the white man's blues' – an idea which proved crucial to the development of rock'n'roll.

Johnny Ace was a sweet-voiced rhythm and blues star who had worked with Johnny Otis, Bobby 'Blue' Bland, Junior Parker and B. B. King. He had R&B hits in the early fifties, but died bizarrely during the intermission of a concert in Huston's City Auditorium on Christmas Eve, 1954, whilst playing Russian Roulette. In 1955 his posthumous release, *Pledging My Time*, topped the American R&B charts. Bob Dylan once commented that 'the singers and musicians I grew up with transcend nostalgia – Buddy Holly and Johnny Ace are just as valid to me today as then'. It was not merely clever talk to say that Johnny Ace and Hank Williams parenthesize rock'n'roll. It is all there in their lives and deaths – sweetness and bitterness, darkness and light, black and white, anger and joy, success and failure and, above all, the tragedies and pleasures of youth.

While teenagers saw their fifties idols as symbols of a positive rebellion against the sterile and passionless world of their elders, many adults were plainly shocked by the lives and works of their children's new heroes. Rock'n'roll music blared from the ubiquitous radio and the increasingly commonplace phonograph. It seemed like a precise statement of the rootless and narcissistic hedonism that they thought sexual awareness might unleash in their children. Songs about 'shaking', 'rocking', 'rolling', 'loving' and 'playing' were sung by young men whose actions and attitudes were unmistakably *dirty* and whose style was borrowed wholesale by the young and worshipped as in some latter-day idolatry.

The music often sounded to adult ears like a caterwaul. Lyrics seemed nonsensical if not obscene. The *Encyclopedia Britannica Yearbook* for 1956 described rock'n'roll as 'insistent savagery . . . deliberately competing with the artistic ideals of the jungle'. The following year, Frank Sinatra refrained from mincing even more words when he described it as 'the most brutal, ugly, vicious form of expression', a 'rancid-smelling aphrodisiac' and 'martial music of every delinquent on the face of the earth'. A Chicago radio station instituted a regular and highly publicized practice of breaking rock'n'roll records over the air. Juvenile delinquency, a legal catch-all that had caught the imaginations of fifties sociologists and criminologists, was blamed on rock'n'roll and records were banned by Crime Commissions. Britain, which at first had nothing significant in the way of home-grown rock'n'roll, was astounded by the thousands of kids who turned out to greet Bill Haley on his 1957 tour of the country and initial amused tolerance gave way to strident aversion in the face of the gleeful destruction

The King of Rock'n'Roll enjoying some close attention in the way he liked best: from both sides at once.

15

Hank Williams sets the pattern for countless rockers to follow: jailed after yet another drunken binge in Alexander City, Alabama on 18th August, 1952, he's obviously not far from an early death.

itself – in which five people were arrested and at least one stabbed – but the fact that the 25,000 kids included black and white. That was how most newspapers reported it anyway, although their estimates varied from about 60 per cent white to amost totally black. If the public (in the shape of those kids) no longer believed in segregation in music, how much longer could it survive in politics and business at large?

Sam Phillips, who owned a small Memphis recording studio and record label called Sun, found the formula for a more acceptable market crossover in the early fifties. The opportunity to meet market demand while circumventing racist objections presented itself to Phillips in the shape of Elvis Presley, a boy who walked into the Sun studio in 1953 to make a private recording as a birthday present for his mother.

Elvis's talent remains difficult to grasp, his personality an enigma, his biography subject to constant distortion and endless reinterpretation. 'God gave me a voice,' Elvis once said. 'If I turned against God I'd be ruined.' And yet he also recognized the devil's part in his success, saying that 'my voice is ordinary; if I stand still while I'm singing, I'm dead, man'. It was, indeed, Elvis's provocative hip-shaking that caused most consternation among critics of rock'n'roll. *Look* magazine was fairly polite when it opined that Presley's 'gyrations, his nose wiping, his leers were vulgar'. (Nose wiping?) The novelty, of course, was that unlike his equally 'vulgar' predecessors, Elvis was young, white and pretty – not a model rapist but a model seducer.

Elvis was well aware of the sexual delights he con-

Sure enough, it is only four months later that thousands file past Hank's open coffin at Montgomery's Municipal Auditorium.

of cinema and concert-hall seats wherever rock'n'roll inspired the urge to dance.

The traditional combination of racial prejudice and sexual jealousy encouraged hatred of the music and its exponents. The well-spring of rock'n'roll was, after all, black music with its bawdy lyrics, its sensual rhythms and expression and its general air of the barroom and brothel. Even the phrase 'rock'n'roll' was composed of two sexual metaphors common in black music. It was predictable when, in 1956, the Secretary of the North Alabama White Citizens Council condemned rock'n'roll as 'a means of pulling the white man down to the level of the negro'. But it was harder to understand why the reputable entertainment trade paper, *Variety*, offered that same year 'A Warning To The Music Business', guarding them against a music that turned 'dirty postcards into songs'.

No doubt, the music business (and *Variety*) saw itself as more of a conservative industry with established marketing arrangements than a guardian of the moral order. What *Variety* was really objecting to was market crossover – the tendency for white kids to search out 'authentic' black music. When 30-year-old Alan Freed, the Cleveland disc jockey, organized his first rock'n'roll concert featuring black artists in his home town in 1952, and 25,000 kids turned up to chase 10,000 seats, what frightened the music industry and the rest of the establishment was not the ensuing riot

jured up. But the sexual power of Elvis the performer gradually infused his off-stage world. His own sexuality was soon reduced to power alone and Elvis, voyeur and masturbator, found it impossible to handle one-to-one relationships. In the early days, his most satis-

'All that glisters . . .' Elvis's gold suit conceals the corruption within.

Even Presley couldn't be kept out of court in the early years: on 19th October, 1956, Elvis (third from right) explains how a scuffle with two garage attendants (left) led to a charge of assault.

fying 'sexual' relationship was with three teenage girls who regularly and collectively assisted him in re-creating innocent adolescent horseplay in the privacy of his own bedroom. In the sixties, his home was the venue for regular orgiastic parties, climaxing in the King getting carried away by the sight of two or three girls wrestling naked but for tight white panties stretched over their crotches. He also enjoyed filming his and other people's performances. By the seventies – wrecked by drugs and gross over-indulgence – Elvis's appetite could only be whetted by the sight of other people exciting themselves. Sometimes it was men and women. Mostly it was women only. The furtive voyeurism of a few years earlier became a deadening ritual in which three or four chorus girls would, by special arrangement, perform for Elvis and his video cameras in one or other of his sumptuous bedrooms. Meanwhile, he continued to have curious 'love affairs' with individual women which rapidly became purely platonic and which were almost always directed towards marriage. It is characteristic that the only woman he actually married, Priscilla Beaulieu, was just fourteen when they first met. It was inevitable that, grown up and a mother, Priscilla would leave Elvis (for the Presleys' karate coach, Mike Stone). Elvis, equally inevitably, became so distraught that he seriously planned to murder her lover.

Elvis lived in a fantasy world of power in many forms. He dreamed of demolishing large buildings; he had a mania for collecting all manner of guns – rare, antique, finely-tooled, efficient weapons of death; paranoid about potential assassins, he even reached the point of packing a derringer on stage during performances; he collected police and other law-enforcement agency badges and the honorary titles that went with them as shamanic tokens of his in-vulnerability. In 1970, after prolonged negotiations, President Richard Nixon agreed to see the drug-soaked Elvis and appointed him as honorary narcotics agent. Most cynically, it was good press for Nixon; most realistically, it suited Nixon's political effort to deflect the efforts of the anti-Vietnam War movement by promoting a 'greater' evil – the 'drug menace' – and one that conveniently also attacked those people most vocal about America's need to get out of Indochina. For Elvis, the schizoid gesture of a drug-happy rock'n'roller becoming a fighter against drug abuse was but another indication of his terminal notion that he could bend reality to his will. The King and the Emperor stood together for a while, and nobody can be sure who had the newest clothes.

His personal relationships were infused with a sense of his own godhead. He expected instant obedi-ence from his minions – not tolerating the slightest demurral to even his most outlandish demands. He strode through his mansions like some despotic, frightened Khan – supervising orgies and violent, childish games with names like War and the Whip, taking vindictive and petty revenge on those who enjoyed themselves too much or displayed the sin of

18

Priscilla Beaulieu was a fresh-faced schoolgirl of just fourteen years when Elvis first set greedy eyes on her – ten years before their marriage in 1968. The bride wore white, the groom didn't.

lèse-majesté. He would take women home and cajole them into taking drugs he had come to depend on; he used his friends to experiment with LSD in 1964 (evidently eager to learn of the new drug's effects but too scared to risk his own delicate balance by experiencing them himself). Of course, he could be loving and kind (sometimes, if we are to believe some of his associates, to a rare degree) but, if he could not be God, at least he could be His Second-In-Command. His former bodyguards, Red and Sonny West and Dave Hebler, recalled him reading out selections from the Bible, and taking special note that when Jesus said 'It is harder for a rich man to enter heaven than for a camel to go through the eye of a needle', the Messiah was definitely not referring to Elvis.

Elvis's attempt to cope with the illusion of sexual omnipotence fostered by rock'n'roll stardom was to try and become divine – an attempt whose very audacity was only possible because Elvis, as his early friends and colleagues remember, was a colourless youth with little in his life but his burning ambition to succeed. And his success was not based on any extraordinary ability to be everything, but on his need to be nothing but the passive instrument of his own myth.

The truth about Elvis is that this myth was the realest thing about him. His image and even his style were carefully nurtured by men like Phillips, Colonel Tom Parker and Steve Sholes of RCA Records (who bought his contract from Phillips for the then unpre-cedented figure of $35,000). Colonel Tom, the quintessential showman, was one of those who recognized Elvis's ability to appeal to both sides at once. He even manufactured 'I Love Elvis' T-shirts and 'I Hate Elvis' badges at the same time. It was Parker too who engineered the subtle change from rebel to nice guy.

When Elvis's 'bumps and grinds' started getting flak from the press and the pulpit early in 1956, after appearances on the Dorsey Brothers' and Milton Berle's networked TV shows, Elvis appeared on the Steve Allen show, in July that same year, standing still, dressed in white tie and tails and playing a little light comedy as well as singing *Hound Dog*. Ed Sullivan, whose show on another network was in direct competition with Allen's, had at first refused to consider featuring the singer. But Elvis's success on Allen's show persuaded him to change his mind, if Elvis would agree to be shown from the waist up only. Elvis, and Col. Parker, were happy to agree. For some even this was not enough. The *New York Times* TV critic, Jack Gould, complained about Elvis's 'singularly distasteful . . . movements of the tongue' during the Sullivan show in September 1956. But the Elvis camp had an answer for all objections.

They announced that the first thing Elvis did with all the money he was making was buy a new home for his parents. See, they said, he really was a home-loving, parent-respecting boy. On the Ed Sullivan show, Elvis announced his first movie and sang the title song, *Love Me Tender*. See, he really was gentle and believed in Romantic Love and marriage and that stuff. Elvis's output of rock'n'roll numbers declined and his output of ballads and religious songs increased. See, he was as good as any singer *and* he was a Christian. In 1958, Elvis was drafted and meekly joined the army accompanied only by a mammoth press campaign. He had his hair cut to regulation length. See, Elvis was a patriot. After his discharge in 1960, Elvis appeared on TV arm-in-arm with his arch-rival Frank Sinatra (yes, the one who thought rock'n'roll was a rancid aphrodisiac). See, Elvis was just another pillar of the show-biz establishment.

Thus, Elvis came to obey all the commandments that Americans hold dear. He was once poor but now he was rich. He loved God and his mom, but boy did he know how to party. He resolved America's contradiction between the desire for pleasure and success and the need for guilt and failure just by being Elvis. And in his private imagination only the myth could compensate for or explain the confusing reality. So, helped by the drug habit he had picked up in the army – where his platoon was regularly issued with benzedrine to help it through manoeuvres – Elvis grew to believe the myth and it grew to kill him.

Fifties rock'n'roll couldn't have produced two stars like Elvis, although that didn't stop performers and record companies striving for comparable success. The $35,000 RCA paid Sam Phillips for Elvis's contract helped Sun promote the careers of a number of contenders – all of them, like the title-holder, country-

Self abuse with drugs and junk food turned the King into a sweaty hulk of blubber which, by 1977, the year of his death, he'd given up trying to hide.

Elvis taking his shots in Germany before joining the Army there in 1958. He picked up his prodigious drug habit in the Army, where troops were regularly dosed with benzedrine to keep them going on manoeuvres.

bred, poor Southern whites. Carl Perkins might have made it, except that he was a little too old, a family man without the required youthful good looks. Besides, a car crash in 1956 on the way to a gig put Perkins out of action for several months at a crucial stage in his career. He had just released a record of his self-composed *Blue Suede Shoes* and was scheduled for all important appearances on the Perry Como and Ed Sullivan TV shows. The crash killed Perkins' manager outright and led to the death from injuries of his brother Jay, a member of Perkins' band. The singer took a long time to recover from the crash emotionally and professionally. His career began to flounder as he relied increasingly on the bottle. The Beatles subsequently recorded some of his songs, but Carl had missed his early chance for stardom.

The nearest Carl Perkins got to greatness in the fifties was when *Blue Suede Shoes* was also recorded by Elvis. His success with the song helped to payroll Sun for some time. Sam Phillips was so grateful to Perkins that, star or not, he held a party in the songwriter's honour, during which a very drunk Carl was presented with a pink Cadillac, the very accolade of achievement in fifties rock'n'roll. Since Elvis's death, Carl Perkins had made several tentative comebacks, and in 1987 was inducted in the US Rock'n'Roll Hall of Fame, but his most notable achievement in recent years was a small role as a heavy in Jon Landis's 1985 film *Into The Night*.

Roy Orbison, hugely successful in the sixties, found it difficult to accept Sam Phillips' dictat in the fifties. His records on Sun did not sell well – and in any case, his squirrelish face and horn-rimmed glasses were not the stuff of which Presleys were made. He seemed, if anything, a misfit – and it was only when he developed a style to match his loser image that he met with, success. The songs, with titles like *Only The Lonely* and *It's Over*, exercises in melodramatic emotionalism and delivered with heaps of saccharin and soya sauce feeling, were perfect accompaniments to adolescent crises in the early sixties. Orbison's looks and his dark glasses (adopted after leaving his ordi-

nary glasses at home, so he said, when touring Britain in 1963 with the Beatles), seemed to confirm a truth behind his whinnying, strained vocal agonies. But when real tragedy struck, it revealed in Orbison a mixture of independence and callousness.

His wife Claudette was killed in a motorcycle accident in 1966, and two of his three children died in a fire at his house two years later. Orbison continued working, his attitude – expressed some years later – was that tragedy should not be allowed to 'turn you all the way round'. 'My object is to be stable,' he said, 'to not let anything throw me too far.'

In the eighties, the Big O strode to success again on the back of soundtrack appearances on movies from cult directors Nicholas Roeg and David Lynch, and an up-market scratch band, the Travelling Wilburys, with George Harrison, Jeff Lynne, Tom Petty and Bob Dylan. But, made for tragedy, the 52-year-old Orbison keeled over and died from a heart attack in December 1988 with his first really successful album, *Mystery Girl*, on the point of release.

Johnny Cash was more obviously the stuff of stardom in the first phase of rock'n'roll. But he became hooked on pills, taking them first, he said, 'So I wouldn't be shy when I went on stage.' A promising career went sour as Cash began to rely more and more on 'artificial energy'. He became increasingly ill as a

Roy Orbison, determined not to be lonely after the motorcycle crash in 1966 that killed his wife Claudette at Galattan, near the Orbison home in Nashville, Tennessee. Big O interviews nice English nannies to look after his three children while he goes on tour.

Just two years after the death of Roy Orbison's wife, on 15th September, 1958 rescue workers remove the body of eleven-year-old Roy Orbison Jr. from the burnt-out Orbison home in Hendersonville, Tennessee. Orbison's six-year-old son Tony also died in the blaze.

Hell-raising Johnny Cash winds up in handcuffs at a court in El Paso, October 5th, 1965, charged with illegally importing over 1,000 pep pills and tranquillizers into the United States from Mexico.

greater sense of sin. He shared Presley's Christian background. Unlike Presley, however, Jerry Lee tried to practise what he had been brought up to believe. His faith – profound but inarticulate – led on at least one occasion (the recording session for the undeniably blasphemous *Great Balls of Fire*) to a hold-up in the proceedings while he and Sam Phillips argued at length about the propriety of turning divine imagery into a blatant sexual metaphor. 'I have the devil in me!' Jerry Lee confessed on the tape of the session, while Phillips tried to argue that Lewis's music 'can save souls'. It sounds like a combination of theology seminar and revival meeting and, although Jerry Lee eventually agreed to make the record, you can tell he still thought it evil. Even so, the result was definitive rock'n'roll.

The curiously similar Little Richard – he too assaulted his piano, seemed to talk in tongues ('A Wop Bop A Lu Bop, A Wop Bam Boom'), was possessed by sexual devils and hid behind a façade of aggressive and flamboyant arrogance – 'gave up rock'n'roll for the Rock of Ages' after, so he says, a divine revelation of uncertain nature. Some say the retirement in 1957 at the peak of Richard's success was in order to avoid the ravages of taxation on massive earnings. Richard's own version of the story, which varies from telling to telling, locates his impulse in a dramatic vision received while flying over Australia during a tour. Apparently, the plane was in difficulty and Richard's resolve to abandon rock'n'roll in the wake of a glimpse at his own damnation acted as a sort of spiritual turbo-prop. Safely back on firm ground, the former gospel singer threw his whole supply of garish jewellery into the sea and made more-or-less straight for an Alabama bible school where he trained for the evangelical life. His record company, meanwhile, continued to release Little Richard records from earlier sessions or radio shows as if nothing had happened. Richard himself returned to rock'n'roll seven years later – never having been able to give up completely the fleshly delights of secular music. His career floundered as it swung between periods of ever more grotesque and sacrilegious display and frequent interludes of public self-chastisement.

In those days such behaviour was often considered no better than could be expected from an 'uncivilized' black man. Jerry Lee Lewis, being white, was never allowed the liberty of his own self-doubts. When it was revealed in May 1958, during a tour of Britain, that he had married his thirteen-year-old cousin Myra, the media-led scandal that erupted drove him out of England, out of the charts and almost out of work. Elvis's subsequent relationship with Priscilla Beaulieu, whom he met in Germany when she was still a schoolgirl, and Buddy Holly's marriage to a Mexican woman (also in 1958) were both closely-guarded secrets. Lewis had tried to keep his marriage a secret too, even

result. He crashed his car, sustaining minor injuries. In the mid-sixties he had several brushes with the law. In October 1965, he was busted for illegally importing pills; in 1966, for possession of marijuana; and early in 1967 he was kept in prison overnight on a vagrancy charge. By this time, his career and his first marriage were in shambles. A reputation for unreliability and hell-raising, (he once painted an entire motel room black, and on another bender installed a donkey and a supply of hay in a rented room), preceded him. His friend Waylon Jennings considers that Cash came near to death on a number of occasions. There was also a suit for damages resulting from a forest fire in 1966. Cash was blamed for starting the fire but it was in fact two years before the case was settled and he was eventually fined. When his family decided they wanted to hospitalize him, and after he had been arrested for the third time in 1967, Johnny Cash finally got a grip on himself and began to climb back, achieving great success as a country musician.

On the other hand, one of rock'n'roll's most desperate victims could easily have been Sun's greatest star. Jerry Lee Lewis was a true rock'n'roll primitive; flamboyant, menacing and mischievous on stage and on classic recordings like *Whole Lotta' Shakin' Goin' On* and *Great Balls of Fire*. Lewis would smash up or even burn his piano, throw chairs on stage and abuse his audience. He had none of Presley's manners but he probably had more passion – and he certainly had a

The devil looks after his own – has Jerry Lee Lewis survived the ravages of the rock'n'roll life style by playing the devil's music?

POLICE CHECK UP ON CHILD BRIDE

Get out, Lewis!

Little Myra Lewis spoonfeeds the Killer. When Jerry Lee Lewis arrived in Britain in 1958, he barely managed to play a note before word got out about his marriage to Myra Gale Brown, his thirteen-year-old second cousin. Literally booed off stage, Lewis returned to America, unrepentant but in disgrace, and his career took a nosedive. At the time of the scandal, fellow musician Ronnie Hawkins commented: 'We didn't know what the fuss about Jerry marrying a thirteen-year-old was all about. All us Southern boys knew she was only twelve.'

CHILD BRIDE MIX-UP MAY CUT JERRY'S TOUR

POLICE TO ACT IN CASE OF Mrs 'ROCK' AGED

though Myra wasn't underage in the State where the ceremony took place, but once the fuss ensued he went out of the way to show her off. She was his third wife.

Lewis had started to drink heavily in his early teens. Like so many early rockers he got into speed, too. Tragedy followed him throughout his life. His and Myra's son was drowned in the family swimming pool in 1962, aged only three. In 1970 Myra left him; he says she caught him 'cheating'; Jerry Lee was highly sexed or promiscuous, depending on your point of view. The wrath of the Lord continued to dog him – his other son, Jerry Lee Jnr, died in a car crash in 1972, aged only seventeen. Jerry himself crashed his Rolls Royce in 1976, and, in that same year, accidentally shot bassist Butch Owens with a .357 Magnum. Jerry was hospitalized in 1977 for gall-bladder removal, collapsed lung, pleurisy and back trouble, and broke up with his fourth wife some time later. In 1981, he almost died from an ulcerated stomach. Hospitalized again and on the critical list for some weeks, Lewis nevertheless pulled through – at least, for the time being – and declared himself irrevocably committed to gospel music. From the mid-fifties to the time that rock'n'roll sends him to hell – as he is certain that it will – Lewis has been and will remain a survivor. Or, in his own words, 'a drunken oaf who thinks he's the best' and probably is. The final irony has been a running battle with the IRS (Internal Revenue Service) who twice

Difference of opinion among the Lewis family and their advisers. On 30th January, 1959, Jerry Lee asked a court to reduce alimony payments to his second wife Jane, and get custody of their two children awarded to his parents. L. to r.: manager Jud Phillips, Jerry's father, Elmo, Lewis himself and his lawyers, Harry and Allex Barnett.

Steve Allen Lewis, three-year-old son of Jerry Lee and Myra, who toddled into the family swimming pool and drowned on 22nd April, 1962.

25

Bible-thumping Little Richard thinks there's nothing better than curling up in bed with The Good Book. He may have thrown his jewelry into Sydney Harbour in 1957, but by 1964 he was back rocking in the service of the Lord.

confiscated all his cars for non-payment of taxes and have since led him to auction some of his historic memorabilia in order to meet a bill he should never have been unable to pay in the first place.

Unlike many other early rockers, Chuck Berry, arch-stylist of the teen scene, clearly had a substantial hand in determining his own orientation. Berry – perhaps the greatest of the rock'n'roll lyricists – made the point when he said, 'I didn't write *School Days* in a class room. I wrote it in the Street Hotel, one of the big, black low-priced hotels in St Louis.' He deliberately moved away from his black R&B roots in his lyrics and approach, if not his musical style, towards images of Middle American teenage life with an attitude to sexuality distanced by comedy or sentimentality. It was always Berry's technique to cover his tracks with laughter, using teenage slang to talk about things no teenager's parents would have wanted to hear. His car imagery was particularly revealing. His first hit, the countrified *R&B* number *Maybelline*, used the metaphor of competitive car driving ('As I was motivating up the hill/I saw Maybelline in a Coupe de Ville'.) The words touch the perennial concern of teenagers with driving but are clearly designed also to stand for fucking.

Chuck Berry has revealed over the years an astute commercial mind, able to gauge precisely the concerns and attitudes of his audience. 'The dollar dictates what music is written,' the former Baptist choirboy and apprentice hairdresser once said simply. 'In my case musical and mathematical aptitude go together,' he said in typically immodest fashion in 1964. 'I manage my own affairs, including my investments.' By 1981, Berry's investments – including apartment blocks, houses, a recording studio and a 98-acre country club and leisure zone called Berry Park, situated near Chuck's home-town of St Louis, Missouri – were estimated to be worth around $20 million. Despite all of which, in 1979 Berry was actually jailed for tax evasion (the alternative was a large fine) after under-reporting his annual income for 1973 (in excess of half-a-million dollars) by more than $200,000.

This may demonstrate no more than Berry's legendary meanness. 'My contract is my Bible,' he says – and he has a pretty fundamentalist interpretation of it. In 1975 there were angry scenes after Berry left the stage at London's Hammersmith Odeon, according to fans who were present, 'about eight numbers into the set'. Without doubt, he had fulfilled his contract (in fact, he claimed to have played 58 minutes against a required 45) but the performance was desultory. 'You learn to live with it all,' Berry replies to those who condemn his performances. 'Remember they criticized Jesus as well.'

This latter-day Christ seems to have taken the American Dream to heart in a big way. On one tour outside the US, Berry is said to have checked the exchange rate of the dollar against the local currency every morning, insisting on a cash supplement to cover any devaluation of his fee before setting foot on stage. One night this supplement came to around 25 cents – but he still insisted on full payment.

But there are good reasons for Berry's cussedness. There's no doubt he had a tough past. A poor black who, but for rock'n'roll, would have become a ghetto hairdresser or followed his father's trade as a carpenter, he has been a victim of America's general racism and the music business's exploitative practices. At fifteen, he was sent to reform school for attempted robbery: in 1959, he was arrested in Mississippi for trying to pick up a white girl; and that same year saw him arrested on a statutory rape charge under the Mann Act. Berry had brought a fourteen-year-old Indian prostitute to St Louis to work in his night-club as a hat check girl. He says she told him she was twenty and that he had no knowledge of her profession. He subsequently sacked her for being involved in a fight but she went to the police with her story.

Berry's first trial was abandoned because it was openly racist. The judge persistently referred to him as 'this negro'; meanwhile the press ran riot: 'ROCK'N'ROLL SINGER LURED ME TO ST LOUIS SAYS 14-YEAR-OLD' screamed the headlines. A second trial in 1962 convicted him and he was fined $5,000 and sent to jail for three years, ultimately serving sixteen months. In 1964, Chuck Berry claimed he owed his then current popularity to the jail sentence. 'My only consolation was to think about music,' he said. 'I made notes of new songs and now think the public will forget and accept me as a performer, not as an ex-jailbird.' By 1972, Berry was denying that he was ever jailed. 'I was acquitted,' he said, claiming that the affair was connected with a rivalry between his club and a whites-only club 'across the street'. The vehement denials that he had ever served time had disappeared by 1975, but not the suggestion that his trial was 'a frame-up to ruin me and drive me out'.

What are we to make of Berry's contradictions? He's been married to the same woman since he was 22 but is persistently seen in the company of pretty young blondes. Within the space of a few months, he can deny knowledge of Mick Jagger and Keith Richard, who helped to resurrect Berry from an early decline, and then profess admiration and love for those same

Chuck wouldn't name the pretty blond accompanying him back home to the USA from London in July 1979 to face a jail sentence for tax evasion, but it certainly wasn't his wife of 22 years' standing.

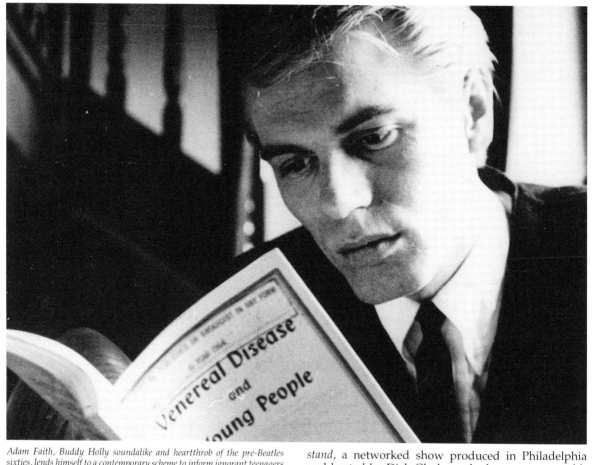

Adam Faith, Buddy Holly soundalike and heartthrob of the pre-Beatles sixties, lends himself to a contemporary scheme to inform ignorant teenagers of the dangers of venereal disease. At the time, rock'n'roll was considered just as dangerous.

two rock'n'rollers. He could be short-tempered to the point of violence: he once destroyed the camera of a fan who annoyed him by trying to take his picture before a performance; in 1981, he punched Keith Richard, when Keith approached him while he was leaving a club. Richard, bearing no grudge, went on to organize a star-studded sixtieth birthday bash for Chuck in 1986. Like Elvis, but in a different way, Berry embodies both the disturbing dreams of rock'n'roll and the comforting dreams of the 'average American'. An ardent believer in free enterprise, democracy and the motor industry, perhaps Berry just cannot accept his rebellious soul. 'At times I become very hot and cold, moody, very schizophrenic,' he once said. 'It's really controlled schizophrenia, and I'm controlling it.'

Without Berry there would have been no clean rock'n'roll. The record industry majors had a lot to thank him for. Shorn of its unmistakeable lyrical *doubles entendres* and its most lascivious bodily movements and vocal inflections, rock'n'roll turned into pop music. Television was especially influential as a launch pad for clean rock'n'rollers. *American Band-*

stand, a networked show produced in Philadelphia and hosted by Dick Clark, pushed numerous would-be stars up the ladder of success. Most of them were called Bobbie or Frankie. Few had much talent and even those who had, suffered from the trivializing impact of relentless TV exposure. This was the much lampooned era when good-looking boys were virtually pulled off the street and asked if they wanted to be stars. The record industry buzzed with the sound of white boys with Latin looks and duck's arse hairstyles scratching their names on contracts. With Elvis in the army, there was now to be an army of Elvises.

Fabian (real name Fabiano Forte Buonaparte) was thirteen when he was signed up by two local Philadelphian entrepreneurs. He was happy to admit that he couldn't sing (one legendary recording session lasted for 88 takes before Fabian got it right) but that did not matter. Fabian looked great.

Bobby Vee (real name Robert Velline) had the good fortune to be in the band that stepped into the empty spot left in the show at Moorhead, Minnesota, after Buddy Holly's plane crashed. Subsequently, producer Snuff Garrett heard a record by Vee's group (the Shadows) and took them under his wing. Vee – with the right, boyish puppy lover looks – was groomed for a solo career and even teamed up with Holly's old backing-group, the Crickets, to capitalize on the Holly mystique.

Rock'n'roll in Britain was, at first, hardly more than a marketing operation, a calculated response by the entertainment industry to bridge a gap in the market. The first big star was Tommy Hicks, whose assumed name, Steele, set a pattern to be followed by almost all the other singers managed by the man who virtually ran the British rock'n'roll scene for two or three years – Larry Parnes. Parnes had a penchant for calling his 'stable' by names crudely suggestive of sexual characteristics. There was Marty Wilde, Billy Fury, Vince Eager, Dickie Pride and Johnny Gentle – to name but a few. At one point, Parnes was managing sixteen performers, but by 1961 he had released all of them, bar Steele, Wilde, Fury and Joe Brown – preferring to concentrate on his first love, the 'straight' showbiz of managing theatres and promoting stage shows.

With an evident relish for the theatrical world, Parnes was also attracted to the histrionic posturing of rock'n'roll. As his talent for creating stage-names suggests, rock'n'roll only meant anything to Parnes as a form of theatre. In the mid-fifties, he was running his father's tailoring shops in London and had invested in the partnership of a small club frequented by show people. He bought an interest in a touring play – the publicist was a man named John Kennedy. Kennedy became interested in managing a singer he had seen in London's 2I's coffee-bar, where a number of Britain's skiffle acts and rock'n'rollers made their debuts. The singer was Tommy Hicks, a young merchant seaman, and Kennedy persuaded Parnes to join him in promoting the lad. The two remained partners until 1961, when a dispute over a five hour, £3,500 poker game caused them to fall out – although Parnes' sardonic comment at the time was simply 'I do the business. Kennedy does the publicity. It isn't essential to confer.'

Parnes and Kennedy saw rock'n'roll as a launch pad for more rounded careers. Accordingly, Tommy Steele only made two records with any pretensions to rock'n'roll (*Rock With The Caveman* and *Doomsday Rock*) before beginning the transformation to film-star, actor, cabaret-performer and TV personality which has been followed equally by Cliff Richard and Adam Faith. Commenting on his own success, Tommy Steele said, 'Someone was looking for an exponent of rock'n'roll, and I was there.' TV producer Jack Good's comment on Cliff Richard was even more succinct: 'He was malleable!' But for others, things were less simply encapsulated. Many were unable to cope with the manipulation of their personalities and were therefore unable to cope when their rock'n'roll moment passed. Marty Wilde, who continued to have hits into the early sixties, nonetheless found his earnings dropping from '£10,000 a year to £1,000' in the wake of a much publicized marriage. In 1961, at the age of twenty, Marty was obliged to announce his first come-back.

Billy Fury, despite being the best of Britain's early rockers with a stage act that even the *New Musical Express* described as 'downright disgusting' (those were the days), suffered from acute depression. Having inveigled his way into Marty Wilde's dressing room at a 1958 gig in Birkenhead, in order to play the star some of his compositions, Fury was catapulted to stardom himself by the ever-rapacious Parnes, insatiably in pursuit of new blood. The would-be songwriter was transformed, Cinderella-style, into a sexual demon. Even Jack Good was moved to comment that, 'Frankly, there are one or two things that Billy does that I would rather he didn't.' He did not elaborate.

Fury's career – parodied in the seventies' film *That'll Be The Day* – was suitably summed up by the name of the character he played in it, Stormy Tempest. He continued in the public gaze until almost the end of the sixties and subsequently made a couple of abortive comebacks (one ruined by his illness on the eve of a rock'n'roll revival package tour and one as recently as 1981). His image was that of an English James Dean. He was shy but passionate, a lover of animals ('Billy cries whenever he sees an animal hurt,' said the press), infatuated with speed and fast cars (he was pulled up for speeding in 1961, 1962, 1963 and 1968), yet lacking the confidence to talk to girls. (Parnes claimed to have written a script for Fury to use once when breaking up with a girlfriend.) Without doubt, Fury was an erotic performer (even without his gold lamé suit) and a victim of his own melancholy. The idea of simultaneous weakness (he suffered from rheumatism, kidney trouble and bronchitis) and strength (sexually and otherwise – he had been a tugboat man), of sensitivity and aggression (he read poetry as well as raced cars), was immensely attractive. But Fury actually seemed to prefer his quiet life studying ornithology and owning race-horses to the rigours of the public life as a rock'n'roll performer.

Larry Parnes (centre) gloats as shy, pet-loving Billy Fury, the latest addition to Parnes' rock'n'roll stable, copes with the clamour of his fans. Fury's act was described at the time as 'downright disgusting'.

Britain's answer to Elvis? But Cliff Richard doesn't know where to put his hands when faced with a kiss from delectable Janette Scott. Nowadays Cliff claims to have been celibate since the sixties.

Parnes was not slow to drop those who did not pull their weight. Vince Eager went on the grounds that he never made hit records. Dickie Pride, who wore pork pie hats and battered leather jackets, was one of the few early rockers to become a heroin addict. He drove a much used sports car and once test-drove a motorcycle through the show-room's plate glass window. Parnes needless to say dropped him because he was a liability and he died in obscurity of an overdose. 'I'm only going to retain the ones who give me whole-hearted co-operation and put themselves completely in my hands both on and off stage,' was Parnes's explanation.

The combination of traditional British showbiz attitudes and rock'n'roll's iconoclasm spawned some eccentric talent on the eastern edge of the Atlantic. The most eccentric were often managers, record producers, songwriters and engineers – many of whom, like Joe Meek and, subsequently, Brian Epstein – were drawn to rock'n'roll at least in part because of an emotional attachment to their young male performers.

Meek's was a particularly tragic case. A country boy who came to London after his National Service, Meek worked as an engineer at a number of independent recording studios in the city. He engineered records by almost all the UK's leading vocalists of the fifties – Frankie Vaughan, Denis Lotis, Lita Roza, Shirley Bassey, Petula Clark and Harry Secombe – and, after 1956, worked with some of the best known skiffle and trad jazz performers in the country – including Lonnie Donegan, Chris Barber and Humphrey Lyttleton. His work on songs like Donegan's 'Cumberland Gap' and 'Don't You Rock Me Daddy-O' put him in a direct line to Britain's vigorous R&B scene.

But Meek was ambitious – driven, according to some of his colleagues – and, in 1960, built his own studio above a leather goods shop on the seedy Holloway Road in North London, and started his own label, Triumph. In Britain, where the market was controlled by just three companies, this was a brave move. In fact, the label was a failure and Meek soon settled into a role as independent producer.

His studio was equipped at a budget price, using secondhand equipment held together, as often as not, with chewing gum and matchsticks. Nevertheless, Meek's ideas were anything but secondhand. He used recording technology to great effect in a series of earcatching hits by John Leyton ('Johnny Remember Me' and 'Wild Wind'), Mike Berry ('Tribute To Buddy Holly'), and – most notably – the Tornados ('Telstar'). 'Telstar' reached Number 1 in the US and in Britain, at that time a remarkable feat. Meek continued to have more-or-less intriguing hits with tracks by the Tornados, Mike Berry and the Honeycombs (whose 'Have I The Right', with female drummer Honey Langtree, prefigures punk) into the onset of Merseybeat.

But Meek's star waned as the sixties progressed. His homosexuality was a problem for him and he became increasingly paranoid, a paranoia which took the unlikely form of an obsession with Buddy Holly. By 1966, he had reached bottom and, following a hitless twelve months, he blew his brains out with a shotgun. It was 3 February, 1967, eight years to the day after Holly's death.

Terry Dene was the next most likely to succeed on the British rock'n'roll scene, after Tommy Steele. He was spotted, by Jack Good, singing between bouts of a wrestling match in 1957 and Good decided to put him on his TV show. At eighteen, Dene was a classic teen idol – fans chased him down streets, tearing his clothes and hair; he was obliged to make elaborate getaways from stage shows through dressing-room windows; even his mother was knocked down by the screaming hordes. From a £3.50-a-week record packer he was transformed into a public sensation. He lost his head. He took to smashing plate glass windows on impulse, throwing motor-bikes around if he did not like the way they were parked and, on one occasion, smashing a telephone kiosk because he had no money to call his girlfriend, the singer Edna Savage. When he married Edna in 1958, it caused a sensation in the press – two of the country's biggest stars falling in love with each other. In fact, the young Dene had only fallen for a face he had seen in a spotlight and, on their wedding night, the bride waited in vain in her room for her young husband, while he went off on a motorcycle ride that lasted three weeks.

The couple's very public rows invariably made the news. There was even a joke about them ('Does Terry Dene make Edna savage?'). They lived in the whirlwind of their own fame, spending their easy money and cheap emotions like there was no tomorrow. Needless to say, the marriage did not last very long.

A few weeks before marrying Edna, on the very day that Elvis Presley reported for duty in the US Army, Dene had received his draft papers for the British Army. It was a golden opportunity for his publicists – and for the Army. 'I wanted to go like any other man,' says Dene, 'but the publicity boys thought otherwise.' He hoped that the army would offer a refuge from the pressures of showbiz. But his 'advisers' fought the call-up and in a month Dene was in court on a drunk and disorderly charge. Eventually, Dene was required to report to the barracks, and a posse of reporters and photographers went with him. After they left, he recalls, 'I broke down and wept.' Not even the Army could rescue him. He was sent to hospital for psychiatric tests and two weeks later was sent to a civilian hospital, suffering from a nervous breakdown. Nine weeks after entering the army, Dene was invalided out. Questions were asked in Parliament.

At home, Dene started to read the Bible and began to calm down. But at a comeback performance in Blackpool, he was booed off the stage – the British can never tolerate an out-and-out weakling. He started drinking again, a has-been at 21. Then one night in 1964, he 'was walking the streets, alone, fed-up and lost'. In London's Trafalgar Square he was approached by an evangelist. 'He took the time to talk to me about Jesus,' said Dene, announcing his conversion.

Gene Vincent, though American, can fairly be linked with these British names since his most sustained success was in Britain where, again under the guidance of Jack Good, Vincent was given his definitive black leather image. With one massive hit to his name, *Be Bop A Lula*, Gene and his band, the Blue Caps, caused riots in Australia and the U.S. They drank a great deal, destroyed hotel rooms and generally caused havoc. A hotel manager once asked for a $50,000 deposit against breakages and Vincent's unpleasant temper when drunk (which he was most of the time), led to feuds with his managers and numerous other problems for his career. He was a naïve working-class kid, unable to cope with success. 'I didn't know how to handle a hit, I was only a child, a boy,' he once reflected. The major injury he suffered to his left leg (it was nearly severed at the shin in a motorcycle crash in 1955) was never properly treated. He never took care of his tax situation after his first success. His membership of the American Musicians Union was revoked for unprofessional behaviour. On top of all that, his record company were bent on exploiting him as a new Elvis, while Gene himself found it immensely difficult to talk to DJs or to do interviews – which did not endear him to the publicity machine. Finally, a court case between his management and his agency forced him off the road for three months.

Yet Gene Vincent was a born performer and when things got too difficult in America he simply moved to Britain. Jack Good took him under his wing and played up the sense of ugly menace in Vincent's personality. The black leather was one aspect. Good also remembers standing in the wings during one TV show exhorting Vincent to 'Limp, you bugger, limp!' Vincent became one of the biggest ballroom draws in the country (in fact, his compere, ex-singer Don

Don and Phil Everly pass on the experience of several years already spent on the road to a green Cliff Richard, whom they met during a 1958 tour of Britain. The filial harmony was only skin deep.

Arden, became his manager and built an empire from there, eventually centred on the Electric Light Orchestra). But the 1960 crash which had killed Eddie Cochran worsened Vincent's leg injury, and by 1964 the pain and the drinking were beginning to show in Britain. His private life was a public shambles – involving press stories of drunken brawls with and without his wife. His leg desperately needed treatment. For four years he was altogether out of the limelight and his life grew more and more chaotic. He sank into a permanent, Martini-induced haze, came back to Britain in 1969 and was greeted by alimony proceedings instituted by his wife. He was fat and debilitated. In 1970, grateful to a faithful French fan, he was reduced to playing village *fêtes* around the countryside of France and, the next year, he fled Europe for the home of his birth, only to die a few days later of a seizure resulting from a perforated ulcer. Performing and dying were two things that came easiest to him. When he could no longer do one, the other was inevitable.

In America, the manipulation of young, *ersatz* Elvises was seen as something that had happened to a spontaneous form of musical expression under the influ-

ence of a controlling industry. The 1959 Payola scandal and the various fates of rock'n'roll's most creative artists – Elvis, Chuck Berry, Buddy Holly, Eddie Cochran, Jerry Lee Lewis and Little Richard were all either killed or effectively silenced – helped that interpretation of events. While British kids believed that real rock'n'roll had been denied them, their contemporary Americans assumed that it had been co-opted.

It was not always as simple as that. The worst victims among America's younger rock'n'rollers were often street-wise kids whose ordinary lives were surrounded by a routine terror. Dion Di Mucci was Bronx-born and started singing at the age of five. By the age of fifteen, he was appearing on TV and, at nineteen, in 1958, he formed Dion and the Belmonts who had a massive hit with *Teenager In Love*. Dion was already using heroin. His neighbourhood was tough and drugs, guns and car crashes were common hazards. Dion took to the drug to 'fill the gap' between what he later described as 'your public and your private face'. It enabled him to cope with everyday life, not just with fame. Certainly, being persuaded by his management to go solo in 1960 – a move which saw him have massive hits with songs like *The Wanderer* – created extra pressures, and by 1964 Dion had dropped out of sight to go through the painful process of overcoming his addiction. On the one hand, heroin had helped him deal with the problems of stardom; on the other hand, however, stardom may well have given him the money and the motivation to throw off

Don Everly arrives in New York with his second wife, Venetia Stevenson, after collapsing from a drug overdose in Britain, in 1962. A doctor had prescribed 'vitamins' to help the Everlys on tour, but they turned out to be amphetamines.

year, a doctor prescribed drugs to the brothers to help them through an arduous tour. The drugs, thought to be some sort of vitamin, turned out to be amphetamines and Don became hooked. While playing in Britain in late 1962, Don was taken to hospital twice in twelve hours. His condition was reported variously as 'food poisoning', 'nervous exhaustion' and – more accurately – 'an overdose of drugs'. He flew home, leaving Phil to complete the visit alone.

A suicide attempt followed before Don successfully came off speed, but the pressures continued. In the early seventies Don fell in love with a woman suffering from spinal meningitis. 'She recovered,' he recalled, 'and I decided she was the most important thing in my life.' After his two previous disastrous marriages, he opted to retire from the Everly Brothers and marry again. Phil had also discovered how difficult living with someone could be. 'I reached the point where I wasn't sure love really existed,' he said after two unhappy marriages. Regrettably, common experiences had not led to common understanding and, at their last show together in 1973, Phil smashed his guitar on stage and walked out of a sixteen-year-old act that had, in Don's words, 'died ten years ago'. Both eventually returned to performing separately, while maintaining their long-lived mutual hostility.

an addiction that might otherwise have proved fatal. Fortunately, his withdrawal was successful and he eventually returned to performing.

One example from the early days of rock'n'roll does seem to indicate clearly how commerce can ruin careers and lives. In 1960, the two brothers, Phil and Don Everly, left the small Cadence label, with whom they had had a string of hits, after a dispute over royalties. They went to the potentially greener pastures of Warner Brothers and, a year later, they also broke acrimoniously with the production-management-writing team that had previously provided them with so many hits. In 1962, they were still being described as 'the world's most successful and richest singing team', but the cracks were beginning to show.

'Everyone has the feeling that all you have to do is to achieve stardom and once you're there you can relax,' said Phil in 1981. 'It's just the opposite. Once you get there, then the war really starts. The pressures get larger because getting hit records is a miracle.' The brothers began to argue, travelling separately, staying in different hotels, eventually hiring separate managers, agents and lawyers. For successful close harmony singers they were the least harmonious of couples. Don, the elder by two years, was married in 1957 and divorced in 1961. He married again in 1962 and within a year his wife was threatening to sue him for divorce on the grounds of mental cruelty. That same

Faced with a host of lookalike/soundalike pretty boys controlled by sharp entrepreneurs it is not surprising to find American kids in the early sixties deserting rock'n'roll for less commercial musics like jazz and folk.

In Britain, kids had all along been fed on largely second rate pap. They rejected the British pop establishment and looked for authenticity overseas in the land of Elvis, Chuck and Eddie. British musicians have always acknowledged this spontaneous searching out of American music for more meaningful forms. Some got caught up in a quest for rock'n'roll, R & B and blues roots – others found inspiration in the emerging soul music which, they believed, ran in a direct line of development from rock'n'roll. In every case they saw that 'black' music (which ironically was often written by whites) stood for a liberation they urgently wanted *and* they saw that rock'n'roll had shown a way in which whites could interpret black soul. Here is the real link with the sixties – for among their number we can count John Lennon, who acknowledged Elvis's influence; Keith Richard and Mick Jagger who, legend has it, first got together over a mutual admiration for Chuck Berry; George Harrison who followed Eddie Cochran around England watching his guitar technique; and Eric Burdon and the Animals, whose Bo Diddley impersonation was admired by Bo himself. After the nightmare race run by the first rockers against the short memory of their public, it was these mainly British artists who revitalized rock music, but who in turn had to face many of the same kinds of battle. Only now it was the sixties, and this was a whole new war.

SEX AND DRUGS AND ROCK'N'ROLL

Serious drug-taking has always had some part in the rock'n'roll landscape. In fact the excessive use of stimulants and depressants of one sort or another has been associated with the rebel image and with music-making since well before the first bohemians walked the boulevards of Paris. For rock musicians, trapped by tough schedules, unnatural hours and the expectations of entertainment-hungry audiences, drugs can also be a necessary tool of trade. Even back in the Beatles' early years entertaining the thirsty patrons of the Hamburg Reeperbahn bars, John Lennon recalled the need for drugs: 'The only way to survive in Hamburg to play eight hours a night was to take pills. The waiters gave you them . . . the pills and the drink.'

The story was the same wherever the rock music of the sixties was being born. In New York's Greenwich Village, the coffeehouses echoed to the folksy sounds of Bob Dylan, Jim McGuinn, Steve Stills and John Sebastian. In London there was less folk, but more blues, R & B and soul, fuelled just the same by plentiful supplies of booze, speed, marijuana – and sometimes by something a little more exotic, like amyl nitrate or cocaine. One rock star used to surprise fellow performers on British TV's early sixties' show, *Ready, Steady, Go!*, by popping amyl nitrate ampoules in front of their faces just before they went on. (Amyl nitrate is a heart stimulant administered in vapour form. The startling effect of the drug is due to a sudden surge of blood to the brain.) For some die-hards there was always heroin, and for others as the sixties progressed there was LSD.

Rock people who take drugs for fun rarely stop at one kind. There is often a tendency to take combinations of drugs to see what the effect will be and almost every user of an illegal drug will experiment with something new. After all, once the barriers of illegality and fear have been broken down, there's not much besides lack of opportunity to prevent you. Rock stars, with their wealth and their unique access to the underworld of late-night clubs and the pushers who frequent them, have had endless opportunity. They have taken it – partly because they needed it to keep going, partly because it was expected of them as vanguards of the new liberation of youth. The result for too many has

been the trap of addiction and self-abuse, ending in death.

Two days after Janis Joplin's death from a heroin overdose her friend and musical colleague Nick Gravenites talked about the inevitability of death among the rock fraternity. 'There's a lot of people using junk on the rock scene and they're on death row . . . You know they're going to die, you know it. So people were just figuring out ways to cushion the blow when it happens.' This was in 1970 – by this time the list of drug- and booze-related deaths among rock stars had grown so long that it wasn't really a surprise; feelings were numbed and each one was, as John Lennon said of Brian Jones, 'just another victim of the drug scene'. Janis Joplin had been part of the West Coast rock scene, where LSD ruled.

LSD, whose effects were first noted in 1943, gained immense popularity in the sixties thanks largely to the proselytizing efforts of two Harvard university researchers, Drs Timothy Leary and Richard Alpert. Both men were sacked by the university in the early sixties for their very public espousal of the drug. For Leary in particular, LSD became a messiah whose gospel he preached across America, wherever there were people adventurous enough to look for new experiences.

The inheritors of rock'n'roll's rebellious spirit – musicians and other outsiders from Los Angeles, San Francisco, New York and London – were just such people: politicians of pleasure, enemies of the establishment and mostly practised drug users already. They took to LSD like ducks to water. It was an excuse to throw aside the old conventions, a drug that changed you, as Hunter S. Thompson said, 'at the place of definitions'. It certainly changed the style and image of rock music.

1965 was the year. The Beatles (who famously smoked pot in the toilets of Buckingham Palace before collecting their MBEs) and the Rolling Stones (three of whom had more famously been fined for pissing against a filling station wall) had made it in the USA. From out of Greenwich Village, a politically committed nasal folk-singer named Bob Dylan had become – quite unpredictably – a star. As it happened it was Dylan who turned the pill-popping Beatles on to marijuana's more meditative buzz in 1964. It showed in the music – rock'n'roll started to look into itself and created a sound that was built for LSD. By the time the Beatles played San Francisco in 1965, Leary was proclaiming them the advanced guard of his psychedelic revolution, 'mutants' preparing for an imagined golden age.

Sid Vicious doing it his way. Vicious, the archetypal punk – angry, inarticulate, and given to self-mutilation – was thrust into the limelight with the Sex Pistols. Sid, a homosexual and habitual drug-user, couldn't cope. In 1978 he killed his groupie girlfriend, Nancy Spungen, and subsequently died of a self-administered overdose on 2nd February, 1979, before coming to trial for murder.

35

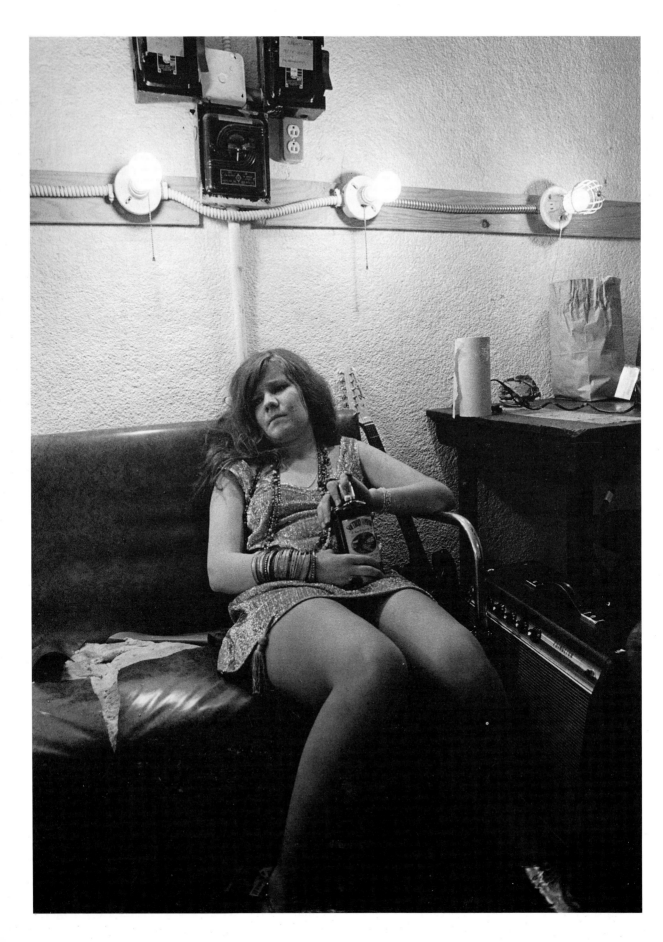

WILD GIRL OF POP DIES

Singer Janis Joplin is found in a Hollywood hotel .. killed by drugs overdose

Janis, ...ushing rings and singing as the fans liked her best . . . loud, agonised and electrifying.

The drug culture was nurtured especially in the fertile ground of California – where LSD remained legal until as late as October 1966. David Crosby, a founder member of the Byrds, remembered the time he spent in San Francisco's North Beach, in Sausalito and further south in Venice, while the Byrds were being born in 1964–65. 'Dino Valenti and David Freiberg and I were dropping acid together years ago,' Crosby said in 1970, recalling times spent hanging-out and playing music with key members of the Californian rock scene. In Venice, Crosby and Freiberg hung out with Paul Kantner – founder member of the Jefferson Airplane. Drifting around the coast there were plenty of other musicians – Jerry Garcia (friend of

Janis Joplin, the wild girl of rock, cuddles her most constant companion, a bottle of Southern Comfort, backstage at San Francisco's Winterland in 1968. The ugly duckling from Port Arthur, Texas, became a swan on stage, but to help her fly she needed vast quantities of booze, speed and, ultimately, the heroin which killed her. The tawdry surroundings of her dressing-room are a long way from the quiet, middle American backwater of Port Arthur – and Janis, who made the journey, never quite knew why or how she'd made it.

novelist and LSD-experimenter Ken Kesey), Ron 'Pigpen' McKernan, Grace Slick, Janis Joplin, Spencer Dryden – all folk, jazz or blues people who now heard the call of rock'n'roll and would soon become familiar names in the first family of San Francisco bands: the Grateful Dead, Jefferson Airplane, Moby Grape, Big Brother and the Holding Company, Quicksilver Messenger Service.

In the Bay Area, LSD quickly became part of a dramatically radical scene which moved from North Beach to the notorious Haight-Ashbury district of San Francisco. There were revolutionary students from Berkeley campus, the Sexual Freedom League, dance troupes, mime troupes and a burgeoning commune movement. The mid-sixties saw a variety of dances, festivals and benefits (among them, Ken Kesey's famous 'Acid Tests') at which musicians, poets, face-painters, Hell's Angels and even ordinary people were piled into one large room dosed with LSD, dazzled with light-shows, seasoned with music, films, make-up and exotic costumes and left to simmer all night. 'Fluid' was the word that fitted.

Jerry Garcia, sometimes known as Captain Trips, and some of his LSD-soaked friends, played music at the early Acid Tests. They were known as the Warlocks, later they became the Grateful Dead. In those days, the band took plenty of drugs – dropping acid, so it was said, before *every* show. For a while, the band was being supported by one Augustus Owsley Stanley III, a drop-out engineering student who had set up his own laboratory and supplied much of San Francisco's LSD. Owsley poured his profits into a sound system for the Warlocks of such unparalleled power and complexity that it took three or four years for the rest of rock to catch up.

'Acid has changed consciousness entirely,' Garcia said at around this time. 'The US has changed in the last few years and it's because that whole first psychedelic thing meant: here's this new consciousness, this new freedom, and it's here in yourself.'

Although the electric heroes of rock were among its first and most avid disciples, by no means all rock stars favoured LSD. Janis Joplin and the Grateful Dead's Ron 'Pigpen' McKernan, for example, rejected LSD in favour of booze, speed or heroin. They seemed scared of LSD's disorientating effects, and sought other drugs and drink in order not to 'expand their consciousness' but to shut it down. But, LSD or not, everyone shared the common attitude of experimentation, hedonism and excess.

With typical exaggeration, somewhere between exuberance and calculated image-building, Janis recalled her mood on arriving in San Francisco in 1963. 'I'd've fucked anything, .'. . I did,' she told David Dalton. 'I'd lick it, smoke it, shoot it, drop it, fall in love with it.' She tried acid only once in those days. Sometime later when she inadvertently drank LSD-laced wine, she forced herself to vomit rather than endure the trip.

Yet her consumption of drink and other drugs was prodigious. Within a few months of leaving her Texas home-town in the early sixties she had become heavily dependent on speed; her death in 1970 was due, according to the inquest, to a self-administered heroin overdose; an open bottle of tequila or Southern Comfort had been a permanent companion on and off-stage. As with many other rock stars, the drugs and drink all but eclipsed the music. Janis's later performances became caricatures of the woman she had then become – drunk, drugged, pained and passionate, trapped between torture and orgasm and screaming hoarsely for release. 'It's not what isn't, it's what you wish *was* that makes unhappiness,' she said. 'The hole, the vacuum . . . I think I think too much. That's why I drink. . . .'

If she could hold back, she preferred not to drink till a few minutes before going on stage because she felt that her best times were when performing and she could never remember them if she was too drunk to start with. Running on stage at 'full-tilt boogie' was, for her, as good as an orgasm – 'better than it has been with any man'. Performance was the key term in her personal equation between sex and drugs and rock'n'roll. Lonely and desperate for love, she found solace in men, women and – best of all – anonymous audiences who alone seemed to promise an uncomplicated release.

But release never came – the common ambivalences of her soul were magnified by the heights of adulation she attained. She once commented in evident amazement that her fans paid her $50,000 a year to be like her. And like her they were – especially if they were women. More than anyone else, she was the cultural symbol of a need for liberation that women were only beginning to rediscover and from which men would ultimately gain. She stood for the future, yet she never overcame the memory of her own past – an unpopular pupil at school, an unhappy and alienated child at home. She couldn't admit her stardom; she liked to be 'one of the boys' but needed to be treated as a helpless little woman; she had dreams of marriage and, according to a former boyfriend, Country Joe MacDonald, wanted children, but she lived and died a child herself and a faithless woman among faithless men. Booze and speed charged her up; heroin blanked out the despair. And though she tried to sort herself out, even managing to overcome her addiction to speed, the last shot of smack took its toll on a sad and abused body. On 4th October, 1970, alone in her room in Hollywood's Landmark Hotel, she collapsed and died from an overdose, splitting open her troubled head as she fell to the ground. She had been in the middle of recording what turned out to be her last album, *Pearl*: by all accounts the sessions had been going well. It may not have been suicide, but then a self-administered heroin overdose is hardly an accident.

Pigpen – who inspired the Grateful Dead with his passion for the blues – slowly poisoned himself with

Ron 'Pigpen' McKernan – bulky prototype for a heavy metal kid in 1967 – weighed only 100 lb when he died from drink in 1973, aged 27.

alcohol. Not even the relative anonymity in which he enjoyed success, nor the egalitarian character of the Dead and their relationship with audiences, could protect Pigpen. Like Janis, he was a loner – part of, yet apart from, the San Francisco scene. He too avoided acid, only taking it once – and then because it was daubed on the lip of an unopened drink can. (It was common for the evangelical sixties' acidheads to dose drinks with LSD and give them to unsuspecting victims. Aware of such japes, Pigpen never drank from already opened cans, but that precaution wasn't enough.) In 1971, by the age of 26, Pigpen had ruined his liver beyond repair and illness forced him out of the Dead. He lingered for another eighteen months. On 8th March, 1973, his once bulky body was found in his apartment in Corte Madera, California – his stomach haemorrhaged and most of his internal organs wasted. He weighed just over 100 lbs and looked twice his 27 years.

Acid had also found ready converts in the place already known as Swinging London. Naturally, the rock musicians whose names were almost synonymous with that over-worked phrase were part of the elite band of young aristocrats, artists and photographers, musicians and models, hairdressers and Harley Street doctors' daughters whose names rang out of the gossip columns and who frequented the night-clubs and restaurants of Soho and Chelsea. Money was the great leveller – upwards – and despite the Carnaby Street image of psychedelia on the cheap, the Beatles, Stones and their friends were early on cocooned in a world of privilege where sex was freer, the drugs more available, the clothes and cars more expensive than anything most of their fans could have imagined. 'We were kings,' Lennon remembered. 'We were all just at the prime . . . it was like a men's smoking club, just a very good scene.'

The Beatles tours became, in Lennon's words, 'like Satyricon'. So much money was being made that no one could mock them – and why should they when the boys in the band picked up the tabs for drinks, drugs, meals and whores. Even those who could afford to pay for their own pleasures, felt a need to buy entrance to the most exclusive 'men's smoking club' in the world by offering gifts unavailable to the common herd. In fact it was a dentist who first introduced John Lennon and George Harrison to LSD. Without telling them, he dosed both of them and their wives, Cynthia and Patti, at a dinner party. 'He was saying, "I advise you not to leave",' Lennon said later, 'and we thought he was trying to keep us for an orgy in his house.' (Obviously a common occurrence.) 'We didn't want to know,' added Lennon, and so it was that the trip hit them at a night-club later, with its usual disconcerting delusions. The club was on fire, their table seemed to elongate, and at George's house, John imagined he was in a submarine floating eighteen feet above the ground. George Harrison told journalist Hunter Davies, 'It was as if I'd never tasted, talked, seen, thought or heard properly before.'

Lennon took his second trip in California, during the Beatles' 1965 tour. Jim McGuinn, Dave Crosby and Peter Fonda were there, as well as George, Ringo and the Beatles' road manager, Neil Aspinall. This was the occasion on which Fonda kept whispering 'I know what it's like to be dead', which at least gave Lennon the hook for a song. After that, trips came thick and fast: Lennon claimed he dropped acid a thousand times – all the while taking speed to help get by in recording sessions.

Through 1966 and 1967, LSD spread through the British rock scene like wildfire. Eric Clapton claimed that 'Acid was conducive to exploring music'. After taking it he never played straight blues. The Rolling Stones, leaders of the sixties' rebels of rock, also joined the beautiful people. Brian Jones, who had initially been the drive and musical inspiration behind the Rolling Stones, was particularly prominent. In 1966, the Stones found themselves musically dried up. LSD provided something of an answer, encouraging them eventually to make *Their Satanic Majesties Request*. The only problem was Brian Jones, who spent his time in the studio tripping out in a corner, contributing little or nothing to the recording sessions.

Jones and his Italian-German girlfriend, Anita Pallenberg, inhabited a world of self-obsessive callousness, but on the streets of London they dazzled the world with their androgyne splendour. As part of the underground they were members of a tight little family, whose house magazines were IT (*International Times*) and *Oz*. The 'all-night rave' thrown to launch IT was visited by Paul McCartney dressed as an Arab and accompanied by Jane Asher (the proverbial Harley Street doctor's daughter). Unhampered by intrusive fans, the Beatles, Pete Townshend, Jimi Hendrix and the Stones could visit John Hopkins' club UFO (standing for Unlimited Freak Out), and at the same IT launch party, Marianne Faithfull, with four top ten hits under her belt, could win a prize for 'the shortest/barest costume' dressed as a nun in a bottomless habit, without anyone being uncool enough to make a fuss about it.

But of course they wouldn't be allowed to get away with it. After all, the drugs they openly used were illegal, and though rock stars were cushioned by privilege and wealth, their fans were following suit and were in the eyes of the media being seduced by the easy pleasure of drug-fuelled liberation. Horror stories began to be unleashed on the public – many of them complete fabrications, issuing from government agencies. LSD was made illegal in California in October 1966, and began to be condemned in unequivocal terms: 'The greatest threat facing the country today . . . more dangerous than the Vietnam war' was how the chairman of the New Jersey Narcotic Drug Study Commission described it. Sexual licence and a breakdown in social order were identified, not altogether inaccurately, with the spread of drug use, and a police crackdown began. Rock stars were prime targets – especially once phenomenally popular heroes of the young publicly confessed to having used (and sometimes enjoyed) illegal drugs.

In July 1966, the folksy Donovan, (full name Donovan Leitch, once heralded as Britain's Bob Dylan), was fined £250 for possession of marijuana. 'I would like you to bear in mind,' said the magistrate, 'that you have great influence on young people, and it behoves you to behave yourself.' A London Sunday paper reported that 'evidence disclosed a shocking scene of debauchery at a reefer smoking party in his flat', and, despite claiming to have given up drugs altogether after the case, Donovan's immediate response was to comment that 'I hope it won't hurt my career'. Of course the press was indignant and took great relish in pointing out that Donovan was, at that time, earning £25,000 a year.

An investigation by the *News of the World* followed Donovan's conviction. The investigation had some far-reaching, if unexpected, consequences. In the course of the paper's four-week series, banner headlined 'DRUGS AND POP STARS – Facts that will SHOCK you', it was 'revealed' that members of the Moody Blues had taken LSD, Pete Townshend (who had previously admitted to taking marijuana and pep pills) had taken LSD, Ginger Baker had gone 'from hash and LSD to heroin and cocaine' and that, generally, drug use among pop stars was rife and clearly demonstrated by the titles and lyrics of numerous songs, like Donovan's *Sunshine Superman*, the Move's *Night Of Fear*, the Beach Boys' *Good Vibrations* and even the Mothers of Invention's *Can't Happen Here*, which, the *News of the World* wrote, was said to have been made on a LSD trip, (by whom, one wonders, since the Mothers' leader, Frank Zappa, is one of the few who definitely *didn't* trip out). The paper also

39

Back in 1967, rock stars wore suits to go before the law. On 10th May, 1967, Mick Jagger and Keith Richard run the gauntlet of the Chichester citizenry after electing to go to trial by jury following their arrest on drugs charges at Redlands, Richard's house in the Sussex countryside.

Marianne Faithfull, Mick Jagger's girlfriend, was described as Miss X during the Redlands trial. She was supposed to have been naked but for a fur rug.

revealed the 'inside story' of psychedelic events, paying particular attention to 'bare-breasted girls' at 'a freak-out' – complete with pictures, of course.

Many of the paper's revelations were unreliable – a fact which was dramatically demonstrated when Mick Jagger instituted libel proceedings against it. The paper had attributed to Jagger the substance of an interview about drug-taking that two unnamed 'investigators' had in fact had with Brian Jones. However, the real impact of the articles soon became evident. Jagger's libel suit was lodged two days after the *News of the World* article naming him appeared. Five days later, on 12th February, 1967, Keith Richard's house in the Sussex countryside, known as Redlands, was raided, with the resulting arrest of Richard, Jagger and art dealer Robert Fraser. Eight men were present, 'two of whom were hangers-on', according to one of the prosecutors at one of the subsequent trials, 'and the third a Moroccan servant'. (Persistent rumour maintains that that there was a ninth – George Harrison – but although he had been at Redlands that weekend, Harrison had left before the raid.) There was also one woman present – called 'Miss X' in court, but actually Marianne Faithfull (whose name the Stones wanted kept out of the whole affair). But further harassment was to follow. On the day of Jagger and Richard's committal appearance in court, 10th May, Brian Jones

THE TIMES

PRINTING HOUSE SQUARE, LONDON, E.C.4.   TELEPHONE: 01-236 2000

WHO BREAKS A BUTTERFLY ON A WHEEL?

MR. JAGGER has been sentenced to imprisonment for three months. He is appealing against conviction and sentence, and has been granted bail until the hearing of the appeal later in the year. In the meantime, the sentence of imprisonment is bound to be widely discussed by the public. And the circumstances are sufficiently unusual to warrant such discussion in the public interest.

MR. JAGGER was charged with being in possession of four tablets containing amphetamine sulphate and methyl amphetamine hydrochloride; these tablets had been bought, perfectly legally, in Italy, and brought back to this cou~~~~. They are not a highly danger~~~~ ~~ proper dosage a danger~~~~ ~~~ ~ of the benze~~~~ factu~~~~ stim~~~~ sick~~~~

They were separate cases, and no evidence was produced to suggest that he knew that MR. FRASER had heroin tablets or that the vanishing MR. SNEIDERMANN had cannabis resin. It is indeed no offence to be in the same building or the same company as people possessing or even using drugs, nor could it reasonably be made an offence. The drugs which MR. JAGGER had in his posse~~~ must therefore be treated ~~~~~ as a separate ~~~~~

that JUDGE BLOCK should have decided to sentence MR. JAGGER to imprisonment, and particularly surprising as MR. JAGGER'S is about as mild a drug case as can ever have been brought before the Courts.

It would be wrong to sp~~~~~ ~e JUDGE'S reasons ~~~~~~ It is ~~~~~

~~~~~ ~oming to ~~~~ ~esent the anarchic ~~y of the Rolling Stones' performances, dislike their songs, dislike their ~fluence on teenagers and broadly ~spect them of decadence, a word used ~~~ MISS MONICA FURLONG in the *Daily Mail*.

As a sociological concern this may be reasonable enough, and at an emotional level it is very understandable, but it has nothing at all to do with the case. One ~~~~~ ~k a different question: has MR. ~~~~~ the same treatment as ~~~~ f he had not ~~~~~

'NUDE GIRL AT STONES PARTY'

Jagger leaves jail handcuffs

~an pep pills, ~ but not legally im- Four is

'Stones' get summonses after raid

Daily Mirror

4d.   Saturday, March 18, 1967   No. 19,667

JAGGER IS ACCUSED OVER DRUGS

Jagger—accused.

BY BARRY STANLEY and JOHN SANDIFORD

TWO of the Rolling Stones pop group—Mick Jagger and Keith Richard—have been accused of offences against the drug laws.

Summonses against the two men—both aged 22—were issued after a police raid on Richard's £20,000 farmhouse home at West Witteri~ Sussex.

The summonses, due to be dealt with at Chichester magistr~~ expected to be served early next week. Two other~~~ summoned.

Brian Jones on his way from court on £2,000 bail. He had been charged with possession of cannabis at his Chelsea flat on 21st May, 1968.

With friends like these who needs enemies? Brian, visibly deteriorating, accepts a kiss from girlfriend Suki Potier, and the upright support of fellow Rolling Stones, Keith Richard and Mick Jagger. Brian had just been on the witness stand to deny possession of 144 grains of cannabis. Within a year he was dead.

was arrested on drugs charges at his London flat. The campaign against drug use was hotting up.

Jagger and Richard's trials, held in June 1967, were fated to become spectacular engagements in the phoney war between youth and the establishment. Jagger, charged with possessing four legally purchased Italian amphetamine tablets, was sentenced to six months' imprisonment; Richard, charged with allowing his premises to be used for smoking cannabis, was jailed for a year. On appeal, Jagger's sentence was reduced to a conditional discharge and Richard's was quashed on the grounds that the prosecution put too much emphasis on the role of Miss X. It was felt that the reliance of the prosecution on the evidently carefree behaviour of a young woman who was naked but for a fur rug when the raid took place, suggested moral opprobrium – even prurience – rather than legal consideration. During the trial Jagger was held for two days in Lewes prison, an experience which shocked him deeply.

One exchange between Keith and the prosecution indicates the tone of the original trial. Replying to the prosecution's suggestion that Miss X should have been embarrassed by the state of undress in which she was found, Richard said: 'We are not old men. We are not worried about your petty morals.' The *News of the World* – in a sudden fit of moral rectitude – sub-

sequently admitted passing on information to the police which led to the arrests.

After the Redlands raid and the subsequent trial, Paul McCartney and Brian Epstein both publically admitted to taking LSD – as did Eric Burdon. Burdon claimed to have given it up by then, but later revealed that until 1970 he had spent most of his time on acid. The press and public picked up the smell of vendetta. The role of the *News of the World* in the whole affair raised considerable doubts as to the propriety of the Redlands arrests in the first place. There was a widespread feeling that what highly paid adults did in the privacy of their own homes warranted no intrusion by sensationalist newspapers and killjoy policemen. The picture of Jagger in handcuffs on his way to Lewes prison was a clear image of the victimization of a scapegoat. 'Who breaks a butterfly on a wheel?' asked the *Times*. 'Let him who is without sin jail the first Stone,' said a popular poster.

Restricting people's freedom of movement is one thing, but – as Keith Richard commented about Brian Jones – 'they hounded Brian to death'. At the trial following his bust in May 1967, a psychiatrist described Brian as 'an extremely frightened young man'. A sentence of nine months' imprisonment for possessing cannabis was over-harsh, especially since the sentences passed on Jagger and Richard following the Redlands raid had already been effectively overturned on appeal, following an unprecedented public fuss. But Brian's sentence was particularly stressful since he had already spent some time in hospital, suffering from what was politely called 'strain' and one of the psychiatrists at the trial had commented that Jones had suicidal tendencies. In December 1967, the sentence was at last commuted – to £1,000 fine and three years' probation – but three days later, Jones had collapsed again and was once more in hospital. Six

A floral tribute for Brian Jones from Mick Jagger and Marianne Faithfull who had already left for Australia. While Brian was being buried in England, Marianne was in a coma in a Sydney hospital, after an overdose of sodium amytal tablets.

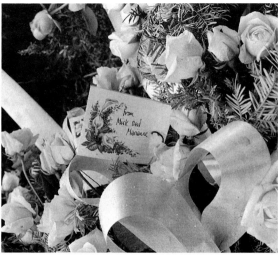

months later, in May 1968, Brian was arrested again on a drugs charge. This time the fine was only £50 but the real punishment was the psychological damage caused by so much police interest.

The harassment accelerated Brian's general decline. The Stones as a whole found it increasingly difficult to work under the permanent threat of imprisonment and Jones himself was rapidly sinking into complete mental and physical stupor. He believed Jagger and Richard were conspiring against him. Even his girlfriend, Anita Pallenberg, had deserted him for Keith. Brian's total insecurity was reflected in the reputation he had acquired for near satyriasis (60 women a month was the figure bandied about) and, believing himself deliberately shut out of the decision-making, creativity and companionship of the Rolling Stones, he withdrew into drug dependence and manic hedonism. His own suspicions turned into a self-fulfilling prophecy. By the summer of 1968, Jack Nitzsche – scoring the music for Nicolas Roeg's film, *Performance*, which starred Jagger and Pallenberg – observed that the Stones had, in reality, turned against their former golden boy. Brian, in his turn, became literally incapable of making music: when he tried to play harmonica, his mouth started bleeding.

In mid-summer, 1969, Brian quit the band, ostensibly to pursue a solo career, in fact because he was a liability. The Stones were planning a tour and Brian was incapable of undertaking it. A month later, on 3rd July, he drowned in the swimming pool of his secluded mansion in Sussex (once the home of A. A. Milne and Christopher Robin) – many of his vital organs suffering fatty degeneration that could, in itself, have killed him. Two days later, his replacement, Mick Taylor, made his first public appearance with the Stones at an open-air concert in Hyde Park. Jagger, looking Byronesque in a white Greek-style tunic dress, released hundreds of butterflies and everybody felt sad. Pete Townshend's response to Brian's death was to comment, 'It was a normal day for Brian, he died every day.' And ten years later, Jagger recalled that 'I felt a bit shocked, but it was really inevitable. The guy was unbearable, but maybe it was us that made him unbearable.' Precisely who 'hounded Brian to death' remains an unanswerable question.

In America, drug-related arrests in the sixties were mainly concentrated on the West Coast – mecca of the drug culture. The Grateful Dead's communal house at 710 Ashbury, in San Francisco's notorious Haight-Ashbury district, was raided in 1967 with the consequent arrest of eleven people for possession of marijuana (not including Jerry Garcia, who was warned of the bust on the street outside the house). Interestingly, the police failed to discover a large stash of grass in a glass jar on a kitchen shelf: in fact, infor-

The Grateful Dead hold a press conference on 5th October, 1967, after the police raided their communal house in San Francisco, acting on a tip-off. This really was the end of the summer of love. L. to r.: Pigpen, Bill Kreutzmann, Phil Lesh, managers Rock Scully (who has since done time for drug trafficking) and Dan Rifkin, Bob Weir, Jerry Garcia (known as Captain Trips), and the group's lawyer.

It took forty of London's finest to arrest John Lennon and Yoko Ono on charges of possession of marijuana – and about as many to escort them from the court the next day, 19th October, 1968. Yoko suffered a miscarriage a week before John was convicted on 28th November, and the conviction led to immigration problems when Lennon wanted to settle in America.

mers had been used so no search was undertaken. Dino Valenti – who had written *Get Together*, the true anthem of the 'love generation' – was busted at this time, as were Neil Young, Richie Furay, Jim Messina and Bruce Palmer, (all of Buffalo Springfield). Palmer was taken three times and, in fact, Messina was brought in to replace him in the group. Eric Clapton, arrested with the Springfield members in March 1968, was acquitted.

At times, the consequences of this campaign on both sides of the Atlantic were no less damaging to careers than the drug-taking itself. John Lennon, busted in 1968 with Yoko Ono, was denied a resident's permit for the United States as a consequence (although the objections to the permit only emerged after he had released *Sometime In New York City*, an openly revolutionary album, in 1972). Lennon finally got his 'Green Card' in 1975, only to be gunned down outside his New York home in 1980, a few weeks after his fortieth birthday.

If addiction turned some rock musicians into liabilities for their fellows, it was a godsend to the police, always happy to increase their arrest figures and hence their public presence by making a few uncomplicated busts. But the circumstances of John Lennon's 1968 arrest, the culmination of two years of 'exemplary' raids by the narcotics division, actually led to questions in

Parliament. How was it, MPs wondered, that it took 40 policemen to arrest two people (John and Yoko) who weren't thinking of running away, and how was it that two national daily newspapers were already present to witness the arrest before the police even arrived? There was more than a suspicion that the drug squad was scalp-hunting and the press had been tipped off. ('Tipping off' in fact worked both ways, however; a showbiz correspondent had warned Lennon some three weeks earlier and John and Yoko had 'cleaned the house out', because, said Lennon, who was on heroin at the time, 'I'm not stupid.')

The theory is still current that John and Yoko's big-time bust was precipitated by reaction against the release of their album, *Two Virgins*, which featured the couple naked on the sleeve. But this is stretching the power of prudery too far. On the other hand, since there was a general feeling at the time that the Beatles (MBE) were actually immune from arrest, the swoop demands some explanation. Even the *News of the World*, eager to explore the illegal drug use of other rock stars, had shied away from tarring the Beatles with that brush. Leading rock groups, like the Beatles, 'derived their success from sheer native genius,' the paper had written in January 1967. 'But others in the pop world needed or sought artificial means to gain recognition.' The clear implication was that the Beatles were above the use of drugs.

However, eighteen months later in 1968, student riots and protests from Paris to Berkeley and back, had made the threat of youthful rebellion seem sufficiently ominous to outweigh these previous considerations. Busts that might have been unthinkable before the Redlands raid and unwise after it were now zealously pursued (although sentences were usually of saner proportions than had once been the case). As far as the Beatles were concerned, it was significant that Brian Epstein was dead (ironically, from a drug overdose), and that the group was in disarray. After the McCartney–Epstein confessions, their image was tarnishing fast. All of which meant that they could now become targets in the war against drugs, with John Lennon being especially vulnerable for his outspoken views and 'outlandish' women.

Paradoxically, the new light in which the Beatles were seen also helped make drug use among rock stars an acceptable, if generally unspoken, fact. As so many times before and since, the moralistic outrage of the press ultimately served only to diminish the hold of its phoney puritanism. Magistrates and judges seemed more and more to regard drug use as a sort of occupational hazard, if not an unavoidable feature of the rock star's milieu. Accordingly, since the late sixties, while the police have opposed rock stars with some vigour, the courts have disposed of them with a sometimes surprising degree of leniency, based on the apparent assumption that the private use of drugs by rock stars is only to be expected.

When, for example, Jimi Hendrix was busted for heroin at Toronto Airport in 1969, his trial defence was that he had unwittingly accepted the drug as a casual gift from a generous fan. The court acquitted him

Jimi Hendrix died in bed on 18th September, 1970, choking on his own vomit after an overdose of pills. Hendrix was the personification of sex and drugs and rock'n'roll; 'he was the heaviest doper I ever met,' said Eric Burdon.

despite (or, perhaps, because of) his surprising confession to have taken LSD, pot and cocaine. Perhaps they believed him when he said he had outgrown drugs, as any number of rock stars seem to persist in falsely claiming. Jimi might have wanted to give up drugs but never did.

After ex-Animal Chas Chandler brought Seattle-born Hendrix to London in 1966, the guitarist's career rocketed. Hendrix's musicianship was stunning, and, of course, he had the added *caché* of black machismo, which he was quite capable of exploiting to the full. But his temper was fearsome and most of his personal relationships seemed unstable. Internal conflicts ensured the eventual break-up of his band, the Experience, after relations between himself and Noel Redding deteriorated completely, and in 1969, Hendrix split with Chas Chandler. On top of these problems, Hendrix's meteoric rise unleashed a hail of reissues and bootlegs. Everyone wanted to get in on the act, and by the end of the sixties, Hendrix was rapidly becoming entangled in a web of legal and business hassles.

Jimi made an attempt to control his own affairs but

British politician Jeremy Thorpe cops a lick from Jimi Hendrix backstage at London's Royal Albert Hall, in 1967. The strange meeting took place before a concert in aid of the Liberal Party, of which Thorpe was the leader before his disgrace and downfall in the seventies, following revelations of his relationship with a homosexual. In spite of this meeting, as far as we know Jimi never made a political speech in his life and Jeremy still can't play Purple Haze.

After the death of Jimi Hendrix, West German skater Monika Danemann, suffering from shock, is helped from her hotel by a friend. Hendrix was discovered unconscious in her hotel suite, but was found to be dead on arrival at hospital.

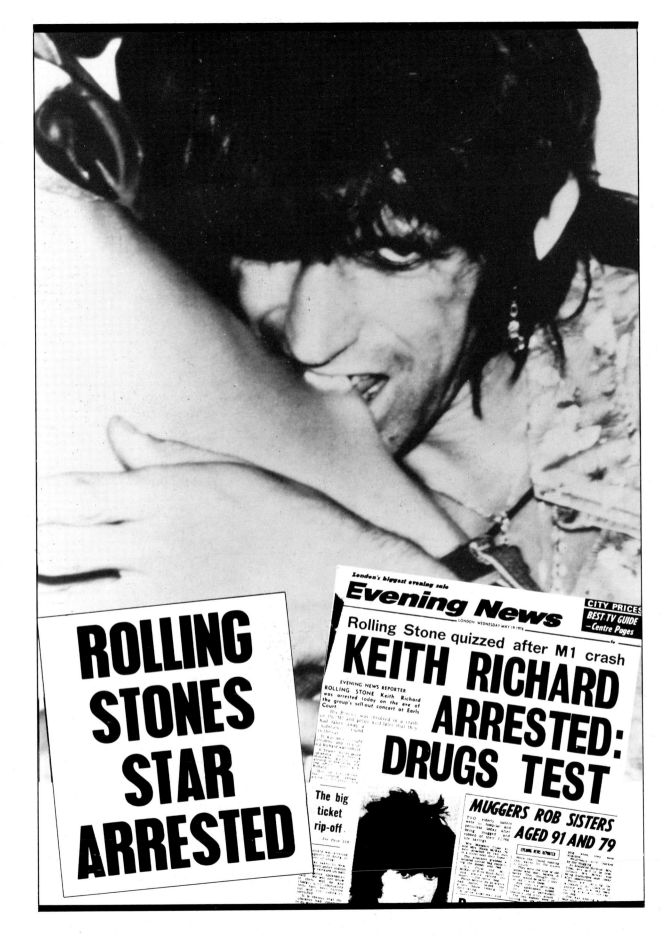

ROLLING STONES STAR ARRESTED

he was temperamentally unable to sort things out for himself. He formed an all-black group (the Band of Gypsies), and also became involved in a recording studio project. But he had neither the time nor the patience to make a success of either. Living in New York after the Toronto bust, he was harassed by the police. He was pulled one way and another by his contractual problems and his somewhat tentative desire to be associated with the mood of black pride. The pressures may have been too great for him, as his friend Eric Burdon suggested, or maybe his death was merely an accident. Whatever the truth, it seemed to occur just when the crest of Hendrix's wave had broken and something had to give.

On the night of 18th September, 1970, a year which had seen him in a downward spiral of lack-lustre performances and recordings, he took a handful of Vesperax sleeping pills, after an evening spent drinking white wine moderately, and smoking a little grass. He died choking on his own vomit as a result of the overdose of pills. The coroner declared an open verdict at the inquest, but Hendrix's death was probably just the result of a momentary desire for some temporary peace of mind.

Less than eight years after Jimi's acquittal in Toronto, Anita Pallenberg was arrested at the airport there while carrying drugs. She was in the company of Keith Richard who was himself arrested a few days later in his hotel room, almost ten years to the day after the Redlands raid. It was Richard's sixth arrest in four countries during the seventies alone – on a variety of

Keith Richard checks he's still alive, while facing the press in Toronto on 20th October 1978, after pleading guilty to the charges brought in 1977.

Accompanied by William Carter, the Stones' US attorney, Keith Richard arrives at the court in Toronto on 14th March, 1977, to face charges of possession of heroin 'with intent to traffic', and with possession of cocaine.

counts from possession of dangerous drugs to assault and weapons charges. Fears that the Canadian authorities' notorious severity on drugs matters would at last put an end to the Rolling Stones were, in the event, unwarranted. The really serious charge of trafficking in heroin was dropped and, to the chagrin of the state prosecutor, the court sentenced Richard to serve a term of probation and to play a benefit concert for the blind on lesser counts of possession. In 1981, Richard himself recalled the Toronto bust as the peak of two years of trouble with the law. 'I was so stoned throughout that whole period,' he commented about the arrests, 'that I just accepted it as part of doing what I was doing. I didn't even bother.'

Since the sixties the Stones have continued to be prime targets for the law and it's often hard to tell to what extent it is the product of their own carefully constructed 'outlaw' image. In Keith's case, we have his own testimony that he and Anita were indeed preoccupied with a variety of illegal substances for a long time, and, while Mick, Bill Wyman and Charlie Watts have remained in low profile, other Stones' associates seem to be at risk by virtue of their very association. In February 1980, Ron Wood and his girl-friend Josephine Karslake, were arrested in the West Indies on charges of possessing cocaine after the alleged suppliers had informed to the police. Even

49

The 219 grams of marijuana found in baggage belonging to Paul McCartney by Japanese customs. 'Imagine smuggling half-a-pound of marijuana in an ordinary suitcase,' went a joke after the Tokyo bust. 'I always knew Lennon was the brains behind the Beatles.'

non-members of the group are at risk. In July 1972, for example, the group's chauffeur was arrested for possession during the US tour, and, in 1975, the year in which Ron Wood joined the Stones, his wife Krissie was busted for possession of cocaine and cannabis during a bizarre early morning raid when the police burst in on her in bed with a dress-maker friend, Audrey Burgon. They were later acquitted.

The war against drug use by rock stars continues, although evidently with a slightly different angle. When, in January 1980, Paul McCartney was arrested on his way into Japan for carrying half a pound of marijuana, at least one London paper was moved to comment that since McCartney had been busted three times for marijuana (in 1973, it was for actually growing the plant at his Scottish home in Campbelltown), the fact that he was a good father, an efficient businessman and a good husband demonstrated that marijuana was not a bad thing.

Even the Japanese – who, in 1973, had refused Mick Jagger a visa on the grounds of his 1967 conviction and in 1975 had banned McCartney, too – seemed less sure that severity was appropriate. McCartney, who was scheduled to play a series of concerts with Wings, had arrived at Narita Airport with Linda and their children. The Japanese customs were at first convinced that the marijuana was in one of Linda's suitcases, until Paul stepped forward to admit ownership. Paul spent nine days in jail, during which time questions were asked in the British Parliament about his treatment and the British Consulate in Japan made every effort to secure his release. Eventually, the Japanese authorities let McCartney go and dropped charges, although they banned him from re-entering Japan for a year. He had bought the marijuana for his

own use, they said, and had in any case suffered nine days in jail and the financial losses due to the cancellation of all his concerts. 'Imagine smuggling half a pound of marijuana in an ordinary suitcase,' went a joke of the time. 'I always knew Lennon was the brains behind the Beatles.'

The police response to *punk* drug use was less sanguine. In March 1980, Hugh Cornwell of the Stranglers was sentenced to (and served) two months imprisonment for possession of heroin, cocaine and marijuana – found in his car during a routine check. The sentence was surprisingly harsh, for a first offence and considering the small amount of drugs involved. The judge, however, echoing the wisdom of his colleagues across the years, told Cornwell that his term in jail would be 'an example to others'.

In fact, the favourite punk drug was often-lethal glue, for those who could afford nothing else, and amphetamine in sniffable powder form ('sulphate') for those who could. In 1978, Sid Vicious and Nancy Spungen were arrested for possessing the particularly powerful amphetamine, methedrine, in their room in a London hotel. Johnny Rotten's public denials that he took drugs did not prevent his flat being raided twice (to no effect). Police activity against punks maintained a particularly high level during the brief period of the music's popularity – and one was irresistibly reminded of the harassment of performers who had been thought equally threatening years ago.

By the mid-seventies, the rock establishment had become inseparably linked to the drug trade. Cocaine and marijuana had become staples of the industry – it was estimated that 90 per cent of all cocaine use in the US centred on the rock and film industries, while 10 per cent of the American population used cocaine and a considerably higher percentage used marijuana. Countries in Latin America producing these two drugs found their economies becoming grotesquely distorted by reliance on this illegal trade. The relationship between rock and drugs in the seventies encouraged law enforcement agencies to take a pragmatic view. In most cases, arrests were directed at clearing up a significant trade, but in only a few did rock stars or their associates suffer greatly.

In 1977, the Grateful Dead's manager Rock Scully was jailed for four months for conspiracy to smuggle marijuana, but he was something of an exception. Far more typical was the 1976 arrest and trial of John 'Scooter' Herring – Gregg Allman's personal roadie. Gregg was offered immunity from prosecution if he testified against Herring – the man who allegedly supplied Allman with the considerable amounts of cocaine he used. Allman accepted the deal, saying, 'I was scared to death to go in there and have them ask me these things, but it was either that or go to jail.' Allman's wife of twelve days, Cher Bono, had sued

Paul McCartney is dragged handcuffed and wearing compulsory sandals into Nakameguro Police Station, after his arrest at Narita Airport, Japan, in January 1980, when customs officers found a bag of marijuana in his suitcase. McCartney spent nine nights in jail before being deported without playing a note.

Blackballed by the Allman Brothers Band after testifying against his personal roadie, John 'Scooter' Herring, in a cocaine trial which brought the hapless Herring a sentence totalling more than 70 years, Greg Allman is seen in court answering reckless driving charges on 4th June, 1979.

him for divorce, she said, after finding out about his drug use, but his testimony in the Herring case helped convince her that he had licked his problem and she returned to him. Other members of the Allman Brothers Band were considerably less affectionate. 'There is no way we can work with Gregg again, ever,' said guitarist Dicky Betts, shocked at the coolness with which Allman betrayed the trust of a man who'd worked for him for two years and, apparently, saved his life twice. Herring had, according to the band, been doing no more than serving Gregg's requirements faithfully. He was sentenced to a total of 75 years (reduced on appeal) and the Allman Brothers Band effectively went out of business.

John Phillips, founder member of the Mamas and Papas, testified against an associate following his 1980 arrest on charges of being involved in a drug ring supplying pills and cocaine. After his arrest, Phillips – a highly successful songwriter and producer – and his daughter went on a lecture tour of the US to campaign against drug abuse. His six year jail sentence was suspended for all but 30 days, much of which had already been spent on remand.

Also in 1980, Fleetwood Mac's John McVie and his second wife Julie Ann were arrested on charges of possessing cocaine following a raid on their home in Hawaii, which also uncovered some pills, marijuana and seven guns. The cocaine charges against John McVie were dropped when his wife admitted possession, although he was convicted on lesser weapons charges. McVie, a resident alien in the US, could have

52

faced deportation on the more serious charges. As it is, he will be able to pay his not inconsiderable US taxes for some time to come.

Once upon a time, drugs were seen as a route to a new form of musical expression. Today, with all the emphasis on 'recreational drugs' as new consumer commodities, drug-taking in quantity is all too often seen as the reward and proof of rock stardom. And between taking drugs to make music and making music to take drugs, the performers, the music and the fans have lost more than the law could ever take.

Syd Barrett, for example, was a founder member of Pink Floyd. He was apparently the first of the band to experiment with LSD, although as Floyd's Roger Waters once said, 'There was so much dope and acid around in those days that I don't think anyone can remember anything about anything.' Even so, it's clear that Syd overdid things. In no time at all, he had taken to a performance style which consisted of playing one chord all night. From then, it was only a matter of time before he learned to stand on stage and not play at all. Sometimes he didn't even appear. On a tour of America in late 1967, the Floyd played 'American Bandstand'. They were meant to mime to their second single, *See Emily Play*, but unfortunately Syd 'wasn't into moving his lips that day'. Two or three months later, Syd left the band and disappeared from view, only surfacing to cut two albums some years later and become the subject of a curious cult which considers him a genius. Meanwhile he has retired once more into obscurity.

Eric Burdon – who found initial success with the Animals – was another acid casualty. Always something of a rebel, Burdon started taking LSD in 1965, and didn't stop until the early seventies. In 1967, he and an Anglo-Indian model, Angie King, were married in London in a ceremony that was widely heralded as *the* 'flower power' wedding. Later Eric remarked that 'the ceremony was great; the marriage was dreadful'. When the Animals split, Eric followed the love generation to its source in San Francisco and recorded *San Francisco Nights* and *Good Times* – paeans to psychedelia. Singing the praises of LSD and meditation in 1968, he said mysteriously, 'I've done a complete circle. I am 21 days behind Bob Dylan.' By the end of that year he was planning to quit rock for a film career. He had suffered a nervous breakdown and the end of his marriage.

Living in Laurel Canyon in a house with his girlfriend, his road manager and a pick-up truck, he wrote elaborate treatments for movies (which no-one else could understand or wanted to buy), and talked about becoming a movie star. Meanwhile his girlfriend made pillow cases to sell for food. Eventually, a couple of management hot-shots informed him that if he wanted to be a movie star, first he had to become a rock star again. Eric attempted a comeback fronting a black group called War, but it was a disaster. He was still heavily into 'change and revolution' and War just wanted to be a funky band. 'The American black group

Eric Burdon abandoned the more exotic substances he once favoured for the mind-numbing effects of cheap Spanish plonk.

I was looking for was not War,' said Eric. When Jimi Hendrix (a friend and profound influence) died in September 1970, Burdon appeared on British television and talked of their trips together, saying that Jimi 'used drugs to phase himself out of this life to go someplace else'. These comments caused a furore. 'I was stoned on MDA (another synthetic hallucinogen),' Burdon explained later, 'because Jimi Hendrix was the heaviest doper that I ever met . . . I felt I had something to say about Jimi . . . I wasn't going to walk on and say how great he was. He was a cunt! He was great, but he was a cunt. That's why I loved him.'

Burdon became obsessed with Hendrix and, during an English tour with War, he convinced himself that he was staying in the same room in a London hotel as Hendrix had once occupied. 'I was so low,' he said, 'and I'd caught pneumonia in Copenhagen.' He took MDA to get up for a gig and started hallucinating. The Hendrix track, *Angel (Came Down From Heaven Yesterday)*, was translated into a vision! This was, apparently, an infinitely more horrifying hallucination than his earlier LSD experiences of talking with Buddha, seeing the crucifixion of Christ, seeing himself aged 103 and, naturally, talking to God. None of it, however, was very funky, and War and Burdon spent the tour at each other's throats – the record company, according to Eric, encouraging the band to leave their front-man. In 1971, Eric and the band split up. 'I'm whoring myself to get to my end medium,' Eric said at around this time, 'which is motion pictures.'

The one picture he cherished was 'a Christ experience film' to be called *Mirage*, which tied up Burdon's half-crazed notions of racial oppression, the exploitation of rock musicians and Hendrix's death. The idea eventually developed into a grandiose mixed-media package including a record and a film. But Burdon's sense of perspective seems to have been dissolved by acid, and his managers were not long in pulling the plug on what they saw as grotesque over-expenditure. A flurry of legal actions followed involving Burdon, his management company (Far Out Productions, would you believe) and his former record company, MGM. 'I lost about $6 million which the Animals earned,' he said in 1973 as a prelude to suing MGM for back royalties. By 1976, Far Out were suing him after he had spent, they claimed, $400,000 on *Mirage*. He was also sued for $17,000 as a result of a car accident, and while visiting Europe, his house in Palm Desert was seized by the State and sold by auction.

The upheaval of all this did have an effect of bringing reality back to his life. Despite being broke and effectively unable to work, Eric had become relatively content. In 1972, he had married a former topless go-go dancer called Rose who, he said, helped him get off drugs. And, with all his legal problems to cope with, the former love child was able to say, 'For the first time I hate somebody.' By 1977, the legal problems were sorted out, mostly in Burdon's favour, and the original Animals were able to record a 'get together' album, titled *Before We Were So Rudely Interrupted*. The next year, Eric was 'totally into music again', and in late 1981 he was planning to form a blues

Joe Cocker faces life philosophically in spite of busts, and management troubles which started in the mid-sixties. Faced with a six-figure tax bill, what else is there to do but shrug?

band in America and star in a film in Los Angeles and Berlin to be called *Comeback* – about a rock singer, who is not Eric Burdon. 'I don't blame it on the drugs,' he once said. 'I just blame it on the mental stress of knowing you are being ripped off by record companies and everybody else and not being able to do anything about it.'

Joe Cocker was busted in December 1968, at the height of his meteoric career. He might have met with visa problems since a first tour of America was being arranged at the time of the bust. Luckily, Cocker's girlfriend, Eileen Webster, admitted the charge of possessing marijuana and the charge against Cocker was dropped. Cocker's legal problems continued, however, especially after his career began to decline. The Sheffield-born rocker had always been a heavy drinker, and in October 1972, he and six members of his tour party were convicted of drugs charges in Australia and ordered to leave the country. Before leaving Australia he managed to drink himself stupid, falling over during one of his final gigs and being evicted from his Melbourne hotel after a rowdy brawl involving his girlfriend, the hotel manager and the police. In 1973 he was busted again for marijuana back in Sheffield, and in 1977 he was deported from America on the grounds of illegal entry, none of which helped his career.

These victims of the drug culture have survived, after a fashion. Although drug-taking may only be a symptom of deeper problems, all too often they have lethal consequences. The list of drug-related deaths in rock'n'roll is depressingly long, reaching all the way from Elvis Presley to Sid Vicious and beyond, and taking in on the way those unfortunates like Janis and Brian Jones and Pigpen, whose sorry tales have already been chronicled. The main agents of destruction are drink, heroin, barbiturates and other depressants, taken either singly or in combination. (Nobody has yet died as a direct physiological result of taking LSD or marijuana and the incidence of death from chronic amphetamine or cocaine use is very small.)

The immediate causes of death vary from foolishness to neglect to suicide and, it has been surmised, murder. Tim Hardin got to the point of making records simply to pay for his habit until he overdosed. Mike Bloomfield – a rich boy who had been lauded in the sixties as America's greatest blues guitarist – spent some time in the seventies towards the end of his life scoring porn movies in San Francisco and recording background music for cremations before being found

Keith Moon holding forth at Paul and Linda, at the McCartneys' midnight matinee held in honour of Buddy Holly's birthday at London's Peppermint Park. The next morning, 7th September, 1978, Keith was dead, overdosed on tablets sometimes prescribed to help alcoholism.

dead himself in his car early in 1981. These two were both heroin overdoses; Bon Scott of AC/DC and John 'Bonzo' Bonham of Led Zeppelin both drank themselves to death like Pigpen. The coroner's report on Bonham estimated that he had the equivalent of 40 measures of vodka in his system at the time of his death. Like Jimi Hendrix, he died choking on his own vomit.

Bonzo's real tragedy was the evident emptiness of his life. He left £855,000 in his will. He had a wife of long standing and two children – Jason, born in 1966, and Zoe, born in 1975. Yet his life was coloured by 'speedballs' (a mixture of heroin and cocaine) and time passed only with the aid of sleepers mixed with booze. In June 1980, the 32-year-old drummer collapsed during a Zeppelin gig in Germany. He had suffered a suspected heart-attack. But he continued to abuse himself, and his last day alive was a desultory progress towards oblivion.

On 26th September, 1980, he began drinking at lunchtime at a pub near his home – four or five quadruple measures of vodka and orange. After lunch – a couple of cheese rolls in the pub – he was driven to Jimmy Page's house in Windsor for a rehearsal. He continued drinking in the rehearsal studio at the rate of two or three very large vodkas and orange an hour. At midnight, he fell asleep on the sofa, having eaten a pie and chips at Page's £900,000 home. He was carried to bed and laid sideways, braced with pillows: 'I'd had experience before of people being drunk,' said one of the men who put him to bed. At 2pm the next day, Bonham had still not stirred. When Zeppelin's road-manager looked into his room to wake him, he found Bonham dead.

Keith Moon died on the day after Buddy Holly's birthday (6th September) in 1978. 'Moon the Loon' did not, as one might have expected from his propensity for wild living, die while executing one impossible stunt too many, but from an overdose of Heminevrin tablets, a drug sometimes prescribed to help patients suffering from alcoholism. On the night of 6th September, Keith had taken a small amount of cocaine and gone out with his girlfriend, Annette Walter-Lax, to a midnight matinée of *The Buddy Holly Story*, followed by a party given by Paul McCartney to celebrate Buddy Holly Week. Back in his flat in Mayfair, Moon found difficulty sleeping. Early in the morning, he woke feeling hungry and consumed a steak in bed. He went back to sleep with the aid of 32 tablets of Heminevrin – more than double the lethal dose. At 3.40 in the afternoon, Annette woke to find Keith dead in bed beside her.

Robbie McIntosh of the Average White Band overdosed on heroin thinking it was cocaine. It was 1974 and the band had recently arrived in America where their white funk sound was being loudly applauded and they were introduced too rapidly into the high life. On 23rd September, they were guests at a plush party, where McIntosh indulged in what he took to be his favourite drug. An eye-witness recorded that the drummer 'turned blue', before gasping hoarsely for breath that somehow wouldn't come. In 1975, the man

who supplied the drug to the unsuspecting McIntosh was arraigned for murder.

Tommy Bolin, who took Ritchie Blackmore's place in the hugely successful Deep Purple and played with them until they split in summer, 1976, was touring the US with a new band, Sailor, when he died in December of that year. His drug problem was severe and, clearly missing the adulation of Purple's audience, he had been hoping to make a comeback and straighten himself out. But that couldn't happen. After an all-night party in Miami Beach he was found dead from the inevitable overdose in his hotel room, by his girlfriend, Valoria Monzeglio. Similarly, Lowell George, who found considerable success with Little Feat, had split with the band – in part because of his heroin addiction. In 1979, while still trying hard to build a solo career for himself, George died of an 'accidental overdose', the details of which, curiously, were kept secret from everyone but his immediate family.

Such stories occur with numbing regularity. One of the saddest declines was Paul Kossoff's. His career peaked in 1970 when Free, his band, had a hit single, *All Right Now*, but it went downhill after that. Kossoff's father, David, is a moderately well-known

---

Tommy Bolin, after Deep Purple and before OD. Heroin consciousness equals a man in a frock with a plastic dog turd.

English character actor who, having carved something of a niche for himself with broadcast and recorded readings from the Old Testament, has struggled to keep his son's memory alive as a warning to all would-be drug users. Unfortunately, David Kossoff has not succeeded too well – partly because he has overlooked both the real problems his son had (which helped motivate him not only to take drugs, but to become a rock'n'roller in the first place) and the pressures under which Paul worked.

Through the early seventies, Free split, reformed and changed its members with disturbing unpredictability. The band's personnel suffered from destructive internal disputes – assisted by the presence of pop success on a group which had been, at first, an earnest blues band. Kossoff himself lived in the shadow of his father's renown and his instability was evident from an early age. In 1972, he left Free permanently and recorded a solo album, subsequently going into semi-retirement for two years in an effort to get off heroin. 'I have killed the drug habit,' said Kossoff in early 1975. His new band, Back Street Crawler, recorded an album for release in the fall and a promotional tour of Britain was arranged. Before the tour could begin, Paul Kossoff suffered a massive coronary and his heart stopped for several minutes. The tour was scrapped but the album release went ahead, and Paul was giving interviews barely six weeks after he had nearly died. His speech was slurred and incoherent, he seemed to be only semi-conscious. And, yet, he played three gigs with Back Street Crawler only three months after the heart attack. A new UK tour was organized for the spring of 1976, but, flying to New York, Kossoff suffered another coronary and died on the plane. Heroin had killed him at the age of 25.

At the age of sixteen, Jimmy McCulloch – a frail-looking Glaswegian guitarist who habitually hid behind dark glasses and enveloping shaggy cardigans – was picked up by Pete Townshend to play in a group he was forming called Thunderclap Newman (after its eccentric piano-player). In some ways the whole Thunderclap Newman concept was a move in a simmering war between Townshend and the Who's vocalist, Roger Daltrey. While Townshend sponsored his creation, Daltrey organized and produced a band called Bent Frame, which included McCulloch's brother Jack, on drums. Thunderclap Newman had one huge success in 1969 with *Something In The Air*, and the war hotted up. Bent Frame were pre-empted when a song recorded by them in demo form, *Accidents*, was released by Thunderclap Newman and became a moderate hit. Townshend subsequently persuaded Jack McCulloch to join his brother Jimmy's band for a planned tour. Meanwhile, Daltrey had persuaded one of the Who's back-up team to join Bent Frame. Not surprisingly, neither band survived this animosity and Jimmy McCulloch moved on to join John Mayall, Stone The Crows (stepping in after guitarist Les Harvey had died) and Blue, before joining Paul McCartney's Wings in 1974. McCulloch, then only 21, harboured a dream to be present at a Beatles reunion, which he fondly imagined might happen

56

Unlike Jim Morrison's earlier experience in a bathtub, Jimmy McCulloch of Wings only fractured his hand in 1976 when he slipped in a bath in Paris. It wasn't until 1979 that he ODed on heroin, following Morrison to an early grave.

while he was with Wings. He also indulged in unhealthy quantities of drink and drugs – putting his 'weirdness' down to 'immaturity' and an inability to deal with people. He was, in some ways, a manipulated child. As a member of Wings, he was more or less an employee of Paul McCartney – despite McCartney's constant protestations that Wings was some sort of democracy. In 1977, after an extended period of quiescence, McCulloch and Wings' drummer, Joe English, left the band.

Jimmy was still drinking heavily, but even so received an invitation to join the newly reformed Small Faces. The Small Faces project was, unfortunately, short-lived and unspectacular. McCulloch left to form his own band, the Dukes – desperate to be part of a real, working group for the first time since he left Scotland. But a few days after announcing the formation of the Dukes, Jimmy went missing. Having failed to turn up at rehearsals, his brother Jack went anxiously round to his Maida Vale flat one morning in late September 1979, to see if he was there. Jimmy was dead on the floor, killed by an overdose of morphine on top of booze and pot. Curiously, the flat had been tidied and the police found no trace of alcohol or drugs or, for that matter, money. An open verdict was recorded by the coroner.

Gram Parsons – former Byrd and Flying Burrito Brother, and close friend of Keith Richard – died on 19th September, 1973, another victim of gross over-indulgence. There was a bizarre sequel to his death. His coffin was hi-jacked on its way back to burial in New Orleans by his friend and associate Phil Kaufman, and another man, who attempted to cremate the remains at the Joshua Tree National Monument. Parsons and Kaufman had once made a pact in which the survivor would ritually burn the body of whichever of them died first.

In spite of all this some have survived – if only just. The albino blues guitarist Johnny Winter came off heroin in the early seventies, as did Eric Clapton. Clapton reckoned to spend up to £1,000 per week on the drug at that time. Clapton, who moved in the sixties from an admired guitarist with the Yardbirds and then with John Mayall to superstardom in Cream, found it impossible to cope with his sudden elevation. The formation of Cream in 1966 was accompanied by a promotional campaign best remembered for the slogan, 'Clapton is God', which appeared as graffiti all over London. Clapton was the one for whom the term 'guitar hero' was invented.

The legend of his virtuosity on the instrument became a reality for fans who took to spraying the graffiti themselves and shouting at concerts 'We want more God.' Clapton, who argued that 'I'm just an unskilled labourer musician' who 'can't see how just being a guitarist is enough', rebelled against the reputation he had somehow achieved as 'the fastest guitar alive'. By 1967, he had discovered LSD and the love generation. He praised the lack of stages and admission fees at 'Be-Ins' in America and enthused over people 'having a gas time with people and not objects'. When Cream collapsed at the end of 1968, Clapton, reacting against the hype that had made him a celebrity, the egotism of the group as a whole and the evident lack of unity between the group and their record company, opted for a period of low-profile performance. He joined the short-lived 'supergroup', Blind Faith, went into tax exile in the Bahamas, moved on to Delaney and Bonnie, for whom he was virtually a sideman, and then started Derek and the Dominoes with a number of musicians from Delaney and Bonnie who allowed him to keep resolutely out of the limelight.

Unfortunately – and cornily – he also fell in love with his best friend's wife: the former model Patti Boyd, who had married George Harrison. (Clapton once claimed that his initial pursuit of Patti was revenge for George 'grabbing' one of his 'chicks'.) The combination of dissatisfaction with his career and the lack of reciprocation from Patti was apparently enough to guarantee addiction to heroin. When Derek and the Dominoes recorded the album *Layla And Other Assorted Love Songs* in 1971, few people realized that the record was a statement of Eric's love for Patti.

Layla is now recognized as a rock classic but, at the time, it went largely unheralded – despite the band's conviction that the album 'would go straight to number one'. Clapton found solace in addiction – rarely moving out of his Surrey home and converting virtually all his money into the deadly white powder for three years. He became known as 'Eric Claptout'. He sold his cars and, at one point he remembers, 'I told one of the roadies to sell the guitars for whatever price he could get. I couldn't get cash from anywhere.' Eventually, broke, unhappy and feeling that he 'didn't want to die', he made the effort to come off heroin. With the help of musician friends – especially Pete Townshend – he crawled his way back, taking a five week electronic acupuncture cure at a clinic run by Dr Margaret Patterson in Sussex (for whom he has played a number of benefits). The cure was 'pretty unpleasant' and cost £60 a day, but it was cheaper and more pleasant than continued addiction. 'Drug taking is escapism,' said Eric – although he managed to exclude booze from that dictum.

In 1975, he was jailed in Tulsa on a drinks charge. In 1976, he took to 'streaking' whenever he was drunk (which was quite often) – and in 1981, he ended up in hospital with a perforated ulcer before a planned US tour. Despite the fact that Patti and Eric finally married

Self-styled 'unskilled labourer musician', Eric Clapton hides his hangover behind dark glasses. The man for whom the phrase 'guitar hero' was coined had come off heroin by 1975, thanks to treatment with electronic acupuncture at a Sussex clinic.

Bloated and defeated, Jim Morrison leaves court on 30th October, 1970, in Miami, Florida, after being found guilty of profanity and indecent exposure. He was sentenced to six months in jail and fined $500, but remained free on $50,000 bond pending an appeal which he didn't live to hear. Eight months later he died in the bath in Paris, aged only 27.

in 1979 in a romantic ceremony in Tucson, he seemed no more able to handle the pressures of his life. After nearly a decade of association, he sacked bassist Carl Radle from his band in 1979. Radle was a heroin addict and died in June 1980, following a kidney infection. 'I couldn't believe it,' said Ron Wood. 'Carl was a lovely guy. He had nothing left in life after the Eric thing.'

The comforting thought for the fans, stunned by all this wasted talent and wasted years, is that all rock star drug addiction and its associated deaths are a form of suicide brought on by the intolerable pressures of stardom. In a way this is true, though self-destruction is more accurate than the deliberate taking of lives. Stardom tends to frustrate noble intentions and distort the stars' grip on reality and their view of themselves. Janis Joplin saw the futility of 'making love to 25,000 people on stage' and then going home alone. Jimi Hendrix complained he could never quite capture the sounds he heard in his head. Jim Morrison of the Doors, who perfectly captured the precise mix of sexual liberation, psychic exploration and political revolt which characterized sixties rock, found his vision clouded by complacent audiences who took him for the thing that he, like Janis, least wanted to be – a pop

Jim Morrison as he would like to be remembered; the Lizard King still plays the erotic politician to thousands of doting Doors fans.

star. He tried to shock and humiliate his audience out of their passivity. On stage he was, without doubt, magnetic – leather-clad, defiantly beautiful, play-acting the dying soldier or the doomed Oedipal lover in a sort of spotlit nether-world that focused all the audience's darkest hopes and fears onto his cathartic presence. The act, as many people have pointed out, was ritual enactment of chaos and anger.

But off-stage, Morrison was a drunken Lothario, a would-be poet cultivating a booze-soaked irresponsibility he might have learned from Baudelaire, Brendan Behan or Dylan Thomas, and finding an endless stream of women with whom he tried to play the 'erotic politician' (his own definition of himself) for real. He explained his fondness for the bottle over less legitimate drugs by saying that 'getting drunk ... is a lot of small choices ... I guess it's the difference between suicide and slow capitulation.' It was usually less romantic than that. On one occasion, at a friend's apartment in New York, he fell into a drunken stupor on a sofa and began urinating on the carpet; a large vase had to be held under his member to catch the flow – it was filled and emptied three times. Meanwhile

59

Sid Vicious playing bass with the Sex Pistols. His heroin tracks are bandaged, so Sid has taken to bleeding through some other orifice.

Morrison remained senseless.

Morrison seemed to be trying out the body and mind of the characters he became on stage in his private life, and the confusion between these personae began to intrude on both. He longed for the opportunity to galvanize an audience into action. At a concert at New Haven, Connecticut, in 1968, he introduced *Back Door Man* on stage by describing how a cop had 'maced' him backstage without realizing who he was. The crowd of course loved it – right up to and including the arrival of a cop on stage to arrest him for 'indecent and immoral exhibition', breach of the peace and resisting arrest. It would not be the last, nor the most serious occasion.

Jim Morrison was extremely impressed by the methods of the Living Theatre, a group of American performers whose techniques were based on psychodrama and the aggressive use of obscenity and violence directed at the audience. Their influence led directly to the famous incident at Miami in 1969 when, after a concert performance, Morrison was arrested for having allegedly exposed himself on stage. There are various versions of the event; one is that Morrison had it all planned and that he was wearing a large pair of boxer shorts under his leather trousers, so that when he took his trousers off, he would not actually expose himself. But fellow members of the band were also reported to have tried physically to restrain him as he began to unbuckle his belt. He was extremely drunk, slurring his words and apparently losing track of

things, so they could not predict how far he would actually go. But what is undoubtedly true is that the kids themselves, roused by Morrison's example, had divested themselves of plenty of clothing. One member of the Doors' entourage remembered that, in the concert hall afterwards, 'Every three or four feet there was another garment.'

Significantly, the concert took place on 1st March, 1969, the day after Morrison had seen the Living Theatre perform *Paradise Now*. The charges made against Morrison were not made until 5th March, long enough for the worthy citizens of Miami to have worked themselves into a lather of hindsighted indignation about the event.

The charges claimed that Morrison 'did lewdly and lasciviously expose his penis, place his hands upon his penis and shake it, and further the said defendant did simulate the acts of masturbation upon himself and oral copulation upon another.' Whether this was true or not, there is no argument that he verbally cajoled and assaulted the audience. During the trial it was alleged that he shouted at them, 'You're all a bunch of fucking idiots. Your faces are being pressed into the shit of the world. Take your fucking friend and love him. Do you want to see my cock? This was the general tone of the evening – and it echoed the general tone of Living Theatre 'happenings' pretty faithfully as well. It couldn't pass without comment in Florida.

Morrison was found guilty of exposure and profanity, but not guilty of lewd behaviour and public drunkenness – an odd irony, since this latter was probably the one thing anybody could have been sure of on that occasion and one he himself admitted at the trial. Eventually, he quit the rock world in disgust and went to Paris to become a poet – apparently unaware that the poets had all left that city years ago. His body was already wrecked by drink at the age of 27; bearded and bloated, he tried to make a Door-less life for himself with his common-law wife, Pamela Courson, but his heart gave out and he died in the bath on 3rd July, 1971. Some say it was heroin, others booze; most agree it was inevitable – unless, of course, they don't believe that he died at all.

The theory that Morrison staged his own 'death' in order to escape his reputation and his past has gripped the imagination of his most devoted fans. It is put forward most cogently by one of Jim's greatest admirers, Jerry Hopkins, co-author of Morrison's biography, entitled, *No One Here Gets Out Alive*. The original manuscript went further even than the published book. Rather than put both sides of the argument together, Hopkins had written two different endings, one in which Morrison died, the other in which he disappeared to start a new life. In a note to prospective publishers, Jerry Hopkins stated: 'There are two "endings" for this book. The press run is to be split equally between them; if the print order is 10,000 copies, 5,000 will close with "End 1" and the other 5,000 will close with "End 2". The 10,000 copies are then to be "shuffled" and randomly distributed without any mention whatsoever of the two disparate endings.' The book remained unpublished for some time, and when it finally came out, Hopkins was persuaded to stick to a more conventional exposition. The book went on to become an international best seller.

The mystery surrounding Jim Morrison's sorry demise rests mainly on the fact that no-one considered sufficiently objective admits to seeing the body, and news didn't filter through to those who presumably thought they ought to be the first to know until nearly a week later. This is understandable given Pamela Courson's less-than-stable state of mind; she was equally a victim of Morrison's stardom and died three years later of a heroin overdose, having conducted a protracted battle to benefit from Morrison's estate. As she died intestate, her family and Morrison's share the still considerable royalties accruing from continued Doors' record sales.

Self-destruction or faked deaths alike are just excuses however. The unpleasant truth is that excessive drug use has become an essential part of the star system. Speed and coke are very common as 'working drugs', (providing, in the words of a Byrds song, 'artificial energy'), and as drugs to heighten sexual pleasure or delay orgasm. Many musicians resorted to heroin to ease their nerves or simply to get some sleep. It becomes easy, as Clapton has said, to 'rationalize it by saying that musicians live on a very intense emotional plane of necessity, and heroin is probably the strongest pain killer you can lay your hands on'. This is the sort of self-image that underlies Patti Smith's contention that there is something called 'heroin consciousness' that some stars have, whether they use heroin or not, (Smith denies that she does). To use heroin (or to look like you do), according to this image, is to acquire artistic credentials, since no-one but a lunatic or a tortured genius would do such a dumb thing. And the aspiring rock musician of recent years often assumes that he or she needs to seem one part lunatic and one part tortured genius to have 'street credibility'. This assumption killed John Simon Ritchie when he came to believe that he was Sid Vicious, star, and not just a deluded kid that had hit lucky as part of rock'n'roll's most self-conscious satire to date. The sorry tale of Sid Vicious's short life and miserable death puts the lid on rock'n'roll drug deaths for all time, no rock star has followed such a futile career with such a violent and yet unsurprising death, and no-one is likely to in the future.

Recruited to the Sex Pistols because of his violent punk image, Sid Vicious fell for the hype completely. ('He believed his own publicity' said Johnny Rotten. 'He was called Vicious because he was such a wanker. He couldn't fight his way out of a crisp bag.') When the Pistols split up, he was just a celebrity with nothing to offer but the myth of his own empty stardom. Drifting aimlessly round London, he was latched onto by an American groupie, Nancy Spungen. Vicious, already a heroin addict, left for New York after she had been threatened with deportation following a brawl with

Goodbye Piccadilly! Nancy Spungen and Sid Vicious with Glen Matlock and Steve New (far right) of the Rich Kids, the night before Sid and Nancy flew off to New York in August 1978. Sid demanded fivers for all from the photographer to allow this happy snap to be taken, but was overruled by his management.

61

The body of 20-year-old Nancy Laura Spungen is carried out of New York's 'historic' Chelsea Hotel on 12th October, 1978. She had been stabbed to death.

some journalists. On landing in New York, Vicious had to be carried off the plane – 'Obviously under the influence of drugs or drink,' said the reports. Sid and Nancy moved into the notorious Chelsea Hotel where Nancy was subsequently found dead, stabbed several times in the stomach.

There were no witnesses to the killing, but evidence pointed to Sid, who was duly arrested on 12th October, 1978, and charged with her murder. Five days later he was released on $50,000 bail, put up by his record company, Virgin. Less than two months later he was back on remand again, this time in the tough Rykers Island prison, after being involved in a night-club fight with Todd Smith, Patti's brother. (So much for heroin consciousness.)

On 1st February, 1979, Sid's lawyers tried to get the charge of murder dismissed, but they failed. They then prepared to take the case into court on a 'Not Guilty' plea, so Sid was released yet again on 2nd February, once more on bail of $50,000. The story was beginning to sound like a game of legal ping-pong – except within 24 hours of Sid's release the ball was finally out of court. He was found dead by his mother and current girlfriend Michelle Robinson, in the latter's Greenwich Village flat. He died from an overdose, after consuming more heroin than his body

Slapped in the face by reality, John Simon Ritchie (a.k.a. Sid Vicious) is taken to be charged with the murder of Nancy Spungen.

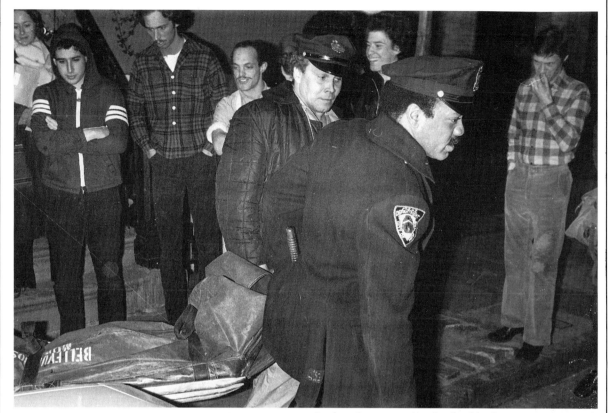

Now its's Sid's turn to be bagged. Last act in the drama, Sid Vicious's body is removed from the Greenwich Village apartment where he died on 2nd February, 1979. He'd been out of jail for one day.

could stand following two months' enforced withdrawal in prison. He was 21 years old.

Back in the movies' golden age, Oscar Levant once said, 'Strip the phoney tinsel away from Hollywood and you'll find the real tinsel underneath.' In the rock world, the real tinsel can still be found in California. There is no illusion of angst among the select group of rock superstars whose success has converted the acid dream into their exclusive reality. Drugs offer not the power to change the world, but merely its paler shadow – the power to change *their* world by changing themselves. Heroin is becoming increasingly popular in the Californian rock community because it is now available in a form supposedly pure enough not to cause the user any danger. After a while, of course, it causes little else, apart from addiction. Cocaine too, has been subjected to refinement for the elite through 'free basing', an extremely dangerous procedure in which commercial cocaine (which is supplied as a chemical compound, cocaine hydrochloride) is dissolved in ether and heated to turn it into pure cocaine. It has a tendency to blow up in your face. Free basing is definitely a hobby for the wealthy alone, since a great deal of the already expensive drug is required to create the more potent 'free' cocaine, and the process also requires fairly sophisticated apparatus. Whichever it is, heroin or cocaine (or both), the constant use of regulated and increasing doses of a highly expensive drug is surely the most convincing demonstration of wealth casually acquired and disposed of.

The Eagles, whose music is the very culmination of California rock, have grown up in the fickle atmosphere of a society devoted to 'changing its mind' by whatever means available. 'I'm not saying I'm an angel or a saint now,' said their drummer, Don Henley, when discussing cocaine in 1979, 'because I'm not. But I've slowed down quite a bit.' Even so, the Eagles are still proud enough of their capacity for alcohol to have invented their own generic term for drunken behaviour. They call it 'to monster'.

And in November 1980, Henley was arrested and charged with possession of cocaine, quaaludes and marijuana. A girl of sixteen was found in the house, naked and, by her own account, overdosed on cocaine and quaaludes. Henley pleaded 'no contest' to the charge of contributing to the delinquency of a minor. He was fined $2,500, given two years' probation, and required to take part in a two year drug diversion programme. Since then he has 'slowed down' even more.

Cass Elliott of the Mamas and Papas once said, 'Pop music is just long hours, hard work and lots of drugs . . .' In July 1974 she died in a London hotel room of gross obesity when her fatty heart gave out. It's been a long, hard trip to the place of definitions.

63

REBELS
WITHOUT A CAUSE

After all the ideals had been exploded in the late six-ties, rock remained simply and solely an entertain-ment, and performances – once they had gravitated towards the mass arena – sought justification in out-rageousness. At its best this was a cry against the distancing effects of stardom, at its worst it was part of a self-contained escalation of rock as spectacle. Since the cry generally went unheard, the worst case came to be the universal one – performances became increas-ingly outrageous because that was what was expected of them.

Outrage on stage was like a return to the time when rock'n'roll's appeal lay in its ability to express the forbidden. But it was a return with a difference – by the end of the sixties, audiences were better educated about the mysteries of the forbidden and more demanding about their thrills. And boy, did the rock-ers work hard to cater for them.

Excess became the watchword. It was partly in terms of mammoth amplification systems, gargantuan light-shows and a general tendency to deafening loudness. (It has been claimed by a colleague of Lemmy of Motorhead, that he is now so deaf that he once failed to notice when his guitar lead fell out of its amplifier; and Ted Nugent, boasting the title of world's loudest musician, wears earplugs on stage.) But it was also in terms of performance style. Mere histrionics were no longer enough. Hendrix burning his guitar and Keith Emerson taking stilettos to his organ keyboard pale into insignificance in the light of subsequent acts. The daddy of them all was of course Frank Zappa, whose 'atrocities' started it. Zappa culti-vated outrage as a rock'n'roll style. Having neither the flashiness nor anger nor sexuality of earlier acts, it was a calculated product of his self-obsessive nihilism. You can see this in the names he's given his children – Dweezil, Moon Unit, Ahmet Rodin and Diva – and the recording of songs like the unforgettable *Yellow Snow*, a warning against the dangers of eating frozen dog's piss.

Zappa's background is instructive. The son of a history teacher who wanted him to be a chemist, he worked for a time as an art director in advertising and for a greetings card firm, helping to hone his sense of the absurd to a sharp point. Having made a few hundred dollars from work on a film, he bought up a sound studio in the small town of Cucamonga, California, shipped in a number of old film-sets that he bought up cheap and set about planning his first

---

What most people prefer under plain wrappers, the Tubes turned into a rock'n'roll show in the seventies.

movie – to have been called *Captain Beefheart versus the Grunt People*. With no money left and surviving on peanut butter, instant mash, coffee and honey, in 1963 he formed a 'blues' trio to play professional gigs locally. While playing in a Chicano club, Zappa was offered an apparently genuine offer to make training films for the San Bernardino vice squad. As he tells the story, he played a member of the force some of his tapes of friends, freaks, locals and girlfriends. Soon afterwards he was approached by a man claiming to be a used car salesman who wanted 'hot tapes' for a party. Zappa and his girlfriend obliged by grunting and groaning in front of a microphone. But no sooner had the tape been delivered than the studio was invaded by photographers and cops and Zappa was busted on a charge of publishing a pornographic record. A six-month jail sentence was reduced to three years probation, on condition that during that time he would not be in the presence of a woman under 21 without 'a competent adult' present. He served eleven days in jail and, as a result, was exempted from the draft.

The atrocities started more-or-less accidentally once Zappa's group, the Mothers of Invention, were well-established. When the anti-Vietnam movement was at its height, Zappa invited some uniformed US Marines on stage during a show. He gave them a life-size doll, saying, 'This is a gook baby, show us how we treat gooks in Vietnam.' The Marines, who rose to the occasion, tore the doll, stuffed limb from stuffed limb. 'After that,' says Zappa, 'we included props in all our shows. I call them visual aids.'

Zappa and the Mothers have had marriages per-formed in mid-show, cajoled members of their audi-ence to make speeches and left the stage completely while up to 30 people from the audience performed and sang in their place. One of their favourite tricks has been to send objects down an overhead wire onto the stage: a spread-eagled doll, for example, followed by a suggestively shaped and well-aimed salami. One specially effective prop has been the 'soft giraffe' – a vast stuffed animal which squirts whipped cream out of its stiffened tail all over the front rows of the audi-ence. 'Sometimes you can't write a chord ugly enough to say what you want to say,' he said in defence of these bizarre practices, 'so you have to rely on a giraffe filled with whipped cream.'

Despite Zappa's self-proclaimed seriousness, those in authority have often found him simply out-rageous. Banned in London's Royal Albert Hall for obscenity in 1971 three days before he was due to perform, he took them to court in 1975. The

65

defendants contended that Zappa wrote 'filth for filth's sake' and Zappa, who would never deny that he wrote at great length about matters sexual, tried to prove that filth is in the ear of the beholder. The transcript of the case (which Zappa lost) reads at times like a subtle farce. 'Would you not say that any young woman who seeks to contact a member of a rock'n'roll group in order to procure sexual intercourse,' asks the Royal Albert Hall's barrister, 'that such a young woman is in a very sorry state?' Zappa (who died of cancer in 1993, leaving a widow whom he once described as a former groupie, 'and an excellent groupie, too'), replies: 'Er, no. I would not.' 'I don't think you can have heard the question,' says the barrister, who has plainly not heard the answer. 'I will repeat it . . .'

By the time the seventies had got under way, the hugely successful acts like the Stones, Led Zeppelin, the Who and subsequently, Rod Stewart, Pink Floyd, Elton John, David Bowie, the Eagles or Kiss, were little more than travelling circuses carting truckloads of equipment round the world, each vying for the title of 'world's most spectacular rock act' (sometimes misinterpreted as 'world's *greatest* rock act'). Jagger's inflatable phallus, the Floyd's light shows, Elton's 'Carmen Miranda' costumes, Kiss's smoke bombs and so tediously on, had become the kernel of their performance. The performers themselves became international jet-setters, flying from all corners of the world to come together for a tour or to lay down backing-tracks on a

Below: Two old troupers, now dead. Nico (once described as the most beautiful woman in the world), suffered a heart attack in 1988 while cycling in Ibiza, and Andy Warhol, who died in 1986, whose New York base, the Factory, was a hothouse of sexual variety, and drug abuse (and a bit of art).

Heroin consciousness for beginners: at Winterland, November 1974, Lou Reed gives an on-stage demonstration.

new album recorded in Munich, mixed in Jamaica, remixed in a chateau on the Loire and mastered in New York. They had become a whole new class of rich people maintaining houses or hotel rooms in three or four different locations, and hanging out in exclusive night-clubs, or else, like the Pink Floyd, maintaining a sturdy indifference to the fans and the glamour and emerging from their reclusive existences only for touring, recording or discussions about their investments.

This sort of rock'n'roll was increasingly soulless and mechanical, inspired only by the need to make money, fill the time and, just maybe, to reinject jaded lives with the frisson of adventure that touring brings. The sad conclusion of success saw the Stones (and entourage), once the bearers of progressive promise, as guests during their 1972 tour of America at the Chicago mansion of chief Playboy, Hugh Hefner. Hef wined and dined the boys in the manner to which they had become accustomed. And then, some years later, the group released an album called *Black And Blue* which was promoted with advertisements depicting a bruised woman, hands tied behind her head and legs spread, bearing the slogan 'I'm Black and Blue from the Rolling Stones and I love it'. Answering vociferous criticism of this promotion, the Stones – once held up as the great pop satirists of sexism – argued that some women liked that sort of thing.

Sexuality became the great playground of rock in the seventies. In fact, everything pointed in that direction: the permissiveness of the preceding decade, the sexual symbolism of performance itself, the need to exploit unconventional morality. Liberation became personal liberation, freedom from oppression became freedom from sexual repression, the democratic urge towards equality and freedom of association became an individualistic quest for guiltless promiscuity. Sex was the great leveller and the means by which the American Dream of power and achievement could be successfully pursued by everybody. Every nook and cranny of erotica was invaded by people in pursuit of the new holy grail. All 57 varieties of sexual experience could be found openly in almost every city throughout America and Northern Europe. It was taken as a sign of freedom and a new moral maturity, but in fact it was all rather joyless and perfunctory, a sort of orgasmic rat-race. It encouraged a notion of sex as a consumer good (even when it was not overtly paid for), the latest product of the 'leisure society'.

The Velvet Underground made much of the running. The band was formed in the late sixties by New York rock'n'roller Lou Reed (an *habitué* of the gay scene who once shocked his fans by announcing his impending marriage to a woman, but later reappeared, reassuringly, with a boy named Rachel in tow), and the classically trained Welsh violinist, John Cale. With the sponsorship of pop-art mastermind, Andy Warhol, and together with a smoky-voiced German chanteuse named Nico (who was the associate and friend of such stars as Bob Dylan, Leonard Cohen, Brian Jones and Jim Morrison), the band went out as a mixed-media event called 'The Exploding Plastic Inevitable'. Nico played the whip-toting Wanda in a song called *Venus In Furs* ('shiny, shiny boots of leather,' sang Lou in the role of Severin); she was, suggestively, a lesbian in *I'll Be Your Mirror*; Lou Reed played a white punk on heroin in *Heroin* and

67

Waiting For My Man; John Cale played a nerve-jangling violin redolent of evil times, low-life and sexual pleasure-pain. The band as a whole was a startling visual and aural assault, virtually defining the seamy New York underworld – 42nd Street, Harlem, a life full of fixing, fucking and masturbatory fantasies in which the operative verb is 'to score': the gutter we all inhabit, as Oscar Wilde once said, from which some of us are looking at the stars.

Of course, the Velvets were no mere titillators, regardless of whether or not their audience got off on voyeurism. Their music was about enslavement, the complete destruction of freedom – but there was something quite thrilling about the extremity of the degradation they pictured and (they were not stupid), there was a reassuring certainty in the music which such a complete denial of freedom offered. Despite the Warhol association (and despite the fact that Lou Reed later recorded a song about Warhol's transvestite 'superstars' (*Take A Walk On The Wild Side*), they were not a Warhol package. But they represented something Warhol understood well – the fascination people have for the bizarre, the decadent, the degraded and the dangerous. They held up that old, old equation between sex and death, pleasure and pain, as a fundamental of rock'n'roll. Not even Jim Morrison learnt to do it as well. The Velvets were selling an image (like Warhol himself) and it was an image that captured the moment (before its time, it must be said) when rock's pursuit of a pastoral idyll would run slap up against the dreadful urban reality.

Throughout the seventies the idea of rock'n'roll representing images from the sexual sub-culture held sway. Former Zappa associate, Alice Cooper, built an entire career on a couple of good hard-rock songs and an act that even as early as 1971 he admitted was '60 per cent contrived'. Among Cooper's contrivances were the name itself (the band was all-male and Alice's real name is Vincent Furnier), whips, leather gear, dolls that were mutilated in the course of the act, a chicken that was 'killed' during the show amid a flurry of prepared feathers, a mock guillotining, even – at one point – the bizarre apparition of Alice dressed in his torn leotard and high boots brandishing a giant toothbrush and chasing a scantily-dressed woman disguised as a tube of toothpaste.

Alice, who had clearly made a study of his mentor, Frank Zappa, was hugely successful and inspired many a later punk rocker with his stage image of decadence refined to complete negativity. Zappa may have been a nihilist, but his sense of morality and humour cannot be doubted. The Alice persona was no more than a hollow shell which enabled the real Vincent Furnier to indulge his favourite activities of golf and drinking. This son of an Arizona preacher hit the green with the likes of Jack Nicklaus and Bing Crosby and hit the bottle with a will. In late 1977, he committed himself to a sanatorium to dry out and later

David and friend: a moment of harmony for David Bowie and Lou Reed, with Mick Jagger taking a back seat. Bisexuality, said Bowie, is 'fun'.

Who was that lady I saw you with last night? David Bowie plays Rosemary Clooney.

company where he would be noticed [...]
sporting shoulder-length tresses and [...]
gowns, could hardly escape attention [...]
coverage given to Bowie and his wife A[...]
fessed bisexuality and 'open marriage' gave cr[...]
to the singer's musical claim to be a child of the [...]
at a time when 'free sexuality' was being passiona[...]
pursued as the most likely candidate to usher wester[...]
industrial society into a golden age. 'It's true – I am
bisexual,' David said some time later. 'But I can't deny
I've used the fact very well. I suppose it's the best thing
that ever happened to me. Fun, too.' Well, that's as
maybe – Bowie's cultivation of image ('I decided to
adopt the masks so I didn't have the humiliation of
going on stage and being myself') has shrouded his
private life in a carefully concealing mist. But, regardless of the testimony of one or two perennial rock
starlets, like Dana Gillespie and Amanda Lear, that
troilism and less mathematically complex activities
were indeed practised in the Bowie household and
ready gossip about David's singular and multiple
activities in New York and Berlin, Bowie and his wife
seem to have been rather less liberated than confused.

In 1974, Angie Bowie spoke approvingly of
groupies – 'the people who make it all worthwhile,'
she said. 'If you can't accept groupies,' she said, 'you

*Angie and friend: Angie Bowie emerged emotionally bruised but still smil-
ing from her celebrated open marriage with 'stud' David, thanks in part to
the help of guitarist Keeth Paul, who saw her through a suicide attempt in
January 1978.*

recorded an album, *From The Inside*, based on his
experiences. 'I was drinking two quarts of whisky a
day,' said Alice after his three month treatment, 'just
to keep going! I was living at 100 miles an hour with
alcohol for fuel.' In two-and-a-half-years, said Alice,
he had *never* been sober. Even early on, the group used
to boast of spending $250,000 a year on booze and
Alice himself would regularly put away 40 cans of beer
in one day. 'In the end,' said Alice, 'I was throwing up
blood.' Alice's sado-masochistic stage twilight stood
in evident contrast to Vincent Furnier's more straightforward reality. After splitting with his lover, Cindy
Lang, Vince married Sherryl Goddard in 1976. 'In two
years of marriage,' he later said, 'she never saw me
sober.' After committing himself to the sanatorium,
Vince expected the worst. But Sherryl came through
with flying colours. She declared that she always
knew that her husband would straighten himself out
one day, and she damn well intended to stay with him!

David Bowie's emergence in the early seventies
was perhaps the single most important influence to
the development of an explicit and outrageous sexual-
ization of rock. The promotion of Bowie as bisexual
superstar and mascot of the eroticists was a carefully
calculated operation. It's no coincidence that Bowie
and Lou Reed (one of Bowie's acknowledged influences) were both signed by RCA in the same year: the
man who signed them, lawyer Dennis Katz, was very
keen to change RCA's image – tainted by association
with the red-blooded defence industry and the heavily
'hetero' country music scene. Bowie's manager, Tony
de Fries, was simultaneously eager to sign Bowie to a

rst place.' David was a
of them were happily
ulture.

ngie and David were at
vorce and the issue of
e marriage may have
, but it seems rapidly
miliar furrow. 'When
recall, 'we were both
ns to have been less
together, she had
downstairs because David was
going off to a rehearsal. Later, Zowie's birth left her
with a cracked pelvis. Unable to cope with the problems and pain of motherhood, she ran off, leaving
David literally holding the baby. In her simpering
memoirs, entitled *Free Spirit*, Angie recalls that 'while I
was in love with David and ready to share him with
anyone he nominated, I still wanted to hold that
privileged and treasured place as his wife'. She
objected most of all to the way news of David's latest
boy and girlfriends filtered through to her via the
gossip columns.

Meanwhile, David was getting heavily into drugs.
'I used to try a new drug every time one came onto the
market,' he said. 'I guess I've been near death a lot.'
During 1975 and 1976 ('probably the worst year or year
and a half of my life . . .'), Bowie's obsessive charac-
terizations and mythologizing about himself (Ziggy
Stardust, the Thin White Duke) became mixed up with
the potent legends of a society in need of salvation.
Helped along by over-exposure to cocaine and Los
Angeles ('That fucking place should be wiped off the
face of the earth,' said Bowie in 1980), he drifted
towards the symbolism of Christianity, Arthurian
myth and Hitlerism. In late 1975, he arrived at Victoria
station in a black Mercedes flanked by blond outriders
giving Nazi salutes. 'Britain would benefit from a
period of fascism,' he said. 'I was in a haze of myth-
ology,' he later explained. 'Mixed up too, of course,
were my own fucking characters.' Bowie fled to Berlin
where he was forced to face up to the reality of
Nazism, not just its nightmare symbolism. Eventually,
he 'came crashing down to earth', but by that time, the
celebrated marriage was in a shambles and David was
spending a great deal of time in the company of a
young German waiter. 'It's been celibate for the past
five years,' Angie confessed in 1979, about her relationship with 'stud' David. She had just recovered
from a heavy dose of sedatives followed by an assault
on her lover, Keeth Paul, and a couple of botched
attempts at suicide.

'I never dreamed that the green-eyed monster
called jealousy would get me – but it did,' said Angie.
David, meanwhile, went to the custody hearings over
Zowie with the claim that Angie was 'an unfit mother
and a drug addict'. He got the child and she got a
£30,000 divorce settlement. By 1980 she was living in
apparently monogamous bliss with a certain Drew
Blood (real name, Bogdan Andrzes Lipka) in a log
cabin in California. Meanwhile David settled in
Switzerland with his son. At home in Corsier-sur-
72

Vevey near Lake Geneva he struck up a friendship
with his near neighbour Oona Chaplin, widow of a
clown greater even than he.

Lou Reed, Alice Cooper and David Bowie opened the
floodgates to a tide of performers more or less dedicated to rock'n'roll's pride of place in the sexual
market. Glitter and glam-rock invaded the charts – a
glaring expression of sexuality as packaging. Flam-
boyance reached new heights of camp elaboration,
with performers like Bette Midler (whose act is liber-
ally sprinkled with crudities), Elton John (who admitted his own bisexuality in interviews in 1976) and
Labelle (who, for a variety of reasons, became mascots
of a certain part of the gay and lesbian scene in
America and Britain). The Tubes developed into one of
the greatest and crudest rock parodies yet. Lead singer
Fee Waybill would come on stage with a false prick and
enormous stack heels as 'Quay Lewd', a totally zonked
superstar, or in leather gear as 'Sado Man', and while
TVs flickered on stage, he would strip and simulate sex
with a female partner on a motor cycle. On one
occasion, the Tubes held a talent contest in Los
Angeles to find an opening act for their show. Among
the competitors were Sister Marie de Sade, the stripping nun; Mr Penguin, who, dressed as the bird itself,
sang 'Hello, I'm Mr Penguin/You do your thing and I'll
do mine'; and – the winners – a group called the Fetus
Brothers who sang 'He's no pansy, he's my lord',
while crucifying a man dressed as a nun.

The Village People, artfully synthesized in New
York, took the stereotypes of the macho gay world out
of the closet and, in doing so, created a comedy act out
of the deadly serious business of fist-fucking and male
homosexual sadism. Even a dreadfully mundane
group like Queen chose their name for its gay connotations, as lead singer Freddie Mercury once said, and
cultivated an act and an image (in Mercury's case, at
least) of such stunningly arch campness that people
were either seduced by it or laughed out loud.

Such apparent sexual freedom was hardly liberat-
ing for women: it only made acceptable a wider range
of male fantasy figures. Cute kids, vamps, virginal
madonna figures and straightforward strumpets have
now been joined by dominatrices and oh so glamorous
lesbian types as stock characters for women to play.
Someone like David Bowie is able to ride out the
storms of his own confusion, even to translate it into a
marketable commodity. Women performers are less
able to do this. Their exploitation by the mainstream
of rock has become, if anything, more subtle and
insidious since the advent of rock'n'roll's overt
sexuality. One all-woman group was named Fanny.
Another – Birtha – had, according to their promotional
material, 'balls'. The Runaways presented the studied
personae of clawing, eyeball-scratching teenage bitch
goddesses. Gaye Advert came on in a leather jacket
and thick mascara. The Slits promised and sometimes
offered a challenge to female stereotypes but appeared

'Sex sells,' says Debbie Harry of Blondie, plagiarizing the Monroe image.

Former Raymond Revuebar showgirl, once known as Peki d'Oslo; writer of 'bullshit biographies'; calls herself a transsexual; Amanda Lear (seen here with Andy Mackay of Roxy Music) knows how to look after herself.

They developed the glitter look into a studied cross-genderism: playing straightforward seventies R&B dressed in pancake make-up, bouffant hairstyles and high-heeled shoes, but usually with a couple of days' growth of beard showing through. The effect was rather like Danny La Rue singing the blues, and almost as offensive.

Wayne County – another influential figure on the New York rock scene – went one further. He was a gawky sort of gentleman who habitually wore a dress and fishnet tights with holes in them, *à la* Monroe in *Bus Stop*, and hair which looked like a bleached blonde fright wig. Wayne once appeared at a party dressed in a delightful frock made of inflated condoms. He also wrote an arch little tips and advice column, entitled 'Dear Wayne', in a New York rock gossip magazine, *Rock Scene*. Towards the end of the seventies he carried his image-building to its logical conclusion and was surgically converted into Jayne County, a move which had little or no outward effect. Wayne said before the final transformation, 'I figure I've lived half my life as a man, why not live the other half as a woman?'

What Jayne did for real, Amanda Lear pretended. This enterprising European disco semi-star made something of a stir in 1976 by claiming to be a transsexual. A distinctly smoky voice and a 'statuesque' figure helped further the titillating illusion. In fact, Amanda had been born a woman – although exactly where and quite how many years ago no-one can be sure – and had been persuaded by former lover David Bowie to play her masterstroke of a hoax. 'I learnt from him to make myself interesting,' she said. 'To stand out from all other girls.' Ten years previously, Amanda had been an undistinguished stripper at London's Raymond Revue bar, working under the name of 'Peki D'Oslo' while claiming to be French. In order to boost herself in the rock marketplace, she released a series of 'bullshit biographies', giving a wide range of exotic birthplaces and parentages. Amanda, who achieved more media coverage as Brian Ferry's girlfriend than she did as a recording artist, brazenly promoted the phoneyness of her image. In 1978, she happily demonstrated this with the immortal statement that 'Disco is the lowest form of music, but the quickest way to fame.'

Maybe all this is a product of popular sexual confusion. But, if so, the quality of rock's permissiveness is no less shabby. Heavy metal, the most consistently popular kind of rock since the early seventies, has made a virtue out of the most strident and offensive male posturing. Curiously the tradition which forms the basis of heavy metal fashions and attitudes most markedly, actually comes from gay male culture. The chained and studded leather outfits, tattooed bodies and 'bike boy' poses that are central to heavy metal style have all been lifted from the world of butch drag – nothing more or less than 'a nice bit of rough'. Not even the strutting cock-rockers like Led Zeppelin, Bad Company, Ted Nugent or Rush could be described as so masculinist as groups like Judas Priest, Saxon, Motorhead or Iron Maiden. In fact, many of the younger

on their first album cover tastefully nude and smeared with a light coating of mud. Deborah Harry, perpetually moaning in interviews about her 'cheesecake' presentation on album sleeves and in the press, has never yet been known to refuse to appear in a mini-skirt, off-the-shoulder dress, tight pants or whatever it takes. One of the early (British) ad campaigns for Blondie presented her in a tight black dress with her hair tied back, under the slogan, 'Wouldn't You Like To Rip Her To Shreds?' (the record was called *Rip Her To Shreds*). Patti Smith – the thinking person's sex object – proudly boasted not just that young boys masturbated over her picture but that she herself had 'jacked-off over the cover of her second album.

But what is even more disturbing than such sexist stereotyping was the way in which male performers, from Bowie onwards, co-opted women's images. The New York Dolls, for instance, were a major influence on the East Coast in the early seventies. They were suitably wasted. Two of them had major problems with heroin and bassist Arthur Kane was almost destroyed by booze. Drummer Billy Murcia died, during a visit to London in 1972, when his girlfriend poured coffee down his throat in a vain attempt to revive him after a particularly heavy night of 'fun'.

Malcolm McLaren and the strong arm of the law. Top-dog in punk management, McLaren was among several revellers arrested after disturbances at a rowdy Thames riverboat party to celebrate the Queen's Silver Jubilee in June 1977.

heavy metal bands have gone beyond masculine exclusivity to outright woman-hating. It's hardly surprising to find among the repertoires of such groups songs extolling the virtues of violence against women, or attempts to elevate the notorious Yorkshire Ripper, Peter Sutcliffe, to the status of folk hero.

'If you want to find out how much freedom you have,' said Vivienne Westwood, 'make some kind of explicit sexual statement and wait for it all to crash down around you.' Vivienne, of course, was the partner in life and commerce of the Sex Pistols' manager, Malcolm McLaren. A fashion designer by training, she was instrumental in creating the whole punk style – an improvisation on themes of death, rape, sado-masochism and bondage. Through their shop in the King's Road, Chelsea, Vivienne and Malcolm promoted their 'provocative' and 'confrontational' theory of clothing. The resulting amalgam of leather, chains, straps, zips and rips made parts of London look like an explosion in a New York gay bar and its blast is still reverberating around the world. The Sex Pistols themselves were another 'explicit sexual statement', designed by McLaren, after his brief period managing the fading but influential New York Dolls. 'Rock'n'roll is not just music,' said McLaren. 'You're selling an attitude too.' The attitude for the late seventies, McLaren discovered, was the glorification of

Thieves and swindlers: the last act of McLaren's 'Great Rock'n'Roll Swindle' took the rump of the Sex Pistols flying down to Rio to record with runaway Train Robber Ronald Biggs in February 1978. L. to r.: Steve Jones, Jim Jetter in SS uniform, McLaren, Paul Cook and shy, fun-loving Ronald Biggs.

powerlessness, soulless despair and nihilistic perversity. McLaren already knew that to make any impact he had to say something that not even the 'progressive' rock world would feel happy to hear. In America in 1974, he had dressed the New York Dolls in red leather, stood them before a giant hammer-and-sickle Soviet flag and promoted them as 'Communist chic' – 'our "better-Red-than-dead" phase,' as Doll vocalist David Johansen said. The late seventies' version was, of course, the Sex Pistols.

After the Sex Pistols finally split-up (amid much acrimony), McLaren approached Adam and the Ants to star in a pornographic video film about a group of

75

kids who start a club to act out sex games, but the idea was axed by McLaren's lawyers and by Adam. Adam and Malcolm parted company after apparently exchanging musical ideas and Adam went off to form the remarkably successful Ants Mk II. Meanwhile, using the nucleus of the original Ants, Malcolm's masterplan produced Bow Wow Wow. Musically and visually, the two bands were remarkably similar – both cultivating a so-called 'tribal' music, which sounds like Gary Glitter's backing group playing in a paper bag, and appearing in heavy make-up and fancy costumes, now as pirates, now as American Indians, now as highwaymen. But Adam (real name Stuart Goddard) has shown greater admiration for the established values of showbiz than McLaren ever did – and he has in consequence seen far more commercial success than Bow Wow Wow.

McLaren, despite some possibly light-hearted claims that he took the pop world with a well-conceived grand strategy, (known as the 'great rock'n'roll swindle'), has always been motivated by a desire to be outrageous rather than anything subtler or better defined. Bow Wow Wow's singer was to be a fourteen-year-old girl called Annabella Lu Win (ostensibly of Burmese extraction, although her mother calls herself Mrs Dunn-Lewin). 'Why shouldn't Annabella be bait for lots of guys to get excited about?' asked McLaren, who planned to feature his new star in a sex magazine for pre-teens to be called *Chicken*. 'Underage sex,' said McLaren, 'is a very splendid thing.' Unfortunately, Bow Wow Wow's record company, EMI (no doubt trying to wipe some of the egg they had received from the Sex Pistols off their corporate face), didn't agree. They pulled out of *Chicken* after reportedly putting up £20,000. When Bow Wow Wow recorded a song advocating home taping of discs, at a time when EMI were vociferously engaged in a campaign against it, the company began politely to ignore the group – despite an investment of £55,000 (according to McLaren). The record (*C30, C60, C90, Go!*) flopped and, in an echo of earlier days with the Sex Pistols, the group ran riot in the EMI offices, throwing gold discs, hurling a clock out of a window, burning contracts and wrecking a revolving door. The group was dropped but, undaunted, McLaren found them another deal (with RCA) and the band went on to make an album which, McLaren thought, should feature a cover parodying Manet's famous painting, *Déjeuner Sur L'Herbe*, only with Annabella and not an artist's model in the nude. Annabella, at that time fifteen years old and still needing a special licence, a governess and a chaperone to perform in public, agreed to pose because she 'wasn't showing enough commitment to the band'. Annabella's mother threatened legal action, however, and RCA dropped the planned sleeve until Annabella was sixteen.

Despite a few inventive studio hits, McLaren's only real success was the Pistols. They, at least, had all the right ingredients at just the right time. The Pistols emerged at the head of the punk movement which seemed implicitly to understand and accept what they

stood for. McLaren's period managing the New York Dolls had taught him something. With the Sex Pistols, McLaren was selling a label which advertised the ingredients necessary for the contemporary rock'n'roll mix – sex and violence. He may not have understood how the very explicitness of this touched a nerve of alienation and despair in the kids, but he did understand that the punk obsession with sex, and especially violent sex, was never more than a pose. There could have been few bands less sexy than the Sex Pistols (especially when Rotten started talking about cutting off his piles). But the important thing was not actually to be sexy or shocking, but to tell people you were, with all the gall of a street trader.

Johnny Rotten was the least musical of the Pistols, but he was the one who best understood the group's hollow image. Accordingly, he became their most celebrated and reviled member – attacked by Teddy Boys, harassed by the police, the person who according to one writer at least, 'almost single-handedly defined punk rock'. His disagreements with McLaren, whom he accused of being a money-grubbing exploiter and who in turn fired him from the band at the end of their one and only US tour, helped to destroy the Sex Pistols. Sid Vicious, Paul Cook and Steve Jones carried gamely on – for a few months. The group, said Johnny Rotten (now using his actual name of John Lydon and in a new band, Public Image Limited), 'was a farce'. Legal action against McLaren revealed that most of the Sex Pistols' money had been dissipated. Not surprisingly, when subsequently questioned about PiL, Lydon said, 'No one in this band is a musician. We all hate the term. We're something close to factory workers. Machinists. Skilled operators.' His ambition for PiL, he said, was the same as it had been for the Pistols: 'To destroy rock'n'roll.'

Outrageous as it was, British punk remained essentially impotent – giving way in short order to only slightly more refined moves by the record industry to control the golden egg-laying goose of music. Despite that, it was seen as threatening by outsiders, and often resulted in actual violence and harassment. This was especially so in Britain's Jubilee Year of 1977, when the Sex Pistols released the distinctly unjoyous *God Save The Queen*, while others waved flags at street parties. Needless to say the record was banned from the airwaves – but it still reached number two.

Johnny Rotten and Sid Vicious were frisked by an over-eager policeman in June 1977; Rotten had been fined for possession of amphetamine sulphate in March; eleven people were arrested on a variety of charges when the Pistols' record company, Virgin, threw a rowdy party on a Thames river boat in June; Rotten and Paul Cook were violently attacked in separate incidents a fortnight later (Rotten suffered knife wounds while Cook was hit over the head with an iron bar); in May, Paul Cook had been fined for theft, and in July Vicious was fined on assault and weapons charges. The Clash, touted as the true revolutionaries of punk – were also harassed, but their harassment revealed the sad insignificance of their personal revolt. Joe Strummer was fined, in June 1977, for stealing

'All our songs are in praise of women,' say the Stranglers, seen here getting on down at an open-air concert in Battersea Park, London in the summer of 1978. Before the police stopped the show, bassist Jean-Jacques Burnel couldn't resist getting in on the act, adding a further appendage to the five-and-a-bit breasts visible.

pillows from a Holiday Inn, and earlier for spraying the band's name on a wall. Topper Headon was fined for stealing a hotel key. The next year, Headon and Paul Simonon were fined for shooting some racing pigeons, while Strummer and Simonon were fined in the wake of a riotous Glasgow gig.

The Jubilee Year also saw the Stranglers ordered off stage at London's Rainbow Theatre because Hugh Cornwell was wearing a T-shirt parodying the Ford Motors logo which actually read 'Truck', but which from a distance could have been read as 'Fuck'. Bob Geldof was attacked on stage at a London club. Kid Reed, singer with the punk group the Boys, was assaulted by Teddy Boys. Meanwhile, Leee Black Childers (manager of the New York group, the Heartbreakers) was attacked by punks because he looked like a Ted.

In Sweden, later in 1977, the Stranglers' show was disrupted by 200 neo-fascists and in the following year the same group was accused of causing a riot in Nice. But despite all the violence and brushes with the law, self-mutilation remains the most potent image of punk, and its ultimate expression was the deaths of Nancy Spungen and Sid Vicious. Perhaps the final comment should come from Malcolm McLaren. 'I didn't make the Pistols famous just for money,' he said in 1980. 'It was a great sexual turn-on too.'

Johnny Rotten dismissed sex as 'two minutes of slurping noises', and for many punks and post-punks

(reacting against the naïve optimism of the 'love generation'), the act itself seemed to have lost all meaning. Sex was an expensive commodity or, heaven forbid, something you had to take your clothes off to do. The late seventies even saw a brief period of trendy 'asexuality', when sex was touted as distinctly boring and, for some people, celibacy was promoted as a radical gesture. Sex was no longer about pleasure and people, but about power and objects. The S&M symbols cultivated by punk resolved sex into power games – and power games are what rock performers play on stage, and rock managers (like McLaren) play off it.

In America, where British punk's sense of irony and despair never had fertile soil in which to root, the 'new wave' picked up where the punk trinity of Lou Reed, Bowie and Alice Cooper left off. A group called the Dead Boys, lead by one Stiv Bators, caused a considerable stir by cultivating a stage act which made great use of S&M imagery. It was widely rumoured that Stiv and his colleagues enjoyed this sort of thing off stage too, although Bator's relationship with Bebe Buell indicated more conventional tastes. Iggy Pop, another of punk's godparents, made a vaunted comeback in 1979 in leather and lacerated flesh.

Not surprisingly, American women performers revealed most keenly the voyeuristic trend. Grace Jones, emerging from the New York gay/S&M disco scene, presented a wide variety of sexual diversions – now she would sing surrounded by a bevy of muscular men in leather jock-straps, now she recorded an album whose very title, *Warm Leatherette*, irresistibly evoked fetishism, now she appeared as a hi-tech androgyne with severely cropped hair. Cherry Vanilla, who once worked with David Bowie's management in New York, created an act of stunning vulgarity

77

making maximum suggestive use of the microphone. She once appeared at a party wearing a chiffon frock and parading a man in a leather mask around on a leash. Patti Smith ensured her own street-credibility by informing the press that, on what one can only presume were good nights, she would have an orgasm on stage.

Most stunning of all have been Wendy O. Williams and the Plasmatics – the ultimate sex-and-violence act to date. Sporting a Mohican haircut, Wendy might come on in a see-through body-stocking or tight black pants and some strategically placed sticky tape and clothes pins – sometimes, she would opt for no more than a couple of blobs of whipped cream to cover her nipples. The all-male Plasmatics looked no less bizarre and the music – if that's the right word – fitted the image. Songs like *Sex Junkie*, *Pig Is A Pig* and *Living Dead* were hammered out with all the subtlety of an

exploding elephant. Guitarist himself over the head with his g televisions, took a chain saw and sliced it in two, and at the group might demolish an entire auto-destruction. This was the of the super-gory exploitation m 'Pornography rock' was how the it. 'I've always been a kind of anarchist,' said Wendy. In London, the group were banned from performing before playing a single show of a 1980 tour because their car-demolition routine was considered too dangerous. In Milwaukee the following year, Wendy was dragged out of a concert hall by police. 'One of them grabbed my tits, another one grabbed my rear end. So I smacked them.' All charges were subsequently dropped, but Wendy commented that, 'I'd have gone along peacefully, but I was outraged intellectually.' Also in 1981, in Cleveland – the city, according to Wendy, with the third highest rape rate and the fifth highest murder rate in the US – she was charged with 'pandering obscenity'. After her acquittal, she emerged from the courthouse proclaiming her victory as 'a big thing for women's rights and the First Amendment'. 'I'm a rock'n'roll singer,' said Wendy. 'I should be able to do what I want.'

US punk star Stiv Bators accepts nomination as a celebrity by kissing Bebe Buell – mother of Todd Rundgren's child and former companion of Rod Stewart and Elvis Costello.

THE BLACK EXPERIENCE

When Frankie Lymon died as a result of his heroin habit in 1968, the tragedy was not just of wasted youth, the fault was not just the record industry's callousness or Frankie's impressionability and inexperience. Frankie Lymon, unlike all the white boys swallowed in and washed up by rock'n'roll success, was a victim of racism as much as he was a victim of a greedy industry or his own too rapid rise.

It was not that he was particularly exploited or ripped-off – although as a black teenager he was certainly a prime target for shady business practices – nor that he was any less able to cope with sudden success than dozens of other ill-educated, street-wise kids who stepped out of junior high school into the back seat of chauffeur-driven limousines. Lymon's tragedy had less to do with rock'n'roll as such than it had to do with being black in a white supremacist society. Not even a string of hit records could undermine the legacy of slavery and ghetto life. Rock'n'roll may have allowed blacks a degree of equality as entertainers (boasting that it broke down formerly rigid marketing distinctions between white and black musics) but rock'n'roll could not give *all* blacks pride, courage or insight into their own situation any more than it could rid the whole of white society of its prejudicial attitudes to blacks. Lymon, in other words, lived and died as a black first and as a rock'n'roll star second.

Like scores of others, the Teenagers (with Frankie Lymon) started as a street-corner vocal group, singing for pennies in Harlem. By the time Frankie was fourteen, the group had released half-a-dozen Top Ten singles – including the well-remembered *Why Do Fools Fall In Love?* and *I'm Not A Juvenile Delinquent.* Typically, black vocal groups have had anonymous members – a feature which not only makes their exploitation easier but also allows personnel to be moved around with impunity.

Frankie Lymon, however, emerged as a star from the Teenagers and left the group in 1956 to pursue a solo career. He was going on fifteen. While not unheard of, it was a brave move for a young black singer – even one whose status at the time was compared to that of Bill Haley, Chuck Berry and, at times, Elvis Presley. But his solo career flopped and Lymon became increasingly dependent on heroin. With the help and encouragement of his girlfriend, Lymon continued to fight his addiction but the relationship didn't last and when the singer went into the Army he also

went back on heroin. After his discharge, Lymon went home to New York and a series of unsuccessful attempts to find and hold a steady job. In February 1968, aged 25, he died of an overdose on the floor of his grandmother's apartment – penniless and forgotten.

Lymon's story, with its combination of themes of golden youth, sudden riches, ambition, addiction, a slow descent back to grinding poverty and eventual death, has become legend – a moral tale capturing the essence of everything rotten about rock'n'roll (comparable to Gene Vincent's sad history). But just as Vincent's tragedy is nothing without his poor white Southern background, so Lymon's resonates because he was black. Though, in the relatively enlightened world of rock'n'roll, the idea that blacks should keep their place may have been abandoned, nonetheless long-standing traditions of racism reverberate in their stories. And the black artists themselves feel this – they too understand the notion of the 'sassy nigger' sashaying through life in defiance of the old white conventions of black subservience.

Other black musicians, like Frankie Lymon, found failure a powerful stimulus to self-destruction. Guitar Slim, born Eddie Jones in Mississippi in 1926, topped the R&B charts in 1954 with a slow blues, *The Things I Used To Do* (featuring Ray Charles on piano). His spectacular act and playing style subsequently drew comparison with Jimi Hendrix and perhaps he was ahead of his time. The respect and admiration of his professional colleagues was clearly insufficient reward and, having failed to achieve long-term success, he fell victim to alcohol, dying in 1959.

Clyde McPhatter was another victim of early success. Born in North Carolina in 1933, he formed the original Drifters in 1953 and had a number of hits with them (*Money Honey* and *White Christmas*, for example), and as a solo performer (*Lucilla* and *Such a Night*) before being drafted in 1954. In 1956, he returned to the business and worked exclusively as a solo singer. He achieved a string of hits, including the unforgettable *A Lover's Question.* But from 1959 onwards, he started switching labels with alarming rapidity and, despite several notable hits (*Ta Ta, Lover Please* and *Little Bitty Pretty One*, for example), his career went into decline. He became an alcoholic and moved to London in the late sixties. Despite a strong personal following, he never achieved the sort of early success he had known. In fact, he walked his way through a series of recording disasters until finally people only put him in a studio out of pity or for the sake of old times. Jerry Wexler once called him 'the great, unique soul singer of all time', and Smokey Robinson said,

Little Frankie Lymon – only fourteen but already a star. He may have jumped for joy at the London Palladium, 1st April, 1957, but heroin finally got him eleven years later.

'He was the man'. But in June 1972, while visiting friends in the Bronx, Clyde died of an apparent heart attack, his liver, heart and kidneys all but destroyed by booze.

R&B star Johnny Ace shot himself through the head on Christmas Eve, 1954, during the interval of a show in Houston, Texas. On the point of breaking through into the mass market with his hit single, *Pledging My Love*, Ace apparently occupied his time backstage with a game of Russian Roulette – the perfect symbol of casual despair in the face of a capricious and hostile fate. In 1973, Paul Williams (one of the original Temptations but no longer with the group) was found, shot through the head, gun in hand and dressed only in his swimming trunks, sitting in his car. The inescapable verdict was suicide. Suicide was also the accepted verdict on Donny Hathaway – an ex-student preacher and gospel singer who had found international success duetting with Roberta Flack. The 33-year-old Hathaway had been recording in New York during January 1979, when, one Sunday morning, his broken body was found on a second-storey roof of his hotel, the Essex House. 'We suspect suicide

82

because the door of his room was locked and there was no evidence of foul play,' a police spokesperson said. Hathaway had either fallen or jumped from the window of his fifteenth-floor room shortly before midnight on the night before. The shock to many friends and critics was not assuaged by the news that the singer had suffered from frequent depressions. But perhaps the man who had once been billed as 'the nation's youngest gospel singer' found it difficult to cope with secular success.

It's not really surprising that many blacks should channel their general feeling of being society's outcasts into self-destructive outlawry. Despite the fact that drug abuse has always been as prevalent among white as black musicians, until the mid-sixties there were far more arrests of the latter on more serious charges and with greater attendant publicity. Louis Armstrong – Whitey's favourite jazz musician – was forced to forego his penchant for marijuana after a particularly harsh bust in the forties. Ray Charles – enormously influential on both soul and rock – was busted at Logan Airport, Boston, in 1964, on his return from a Canadian gig. Charles had been using heroin for seventeen years and this bust, for smack and grass, was his third. He decided to kick the habit. 'Kicking was something I felt I had to do,' he said in his autobiography. 'I didn't quit because the heroin was killing me – maybe it was, maybe it wasn't – but because it was going to bring down my family and maybe even cause me to rot away in some jail cell.'

As it turned out, he was able to avoid both outcomes – because he managed to kick the habit before his trial and because, as he himself says, 'I was blessed: I'd had the bread to buy decent junk, and then I had the bread to buy bail and a high grade of justice.' He was convicted, but was put on probation. Others haven't been so lucky. Blues singer Little Willie John died in jail after being incarcerated for theft. Drummer Buddy Miles – who had played in Jimi Hendrix's Band of Gypsies – was jailed for two years for the relatively minor offence of stealing a parked car (the British call it 'taking and driving away').

When not being attacked by the law, even successful black musicians find themselves entrapped by that negative institution of the law, organized crime. Larry Williams (who had several hits in the fifties and sixties with 'Little Richardesque' songs like *Bony Moronie* and *Slow Down*), ran a highly successful Hollywood prostitution ring. In 1979 he was shot dead – by his own hand, according to the police, by the mob, according to his family. 'King' Curtis Ousley – *the* fifties' and sixties' session saxophonist, virtuoso of the booting, yackety-sax style – was as successful as any black performer of the period. He was stabbed to death in New York in 1971 by a young Puerto Rican with whom Curtis had picked a fight, possibly because he thought the man was a burglar. Curtis came upon the man, 26-year-old Juan Montanez, sitting on the stoop of a brownstone apartment house, owned by the saxophonist on West 86th Street. It was late one Friday night in August, Friday the thirteenth as it happened. According to the police, the two men had a heated

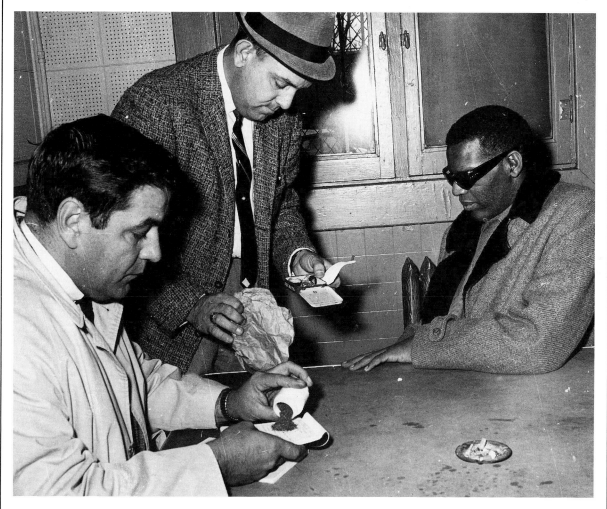

Before the sixties, black musicians attracted more attention from narcotics investigators than whites. Blind Ray Charles sits helplessly as detectives examine drugs and paraphernalia, following his second arrest in Indianapolis, 4th November, 1961.

exchange; Curtis, a heavily-built six-footer, was notorious for his short temper and was known to fly off the handle with little provocation. This time however the Puerto Rican pulled a knife and stabbed the musician. Curtis grabbed the knife and stabbed Montanez four times in retaliation. Montanez managed to run off, but unluckily for him, collapsed later and was taken to the same hospital in which Curtis had by this time already died of his stab wounds. Montanez was then arraigned for the musician's murder.

This whole squalid incident may have been completely attributable to the unattractive side of Curtis's character, but it remains powerfully suggestive of the violence and criminality that surround black musicians. In another incident in 1974, singer Bobby Womack's brother, Harry, was stabbed to death by a woman at the door of Bobby's LA apartment. Harry, who had performed with his brother under the names of the Womack Brothers and the Valentinos, resem-

bled Bobby closely, and it has been suggested that Bobby was the intended victim. The killer may have been exacting some curious revenge for Bobby's marriage to the wife of his former mentor, Sam Cooke, who was also killed in bizarre circumstances.

Not surprisingly for a people whose culture has been exploited, plundered and attacked as much as the black Americans', male black performers rely heavily on *machismo* as a mark of their identity, while many female black performers – Tina Turner, Ronnie Spector, Donna Summer for example – present themselves in a sexually obvious, not to say whorish, way. Of course, sexual stereotypes are one of the most obvious aspects of racism and, while most of the black female performers who have been popular with white audiences have depended on emphasizing their availability, male performers in a similar position have ironically compromised their macho image with emasculating touches (falsetto or high tenor voices, clownish costumes or stylized dance routines). Jimi Hendrix based much of his act on an *explicit* referral to black machismo, but his success was founded in

83

Britain, not America. Eric Clapton explained his appeal. 'Everybody and his brother in Britain still think spades have big dicks,' he said at the height of Hendrix's success. 'Jimi came over and exploited that to the limit, the fucking tee. Everybody fell for it. Shit.'

It's not surprising that the macho image displays an understandable confusion. Al Green, perhaps the leading gospel-influenced soul singer of the seventies, is a case in point. 'Green's style ... becomes the vehicle for a persona that is modest, even fragile, yet undeniably compelling,' gushed Robert Christgau after one performance. What he really meant was Green was sexy. In October 1974, Green was approached by a woman fan – 29-year-old Mary Woodson – who foolishly hoped to marry him. She discovered that Green did not match up to her fantasy image of him. Despite her persistence, she was rejected. Attempting to disfigure the reluctant lover, she tipped a pan of boiling grits down the Alabama-born Green's back. It ranks as an incomparable piece of poetic drama. She then took a gun and killed herself. The tragedy was not just one of unrequited love or burning sexual desire, but of black sexuality as it has been defined in public. Green may not have promoted a he-man version of black macho, à la James Brown, Wilson Pickett or Teddy Pendergrass, but his meaning

Courtroom blues: Ray Charles sits in an Indianapolis court on 9th January, 1962 to face charges made in the previous November. After Charles' third bust, at Boston's Logan Airport in 1964, he gave up drugs to save his family from distress and himself from destruction.

Al Green, one of the great black sex symbols of the seventies, preaching the gospel in Memphis, 26th January, 1980. After his experiences with a pan of boiling grits from an over-eager fan, it's not surprising he retreated into the ministry.

and his moans were intended to be just as clear.

Green's precursors included the far less restrained Jackie Wilson and Sam Cooke, both acknowledged architects of soul music's synthesis of spirituality and carnality. Like most soul performers, Jackie Wilson's recording career seemed shaky and uncertain – never quite sure of its direction, whether it was the Elvis pastiche of *Reet Petite*, night-club standards or high energy storm raisers like (*Your Love Keeps Lifting Me*) *Higher And Higher*. But on stage he was magnetic. Sexual hysteria could reach fever-pitch and engendered a violent intensity which white performers could rarely match at the time. Joe McEwan described a typical occasion at Boston's Back Bay Theatre. In the middle of *Shake! Shake! Shake!*, Wilson jumped into the willing arms of the women clustered round the edge of the stage and completely disappeared in the turmoil. Shirt shredded, he had to be escorted to safety by the police.

In July 1960, Wilson was arrested with six other black performers at a show in New Orleans. This time the police had tried to prevent the singer from 'mingling' with the audience at the all-black show. They only succeeded in creating a riot. The show was stopped and the anger of 5,000 disappointed fans had to be quelled by the riot squad.

85

On 15th February, 1961, Wilson returned home to his New York apartment at about four in the morning. Juanita Jones, a 28-year-old black woman, claiming to be a friend and fan, was waiting for him. As Wilson told it, she knocked on the door and asked him 'to pay her some attention'. When he refused, she threatened to shoot herself and pulled a .38 pistol from her belt. Wilson, a former boxer, said he grabbed the gun and was shot in the back and front during a brief struggle. He ran into the street, crying for help – his hysterical sexual persona turned back on itself. Juanita Jones, arrested for 'felonious assault', could only say, 'I've loved him ever since he cut *Lonely Teardrops*. I hope I haven't hurt him . . . I'm all mixed up.'

Wilson's career was as florid on the way down as it had been at its early sixties' peak. In 1967, he was arrested with a lorry driver for possession of heroin, hypodermic syringes and two loaded guns, after the police had stopped the two men's car in Catskill, New York State. Two years later, he was held as a material witness after an Atlanta waitress and former Playboy Bunny named Karen Lynn Calloway was murdered by her husband, shot five times. Wilson had just completed a six-day residency at the club where Karen worked. Her husband, a hand in a local carpet mill, claimed that he shot his wife because she had become infatuated with Jackie Wilson. Karen Lynn was a 21-year-old mother of two when she died.

Of course, the screaming had to stop sometime and Wilson declined into a parody of banal sentimentalism. He suffered a stroke while performing in New York in 1976 and spent much of the rest of his life in hospital. In February 1978 – a few years before his death – one newspaper recorded that in the course of his flamboyant career, the singer had sold 22 million records and generated around $200 million of revenue from record and concert ticket sales. Broke and unconscious following another stroke, Jackie Wilson had just passed his forty-third birthday, on which the former idol of millions received just six cards.

Wilson lived to see rock'n'roll change utterly from his halcyon days. Sam Cooke, however, was killed at the turning point. The most curious aspect of Cooke's death is the way that, even many years later, people find its manner in stark and worrying contradiction to his public image – invariably described as 'gentle', 'poised', 'graceful' and 'genial'. His death was a profound shock to his millions of fans – 200 people attended the Los Angeles Inquest, 200,000 filed past the body in Chicago and LA. Cooke remains for many whites just a man who composed and sang trite little pop songs like *Only Sixteen*, *Twisting The Night Away* and *What A Wonderful World*, but for blacks he was the embodiment of the drive towards black pride: a black capitalist with his own record company, management firm and publishing organization, a man who controlled his own destiny and could hold his own in the white world, and who openly allied himself with the cause of black liberation.

All this fuelled rumours that his death was not an accident – that he was the victim of some elaborate mob killing because, so it was said, his success made him too much of a threat to the white establishment. Much the same was said about the crash that killed Otis Redding some three years later, and similar rumours have circulated around Jimi Hendrix's death. In 1981, the French newspaper, *Le Monde*, actually carried an interview with an anonymous but self-confessed contract killer who, while denying he had been involved in Hendrix's death, claimed to have known the man who arranged it. As yet, the claim remains unsubstantiated. The evidence in all three cases is thin – but in Cooke's case at least, his death has acquired the resonance of myth. It is a sad fact, however, that the truth is probably as sordid as it seems and the reaction against it was the result of the poor light it shone on Sam Cooke.

The inquest testimony indicated that on the night of his death (10th–11th December, 1964), Cooke picked up 22-year-old Elisa Boyer at a small party at a Hollywood restaurant. Cooke was 33 at the time and married to his high-school sweetheart, Barbara Campbell. After offering to take Boyer home, Cooke drove to a motel in Los Angeles and registered (as 'Mr and Mrs Cooke') with Boyer apparently standing quietly by. 'He dragged me to that room,' Boyer told the inquest, 'and I again asked him to take me home. He turned the night latch, pushed me into bed and pinned me down. He kept saying, "We're just gonna talk" . . . He pulled my sweater off and ripped my dress. I knew he was going to rape.' Boyer picked up her clothes (together, it seems, with Cooke's) and ran out of the motel room. Cooke followed her to the motel office but she had gone to look for a telephone. The motel manageress, a black woman named Bertha Lee Franklin, told Cooke that Boyer was not with her but, after starting his car up, the singer returned to the office dressed only in an overcoat. According to Franklin, he persisted in asking 'Where is the girl?' and, after being told to get the police, he broke down the door of the motel office and attacked the manageress. She pushed Cooke away, grabbed a pistol and shot him three times. 'He said, "Lady, you shot me",' Bertha Franklin told the inquest. 'He ran at me again. I started fighting with a stick. The first time I hit him it broke.'

It was, by the witnesses' accounts, a bloody, brutal and unnecessary death. Sam Cooke's partner, J. W. Alexander, evidently hired a private detective 'to find out what the hell happened to my friend' – with no result. Alexander and his new partner, Barbara Cooke, fell out and Alexander eventually withdrew from the association. Soon afterwards, Barbara Cooke married Bobby Womack.

Naturally, RCA – Sam Cooke's record label at the time of his death – continued to release records by him. The first release after his death was the exhilarating ballad *A Change Is Gonna Come*, written by Cooke after he had heard Bob Dylan's *Blowin' In the Wind*. The song was Sam Cooke's own epitaph. Somewhere in

Sam Cooke, the suave, gentle soul singer of the early sixties, whose violent death belied the poise and geniality of his public image.

200,000 people paid their respects to Sam Cooke's body after his death at the hands of a motel owner on 11th December, 1964. A further 5,000 people attended the funeral service at Mt. Sinai Baptist Church, Los Angeles on 20th December, many having to stand outside in the steady rain.

New York, Frankie Lymon may have been shooting himself full of heroin, but Cooke had known that for black and white alike the times were moving on.

Sam Cooke's hopes for the future of integrated popular music had already begun to bear fruit in the late fifties and early sixties when the formal and informal segregation of music started to break down. This earlier segregation had taken some curious forms. Until the fifties, the US had been a country operating an effective apartheid policy, at least below the Mason-Dixon line. Black musicians playing for white audiences were in many towns required to 'appear' behind a screen. Conversely, white performers on predominantly black tours were not allowed to play at all – one such tour which included Buddy Holly and the Crickets, Paul Anka and the Everly Brothers, found these white performers forbidden to appear in Chattanooga, Columbus (Georgia), Birmingham (Alabama), New Orleans and Memphis. These same integrated package tours, many put together by DJ Alan Freed, would often have to split up when the performers left the concert hall, even if they were actually allowed to play on the same stage, the whites going to one hotel and the blacks to other, inferior, accommodation. Many white performers refused to go

Sam Cooke's widow, Barbara, places a flower on her husband's casket. He died while out with another woman, who claimed at the inquest he had tried to rape her. Cooke's daughters, Tracey (4) and Linda (11) can be seen on either side of their mother.

along with this – Niki Sullivan, who toured with the Crickets in 1957 said that eventually they preferred to stay in black hotels, where, he observed, 'We were accepted'.

The record industry at that time operated a category of 'race music' (under whatever euphemism, usually Rhythm and Blues) which separated the recording, promotion, distribution and sale of records according to the performer's skin. There were black radio stations, black record shops and black record labels serving the black community but generally owned and controlled by whites. Rock'n'roll and British R&B began to change this; one early example involved Buddy Holly and the Crickets again, who, booked to appear 'sight unseen' at one venue, surprised the tour promoter mightily when he found out they were white.

Unfortunately, the de-segregation of musics and audiences made little difference to the practice of exploiting performers. White and black alike were ripped-off, because any inexperienced performer with an inadequate understanding of the business and inadequate advisers was a potential target for bad (or no) royalty deals, shark-like managers and agents, diabolical contracts and Faustian agreements. If blacks suffered more from this institutional cheating, it was because they tended to have less experience of business, less effective representation and perhaps even a lower level of aspiration. On top of that, the 'race' market was smaller and poorer than the white market which meant that deals were usually worse and the ultimate rewards invariably smaller.

The familiar practice of covering 'race' records for the white market was a particularly subtle form of exploitation stemming directly from the segregation of the market. Many white performers made their reputations on covering black records, many of which never sold in the white market at all. Pat Boone, for example, recorded successfully versions of Fats Domino's *Ain't That A Shame*, Little Richard's *Long Tall Sally* and *Tutti Frutti*, Ivory Joe Hunter's *I Almost Lost My Mind* and the Flamingos' *I'll Be Home*, in the middle years of the fifties. Clearly, every sale of one of Boone's anaemic versions reduced the sales of the original. Even where the original performer could expect a writer's royalty, such payments were often unforthcoming. The classic example is that of Arthur 'Big Boy' Crudup, whose *That's Alright Mama* and *My Baby Left Me* have been covered over the years by everyone from Elvis Presley to Rod Stewart and Elton John. But Crudup saw no royalties. 'The company paid my manager, but he didn't pay me,' Crudup said in the mid-seventies. 'I was to get 35 per cent of every dollar he received. Well, I failed to get it.' Crudup's Lester Melrose, died before his client received any money. Legal action resulted in an offer in settlement of $60,000 from the Melrose estate and Crudup's publisher. However, while waiting in New York for the cheque to be paid, Crudup was told that the offer had been withdrawn. The issue would have to go back to court, and Crudup himself died before any final decision was reached.

Similar experiences to Arthur Crudup's were, however, commonplace (and probably still are). They are worse among black musicians and writers but by no means restricted to them. Many of the popular black performers of the fifties and early sixties had to soften their blackness for white consumption. They were aware of the compromises they made. This awareness showed in their attitudes to the business. Sam Cooke and Chuck Berry, for instance, were both clearly motivated in large part by a desire not to be exploited. Cooke had his businesses; Berry had his by now notoriously rigid attitude to his contractual obligations. It's not surprising that someone like James Brown should fight and ultimately win the right to control the whole of his business interests, including management and record production. In the late sixties he risked the accusations of capitulation by black militants and of repetitiveness by rock and soul critics. But the Number One Soul Brother just ignored both; his answer to them has been to keep going in exactly the same, successful way, even at the approach of his fiftieth birthday.

If there was no specific move against racism or for black equality in the early days of rock'n'roll, there was a great deal of feeling that blacks should, at least, assert themselves and protect their own interests. The sixties consequently saw the growth of independent black record labels, song publishers, agencies and managements, and the prime example of this was Berry Gordy's Motown Company.

The Motown and Tamla labels were launched in Detroit in 1960 by Gordy, who had been one of America's most successful and prolific songwriters in the late fifties. With hits by Jackie Wilson, Marv Johnson and Etta James, among others, to his credit Gordy's move into distribution with his own label was – like the subsequent development of the publishing, management and film-making side of his business – motivated by the simple desire to maximize profit. Smokey Robinson, one of Gordy's early co-writers, leader of the Miracles (Tamla's first successful group) and later Motown's vice-president, explained that Motown started because black groups did feel they were being ripped off elsewhere. He said: 'Motown was just local and we decided since nobody was paying us for the national stuff anyway, why not see what the national market could do. So that's why we exist today.'

From the start, Motown was almost exclusively a black operation (unlike, say, the supposedly more 'authentic' black labels like Atlantic, Chess or later Stax/Volt). The company relied heavily on family loyalties – one of Gordy's first associates was his sister Gwen and two other sisters married Harvey Fuqua (of the Moonglows) and Marvin Gaye, both of whom were important members of the Motown team from the early days. Early Motown performers were treated like most of the other black performers scuffling around in the marketplace. Most effort was expended on groups: the Miracles, the Velvelettes, Martha and the Vandellas, the Four Tops, the Temptations, the Supremes were all patterned on the classic vocal group

Diana Ross as Billie Holiday in Lady Sings the Blues. *Once a nameless member of the Supremes, she was groomed for stardom by Motown boss Berry Gordy, who achieved his goal when she played the tragic Lady Day.*

their talents. Motown has always aimed its music at the white market and the company tactic has been to understand the white market and supply what it wants. Successful though it has been, this tactic has not been without problems.

Gordy always seemed eager for his performers to move into the highly lucrative middle ground. His ambitions pointed to Las Vegas, the Copacabana and movies. By the early seventies, however, Motown finally achieved 'intellectual' respectability when the company's two most notable mavericks, Marvin Gaye and Stevie Wonder, produced albums that went against the Motown grain. Gaye's *What's Going On* and Wonder's *Music Of My Mind* were wordy and experimental and, although Gordy had never shied away from topicality or symbolism, Gaye was political and Wonder introspective. In addition, both performers gave themselves almost total responsibility for their albums. The Motown mould had been broken.

Motown's relations with its performers have frequently been criticized – most remarkably, by the performers themselves. As recently as 1981, Marvin Gaye complained that the company failed to treat him as 'an artist . . . a complete entity'. However, Gaye has stayed with Motown while many others have departed the fold, vociferous in their complaints – the Holland brothers and Lamont Dozier, Martha Reeves, David Ruffin and Eddie Kendricks among them.

The conflict which led to these departures is not so much between employer and employees but between the original idea of Motown's operations and the new attitude which began to take over in the sixties. Gordy's vision of a black company directing its product at the white market involved the cultivation of a corporate identity under which individual talent was buried. By the mid-sixties, a number of changes had occurred which overtook this vision. Black consciousness and the success of a handful of vanguard black performers like Sam Cooke were joined with a growing general acceptance that popular music could be an 'art' in the most traditional sense. Gordy and his 'employees' were well aware of these changes, but Gordy's response was to turn his company round from producing a corporate product to cultivating individual talent. Many of his protégées saw their future in terms of personal promotion and even stardom based on the recognition of their individual worth. Inevitably, many would feel that Motown was stifling their chances, while others, like Florence Ballard, would be left behind in the rush to build up the reputations of a handful of individuals.

Florence Ballard was one of the original Supremes (with Diana Ross and Mary Wilson). The three girls, all from the same poor quarter of Detroit, met at a church gospel meeting and sometime later decided to form a professional vocal group. Through Berry Gordy's patronage (and, as legend has it, after painstakingly sewing their own costumes), the Supremes became an immensely successful act. But then Gordy's design changed. In 1967, the Supremes were to become Diana Ross and the Supremes, and would start recording songs with what have been described as 'slightly more

format of much black music. Individual members were kept largely anonymous, which helped when the membership changed, as it frequently did.

The real Motown artists, throughout most of the sixties, were the writers, the arrangers and producers – the performers were moulded to a pattern and, in the end, tended to settle down with one or other team of composers and craftspeople whose conception they faithfully realized. Like the Platters, the Drifters, the Chiffons, the Ronettes or countless other earlier and later vocal groups, they were effectively faceless – it was the Motown *sound* that mattered. And this hard-nosed operation was also extremely paternalistic; Gordy obviously saw himself as some sort of patriarch, running his 'family' with an iron but gentle hand. 'We used to have a school at Motown Records called Artists' Development,' said Smokey Robinson, 'and in order to become a Motown recording artist – before you had been recorded and did any dates at all – you had to be at school. You had to go and you had to learn stage presence, choreography and the girls had to learn hygiene and stuff like that. You learned all about it before we presented you to anyone in the country.' The Supremes were told to finish their formal education before recording; Little Stevie Wonder's royalties were kept in trust until he came of age. Critics have accused Motown of manipulating its performers; Gordy and Robinson have always maintained that they cared for their artists, developing and nurturing socially-conscious lyrics' (*Love Child* and *I'm Living In Shame*, for example). For Diana Ross, a career as an artist, actress and star stretched far ahead. Meanwhile, back in the sixties, Florence Ballard and Mary Wilson were pushed into the background.

Florence – whose contribution to the Supremes before 1967 had been as great as Diana Ross's, and who had recorded eight gold records with the group – did not readily accept such a fate. Despite the flashy accessories of a Cadillac Eldorado and a golden Fleetwood, she later claimed that she only received a weekly allowance through all those hits – a practice which may have been unfair, but was by no means illegal. It was put about that she quit because she couldn't stand the pace of world touring. She told the *Los Angeles Times* in 1975 that she had agreed to leave the group after being offered a million dollar settlement by Motown, but her $8.7 million dollar lawsuit against the company, the Supremes and her former attorney, was dismissed in 1971. By 1973 she was separated from her husband and had lost her home through foreclosure. She moved back to her childhood area and, with support from Aid to Dependent Children, moved into a two-family apartment with her three daughters, mother and sister, in the same Detroit housing project in which she had grown up.

In 1975, she told her story to the papers and received considerable publicity – and probably some much-needed remuneration. But a few months later, in February 1976, the 32-year-old singer was admitted to hospital complaining of pains in her arms and legs. She had apparently been drinking heavily at the same

Above: Florence Ballard in 1965, at the height of her success with the Supremes. By 1967, the group had become Diana Ross and the Supremes and Florence was on her way out.

Below: At Florence Ballard's funeral in Detroit, 18th February, 1976, Diana Ross (left) comforts Florence's daughter, Nicole Chapman, aged 7. Florence's husband, Tommy Chapman (right) cuddles twin daughter Michelle. Diana and Florence began life in the same Detroit housing project.

Just walking in the rain. Marvin Gaye, enfant terrible *of the Motown stable contemplates the difficulties of combining artistic integrity with good commercial sense.*

time as taking drugs to help her lose weight and reduce her blood pressure. She died shortly afterwards.

The accepted myth has always been that Florence Ballard died in poverty. But her sister Pat subsequently claimed that Florence had in fact received an 'unexplained legal settlement' shortly before her death. Indeed, at the time of her death, Florence had been reconciled with her husband and had bought a new home for herself and her family, as well as another Cadillac. The manner of her death may well be a clue to her original problems with Motown and the Supremes – heavy drinking could have made her a liability, hence the excuse that she left because of 'the pressure of touring'. But whatever the reason, Florence never made her dreamed-of comeback, and if she had ever been an embarrassment to Motown and its most successful female star, Diana Ross, the hapless Florence was no longer.

Stevie Wonder stayed with Motown because when he came of age the company released the $1 million they

had held in trust for him. Having satisfied himself that Motown had handled his finances fairly, he signed with them again after securing a higher royalty rate and the right to publish his own material. In 1976 he renegotiated his Motown contract again for a reputed $13 million advance but even Berry Gordy's 'Trilby', Diana Ross, left Motown in 1980 for RCA's pastures, greener it is rumoured by $20 million.

Marvin Gaye also left Motown in the early eighties, his career, blighted by drug abuse and financial troubles, drifting towards a bizarrely tragic climax. Gaye had been married to Berry Gordy's sister Anna – a 14-year relationship which sustained him through difficult times until his divorce in 1976.

Back in March 1968, Gaye's then current singing partner, Tammi Terrell, collapsed in his arms of a brain haemorrhage and died some time later, aged only 24. Gaye was of course greatly upset. More than a decade later he spoke of the internal problems of the company at the time. Gordy and Motown were getting backlash from some sections of the record business because of the success they were achieving among radio stations and distributors. Gaye found the combination of personal and professional pressure difficult and went into virtual retirement.

'I'd become such a creep basically,' he admitted. 'I'd made Berry very angry. I wasn't on the best terms with my wife. There was the Vietnam war still going on.' Eventually he decided he had to come back, and he recorded *What's Going On*, but despite the appearance of having won a personal and artistic victory, things did not improve. By the end of the seventies, Gaye had demonstrated his artistic worth beyond doubt, but he had gone through two divorces and a bankruptcy following a tax bill of more than $2 million.

Unfortunately a growing drug habit inevitably began to make him unreliable. He had already attempted suicide once (in 1976) by ingesting 25 grams of cocaine in an hour. He moved to Europe in the early eighties and left Motown for CBS and a brief but glorious resurgence with the single 'Sexual Healing' and the album, *Midnight Love*. But the cocaine had gripped him and he grew increasingly paranoid, depressed and dependent.

In late 1983 he moved into the LA house which he had bought for his parents, took to carrying a gun and refusing food for fear of poison. In his more lucid moments, he talked of taking his own life, but in the end it proved unnecessary. A violent argument in his mother's bedroom was settled by a shot at point-blank range when Gaye's father – a fire-and-brimstone Pentecostal minister – killed his own son. It was 1 April 1984, but he wasn't fooling. Gaye was one day away from his 45th birthday.

Bob Marley, the first Third World superstar, dedicated many of his performances to Rastafarianism and the cult of the late Emperor Haile Selassie of Ethiopia.

The upsurge of black popular music in the sixties showed the world that it was as wide-ranging in its approach as anything white rock'n'roll could produce. In that respect it paved the way for the growing acceptance of reggae as more than just an exotic dance rhythm from Jamaica. Unlike some other forms of black music, however, reggae has never felt impelled to enter the white market. If whites want to accept it, that's their business; for some Rastafarian reggae artists, in fact, the white acceptance of reggae has been resisted and is seen as an encroachment by Babylon (the Rastas' general term for the whole of the white dominated western world).

Reggae is a fundamental part of Jamaican society's political process – which is not true of black music in the US. While James Brown could sing, 'Say it loud, I'm black and I'm proud', *and* endorse Richard Nixon's presidential campaign, Bob Marley recorded *Get Up, Stand Up!*, supported the socialist Prime Minister of Jamaica, Michael Manley and, in 1976, was shot and wounded for his pains. A different level of commit-

Marley waits to be treated in the hospital, 4th December, 1976, after being shot by politically inspired gunmen who broke into his house in Kingston, Jamaica. Marley was a vocal supporter of Jamaica's leftist premier, Michael Manley. Marley survived this murderous attempt, but succumbed on 11th May, 1981, to the ravages of lung cancer.

93

ment is involved.

Marley's death from cancer in 1981 revealed just how important reggae and Rastafarianism had become in Jamaica. It wasn't just the crowds who turned out for his funeral, or the orations given by Jamaica's leading politicians. More significant by far was the attention paid by countries and commentators outside the West Indies who were unanimous in recognizing Marley as the first 'Third World Superstar', an accolade that had already been bestowed on him implicitly when he was invited to play at the 1980 Independence celebrations in Zimbabwe. Through reggae and its association with Rastafarianism – a belief that holds the late Emperor Haile Selassie of Ethiopia to be a god, uses marijuana (*ganja*) as a sacrament and preaches the eventual return of all blacks to Africa – Marley represented the unity of the Third World countries against the rest.

Bob Marley was also a crucial figure in Britain, giving young, disaffected blacks a focus – many of whom had never set foot in Jamaica, let alone Africa. Some accused Marley of selling out when he came out in support of Manley's regime in Jamaica. But most saw white imperialism as the great enemy, rather than any particular political position. Even Marley's much reported love life – unrestrained by conventional notions of fidelity – and his equally widely publicized penchant for *ganja*, did not dissuade most blacks from the essential rightness of his position. If Whitey paid the piper – as Whitey paid Marley – then Whitey was the only loser.

If black attitudes to reggae were equivocal, that is no more than can be said for white attitudes. After 25 years, the experiences of the mixed American tours of the fifties were being depressingly repeated in England, but in a much more unofficial way. Reggae attracted the attention of neo-Nazi groups in Britain when this style of music, along with its West Indian influenced predecessors, Ska and Blue Beat, were adopted by a variety of black, white and mixed bands in the early eighties. The punk explosion threw a new ingredient into the usual mix of rock audiences. The disaffected youth who coagulated around punk have always been a prime target for fascist and racist organizations, and in short order such organizations were openly trying to impose their version of rock'n'roll on the new wave. Things came to a head in July 1979, when the arch-populists of punk, Sham 69, played at London's Rainbow Theatre amidst Hitler salutes and in the face of a running battle in the auditorium. The stage was invaded by neo-Nazi kids (mostly skinheads), and the band was forced to retreat, convinced that they had been betrayed by their fans. Sham's singer, Jimmy Pursey, proposed a 'music strike' until the kids realized that such demonstrations were not on. Unfortunately, Pursey's ambitions tended towards punk-without-politics, while all around him Rock Against Racism, the organization formed to fight racist attitudes from within the rock industry, and the two main neo-Nazi organizations, the National Front

Marley taking (or toking) the sacrament of ganja, the rastaman's word for marijuana.

94

Bob Marley's family watch his coffin being carried into the National Stadium in Kingston, Jamaica, for the public funeral on 21st May, 1981, following a private family service earlier in the day. Thousands of people turned out to watch Marley being buried in a specially constructed grave near his birthplace of Nine Miles in St Ann's.

and the British Movement, were busy demonstrating the opposite.

Jealous of RAR's success, the extreme right-wing National Front started a woe-begone organization called Rock Against Communism, which put on one gig (headlined by a lamentably bad group called White Boss), before collapsing with hardly a murmur. Meanwhile, the new breed of skinheads latched onto the two-tone dance bands like the Specials, the Beat and Madness. A tour by Madness in 1980 was called off because the band realized the rowdy element it was attracting was not merely composed of 'skins' having a good time, but included substantial numbers of mindlessly violent neo-Nazi thugs. For similar reasons, the Specials resolved not to play live again.

Deserted, as they saw it, by bands like Sham 69 and Madness, the 'skins' looked for an alternative – a raucous, rowdy style of music which was dubbed, by Gary Bushell of *Sounds*, with the unaesthetic, highly descriptive and totally artificial generic term, 'Oi'. His paper encouraged the music throughout early 1981 as some sort of grass roots phenomenon, as punk had once been. In fact, Oi seems to have been more a media invention than anything else. On the other hand, a number of the groups and fans connected with it were the very same neo-Nazis who had earlier disrupted punk and two-tone gigs, who were only too glad of the unaccustomed publicity they were being given. Criticism of Oi's supporters in the media (issuing, in the wake of a riot in the London borough of Southall, most notably from the London *Daily Mail* and the *New Musical Express*), led the editor of *Sounds* and Gary Bushell to institute libel proceedings. Against accusations of incipient or aggressive fascism, they countered with the argument that Oi was and remained a genuine expression of the despair and disaffection of working class kids and, as such (and only as such), they supported it.

While reggae developed its curious, millenarian and mystical political stance, much North American black music developed into the sterile repetition of disco. On the floor of ultra-exclusive clubs like New York's Club 54 (money was not enough to gain admission, you had to have a face too), the ultimate irony was worked out. Black music had arrived through its various phases of struggle and reached the arsehole of respectability.

Disco is black music as a parody of itself. There was no longer any sense of a struggle, only the exploitation of the tired old myth of 'natural black rhythm'. The whole orgasmic thrust of disco stars like Grace Jones or Donna Summer played on the assumption of black women's availability to men – as it always had done. The male counterpart tends to suggest sexual blockage and, once again, the image of most of these performers echoed the necessary personae of black male performers twenty years ago and more – clownish, macho, faceless, romantic.

'ROCK' STAR DIES IN CRASH

● PICTURED ABOVE: Singer Eddie Co...
LEFT: The wreckage of the car after the ... which killed him.

By NED GRANT

AMERICAN rock 'n' roll singing star Eddie Cochran, 21, died yesterday after a car taking him to London Airport crashed.

Among the three other passengers in the car when it crashed at Chippenham, Wilts, on Saturday night were two Americans—"rock" singer Gene Vincent, 25, and girl song writer Sharon Sheeley, 20.

Last night Miss Sheeley—she wrote the hit song "Poor Little Fool" when she was seventeen—was in "fair" condition with a fractured pelvis in hospital at Bath, Somerset.

Her mother, Mrs. Mary Sheeley, sobbed in Hollywood last night when she heard of the crash.

The news was broken to Mrs. Sheeley by the mother of Ritchie Valens—the "rock" star who was killed at the age of sixteen last year in an air crash soon after recording one of Sharon's songs.

Mrs. Sheeley said: "Eddie Cochran and Sharon had been

Sharon Sheeley

going steady since they met two years ago.

"Eddie was the first and only boy friend Sharon ever had. They were terribly in love, and were planning to marry. They were unofficially engaged."

The car's driver, George Martin, of Hartcliffe, Bristol, was unhurt.

Cochran—with Sharon, Gene Vincent and the fourth passenger, Camberwell theatrical agent Patrick Thomkins, 29—was taken to hospital.

America-bound

Just after four o'clock yesterday afternoon, Cochran died.

Cochran—his record hits have included "Summertime Blues" and "C'mon Everybody"—was travelling from Bristol, where he was starring in variety, to catch an America-bound plane at London Airport.

He had been in Britain since January, appearing on the stage and in TV shows—including I TV's "Boy Meets Girls."

Gene Vincent, whose first big song hit was "Be-Bop-a-Lula," planned to fly with Cochran.

He said in hospital last night: "I hope to be out in two or three days."

● Cochran's last record will be issued according to schedule in the next few days, his British impresario, Larry Parnes, announced yesterday. It is called "Three Steps to Heaven."

The toll: 33 dea... 632 injured so f...

AT least thirty-three people have been killed and 632 injured on the roads since the Easter Holiday started on Good Friday.

And last night the Automobile Association made an urgent Bank Holiday appeal for safety on the roads.

First reports of YESTERDAY'S ACCIDENTS showed that twelve people were killed and sixteen injured.

Provisional figures for GOOD FRIDAY and SATURDAY announced by the Automobile Association were: Twenty-one dead and 616 injured.

Last year's figures for the same two days were: Fifteen dead and 460 injured.

In their appeal last night, the AA said: —

● These figures tell their own sorry story, but they do not reflect the grief and misery in thousands of homes. An all-out effort will be required by eve... the toll on the... not to be greate... last Easter.

Bank Holiday... conditions call f... bit of concentra... the part of... cyclists and pede...

A second's care... could mean... lost life.

The margin of... allowed by co... roads and heav... is so small that... can afford th... slightest mistak...

● BUMPER "PA... TO THE S... Back Page.

ROAD FEVER, STAGE FRIGHT

The Eagles' guitarist, Joe Walsh, had a motto to tide him over the long weeks of touring. You could often find it scratched into the furnishings of the hotel the group has just left. It read: PARTY TIL YA PUKE. When on tour, the group always set aside a large suite at the hotel for post-gig parties. They called it 'the Third Encore' and it was invariably changed utterly after the group, their friends and their entourage had all taken their bows. The group's manager, Irving Azoff, bought Joe Walsh a chain-saw one Christmas. The guitarist took it with him on the road – just in case something begged to be rapidly and completely destroyed. (The opportunity has not yet arisen.) Similarly Ian MacLagan, the former Faces' keyboard player, always carried an axe about on tour to dispose of any concert-hall pianos that didn't meet the stipulations of the group's contract. Nothing but the best for the big boys – and then some. It's a case of conspicuous destruction, of knowing, as the Eagles' road manager said, that 'we're going go pay for everything'. The Eagles called it 'life in the fast lane'. Everybody else knows it as 'road fever'.

Road fever takes many different forms – partying, practical joking, physical assaults, the sort of obsessive gambling that Buddy Holly, for example, used to indulge in to while away the hours between shows, or the apparently senseless activities of the likes of country rock star Waylon Jennings and his band, who once barricaded themselves in their hotel room all night for no apparent reason other than to play 'Fort Apache' or 'Beau Geste'. Usually it is fuelled by plenty of drinking and not a little drug taking. It can be the result of boredom, exuberance, frustration or plain annoyance, but it is always about the routine of the road, the sweat, the long and anti-social hours, the pent-up emotion of most performances, the isolation of rock stars and their entourages in unfriendly hotel rooms, on unfriendly stages, in claustrophobic trains and planes and limousines with black-tinted windows.

The pressures of touring have been a central part of the rock scene since its very beginning. More than any other kind of popular music or entertainment, rock'n'roll has always involved getting the message across to the most people in the shortest time. 'In this business it's not so much making it as fast as you can,' said Led Zeppelin's bassist, John Paul Jones, 'but making it *while* you can . . . The touring makes you into a different person. I realize that when I get home. It takes me weeks to recover after living like an animal for so long.'

Sometimes the pace can be literally killing, because most tours are organized into tight and exhausting schedules in order to cover what may be thousands of miles of travelling as quickly as possible. The deaths of Buddy Holly, the Big Bopper and Richie Valens in 1959 certainly indicate the dangers of constant touring. Had Holly not wanted to get to the next gig as quickly in order to make some last minute arrangements, organize some clean laundry and get a good night's sleep, neither he nor his companions would have bothered with the fatal plane journey. Talking in 1980, Buddy's widow, Maria Elena, recalled that the singer had never wanted to go on that tour at all. He was broke at the time, however, having recently split from the other Crickets. Perhaps more importantly, Maria Elena was pregnant after six months of marriage. 'He was unprepared,' she said, 'and everything was organized at the last minute. But we needed the money.' There was a further tragic twist to the story – the shock of her husband's death caused Maria Elena to suffer a miscarriage.

Many others have met with similar accidents – to a degree probably consistent with the uncommon mileage covered by rock musicians. Carl Perkins wasn't the only rocker to have his career interrupted by a road accident. 21-year-old Eddie Cochran, hugely popular in Britain, started a twelve-week tour of the country in January, 1960. The tour was so successful that it was extended for a further ten weeks. Cochran, Gene Vincent (appearing on the same bill) and Cochran's fiancée, Sharon Sheeley, were travelling to London Airport for a break between the first and second halves of the extended tour. Vincent was scheduled to play some dates in Paris, while Eddie and Sharon intended to fly back to America to get married. Twenty miles outside Bristol, travelling in a chauffeur-driven car after a show at the Bristol Hippodrome, a tyre blew out and the car skidded backwards into a lamp-post. It was just after midnight on April 17th. Cochran was flung from the car, amid confetti, photographs and his own guitar. He died the following afternoon at a hospital in Bath. Sharon Sheeley and Gene Vincent were both injured, and in Vincent's case the effect was to worsen considerably his earlier leg wound. Sharon, who had crawled around in the wreckage of the car, crying 'Where's Eddie?', seems never to have quite recovered from the trauma. She had only been visiting England for a week. Ironically, Eddie's next scheduled release was a medium-paced love song called *Three Steps To Heaven*. Immediately after his death, it shot into the British Top Ten and stayed there for two months.

Buddy Holly's last tour ended early in the morning of 3rd February, 1959, when the single-engine plane carrying him, Ritchie Valens (whose body lies in the foreground) and the Big Bopper, crashed in a snowy meadow near Fargo, North Dakota.

Four members of the Lynyrd Skynyrd entourage, the pilot and co-pilot were killed outright when their private plane crashed *en route* to a gig in 1977 (two roadies later died in hospital from their injuries). Apparently the plane – a Corvair 240 prop – ran out of fuel 200 yards from an open field near Gillsburg, Mississippi, where the pilot intended to land. On an earlier flight, one engine had nearly burst into flames, and several members of the band had planned to vote on whether to continue using it. Singer Cassie Gaines had been talked out of travelling in the equipment truck that day. The band and their entourage (amounting to about twenty people) were all close friends, whose tours more often resembled wild private parties than business trips. Both Cassie and her brother Steve died, along with the band's leading light, Ronnie Van Zandt, and their road manager, Dean Kilpatrick.

In December 1967, Otis Redding and five teenage members of his backing group, the Bar-Kays, died in similar circumstances when Otis's brand new private plane crashed into an icy lake just four miles from its destination. Clarence White, brilliant guitarist with

Left: The second step to heaven? Eddie Cochran, bridging the gap between fifties rock'n'roll and eighties new wave, died on 17th April, 1960 on his way to London Airport with his fiancée, Sharon Sheeley, who survived the accident. His latest release, Three Steps To Heaven, *climbed to the top of the charts within two months of his death.*

the Byrds for a time, was the victim of a hit-and-run accident while loading a van with equipment after a concert. And there have been many other fatal and near-fatal accidents. Bob Dylan crashed his motorcycle on a road near his Woodstock home in July 1966, breaking his neck and dropping out of circulation for some eighteen months. The crash and Dylan's subsequent silence only served to deepen his mystery for many fans. Many of them speculated that it was an attempted suicide, brought on by the heavy intake of drugs Dylan relied on to keep him going during his heavy touring schedule in the sixties.

Stevie Wonder's car collided with a logging-truck in North Carolina in August, 1973, four days after the release of the enormously popular *Innervisions* album. Stevie received head injuries which were happily less serious than had at first been feared, and he was back on stage by September. Phil Spector, whose eccentricities were already becoming legendary, apparently suffered burns and multiple head injuries in a car crash somewhere between Los Angeles and Phoenix in early February 1974. Rumours that Spector had faked the crash in order to 'get away from it all' (or even to undergo a furtive hair transplant) were fuelled by the lack of information about it and by Spector's subsequent behaviour – he became reclusive to the point of paranoia. Of course, the crash itself could have been

A rescue worker finds a publicity photo of Lynyrd Skynyrd among the tattered remains of their baggage. Three members of the band died when their Corvair 240 crashed into woods near McComb, Mississippi, on 21st October, 1977, while on a tour of the States.

A physical wreck even before his fatal car crash in September, 1977, Marc Bolan's youthful glitter image belied the killing effects of the rock life-style. Even the teeth were false.

responsible for just those symptoms – but Spector, like Dylan, is the stuff of myth.

Later stars have fared no better. Robert Plant of Led Zeppelin, and his wife Maureen, were both seriously injured on the island of Rhodes in 1975. Their car left the road, plunged down a precipice and was caught in a tree. Among other Zeppelin disasters, John Bonham was involved in a car crash, breaking three ribs, in 1977. Eric Clapton, too, suffered a car crash in 1975. On his return from an exhausting tour of Australia and New Zealand he climbed into his silver Ferrari for the first time in weeks, only to crash into a lorry in a narrow lane near his home in Ewhurst, Surrey. The car was a write-off and, though uninjured, it took firemen twenty minutes to cut Clapton out of the wreckage.

In 1976, *en route* from a gig in Stafford, Keith Richards' Bentley ploughed through a motorway barrier at five in the morning. The car was carrying Keith, Anita Pallenberg and their son Marlon – but the only victim was Keith himself, who was busted by the police when they discovered cocaine and marijuana in the car on arriving at the scene of the accident.

Yet others were not so fortunate as to escape with their lives. Fairport Convention's Martin Lamble and clothes designer 'Genie the Tailor' (for whom Jack Bruce recorded the album, *Songs For A Tailor*) were

Otis Redding's body lifted from the icey water of the lake near Madison, Wisconsin, where his plane crashed, 10th December, 1967. Ironically, his posthumous hit was titled Dock Of The Bay.

killed when their car crashed in June, 1969. Duane Allman, whose talent for the guitar was matched only by his drug consumption, crashed his motorcycle in Macon, Georgia, swerving to avoid a truck. It was October, 1971, and Allman had just left bassist Berry Oakley's home. Just over a year later, Oakley himself crashed his bike along the same stretch of road. He smashed into a city bus and, having steadfastly refused hospital treatment, died of a brain haemorrhage

The car in which Marc Bolan (real name Mark Feld) died on 16th September, 1977. It was being driven by his girlfriend Gloria Jones, who suffered face injuries when the Mini ploughed into a tree on Barnes Common. Bolan was killed outright.

in November 1972. Allman and Oakley are buried side by side in the Rose Hill Cemetery in Macon – a place that inspired many early Allman songs.

Marc Bolan, returning home from a club with his girlfriend Gloria Jones at the wheel, was killed when the car they were in wrapped itself round a tree in September, 1977. Gloria, only slightly injured, was later charged with drunken driving.

It's fascinating to note that transport accidents (planes, cars and motorcycles especially) cause as many, if not more, deaths and serious injuries among the rock fellowship as drugs and alcohol. While some are the result of straightforward occupational hazards – fatigue and tight schedules – other accidents may be put down to a fatal fascination with speed (both sorts) which attracts so many musicians, dissolving caution and persuading them to chase that extra buzz of adrenalin in their implacable desire to live life in the fast lane.

Road fever is not just the product of the wearisome schedules that have plagued performers since those early days of the fifties, when rock'n'roll package tours first snaked their way across continents. Even so, road fever proper belongs to the era of mammoth tours by single acts, from the mid-sixties to the pre-punk seventies. If today there are hotels and local worthies who go out of their way to court rock musicians (a sign in the reception area of the Continental Hyatt House hotel in Los Angeles shows a typical 'long-hair' with the caption underneath: 'Be courteous to him, he may just have sold a million records'), things were different then. Nowadays wanton destruction may be part of the image, and hotel owners know that it will be paid for (plus). The time was, however, when road fever was less a rich man's hobby and more a sort of hooliganism, inspired by the absence of friends and the friendlessness of those who are present.

'You've been standing around an airport, had some accommodation problem because someone's hair's too long, or you've been on some vehicle for hours without sleep and have only three hours till you go on stage,' Grace Slick said, pointing out the hassles of performing under such circumstances. 'People in the group start getting uptight, and music's an emotional thing too, you know, so everybody's backstage yelling and screaming ... People get really strange getting on and off buses and talking to a lot of different people all the time.'

The feeling of strangeness is a product of the musician's very peculiar circumstances on tour. A tour offers freedom from the constraints of normal domestic routine combined with a sometimes threatening sense of unfamiliarity and isolation. But the musician on tour is also working – often very hard. Even worse, musicians on tour are working to a mirror-image of most people's daily time-tables. No wonder the experience of touring is disorienting and no wonder musicians fall back on their own company, or the company of other musicians and on the sense of bonhomie and solidarity associated with childish

102

pranks. No wonder, either, that some musicians on tour are driven to protest their curious situation in the most physical ways possible – fighting, fucking or wrecking.

When the so-called 'British Invasion' brought a tidal wave of musicians over from Britain to America, they found themselves in stranger situations than Grace Slick could imagine. They were, after all, not just hippies, Easterners or long-haired moral degenerates to those who disliked them – they were aliens and, as such, loved and hated, freer and more constrained than their American equivalents. Passions were higher, tensions greater, isolation more acutely felt. 'We usually take a party of four road managers, a production manager, a booking man, there's usually ten Englishmen going round in the States,' the Who's John Entwistle said in 1971. 'Americans have a different sense of humour, their whole way of life is different. If they're not in your business or if they don't come to your concerts they're boring. They're aliens and you're aliens to them and you can't mix with that sort of person, so you're thrown together and you spend a lot of time in hotel rooms and so on.'

The Who were one of the first groups to get a reputation as hotel wreckers – no doubt connected with the unprecedentedly violent nature of their stage act. 'The Who on tour is a very difficult trip,' said Pete Townshend in 1968. Aware of the implications of all this violence on their private lives, the Who tended to channel it into zany humour. 'If we were serious,' said Townshend, 'we'd admit that we don't like each other. But because we're not serious, we don't have to admit it.' The Who were by no means the only group to have a reputation for 'insanity' (as Townshend termed it) on the road. The Beach Boys were particularly wild, as were the Rolling Stones and, until they retired from touring in 1966, the Beatles. But thanks to Keith Moon (known universally as Moon the Loon), the Who will probably hold in perpetuity the title of 'Most Disruptive Rock Group On Tour'.

It all started back in 1967 when the group spent weeks of arduous touring in America trying to hit the big time. In the process they lost huge amounts of money and a substantial portion of their sanity, proving conclusively Townshend's dictum that the way to 'stop taking life seriously is to go out on the road'.

The group's first tour of the US set the pattern for the future. Moon discovered Cherry Bombs – a particularly explosive variety of firework – and began a long and fruitful association with havoc. As a younger man, Moon had been content to take out his destructive urges on a drum-kit. But a growing intake of booze and pills and the infectious insanity of road life soon expanded his horizons. In no time at all, he was blowing out hotel room doors with Cherry Bombs, pitching

Backstage hi-jinx with shock-rocker Alice Cooper, friends, and Stacia from the Heavy Metal band, Hawkwind. The Cooper band once boasted of spending $300,000 a year on booze. This sizeable drinks' bill may be partly explained by the curious use for a bottle of beer devised on this occasion. Alice Cooper eventually committed himself to a sanatorium to overcome alcoholism.

Who's who? Keith Moon and Pete Townshend (right) keep the good times going on board a Rally Escort. Life on the road isn't always so comfortable.

televisions out of windows onto the street below and blowing up toilet bowls ('This Cherry Bomb was about to go off in my hand,' he explained once, 'so I threw it down the bog to put it out').

During the 1967 tour, the Who found themselves in the Gorham Hotel in New York – a popular hang-out for visiting groups. In the middle of the night the hotel residents were disturbed by the sound of police tramping through the corridors and sirens wailing outside. Townshend woke up thinking that one of the Who's party had been busted for pot. While taking the elevator to the appropriate floor, he heard the last of what must have been a number of explosions. The elevator stopped and the doors opened. The corridor outside was filled with smoke, so Townshend got back in to resume his journey. As the elevator doors were closing, Moon walked past, his mission accomplished. He had just blown up the hotel manager's wife's room.

Latterly, Moon took to destroying hotel rooms artistically. With little or no noise he would methodically take apart the furniture and rearrange the room to look as if it had been wrecked. Sometimes, he would

John Entwistle – the one member of the Who you don't usually hear about. But he's suffered his share of road fever, too. John (below) was arrested in Houston, Texas for disorderly conduct at a party marking the start of the Who's 1975 tour of the US on 20th November, 1975.

Harmless loon or unpleasant buffoon? The tasteless Keith Moon arrives at a Los Angeles premiere dressed as Field Marshall Rommel giving a Nazi salute, 12th November, 1976. He once enraged the Jewish community of London's Golders Green by parading in similar gear down the high street on a Saturday.

pour tomato ketchup in the bath and stick a pair of plastic legs in it. At other times, he would disturb other members of the Who or their entourage (or complete strangers) with itching powder, stink bombs, smoke bombs, plastic insects or whatever loathsome device he could find in the local joke-shop. Moon considered no town complete without such a shop. On one occasion, after playing a pier-end concert hall in Asbury Park, New Jersey, Moon decided he wanted the company of a groupie on the band bus. Everybody else said 'no' – earlier in the tour some girls had spirited away a few thousand dollars petty cash in the course of a stoned hotel room party, and the band wanted no repetition of that event. But Moon insisted and the band's dressing room – which happened to swing out over the sea – echoed to the aggressive sounds of yet another post-gig Who fight. Moon could be deadly serious about some things if he wanted to be, and it was scary to watch him then because you could see a genuine malice in his eyes, even though he often tried to defuse the situation with a joke. He was serious this time. 'She comes with me or I jump!' he shouted, leaping to the windowsill and, without further ado, he jumped. They searched for hours, they sent for the Coastguard and the cops, they called out to him. But Moon was nowhere to be found. When at last all hope had been abandoned and the group were

preparing to face the future without their drummer, a tiny voice wafted up from the pier rafters below. 'Thought I'd never do it, did you?' It was Moon.

If Keith was an obsessive practical joker with a fondness for shocking that sometimes plumbed the depths of tastelessness (as when he and Vivian Stanshall dressed up as Nazis and paraded up and down Golders Green in London, deeply offending the Jewish population there), he was also a maniac for transport. At his home in Chertsey he kept about a dozen vehicles from Rolls-Royces to a personal hovercraft. He thought nothing of driving an expensive Rolls into a swimming pool. Tragically, his chauffeur, Neil Bolland, was run over and killed by Keith's Rolls when the drummer, desperate to escape a rowdy crowd outside a disco in Hertfordshire, backed the car out in too much of a hurry. Moon was charged with drunken driving.

Moon was the soul of the Who's live performances. The other three always had other interests and shifting views on whether they liked the road or not. For Moon, rock'n'roll *was* the road – he was always on the move, the homeless one, the one who was constantly searching for something else to satisfy his roving soul. For him, the Who were live performance and live performance was loud. So, one day in a hotel in Los Angeles (that 'meat market' as he called it), he was playing a tape of a Who album very loud – as it should be. The manager's attention was drawn, inevitably, to the disturbance. He complained to Moon. 'It's a noise,' said the manager, instructing the drummer to turn down the volume. Keith obeyed, but a short time later the hotel was shaken by an explosion that blew the

Rod Stewart woz 'ere ... the first-class lounge on Stewart's flight to London, 23rd December, 1977, after he and his party had finished pouring drinks on the carpet, smearing seats with jam and butter and dumping gourmet dinners in the aisle.

door of Moon's suite off its hinges. Seeking the by now enraged manager, Moon explained: 'That was a noise. What you heard before was the Who.'

Officiousness and bad service have inspired some awesome moments of road fever. Boredom, too. 'Sitting in a hotel room for a week is no picnic,' said Jimmy Page. 'That's when the road fever starts and that's when the breakages start.' Writer John Pidgeon kept a diary of the Faces' 1972 tour of Britain – a tour which was crucial to the band's success. Pidgeon was an acting roadie on the tour – it is often the roadies, who do most of the work for the least glory, who are hardest hit by road fever in their odd hours of relaxation. Pidgeon tells of how the band and entourage booked into an appalling Blackpool hotel.

'The lights on the second floor corridor had fused, the room phones were out of order ... the bedside lights wouldn't turn on, neither would the heating, and there were pubic hairs in the bath. We couldn't eat in the restaurant without a tie and we were only allowed into the informal, ghastly Cabaret Grill on the say-so of a receptionist.' After a pleasant night drinking a local bar dry of brandy, two of the Faces' senior roadies decided to make some 'alterations' to the

'Don't give me any of your lip.' After falling over on stage during a San Francisco concert, Rod Stewart, with stitched lip, flew to London for his traditional Christmas shows, 23rd December, 1977. Clutching a glass of brandy, Rod arrived singing, 'I'd walk a million miles for one of your legs.'

hotel's fixtures and fittings. During the show the next night, fans invaded the orchestra pit and the police were called. Rod Stewart himself talked them out of stopping the show. Back at the hotel later 'some further alterations' were made – despite a snarling guard-dog. Next morning, one of the roadies drove the band's truck away. 'He meant to nudge the concrete ball off the gatepost,' Pidgeon recorded, 'but we whapped the pillar so hard it collapsed, bringing ten feet of brick wall down with it.'

This kind of deliberate destruction is a revenge for not having a good time laid on. In fact, there is little to tell between the good and bad times on tour – under the pressure of touring everything seems to take on a curiously joyless and perfunctory air, as if good times offstage were just another part of the job.

'We had another party planned after the show in Sheffield,' said Pidgeon. 'By the time we'd finished packing the truck, the girls we'd lined up had left and the mood at the hotel was drab.' They recovered their party spirits however and 'decided the Warner Brothers' man's room was as good a place as any to celebrate. Woody (Ron Wood), Mac and Rod thought so too, although our host didn't. He had eyes for two girls and was nervous they would be lured or, more likely, frightened away. He was right. Woody and Rod hauled one of them into a wardrobe. When she escaped she ran right out of the room, so they treated us to a closet cabaret routine of songs, jokes, even dancing, mostly from inside. Mac gave a practical demonstration of how to dismantle a cheap armchair, lecturing us on its construction faults as he did so.'

Pidgeon continued: 'Everyone had a *smashing* time. Except the Warner Brothers man, who grew increasingly frantic as he tried to figure out how he could explain away his room bill as a business expense.' He needn't have worried – as is always the case after these bouts of road fever, remorse set in the morning after, and the group took care of the bill.

And so it goes, from one dreadful hotel room to the next, from one disappointing gig to the next, from one grey town to the next, from one tour to the next. Some groups, or at least certain members of them, seemed to thrive on the high pitch of excitement which characterizes and surrounds rock performance and life on the road. Until, that is, the concert tour routine began to become more and more elaborate as the seventies progressed. Then the whole basis of road fever began subtly to change. The tours themselves became big money operations, like military manoeuvres organized by teams of expert managers.

During the 'Diamond Dogs' tour of 1974, David Bowie used an entire theatrical set – scaffolding hung with painted flats to show an expressionist version of a modern city, an enormous lighting rig, towers to carry loudspeakers, a moveable bridge and chair attached to a motorized steel beam which could raise and lower Bowie on the stage or up to 30 feet into the auditorium. There was also a giant mirrored perspex egg called the Diamond Module, with a motor and wheels to transport Bowie about the stage, opening up to display the artist in all his finery. All this added some $200,000 to the cost of the tour. A travelling road crew of fifteen was housed in a bus complete with bunks, a stereo, colour TV and bathroom. They, and a local crew of about two dozen, spent up to nineteen hours a working day (discounting travel time) erecting, supervising, dismantling, loading and unloading equipment. Whatever Bowie and the musicians were doing, the crew had little time to party. 'After five or six days,' said one of them, 'a large shipment of cocaine arrived, which initially cut the working day to fourteen hours, but no-one got any more sleep than before, because we were all wired and sat up babbling; after a couple of days, the working day drifted back to 21 hours and remained that way. Fortunately, I have forgotten what it felt like to be that tired but everyone was in a constant state of near-psychosis and hallucination.'

Through all this, the rock stars themselves became increasingly pampered. The private jets that had once seemed such a luxury were now *de rigueur*. By 1973, Led Zeppelin were in a position to have $180,000 in cash stolen from their hotel safe at the end of the tour – money that had apparently been earmarked to pay for hotel rooms, a film crew and the hire of an airplane. By 1978, the Rolling Stones were playing to a total of 760,000 people on one tour, taking more than one million dollars gross at some shows, and paying out a minimum of around $25,000 in expenses for even the smallest show (a gate of about 2,500). The Stones' hotel bill for a few nights in Texas came to $17,000, food and drink for *one* show to more than $2,000.

At these exalted heights, the rock star on tour is insulated from the hostility and disappointment that might once have greeted him. In fact, he is insulated from almost everything. 'It's a real hassle to go out,' said Keith Richard. 'You got all you needed from room service, sent out for it . . . You're getting really cut off.' Entertainment can be bought, and even the opportunity to run riot comes quite cheap. 'It's strange how success and room-wrecking seem to go together,' ELO's Bev Bevan remarked. 'For years we never destroyed so much as a toothbrush holder and it was only when we were playing every night to sell-out crowds of anything from 20,000 to 72,000 did we get trouble.'

This kind of conspicuous destruction reached its peak with Led Zeppelin. 'From the shit holes to the classiest hotels,' said Robert Plant, 'it's all been fun.' But even Plant grew jaded. Seven years after the group's first American tour, he looked back with something approaching yearning. 'It's been a long time,' he said. 'Nowadays we're more into staying in our rooms and reading Nietzsche. There was good fun to be had, you know, it's just that in those days there were more people to have good fun with than there are now.'

'There were a lot of fun-loving people to crash into,' Plant continued. 'People were genuinely welcoming us to the country and we started out on a path of positive enjoyment. Throwing eggs from floor to floor and really silly water battles that a nineteen-year-old boy should have. It was just the first steps of learning how to be crazy.'

110

Stage fright: Bill Wyman suffered a severe electric shock at a rehearsal for a Stones concert in Oclense, Denmark, 27th March, 1965. Wyman, Mick Jagger and Brian Jones were all affected when a 'live' microphone shot 220 volts through them. Bill Wyman was unconscious for several minutes.

Increasingly, boredom is cited as the major reason for the callous destructiveness that rock superstars seem to rely on to lighten the load of performance. But destruction is also a status symbol, demonstrating their ability to disregard material values, to acquire the most exotic toys that money can buy. Rock stars can realize their fantasies. But when a fantasy becomes real it also becomes subject to the tedium of everyday life. And more exciting fantasies just become harder and harder to think up.

Performance itself remains the arena of rock's most potent fantasy – the fantasy that audience and performer can become one. 'We all share the simultaneous experience of forgetting who we are at a rock concert,' said Pete Townshend, 'losing ourselves completely. When the music gets so good . . . everybody for a second forgets completely who they are and where they are . . . If you have experienced that enough times, it starts to become something that you strive for, because it is so sweet.' Yet the undercurrent of pain and aggravation in the Who's stage shows has led to aggressive outbursts on stage that show the act of striving itself can be most bitter. Townshend

Patti Smith's acrobatics led to serious injury when she fell off stage in Tampa, Florida in 1977. 'All I know is that in some moment every night, I'm so committed that I piss myself or I come on stage,' said Patti – seen here with her head in the air.

whacked 'youth revolutionary' Abbie Hoffman over the head with his guitar when Hoffman's acid dream led him to take the stage at Woodstock, interrupting the beginning of the Who's set. Hoffman, half-crazed, demanded that the half-million strong audience march down to free the jailed John Sinclair and Townshend couldn't take it. I have seen Townshend leap off stage and half throttle a kid whose only crime has been to keep requesting a song.

But Pete Townshend has an answer to this too. 'There is a particular attitude I call the "tour armour",' he told Greil Marcus in 1980. 'When you go on the road you throw up an armour around yourself, you almost go into a trance. . . . When I say armour, I mean armour that actually *allows* you to be more abandoned, and freer, that allows you to be tougher, harder . . . I'm not trying to glamorize it and it's not something I'm necessarily proud of.'

Tour armour does not however save the performer from the dangers of actually performing on stage, many of which result from a too-hurried setting up or too eager exit. Stone the Crows' guitarist, Les Harvey, was killed in front of 1500 fans when his guitar electrocuted him on stage at the Top Rank ballroom in Swansea, in May 1972. He had done no more than start to play. In a rush to set up the gear, nobody had bothered to check whether the guitars and microphones were safely connected and Harvey's guitar became live. In October 1974, Uriah Heep bassist, Gary Thain, was similarly electrocuted on stage in Dallas. He was ordered to rest for two weeks, but the effects of the accident, combined with heavy drug use, made him increasingly unreliable. He was sacked from the band and in February 1976, he was found by his Japanese girlfriend dead from an overdose, in his bath at home. Even the Rolling Stones have suffered electrocution, once causing Bill Wyman to spend several minutes unconscious. Tom Petty is another performer who suffered an admittedly minor shock on stage. But with so many electrical connections to come adrift during a stage show, it is surprising that so few of these accidents occur.

Needless to say, the suicidal possibilities of the electric guitar have also been explored. Keith Relf, focus of the Yardbirds, whose career floundered after that group mutated into Led Zeppelin, was found dead in his West London house in May 1976, holding a live electric guitar. An open verdict was recorded on John Rostill, who had joined the Shadows to replace bassist Brian Locking in 1963. He joined the Shadows as a complete unknown after an audition, and remained a background figure until the Shadows effectively disbanded in 1968. In November 1973, Rostill was found apparently electrocuted by his own guitar. His death remains a mystery, because it occurred shortly before a planned reunion of the Shadows. In the event, the reunion went ahead without him and led to a resurgence of their popularity.

The stage itself is, of course, responsible for numerous minor injuries. Serious injuries (when not the result of missiles accurately aimed by members of the audience) are less common. In 1971, Frank Zappa

was hurled from the stage of the Rainbow in London by an irate fan jealous of his girlfriend's enthusiasm for the American star. Zappa fell into the orchestra pit and broke his leg so badly that he had to perform wearing a steel brace for a year. Now he has an ex-policeman as a permanent bodyguard. 'You get a lot of very strange people at any rock concert,' he says, 'and the drugs people use at the moment increase the risk of a crazy, violent attack.' In 1977 Patti Smith – whose extrovert performances inevitably skirt major injury – broke her neck and needed 22 stitches after spinning on stage until she got so dizzy that she tripped over a monitor and was pitched head-first towards the audience at the Curtis Nixon Hall in Tampa, Florida. Typically, Patti denied that she had been on any drugs at the time – although the performance commenced with a vitriolic and gratuitous diatribe against Florida and its people. She claimed to be high on rock'n'roll. 'Performance,' as she says, 'is the drug'.

Performance can call forth complex emotions, leaving the musician floating somewhere between ecstasy and despair. It is always a sort of failure, because it is always temporary. Yet every performer is aware of the power they have, even if it is only half-formed. Performance is, after all, a surrogate sex act, and for some the very act of getting on stage in front of an audience is its own self-contained road fever.

'You were at school and you were pimply and no-one wanted to know you,' Eric Clapton explained. 'Yet get into a group and you've got thousands of chicks there. And there you are with thousands of little girls screaming their heads off. Man, it's power.'

For some, the power itself is both awesome and frightening – not least because when it fails to work (or works too well) audiences have been known to riot and individuals to assault performers. Jimi Hendrix's last, sad performance in America suggests something of what was behind his prodigious partying, his violent arguments with associates and his general tendency to road fever. (After one particularly vicious row with Noel Redding in a Swedish hotel room, Hendrix landed himself in jail – and it had taken three policemen to get him there.) Hendrix's last show was in Seattle, his home town. The guitarist played badly but eager fans rushed to the stage all the same, desperate for their magic moment. Hendrix was reduced to swearing at the audience. 'Fuck you! Fuck you!' he shouted, despite which people began to chant, 'We love you, Jimi!' At the end of the show he flung his guitar down and walked off the stage, only to return dejectedly to the microphone a few minutes later and ask if there was anyone in the audience from his old school. The shouts of 'Yeah' met with a desultory comment from Jimi. 'Far out', he said.

Jim Morrison, too, felt increasingly aggressive towards his audiences. At first he said, 'Concerts are great but it gets into a crowd phenomenon that really hasn't that much to do with music.' As the crowds got greater and eager for more thrills, and as Morrison failed adequately to harness his own stardom, the risk of losing control became greater. Morrison's ambivalence eventually and effectively destroyed the music and turned his concerts into freak shows. And Iggy Pop, who ironically took to exposing himself on stage like Morrison (but without the same legal consequences), remembered at the time of his late seventies comeback how he 'hated the audience, at times, for the things they made you do. They're cunts,' he said. 'Why did they come and see me?' Iggy, of course, used to assault both his audience and himself. He would dive into them, provoke fights, daub them with peanut butter. He ripped his own body with broken glass and invited audiences to invade the stage. He played the sound of amplified toilets. But he was addicted to heroin at that time, and was sometimes unable to perform without a massive shot of methedrine beforehand. (He remembers how, on one memorable occasion, a gorilla walked on to the stage and held him in the air while he was singing – he was heavily dosed with speed. 'I was out of my mind with fear,' he says – but the gorilla turned out to be Elton John in an ape-suit paying a friendly, if rather mistimed, surprise visit.)

'When I'm on the road, you know, it means I'm away from somebody I love,' said Patti Smith. 'It might

mean I'm alone for the night, it might mean I'm not gonna be making love for a month, and so I have to get that shot on stage ... All I know is that in some moment every night I'm so committed that I piss myself or I come on stage – once I even shat myself on stage, I was pulling in so much to try and hit a note or try to hit a sensation or hit a word that I just lost control of myself.'

Smith sees the rock star's role as a mirror for the audience. 'You give them a lot of fantastic energy and they eat it and spit it out,' she announced. 'They're like loving vampires or something.'

Patti Smith is a performer committed to herself as a performer. Her moment of fever is on stage. Mick Jagger knows the same power she does, but he is too cynical, possibly less pretentious and certainly too distant from his audiences to accept performance as anything more than an imperfect imitation of life. 'I don't understand the connection between music and violence,' he has said – a trifle disingenuously. 'I just know that I get very aroused by music, but that it doesn't arouse me violently. I never went to a rock'n'roll show and wanted to smash windows or beat anybody up afterwards. I feel more sexual than actually physically violent.' Maybe the feeling only lasts five minutes as Jagger says it does – but it is still a strange sensation. The road is long for people prey to such volatile and strident emotions and, like snow-blindness to the Antarctic explorer, road fever is the malady they develop as a result.

'It's big,' said one authoritative source, 'but not that big.' Mick Jagger once said, 'I get very aroused by music', but is his sexual image just so much hot air?

STAGE-DOOR SEX

Somewhere at the heart of rock'n'roll's magic is the groupie – whether nameless fan or glamorous socialite – who converts music into the currency of the orgasm and spends freely. She (it is almost invariably a woman) is a central character in the myths and legends of rock – proof to fans and observers that rock stars have found the modern holy grail of guiltless promiscuity, evidence that people's dreams of release, refuge and reward can be made real. But to rock stars, groupies are little better than a demonstration of power, expressed through sexuality – success symbols. 'You won't make much money,' Ronnie Hawkins promised Robbie Robertson when recruiting him to his band, 'but you'll get more pussy than Frank Sinatry;' a promise which puts the groupie on about the same level as a free meal.

Backstage or in hotel rooms, the Beatles lived at the centre of a hive of grotesque sexual hyper-activity. John Lennon told Jann Wenner: 'Derek's (Derek Taylor) and Neil's (Neil Aspinall) rooms were always full of fuck knows what, and policemen and everything. *Satyricon*! We had to do something, and what do you do when the pill doesn't wear off . . . If we couldn't get groupies we would have whores and everything, whatever was going.'

Chrissie Shrimpton – model Jean's little sister – gained fame for a while as Mick Jagger's girlfriend, a title later bestowed on the hapless Marianne Faithfull. Chrissie delighted in telling the press that she knew from experience that the Stones were not homosexuals. Marianne Faithfull remembered her determination to have 'a Rolling Stone as a boyfriend'. 'I slept with three and then decided the lead singer was the best bet.' But she fell in love with the lead singer, this nice upper-class, convent girl who believed, like so many others, in the myth that rock'n'roll would lead her to liberation. Her liberation, it turned out, was the freedom to become captivated by Mick Jagger's lusty image. She followed him around like a lap-dog, they made love in the changing room of an exclusive clothes shop, her name – kept out of the trial following the Redlands raid – was dragged through the gutter-minds of randy young boys obsessed by the sexual riches at Jagger's disposal. She and Jagger had been caught at Redlands *in flagrante delecto*, it was whispered rather loudly, having discovered a novel use for Mars Bars as an accessory to cunnilingus. Assuming

this curious rumour was invented (and it surfaced in America with minor but significant changes – the place was Woodstock in upstate New York, the chocolate bar was an acid-infused Baby Ruth), it still defined Marianne as a horny fantasy figure: the whore with the looks of a virgin (even an angel): the willing victim.

But Marianne was learning to suffer. 'Once you start to care about anything or anybody,' she said, 'it always fucks ambition up.' Four hit records had crystallized her ambition. Mick shattered it. 'He had me on a pin,' she recalled, 'and he was watching me flail and writhe, but it was something that fascinated him as an artist.' Marianne became hooked on heroin, overdosed in Australia in 1969, once walked into a plate glass window and later miscarried Mick's child. She broke with him, and after ducking the rock limelight into acting married another musician, Ben Brierley (the Bride Wore Scarlet', said one press report), and re-emerged quite successfully as a recording artist again in the late seventies.

There can be little doubt that the image of Marianne hanging over from those heady days is still potent enough for her to exploit to her own advantage. In 1977, tentatively cast to play Sid Vicious's incestuous mother in a fictional Sex Pistols film, she described a planned nude scene with Sid as 'pretty disgusting', while admitting that 'basically, I suppose I'm still a dirty little girl'. On the other hand, she has struggled to come to terms with her own complex emotions, recording a song about sexual jealousy on her 1977 album, *Broken English*, which was explicit enough to invoke the displeasure of the BBC. About Mick Jagger she says that 'no-one was deserted. My relationship . . . just came to a natural end.' And, insisting that she 'was never a victim', she said in 1981 that 'perhaps I can get hurt easily, but on other levels I'm very strong.'

She rejected promiscuity ('People tried all that in the sixties and seventies,' she says, 'and it didn't work'), and tried, less successfully, to renounce heroin on several occasions. Her addiction led to her losing the custody of her child, Nicholas, to his father, John Dunbar. She was busted as recently as early 1981 for possession of fifteen milligrams of heroin and was fined £100, after claiming that 'a friend called Nicky' left it in her bedside cabinet.

'I've got over the drug problem,' she said, 'but even now I get tempted, especially when I'm down, or on my own.' The past itself is perhaps the most potent drug and, even today, Marianne is still 'the former girl-friend of Rolling Stone Mick Jagger' to the world's press.

Bare hug. Once hailed as the world's highest paid model, former Vogue *cover-girl Jerry Hall, naked but for her jewels, shows her love for Mick Jagger.*

Above: Marianne Faithfull confirming her public image as the whore with the looks of a virgin (even an angel): every adolescent's horny fantasy figure.

Above right: The beautiful and the damned. Mick and Marianne arrive at Sydney Airport, 6th July, 1969, for the filming of Ned Kelly. For Marianne, who had endured two years of reflected glory and legal hassles in the company of the Stones, it was nearly the last landing.

Below: The tears gone by. Marianne Faithful in intensive care in a Sydney hospital, following an overdose of 150 sodium amytal tablets on 8th July, 1969. Her heroin addiction, the death of Brian Jones five days earlier and a troubled relationship with Mick, had resulted in an attempted suicide. Marianne had seemed the epitome of the swinging sixties, but as that decade ended, its glossy veneer cracking, Marianne arrived at death's door and almost entered.

Miss X riding high. The Redlands raid and her role in Girl on a Motor-cycle *(1967) with Alain Delon (shown here) killed off Marianne Faithfull's virginal image.*

Although the word 'groupie' is relatively new, similar camp followers have existed for centuries. Fame itself is not necessarily the magnet, but the sort of renown associated with those men whose lives carry some sort of risk, threatening to be short and therefore (so the theory goes) lived at a high pitch of excitement. The sexual activities of such women can be called acts of generosity, services to the lonely, tired and tragic, whose relationships are always tenuous and usually short, shots at vicarious excitement and fame, or simply whoring. In a sense, all these descriptions demonstrate the same underlying motivation – the desire to flirt with death and life, taking the dangerous chance that a temporary sexual association will turn into a permanent emotional attachment. For the women, such associations are pale shadows of the

Older and wiser? Marianne re-emerged in 1979 as a singer with a voice that showed her age and pain.

Group grope: David Essex recreates the sexy image of sixties rock'n'roll in the film Stardust.

self-defining experiences of their men. Often, that is all they can hope for.

Among musicians, camp followers have been known as 'band chicks', 'starfuckers', 'snuff queens' (in country music) and, since the sixties, 'groupies'. The big difference between rock groupies and their predecessors and fellows is their infatuation with groups. The Beatles, of course, set the pattern. They were not just stars, they were an exclusive band of brothers, to which people so much wanted to *belong*. Sometimes, the sex came later. The girls hung around stage doors, waiting for a glimpse. If a roadie came out to procure for the Fab Four, it was easy to offer yourself – and, once made, the offer was rarely refused. Later on, perhaps, roadies and concert promoters and local DJs would arrange back-stage passes in return for services rendered. What else could a poor girl-fan do?

It was easy to slip from fan to groupie in the early sixties. The whole atmosphere of rock'n'roll concerts was charged with adolescent sexual electricity. Against the backcloth of fumbled experiences with untutored and ungainly boyfriends, the worldly

Reach for the stars. The nearest most groupies ever came to stardom was to feature in a magazine article or, as here, a film. The shot comes from Groupies *– a semi-documentary of 1972.*

image of the love-toting pop or rock musician was truly seductive. The girl who once stood outside a stage-door and found herself ushered into the holy of holies to minister to the needs of some lust-gripped musician often found the experience worth repeating. The sexual act itself was little more than symbolic. It was a demonstration that the barrier between audience and performer had come down for her, setting her above the crowd. Sex was the show carried on backstage – no longer a surrogate, but the act itself.

Although the groupies quickly developed favourite performers or formed into a hierarchy reflecting the hierarchy of rock stars, their common motivation was more important. This depended on an idea of the exclusivity and alien character of group life, so that while any group might attract groupies, the phenomenon really mushroomed with the so-called British Invasion of America in the mid-sixties.

Young girls from nice middle-class homes quickly latched on to the idea of becoming groupies. They were 'often well-heeled, living on Daddy's money, a solid educational background', the Electric Light Orchestra's Bev Bevan remembered. Many British groupies were inspired by the fuss that was made about Chrissie Shrimpton, Marianne Faithfull, Jane Asher (Paul McCartney's girl-friend for a time in the sixties) or Patti Boyd (the model who became first George Harrison's wife and then Eric Clapton's). Others were content to enjoy what the moment seemed to offer. 'You get to ball the prettiest boys, smoke the best dope and meet all the most far out people,' said one girl known as Patti Cakes. 'You're there three or four days, waited on hand and foot, and there's just all the dope and food you can eat,' said Anna, from San Francisco, 'and all the people paying attention to you and your lover. It's very beautiful.'

Whatever a groupie was after, her sexual services were clearly a marketable commodity – even if the price she was paid was often insultingly low. Sherry, a Los Angeles groupie (now retired), would cruise Sunset Strip looking for long-haired boys on hotel room balconies. She would shout up and ask them their room numbers. She also had engraved visiting cards printed with messages like 'I want you' or, more circumspectly, 'Let's get it on'. Another groupie from Cleveland spent many a night chasing likely looking limousines. One hopeful wrote Mick Jagger a note beginning, 'Can you move your prick/As well as you kick/When you dance, Mick?' and signed it with her name, address and phone number. Less artistic efforts have included hiring a helicopter to buzz a house where the Beatles were staying, sending a pair of panties to ELP drummer Carl Palmer accompanied by a telephone message suggesting 'a personal demonstration', plain lying and, of course, setting a sexual sprat to catch a mackerel.

Anybody with the right sort of connection would do. For example, there is the story of the sixteen-year-old New York groupie who climbed out onto the ledge below a sixth-floor hotel room occupied by a journalist travelling with the Rolling Stones. Having entered the room through a window and ascertaining that she was indeed dealing with a friend of Mick and the boys, she stripped and got into bed. In Robert Greenfield's account of the Stones' 1972 US tour, *Stones Touring Party*, we are introduced to Renée, a 'fresh-faced' nineteen-year-old secretarial student who lies her way backstage at a Philadelphia show, into the beds of a roadie or two and onto film as a featured player in Robert Frank's unreleased documentary about the tour, *Cocksucker Blues*. In this she agreed to let herself be filmed with her fresh-face stuffed with the genitalia of Stones' associates. Renée was not a top groupie – as she herself said, 'The Stones should have had the Butter Queen, Suzy Creamcheese or Cherry Vanilla there' – but she understood her role well enough. 'I think a tour makes it easy on a chick,' she said after the tour was over. 'She doesn't have to bother putting the make on anyone. She's there just to say yes.' It's a comment worthy of Jagger himself, for whom 'there's really no reason to have women on a tour unless they've got a job to do; the only other reason is to screw'.

'Girls come round and pose like starlets, teasing and acting haughty,' Led Zeppelin's Jimmy Page once complained. 'If you humiliate them a bit they tend to come on all right after that.' A groupie's job was to serve, to be available – and it is in the nature of her availability and service that she will be humiliated. This is one reason why fellatio ('blow jobs', 'giving head', 'cocksucking') is the preferred mode of backstage and hotel room sex (another is a not unrealistic fear of venereal disease). By itself, the act is the epitome of sexual servility.

Bev Bevan tells of a strange encounter with four groupies in the bar of a Holiday Inn in Salem, Oregon. It was 9.30pm and the group retired there after playing the opening set at a Wishbone Ash concert. Apart from themselves, a bored barman and a piano trio playing a medley of show tunes, the bar was empty. Four girls, dressed in best Basin Street brothel finery, strode in purposefully. They were very self-assured. Their leader, Penny ('double for a young Mae West' according to Bev) introduced them. 'We call ourselves the Flying Garter Girls and, honey, I run the finest academy for oral sex on this side of the Rockies.'

Soon, in the interests of 'laying it on you', as Penny assured them, she and 'Miss Memphis' were dancing with two members of the group, while the other girls (Cheryl and Cindy-Lou, would you believe), were making love to each other on the floor of the bar. 'We're AC/DC,' Penny is said to have explained. 'We like each other's company as well.'

Voyeurism, group sex and a little bit of mild sadism are all important parts of the groupie scene. The rock stars maintain the proper distance of a discerning consumer, while the groupies maintain the high standard and wide range of services one might expect of a good department store, an ice cream parlour – or a brothel. Breaching the etiquette runs the risk in extreme cases of fathering unwanted children. Brian Jones is said to have managed six in his time (two admittedly before he was a star); Jimi Hendrix (who coined the derisive term 'Band Aids' for groupies) is supposed to have left

Sunday People EXCLUSIVE

NOVEMBER 30, 1980   No. 5158   20p

Erika Hubers: "Love affair"

I AM BEATLE PAUL'S SECRET CHILD

By HARRY WARSCHAUER
in West Berlin

A YOUNG German girl last night revealed her startling belief that she is the daughter of ex-Beatle Paul McCartney.

"I hope very much to meet my father one day", said 17-year-old Bettina Hubers at her home in West Berlin.

Her mother, 38-year-old Mrs Erika Hubers, claims that Bettina is the result of an affair she had with McCartney while The Beatles were appearing in Hamburg early in their career.

"On December 19 the whole world will have great fun as it is Bettina's father," she told you.

On that date her 17th birthday, Bettina comes of age.

Amazing claim by Bettina aged 17

Bettina and a Paul McCartney poster: "You may see a certain resemblance — for example, the mouth," says lawyer.

Continued on Page 2

TWINS WHO SPEAK THE STREET OF LOVE **THE GHOST THAT**

Little Jimi, aged six, pictured with his mother, Eva Sundkvist, six years after Jimi Hendrix's death. The Swedish courts supported her claim that he was Hendrix's son.

Marianne had a miscarriage, Bianca had Jade. Marsha Hunt, squeezed between the two in Mick Jagger's affections, found time to have Karis in 1970, and settled paternity with him out of court.

a trail of children and threatened paternity suits across Europe and America; in 1980 a Berlin woman, Erica Huebers, claimed that her seventeen-year-old daughter is Paul McCartney's child, the result of a supposed liaison during the Beatles' night-club days in Hamburg ('Paul has no recollection of this lady,' said his publicist); Marsha Hunt settled with Mick Jagger out of court over the contested paternity of her child, while he admitted fathering the child that Marianne Faithfull miscarried.

'You look for certain things in certain towns,' said Jimmy Page. 'Chicago, for instance, is notorious for sort of two things at once. Balling two chicks, or three, in combination acts.' When *Rolling Stone* ran a groupies' issue in 1969, there was some criticism that they hadn't written about New York groupies, who were, it was said 'a different breed'. According to Jimmy Page, San Francisco groupies are 'like friends', while New Yorkers and Angelenos 'make a religion out of how many pop stars they can fuck'. Eric Clapton remembered playing the *Murray the K Show* with the Who in New York, 1967. 'There were just tons of them around then,' he told Steve Turner. 'I mean, pretty ugly ones but some fair ones, too. There were both ends, really – horrible spotty scrubbers and really nice looking middle-class chicks. Or just nice chicks who didn't realize they were making themselves into groupies – they were pretty innocent.'

The callous classification of women has been something that groupies themselves have always done – at least, since the idea became current that being a groupie could be a full-time occupation. Jenny Fabian, who used her experiences with a number of English groups as background material for her novel *Groupie* (co-written with Johnnie Byrne), suggests how competitive the groupie scene was.

At the bottom of the groupie heap were those who were totally disposable. They received no payment, no thanks and no second chance. They were room service or 'in-flight entertainment' – ready and willing to be used or abused as fancy dictates. 'We're the ugliest band ever born,' claimed Bobby Colomby, drummer with Blood, Sweat and Tears. 'We have the funniest groupies in the world – real bottom-of-the-barrel stuff.' Led Zeppelin were plagued by two particularly unattractive but persistent Detroit groupies. Members of the group once conceived the idea of taking them to one of the group's motel rooms and pelting them with cream-filled doughnuts. In the event, Robert Plant couldn't find an open doughnut shop so it never happened. Then there was Renée again, doing her stuff on board the Stones' plane. The guy she was with wouldn't come and Renée was naked and hot and tired. Another member of the entourage came up to her with a drink in his hand and Renée asked for a sip. 'Not after what you been doin', man,' he said. Eventually, he magnanimously handed her his empty glass. Moments before, he had been watching two other groupies performing and shouting, 'Get me some orange juice. Get me something wet I can throw!'

But at the top of the pile are the groupies whose attentions are prized. Some of them may not even consider themselves groupies, since they are treated rather like wives or high-class prostitutes, (but without the legal protection of either). 'It doesn't matter what their motivation is,' Country Joe MacDonald said in the sixties. 'There are times when they come around after something and you're after something, too, so you get it together and everybody's happy. Groupies are beautiful. They come to hear you play, they throw flowers and underpants, they give you kisses and love, they come to bed with you. They're beautiful.' Living in Topanga County in 1968, Neil Young had observed that 'there are about eight girls who go around, keeping house, cooking food, and making love to everyone.' It was, he agreed, 'beautiful'.

'As a rule, they're the most incredibly warm people,' said Eric Clapton about groupies in the early days. 'If making love to you was going to make you happy, they'd make love. If you were tired and didn't want to make it, they'd cook you a meal and make you feel at home. They really were ports of call.' Hendrix said much the same thing. 'Instead of saying, "We're part of the love scene", they're actually doing it,' he once remarked. 'They take you around, they wash your socks and try to make you feel nice while you're in town because they know they can't have you forever.'

Behind this romantic fiction lies the brutal reality of male chauvinism. Hendrix's 'love scene' consisted of

this: 'He had an incredible sexual appetite and would often sleep with three or four girls in the same night,' said Kathy Etchingham, one of Jimi's long-term companions. His casual attitude was legendary – the only surprising thing being how readily it was accepted, by colleagues, friends, fans and lovers alike. 'One night after a concert in Manchester,' said Kathy, 'I even found him in the ladies' loo with a chick. She meant nothing to him, and it meant nothing to me – apart from the fact that I had to tell him to hurry up or we would miss the train back to London.'

Jimi, apparently, was as over-indulgent with women as he was with drinks, drugs and music. And, like most men, he enjoyed a double standard. 'When we first started living together I was very young and kind of wild,' Kathy recalled, almost apologetically. Eventually, Hendrix locked her in the bedroom as a punishment, and spent 'many hours of patient explaining' how she was 'supposed to act', according to Kathy, 'both as a woman and when I was living with someone I love.'

In fact, the gallant Jimi often relied on a more basic teaching method. One night in the Bag O'Nails, a London nightclub, Kathy left Jimi at his table to go upstairs and phone a friend. After a while – longer

Exits, bold as love. Hendrix associate Alan Clark comforts New York supergroupie Devon as they leave the Seattle funeral home where Jimi Hendrix's body awaits burial on 18th September, 1970. Devon was more than just a groupie to Hendrix, and she only survived him by two years, overdosing in 1972.

than Hendrix approved of – he came upstairs and, assuming she was talking to some male competitor (she wasn't), he grabbed the phone out of her hand and started beating her about the head with it. Kathy was screaming when, luckily for her, those two well-known tunesmiths, Lennon and McCartney, happened to be passing and pulled the gallant Jimi off his lover. 'That may have been the first of our many fights,' said Kathy. On one occasion her nose was broken in three places by a well-aimed kick from Hendrix.

'Jimi Hendrix was a genius,' said one of his most intimate associates, Eric Burdon, in 1976. 'But one minute he's on stage singing about the mass of underdogs in America and the next he's kicking the hell out of some poor chick in a back alley.' Perhaps Jimi Hendrix's best-known companion was the New York 'supergroupie', Devon. She was, said writer Al Aronowitz, 'the closest thing Jimi had to an old lady . . . one of the most beautiful and sensuous of the groupies and one of the most successful.' In the late sixties there were (according to Devon's friend, Pat Hartley) 'four or five sort of famous groupies and Devon was one of them, but she never lasted long with anybody. She didn't want to live with anybody, it was just a real status thing . . .' Devon was a rock star's favourite. She went through Brian Jones, Mick Jagger, Jimi Hendrix. 'Whenever a rock star came to New York,' wrote Al Aronowitz, 'chances are you'd find Devon in his hotel room.' Her services were recommended. Jagger phoned her up after getting her number from a friend and invited her to go to Philadelphia with him for a concert. 'After the Philadelphia gig,' she remembered, 'we spent the week together in New York. Six beautiful days and nights . . . If I wanted to go to Boston with him, I could. Or I'd wait for him to come back. I just felt beautiful . . . I'd get calls from my friends who'd congratulate me and say "Hey, you did it!" Like *heavy* score, right?'

The congratulations had something to do with the fact that Devon was black. She was also Jimi's girl – she even wanted to marry him. And she provided the extra service of pimping half-a-dozen other girls for Hendrix. Pat Hartley recalled 'all kinds of weird shit going on and telephones ringing and girls being kicked downstairs and all kinds of nonsense . . . very late night acid trips and things like that . . .' Jimi, said Pat Hartley, 'was shy, but that doesn't mean he wasn't going to beat you up if you took too much of a liberty with him . . . some of it was an absolute horror.'

As for Devon, she was happy to be wanted. But it was all somehow so sad and empty. She lived for the next date, to get her photograph in the papers, to have journalists like Al Aronowitz write columns about her. Truly bereaved after Hendrix's death, she killed herself with an overdose less than two years later.

Chris used to be another top-flight groupie. But she actually fell in love with Lynyrd Skynyrd's road manager Dean Kilpatrick, who died tragically in the Skynyrd air-crash in 1977. She'd been through some

Soft surfaces and hard edges. Anita Pallenberg shows her form.

123

shit even before that, though. 'Woodstock was the first time I was away from home with the licence to be totally free,' she told writer Michael Segell. 'I was very drunk, very high all week,' she recalled. 'I had smoked some before but had never tried heavier stuff. And I made it with a lot of people. I can't even remember who.' When her boyfriend arrived, he didn't like what he saw. Chris walked off with another man – a performer at the festival. When they got to the Chelsea Hotel in New York, the week's intake of drugs and drink (including Woodstock's notorious acid-spiked punch) was taking its toll. Her companion was having none of her explanation of fatigue and sickness. He tried to rape her and beat her so badly that she had to be hospitalized.

Yet she continued as a groupie for a while, even through further brutalization by other musicians. Eventually, she won the demeaning accolade of being voted Cleveland's top attraction. 'I always imagined I had some great purpose in life,' she told Segell, 'to fulfill someone's dreams or help someone or do some segment of mankind a great deal of good ... In retrospect it didn't have much purpose. I just learnt a great deal about life.' When Kilpatrick was killed, she gave

'Would you let your daughter go with a Rolling Stone?' Right: Anita Pallenberg with Brian Jones in 1966 – the ice princess. Far right: Anita holding Marlon, her first child by Keith Richard – maternal but insecure. Italian-born Anita was told by the British authorities in 1969 'Marry or Leave,' so she flew off to America. She and Keith never married. Below: Anita passes a joint to Mick Jagger on the set of Performance. *Her seduction of Jagger during a shooting break made her Stones score equal with Marianne Faithfull's.*

up the rock world for ever, and went to work as a receptionist in a law office, returning home each evening to live quietly with her parents.

The enhanced status of the 'rock'n'roll old lady' is an illusory triumph. She may win her way into the holy of holies, but she always does it as a sacrifice. Marianne Faithfull found that out – in time, perhaps, to save her life. Anita Pallenberg, too, has found it difficult after her long association with the Rolling Stones. Anita, a teutonic beauty as a young woman, first entered their lives as Brian Jones's girlfriend, in the mid-sixties. The couple's relationship was stormy, to say the least. Brian would beat the hell out of Anita; Anita would support Brian in his paranoid fantasies. She joined him on his trips. On one occasion, Brian dressed up in a Nazi uniform and had his photograph taken grinding a doll into the ground with his jackboot – Anita suggested he send the picture to the newspapers, telling them it was 'an anti-Nazi protest'.

In 1967, Anita left Brian for Keith Richard. While on a drive to Morocco, Brian fell ill and was left behind in hospital by the rest of the vacationing group. Keith and Anita got together in Valencia, but kept it a secret from Brian. 'He was becoming increasingly vicious,' Keith explained later. Joining them in Morocco, Brian paid a trip to a local brothel, brought back two prostitutes and demanded a scene with them and Anita. Keith, in a sudden fit of revulsion at all this excess, threw Anita into a car and drove off. 'I was disgusted with the way Brian treated her,' he said.

But Anita herself was no angel. She was at one time dependent on drugs, notably heroin, although she

even[...]
many[...]
occul[...]
ance,[...]
assoc[...]
being[...]
lawy[...]

I[...]
sion[...]
seve[...]
Anit[...]
thro[...]
revo[...]
bed[...]
old [...]
had[...]
blow[...]
beco[...]
noise of shooting and she had turned Scott over onto his front. Anita said that she had heard a click, then a shot. When examined, the .38 was found to contain three bullets – one discharged and two live, one of them nicked as though it had been hit with the firing pin. The boy had, according to Anita, been discussing Russian Roulette earlier – he was depressed, didn't get along with his father and felt considerable remorse about his mother's death which had occurred some six months earlier. The two of them, Anita said, had been drinking white wine all day and Scott had been smoking a lot of marijuana.

Scott's father, Robert Cantrell, said that Anita was desperately in love with his son and had seduced him. But it was also pointed out that some time earlier a police patrolman had reported the noise of chanting from bushes not far from the house. The police report of the incident said that the patrolman was jumped on by a robed and hooded man, resembling Scott Cantrell in height and weight. Was he involved in occult practices with or without Anita? Inside the house, police noted a hangman's noose – holding up a hammock – and a 'voodoo style doll depicting Elvis Presley' on the mantelpiece. It is not surprising that Anita Pallenberg was cleared of any part in Scott Cantrell's death, although she was charged with the possession of one stolen gun (the .38) and with criminal possession of an unregistered automatic, also found in the house.

Whatever the truth of Anita's bizarre life, her tragedy seems much more straightforward. As a rock'n'roll girlfriend, she had been prey to the gross enlargement of conventional insecurities. Her sexuality had become, for a time, the essential prop in her life.

How far Anita's condition at the time of Cantrell's shooting was attributable to the state of her relationship with Keith Richard can only be surmised. However, Richard's constant companion through most of 1979 was the Swedish model Lil Wenglas Green, who had lived with him in Paris for a year. But Richard's publicist, commenting about Keith and Anita at the end of 1979, said that 'Keith's position was that they never parted. Only the press said they did.' Indeed, within a few months of the shooting, Keith was back

Life with the Stones can seriously damage your health. After the Scott Cantrell shooting, when Anita left court in Lewisboro, N.Y. on 24th July, 1979, charged with illegal possession of a gun, she looked bloated and vacant.

with Anita. But, as one of his friends has commented, 'The person Keith really loves is their son Marlon.'

The Stones of course have attracted the most distinguished of all followers. Margaret Trudeau, then wife of Canadian prime minister, Pierre Trudeau, was one of them. Just after Keith and Anita were busted in Toronto for heroin in the summer of 1977, 'Madcap' Margaret (as the press knew her) became entangled in their magic. 'I didn't encourage or dissuade her,' said Mick Jagger after she had spent some time pursuing the group to New York. 'It would have been difficult to kick her out. She had six security men with two guns each. No, thank you. She was a very determined young lady – er, older woman. I think she was just a very sick girl in search of something. She found it, but not with me. I wouldn't go near her,' he added, 'with a barge pole.'

Evidently the 27-year-old cement millionaire's daughter was going through a bad patch in her six year marriage to 56-year-old Pierre. After meeting the Stones, she followed them to New York, booked herself into their hotel and attached herself to their party. She returned to Canada some time later with a black eye, the last chapter of her 'modern girl' autobiography, *Beyond Reason*, and an extraordinarily contradictory testimonial from the Satanic Majesty himself (who was, at the time, separating from his own wife, Bianca). 'I have no relationship with Margaret Trudeau,' said Jagger, 'just a passing acquaintance for two nights.'

The women who best survive in the male-dominated rock world are not groupies at all. Jenny Fabian, for example, said Family's vocalist Roger Chapman who knew her well, 'was just a part of that whole underground scene'. Deborah Harry spent the late sixties in a flower power group called Wind In The Willows and always harboured a desire to be a performer. For a while she worked as a Playboy bunny although waiting on table at Max's Kansas City in New York was more rewarding, allowing her to hang out with musicians and nurture her own talent. While she would admit, in 1981, 'that sex sells and I do exploit my sexuality', she could also argue, with an eye to her own position, that 'women are going to be the new Elvises. That's the only place for rock'n'roll to go. The only people who can express anything new in rock are girls, and gays.'

For Linda Eastman, photography was both an occupation in its own right (she worked for *Eye* Magazine in New York) and a means of access to musicians. The two things were never, of course, entirely separate, but when she met and married Paul

What's up, Deb? Harry as bunny – but where's the carrot?

126

Photography brought them together, but Paul and Linda sometimes prefer photography to leave them alone.

that he had made it all up 'on the spur of the moment'. 'Sometimes I don't think he is very truthful,' said Britt, disingenuously. 'But it's not because he means to lie. It's because he wants either to confuse people or to please them.' Quite which member of the Britt and Rod team was living in the other's fantasy world is not clear, but, apparently, morality and judgement were infrequent visitors to the couple's glamorous household.

Britt claimed that Rod was excessively mean with money. However, seasoned commentators of the rock scene have long remarked on Britt's obsessive love of shopping. Rod's former girlfriend Dee Harrington, and his present wife, Alana Hamilton, have both leapt to his defence. But despite their protestations, Rod himself has shown that where Britt was concerned, he'd spent as little as he could get away with. He even confessed to stealing a copy of *True Britt* from an airport bookstall. 'Well, I was damned if I was going to pay for it,' he said.

When it came to the separation, Britt claimed that Rod and she had a verbal agreement to pool their 'earnings and abilities', and as such she demanded some recompense. Everything, she said, should have been split down the middle and, considering how she had sacrificed her acting career to help Rod, she felt she deserved £6,000,000 – especially, she said, since Rod was about to sign a £13,000,000 deal when he left her. As an interim award, Britt asked for £2,750 a month while her claim was being assessed. But her arguments were rejected by the courts.

Rod, eventually, married Alana Hamilton, the former wife of the actor, George Hamilton, whose name had earlier been linked with Lyndon Johnson's daughter. Alana and Rod first met in 1977, after which he got his press officer to phone her up and ask for a date. 'I found him sensitive, witty, intelligent, sexy and shy,' said Alana. Apparently, on their first date, they sat up most of the night talking.

Flying between famous men, such women tend not even to be celebrities by virtue of their celebrity, but rather because of their men's. They are, as a result, the staple of gossip columns – that journalistic domain where all that matters is who was with whom and when. Living from star to star is the tedious routine of these lives. Bianca Perez Morena de Macias, a Nicaraguan model and former girlfriend of Michael Caine, looked promising when she told the press after her first meeting with Mick Jagger that 'I have no name'. Once she had been granted her husband's, however, she soon took up the regular sport with a vengeance. 'Bianca,' said Andy Warhol, 'is the greatest movie star who's never made a movie.' Towards the end of her marriage to Mick, she began to be seen in the company of numerous gossip column items – Ryan O'Neal, Princess Margaret's friend Roddy Llewellyn and a number of art dealers, oil tycoons and other businessmen. For a few weeks she ran the hectic

McCartney in 1969, the rapidity with which she gave up professional photography for a place in McCartney's new group, Wings, suggested a certain lack of application at the time. 'We met in a club in London called the Bag O'Nails,' Linda recalled three years into marriage. 'It was a real pick-up job. Georgie Fame was playing and I saw Paul and I just felt I had to meet him. So I managed to get talking to him and afterwards we went to another club called the Speakeasy with Keith Moon and Roger Daltrey from the Who . . . We considered living together, but it wasn't really on, so we got married.'

If Linda's description sounds rather like the perennial approach of the groupie, it must be emphasized that her marriage to Paul has been successful. Having already had one child, her daughter Heather, by a previous and brief marriage when she was still a student, Linda once remarked thoughtfully, that 'you've got to love someone a heck of a lot to stay married.'

Britt Ekland, a Swedish starlet, moved from Peter Sellers to Lou Adler to Rod Stewart. With Sellers, she recalled, there was no love in the marriage, and despite the fact that he fathered her daughter Victoria, she has said that she only learned to love him after they had separated. Lou Adler, the emperor of the West Coast rock scene, fathered her son Nicolai. But Britt's greatest love appears to have been Rod Stewart. After they split, he said ruefully of her memoirs, *True Britt*, 'The book made me feel sorry for her because she's a born loser. She's always the one that's jilted and always the bridesmaid.'

While Rod and Britt were together, he once claimed to have fathered a child in 1963, only to confess later

Do you think I'm sexy? Rod Stewart gropes his wife, Alana, during a 1980 post-gig party at London's Embassy Club. Having replaced Britt Ekland in Rod's affections, Alana soon replaced her in Rod's bed.

route of New York high-life revolving at the time mainly round the ultra-exclusive disco and haven for coke users, Studio 54.

Her split with Mick was hotly denied at the time (in 1977) and legally complex afterwards. Having married him and mothered his daughter, Jade, Bianca had a legitimate claim to alimony. She claimed $12.5 million – calculating Mick's earnings in their eight-year marriage at $25 million. After some haggling out of court, Mick sought to have the case heard in Britain, where divorce settlements are generally smaller than in the US. (Bianca's lawyer, Marvin Mitchelson, had already represented Marsha Hunt in her paternity suit against Jagger.) While this attempt was in process, Mick was ordered to pay Bianca over $3,000 a week in expenses (including $500 a week for transportation, $250 a week for entertainment and $1,000 a week for rent or mortgage repayments). Eventually, the courts decided the divorce case should be heard in London. An interim payment of some £25,000 was awarded to Bianca but the case dragged on even after a decree nisi had been granted. A year later, in November 1980, a judge in

Above: Sweet nothings and rich somebodies. Mick and Bianca celebrate the Hon. Colin Tennant's fiftieth birthday on Princess Margaret's hideaway isle of Mustique.

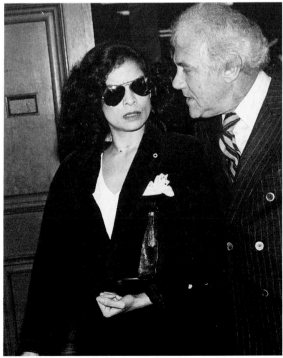

Left: Admitting no impediment to a marriage of true minds, Bianca Jagger struts her stuff at the reception to celebrate her wedding to Mick, 12th May, 1971.

Right: The price of Love? Specialist divorce lawyer Marvin Mitchelson suggesting to Bianca that it might be $12,000,000, outside the Los Angeles Superior Court, 8th May, 1979. The Jagger divorce was finally settled privately under British jurisdiction by a judge in chambers, for an alimony figure rumoured to be around £1,000,000.

chambers fixed the final amount of the settlement in private – a figure which has never been revealed but is estimated at £1,000,000.

Somehow, Bianca retained a certain degree of perspective – demonstrated in the early eighties by her efforts in support of her Nicaraguan compatriots, who had suffered enormously in the struggle to overthrow the oppressive Somoza regime and the battle to defend their new democracy. (She had already given much time and money in their aid back in 1978 when a severe earthquake devastated the country.) She has also spoken up for the freedom fighters in El Salvador. 'The rock business is like a secret society run by men,' she commented in 1981. 'Every woman is treated like a second-class citizen.' Women, she said, became their own worst enemies by virtue of the competitiveness with which they regarded each other – as she herself had proved when she declared her dislike for Mick Jagger's new companion, Texan model Jerry Hall.

Jerry Hall, six foot and a former *Vogue* cover girl, was once said to be the highest paid model in the world. Bryan Ferry, the elegant son of a Durham miner who fronted Roxy Music in the seventies, saw her on *Vogue* and used her for the sleeve of the Roxy album, *Siren*. Then he fell in love with her and the couple got engaged. He was, not unnaturally, hurt when Jerry went off with Mick Jagger in October 1977. After all, among Jerry's admirers could be counted the former Shah of Persia, and Bryan – who liked nothing better than to Christmas on shipping heir Takis Theodarakis's yacht or to holiday on Princess Margaret's hideaway island of Mustique – could aspire to nothing higher than a woman who was admired by the richest man in the world. 'I do not like being accused of going uptown,' said Ferry after recovering from the Hall affair. 'I like social exploration.' The trouble is that in the social stratosphere inhabited by the likes of Ferry, very little exploration is possible. In the end, what is the really significant difference between Jerry Hall and, say, Amanda Lear (another of Ferry's girlfriends), but the precise list of celebrity names appended to their's in the gossip columns – even their memoirs are tediously similar re-runs of the same sort of tittle-tattle. Perhaps concern for wealth and fame sets these people apart but (as Bianca suggested), to male rock stars all women are potential groupies.

Meanwhile, the dedicated groupie, following the dictum that 'if he doesn't strum a guitar and sing like a sex maniac, he's nobody,' concludes that doing those things qualifies almost everybody as a somebody. The dedicated groupie plays the field, collecting musicians and groups like other kids collect stamps or train numbers. The memorable Plaster-Casters of Chicago carried the collecting mania to the level of artistry. The Plaster-Casters – Cynthia, Dianne and Marilyn – made a unique collection of plaster models of the erect penises of rock stars. They started in late 1967 when Cynthia was about twenty. She had been 'chasing groups' since 1965, but 'wanted to stand out from the other groupies and get to meet the groups first'. The first group she met was the Stones. 'Since then,' she says, 'well just about everybody, I guess.'

The Plaster-Casters' technique was simple, direct and unashamed. They would approach a group with an unusual degree of openness. They carried their equipment in a briefcase marked 'Plaster-Casters of Chicago'. They took their casts around to show prospective 'clients'. They even had T-shirts and visiting cards printed up. A typical session would involve one of them as 'plater', one as mould-maker and plaster-caster and one as assistant. The operation would be recorded in a diary in almost clinical detail. 'He . . . kept his hard for the entire minute,' one entry reads. 'He got stuck, however, for about fifteen minutes (his hair did), but he was an excellent sport – didn't panic . . . he actually enjoyed it and balled the impression after it had set. In fact, I believe the reason we couldn't get his rig out was that it wouldn't get soft.'

The last gasp of the traditional groupie was blown on to the 'pretty boy' teenybopper idols of the seventies, like Marc Bolan and the Bay City Rollers. Even David Cassidy claims to have enjoyed the services of groupies. It gave him credibility as a rock musician. 'On the road there was always this one room where we'd corral a handpicked dozen of the most beautiful,' he said in 1977. 'After the show, I'd go up to this room, pick the one I wanted, and let the band divvy up the rest. I was an animal.' But even for him it palled. 'I was tired of strangers in my room, my bed; tired of girls climbing up the fire escape and hiding in my closets, in my shower.'

Today the rock scene attracts a wide variety of sexual opportunists of greater or lesser degree. The innocence of an earlier age, when sex with the stars was usually no more than harmless fun, has disappeared. There are would-be supergroupies who always seem to be at a loss for more famous names. There are male groupies and gay groupies. And for some, close association with rock stars has provided a launching pad or a welcome boost to a separate career. Bebe Buell, having become something of a celebrity as a friend of the stars, recorded an unmemorable album in an attempt to strike out on her own. Paula Yates (daughter of Jess Yates, one-time presenter of British TV's quasi-religious show *Stars On Sunday*, until a scandal with a divorcee lost him his job), met Boomtown Rat Bob Geldof and rode his rocket to a hallowed place in the pop gossip columns. Her career as a celebrity columnist in the music press, Sunday papers, women's magazines and breakfast TV, was assured.

Of course, things have changed since Jimi Hendrix or Neil Young were able to talk of groupies as the practical exponents of hippy love. In the eighties, groupies and musicians alike knew that starfucking is what it's all about. The people who have actually made it to the starry heights tend to find that the hassle of groupies now outweighs any possible benefits. Years ago the people who organised rock stars' lives – managers, agents, promoters – saw provision of groupies as part of the general paraphernalia of the concert or recording schedule. Nowadays, the priority is to protect stars from too much contact with the

Hey, hey Paula . . . Yates, that is, then a 19-year-old 'professional punk', according to the press. Here she is revealing hidden qualities on a chilly July day in 1979.

outside world.

Rock music now means status and exclusivity. Today's big stars would never admit a need for groupies. But for those at the bottom of the heap, groupies are still a sign of some sort of stardom. On the way down, in Dallas, Sid Vicious left the Sex Pistols' dressing room to pick out a groupie. 'I don't want to fuck them all,' he screamed at the guards keeping the girls at bay. 'I just want to fuck one!' (This, from someone who described himself as a sexless monster.) He picked up with an American groupie – Nancy Spungen – when he left the Pistols. Nancy, whose father owned a paper company in Philadelphia, was – according to Malcolm McLaren – 'the first and only girl Sid went out with. Before meeting me' (said McLaren), 'he was a homosexual.' Like the nice American girls who get into sado-masochism because that's what punk groups are supposed to dig, Nancy just wanted to be noticed.

The trouble with being a groupie, one of them once said, is that people are always leaving you. In fact, they never have any intention of staying. It's the groupies who yearn for some permanence – perhaps a reassurance of their own desirability, even in the least promising circumstances. The story goes that Gram Parsons, the rich boy who joined the Byrds, hung out with the Stones and was desperate to be a star, collapsed in his motel room after a typical day of drinking and drugging. Parsons – who regularly ended up financing his unsuccessful musical ventures with his own private income – was himself a sort of groupie. He liked nothing better than to get doped up with Keith Richard. He was desperate for the recognition the Stones afforded him as perhaps *the* founder of sixties' country rock. He was loved by the singer Emmylou Harris and, indeed, recognized by those who knew what he had done. But that was not enough. Drugs, drink and groupies were what he craved – the palpable rewards of stardom.

On 19th September, 1973, Parsons was in the Joshua Tree Inn, California – where he often stayed on his frequent visits to the area, which had an obscure mystical significance to him. 'About ten, I just caught some weird vibes from over in his room,' recalls the motel owner's son. 'When I get there, there was this chick jerking him off, trying to revive him. She was probably in love with him.' Gram Parsons was dead. Three years later, in 1976, girls were still arriving from time to time at the motel. 'They ask if they can have the room Gram Parsons died in,' the owner said.

133

25¢

New York,
December 10, 1980

DAILY ☒ NEWS
Tonight

**LATEST
STOCKS**

TUESDAY NIGHT EDITION

Killer stalked him 3 days

Page 3

Lennon signing autograph for Mark Chapman, before the shooting.   **News photo by Paul Goresh** © Copyright 1980 New York News Inc.

EXCLUSIVE: Lennon & suspect

FAN DANCING

In rock'n'roll's Babylon, the stars occupy the upper storeys of the sacred ziggurat, frolicking desperately among the exotic foliage of their own hanging gardens. Meanwhile down on the street are the people who put them there: the fans. Fans buy their records, go to their concerts, collect their autographs, read their magazines; and above all they identify with their heroes.

The true aristocracy of fandom are the Elvis followers. These people think nothing of filling their houses with Elvis records and Elvis memorabilia. Otherwise apparently sensible, they might spend their last penny on a Nigerian copy of an Elvis Greatest Hits compilation or on a bottle of sweet white wine bearing Elvis's image and the name 'Always Elvis – (Blanc d'Oro)' – utterly regardless of the fact that they might have the same album in seventeen different sleeves already and unworried by the knowledge that Elvis never drank wine ('We feel that this is the kind of wine Elvis would have drunk if he did drink wine,' said a spokesperson for the company that markets 'Always Elvis'.) With Elvis interred – actually, or only spiritually within the walls of Graceland – the Elvis fans have lost all sense of Elvis as a real human being.

Elvis fans can be men and women of almost any age or class. Their obsession is a strange blend of hobby and quasi-religious devotion. They invariably speak of their trips to fan conventions, their holidays in Memphis to visit Elvis's mansion and their pursuit of Elvis live (when he was alive) or on film, as social events, excuses for a bit of fun and occasions to meet like-minded friends. They are often deeply concerned at the exploitative excesses of the Elvis memorabilia industry and yet they are all collectors and avid readers of the vast body of Elvis literature (most of it brazen-faced rubbish). Even so, their illusions about Elvis are treasured – so that, when Albert Goldman's scurrilous biography of the man was published in 1981, the British Elvis fan club boycotted it, presumably on the grounds that either Goldman's *Elvis* was a lie from start to finish, or it must have been a deliberate half-truth designed to tarnish the image of a great man.

Elvis fans talk a great deal about Elvis the man and Elvis the singer, they worry of the future of Elvis's daughter, Lisa-Marie, on his behalf (even donating money to her to help maintain Gracelands) and yet they often discuss him as if he were a candidate for canonization or even godhead, rather than the human being they all pretend to know. One English fan said he'd have given his life for an hour with Elvis – since Elvis was dead at the time, however, it was a pretty safe bet. Most bizarrely, there is a group of Elvis fans who believe that a child in North Carolina, christened Elvis Presley Patterson, is Elvis's reincarnation; there is at least one book, and one song, purporting to be dictated by Presley from beyond the grave, while a sensationalist American magazine about the supernatural ran a story some time after Elvis's death claiming that a half-formed clone of the singer had escaped from an institution where 'scientists' were attempting to control its murderous urges.

Elvis of course didn't have a monopoly on fan worship. There are plenty of other examples of obsessive devotion, bordering on lunacy. There are, for example, the Deadheads; the ninety thousand fans on the Grateful Dead's mailing list who trail around the world after their superheroes, tape-decks at the ready to record every note and nuance of the Dead's performances. Their language sometimes reaches new heights of obscurity as they try to describe their feelings for the band. It is difficult to believe that a fan who talks seriously about 'shifts into hyperspace', 'quantum chemistry', 'stretching the Taos' and similar distillations of psychobabble when talking about a rock group could also be a successful case lawyer, who, according to his wife Michelle, 'has argued final arguments – to juries – behind three nights of the Dead' and 'whose trip is so charged he wins cases'.

On the other hand is this any less weird than the one-man Bob Dylan fan club known as A. J. Weberman? Self-styled inventor of the science of 'garbology', Weberman coined that most useful of critical concepts, the CB (or current bag), for Weberman delights in the analysis of garbage – especially Bob Dylan's. At first, Dylan was amused, even captivated by A. J., but Weberman's desperation to find out the true meaning of the world's most mysterious rock star led him to spy on his subject's house at all hours, concentrating on rifling through Dylan's garbage cans for any clues to the elusive CB. Once, Dylan confronted A.J. and offered him a job as his chauffeur. However the conversation between the two great minds took such a curious turn that Dylan brought it to a close with a touch of typical enigmatic brilliance. 'I'm not Dylan, A.J.,' he pronounced, 'you are.' What greater accolade for the true fan?

'I read the news today, oh yeah.' The ultimate fan, Mark Chapman got John Lennon to sign his Double Fantasy *album a few days before returning to gun him down outside the Dakota Building where Lennon lived. 'Do you know what you just did?' said the appalled janitor. 'Yes,' said Chapman. 'I just shot John Lennon.'*

If only they could talk. The inventor of Garbology, A. J. Weberman, holds an unsmoked cigar and a bag full of diapers removed from the trash-can outside Bob Dylan's Manhattan home on 12th October, 1971. For the ultimate fan, garbage isn't rubbish.

London where his car hit a tree and killed him, and Duane Allman and Berry Oakley's adjacent graves in Macon, Georgia, have become a place of pilgrimage, where fans leave guitar picks and joints as offerings to appease the grim reaper.

In Lubbock, Texas, Buddy Holly's tomb is one of rock's holy places, as is Jimi Hendrix's grave in Seattle. Fans, unable to face the sordid facts of Jimi's death, cling to the curious fiction that Hendrix took his own life as a supreme artistic gesture ('phasing himself out onto another plane of being' as Eric Burdon once put it). Others try to ignore the fact of death altogether. Jim Morrison's acolytes have defended the theory that he staged his own 'death' but is actually still living somewhere under an assumed identity (unlikely, as fellow Door Ray Manzarek drily observed, since 'he hasn't called the accountant recently'.) Even hardened rock journalists fall into the trap. 'Four days after John Lennon was shot,' Greil Marcus wrote, 'I woke up to find Beatles music off the radio and the story off the front page . . . Does this mean, I thought, that it's over? That he's not dead any more?'

It's not really surprising that Lennon's death caused the most widespread trauma among fans, and it wasn't simply the shocking circumstances of the

A desert shrine to the memory of Gram Parsons, whose coffin was hi-jacked by his friend Phil Kaufman and burned near this spot at the Joshua Tree National Monument in September, 1973.

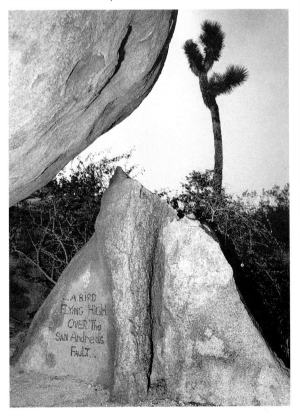

The herd instinct is strong in fans: there's safety in numbers. And there's the community spirit felt especially when a hero's life is cut brutally short. Early death destroys the possibility for ever of the fan and star meeting as equals, but it also has the advantage of enabling the star to be frozen for ever in his ideal image, rather than the often unsavoury reality. More prosaically, nobody has ever been able satisfactorily to explain the morbid curiosity of the general public when any media mogul dies in unusual circumstances. This magic combination of hero worship and morbidity explains why an estimated 1,500,000 people visited Elvis's grave in the year following his death; and why fans rededicated the site of Gram Parsons' illicit cremation at the Joshua Tree National Monument to the memory of the singer. At Joshua Tree, someone has scrawled the dedication, 'A bird flying high over the San Andreas fault' and, from time to time, flowers and other sacrificial items are laid there. Jim Morrison's grave at the St Pierre Lachaise cemetery in Paris is covered over in graffiti. Fans congregate there to leave small offerings, meditate and play music. There's 'Lizard King' graffiti, inscriptions reading 'I Want To Kill', drawings of Morrison scratched onto his tombstone, dedications to acid and, among others in French, the words *'Monstre de sensualité'* and *'Jim, tu les a libéré'*. A similar shrine has been dedicated to Marc Bolan at the spot on Barnes Common in

Stars are also fans: Patti Smith seeking inspiration at Jim Morrison's burial place in Paris. The grave may be unmarked, but fans have made sure that it doesn't go unnoticed.

shooting. Beatlemania was, after all, only the most extreme example of the all-consuming passion of fans to connect. At its simplest, it manifests itself as the sort of sexual frenzy at concerts that once inspired the old showbiz adage that a successful show means 'not a dry seat in the house'. From the days of Johnny Ray, Elvis and Fabian, up to the teenybop days of glitter rock, and right into the eighties' adulation for Adam and the Ants, the sound of pubescent girls screaming has been a constant accompaniment to rock'n'roll. It even came through the TV screen. 'In six minutes,' said Patti Smith of her first viewing of the Rolling Stones, 'five lusty images gave me my first glob of gooie in my virgin panties.' Adam Faith, remembering the girls of the late fifties who adored him, was being realistic when he said recently, 'I'm still that sort to let them wet their knickers on the seats. That's basically what it's all about for me.' Cliff Richard admitted that the first time girls screamed for him (at the Gaumont, Shepherd's Bush, in the late fifties), 'It was nice'. Tom Petty echoed this in the seventies. 'It's always good to have a few screaming girls in the front row,' he said. 'It makes it more rock'n'roll.' And Bill Wyman, the oldest teenager in the business, admitted the Stones' relief that the audiences at their 1981 concerts still contained sixteen and seventeen year old girls.

But the uninhibited sexual attraction that this implies can have disastrous results. The crush of girls trying to touch their idol led to 240 girls fainting at a

Leif Garrett show in 1979. These figures aren't exceptional, and can lead to real tragedy. In 1974, fourteen-year-old Bernadette Whelan died after being squashed against the stage at a David Cassidy concert. She had been trying to get close enough to take photographs of her idol; her camera survived the crush and the developed film shows how near she got; but she didn't live to see the results.

But if young female fans relate to their heroes as sexual objects, young male fans often feel no less pressing a need to get close to the star on stage. Predictably male fans tend to identify with the objects (usually male) of their admiration, rather than feel their idol worship in a sexual form. For instance, heavy metal fans don't just dress like their favourite bands, they often copy them to the point of playing along with songs by strumming along with imaginary or cardboard cutout guitars. Often the mimicking can be dangerous – especially when the act mimicked makes use of potentially dangerous props. In June 1974, at the height of Alice Cooper's mock-hanging act, a thirteen-year-old boy from Calgary, Canada, hung himself by the neck until he was dead at a copy-cat 'hanging party'. (Alice dropped the item from his act after this tragedy.) In November 1978, a male Kiss fan in Baltimore gave himself severe burns trying to copy his favourite band's fire-swallowing act. Disasters like this are, thankfully, rare.

The first time the press and general public became aware of the shocking power at the disposal of an uncontrolled rock audience was at Alan Freed's first concert promotion, on 21st March, 1952, at the Cleveland Arena. With 2.5 people after each seat, the music was all but inaudible. One stabbing and five arrests for drunkenness later, police and fire reinforcements were called in and the concert stopped.

When Bill Haley toured Europe in 1957, seats were smashed at concert halls across the continent and there was a virtual running battle at a show in Berlin. For the most part, the papers treated it all as good, clean fun but, on 5th February 1957, Haley arrived in London's Waterloo Station to be greeted by a near riot. 'You saw all around faces turned upwards, crumpled in fear by now, the ecstasy gone,' wrote George Gale in the *Daily Express*; 'angry faces trying to touch the car and see the face inside; faces bewildered like faces in the panic scenes of Russian films.'

The fans, wrote Gale, who witnessed the 'riot', were 'children tossed like jetsam in the swaying human tide'. Professing indifference to rock'n'roll and Haley, Gale described the scene as 'very nasty'. Next to his column, the paper printed a 'Warning' notice, telling its readers that 'preparations are being made to start a new trend' to replace rock'n'roll. Even something 'very nasty' could be tolerated if it was destined to be short-lived. But the fans knew what they wanted and, although often exaggerated in the press, the delinquent behaviour continued.

After Haley and the fifties came Beatlemania, a curious mixture of riotous assembly, political sycophancy and trendy exuberance in which almost everybody seemed to participate, from Prime

137

Ministers who knew a vote-catcher when they saw one, to society hostesses who knew what made cocktails go with a zing, to crippled teenagers whose earnest guardians persuaded the Beatles to meet their charges for a sort of laying-on of hands. Pop psychologists and sociologists explained that Beatlemania was a natural stage of adolescence, women's page journalists described how, even as jaded thirty-year-olds, they enjoyed a good scream. Almost everybody agreed that rock rioting was probably fun – they all had one reason or another to pretend to be fans.

Even doctors got into the act. Some declared that the Beatles 'were not sexy' – an analysis presumably meant to comfort the parents of teenage girls swept up by hysteria. Another declared that Beatlemania was like 'the frenzied dancing and shouting of voodoo worshippers', learnedly noting that 'beat music has a rhythmic stimulation on the brain' which induced behaviour rather like an epileptic fit. However, such distasteful analogies were not designed to prove that Beatlemania was harmful. On the contrary, sociologist J. B. Mays noted that while he couldn't say whether Beatlemania actually reduced the incidence of juvenile delinquency, 'it does syphon off a great deal of surplus juvenile energy into socially innocuous channels'. Thank heavens for that.

Meanwhile, the police were struggling to contain vast crowds at concerts and before concerts – in one case, taking almost an hour to restore order among fans queueing for Beatles' tickets in Newcastle-Upon-Tyne. An editorial in the *New Statesman* (written by Paul Johnson), described the 'menace of Beatlism' in much the same way as Bill Haley's Waterloo 'riot' had been written about a few years earlier. The Beatles themselves had, by the end of 1963, to travel with 35 guards in tow. Their popularity was such that within a week of revealing a taste for jelly babies, they had apparently received in the post over 100lbs of the confection – not counting the ones thrown to them on stage. As 1964 was about to begin, the owner of the Cavern Club announced that he was intending to break up the club stage and sell pieces of it for charity. 'This is the most sought after wood in the world,' he said, of an event echoed in the late seventies, when Bill Graham, owner of the Fillmore West, did exactly the same with that hall's considerably larger dance-floor.

The Beatles, for all the distaste they inspired in some people, were cultivated as relatively harmless symbols of new, jolly, swinging England. The Rolling Stones, who followed them, were a little less polite and, consequently, their fans were considered a little more dangerous. The Stones inspired riots across the world from Warsaw to Los Angeles and, with each one, a new shock headline. At first, the Stones were presented as part of the rhythm and blues scene, and Mick Jagger made this immortal comment about his potential fans: 'I hope they don't think we're a rock'n'roll group.' But the Stones' attachment to black music was in itself rather shocking, and the rapid abandonment of any group uniform, combined with hair that was noticeably longer than the Beatles' and an act that involved a certain amount of lascivious

138

Below: Beat music. Danish police use batons to quell a riot in Copenhagen following a showing of Rock Around The Clock, 8th August, 1 Rock'n'roll was an instant hit . . .

The New York

Four Young Singers Pay a Call on the Qu

AT DOCKSIDE

*ht: Baby, please don't go. A desperate fan tries for a glimpse of the
ling Stones as they leave the Los Angeles Sports Arena after a show,
December, 1965.*

STONE BONKERS!

*Law and disorder. Beatlemania comes to Atlantic City, New Jersey, in
December 1964.*

movement, especially from Jagger, soon won the Stones the undying hostility of many members of the press. Even the music press was uncertain whether to praise or to bury them. As early as the summer of 1963, one reviewer in the *New Musical Express* could be found comparing the group to 'long-haired dervishes' und in March 1964, the staid *Melody Maker* printed an article under the eye-catching title: 'Would You Let Your Daughter Go With A Rolling Stone?'

The non-rock press delighted in reporting all the bad news about the Stones – they were the ugliest group in the world, they didn't wash their hair, hate mail accused them of being filthy and vicars and country justices remarked on the decline of Britain's moral welfare, as though the Rolling Stones had brought it all about. It must be said that the Stones themselves encouraged much of this, not even displaying the mocking deference that marked the Beatles' early relations with the press and the authorities. As manager Andrew Oldham once said: 'For the Stones bad news is good news.'

The Stones toured the US in 1964 and, in the wake of Beatlemania, found themselves often playing behind a line of policemen. Much of the publicity in America had been generated by a taxing regime of photo-calls and TV appearances, which the Stones undertook with no evident discrimination. Dean Martin, hosting the show featuring the group, introduced them with a tedious series of studied insults. 'Their hair is not that long,' he said, 'it's just they've got smaller foreheads and higher eyebrows.' He joked about a 'Hair-pulling contest with the Beatles' and introduced an acrobat on the show as the group's father. 'He's been trying to kill himself ever since,' said Martin. While Dino was playing up the neanderthal image beloved of the British press, others noted the group's sex appeal. 'To women, Jagger looks fascinating,' said *Vogue*, 'to men a scare.'

It was a combination designed to sell records, and engender fan worship. By the end of the US tour (which had started quietly enough), the group were greeted by a riot at Carnegie Hall. A month after their return to England, 50 fans had to be taken to hospital after a show in Blackpool. A grand piano was pushed off stage and destroyed and chandeliers were wrenched off the ceiling. It took a hundred men to quieten the crowd down. 'It wasn't more than twenty that really started it off,' said Jagger the next day, 'They sort of pushed their way to the front. I saw some girls being punched in the stomach and it was really violent and horrible.' The show had to be stopped and the Stones pulled off, leaving their instruments and

Death in Cincinnati. One of eleven people killed in rock's worst concert disaster to date. Thousands of fans, queueing in near-freezing conditions for a Who gig, stampeded into the Riverfront Coliseum on 2nd December, 1979. The fans thought they had heard the band start to play and trampled the victims to death in a mad rush to get a good position in the hall.

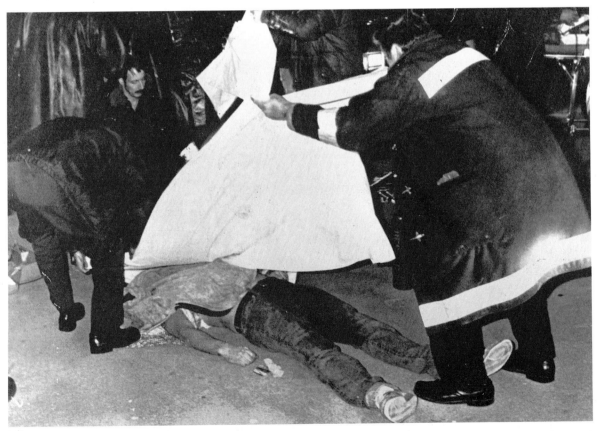

amplifiers at the mercy of the rampaging crowd. There were subsequent riots in Belfast and The Hague and near riots in Manchester and Jersey. In October 1964, 150 fans were arrested in Paris after a Stones concert at the Olympia, as the audience rampaged through the concert-hall foyer and into the streets. The next year, fans rioted when the Stones flew into Sydney, Australia. Twenty girls were crushed, two seriously, as the airport crowd burst through fences in an attempt to get closer to the group. By the time Jagger, Wyman and Brian Jones appeared in court in July, 1965, charged with insulting behaviour after pissing against a garage wall on their way back from a gig, the Stones were well on the way to becoming a fully-fledged 'public menace'.

Beatlemania and Stonesmania meant that rock rapidly acquired an elaborate paraphernalia of control – high stages, security guards, crowd barriers. These were anathema to fans and their very presence often turned the rush to the stage into the riots the security measures were supposed to prevent. The Beatles retired from live performances in 1966, but the paraphernalia surrounding their big venues has remained. So have the riots, which have become a regular feature of rock shows wherever they're held.

Between 500 and 1,000 Led Zeppelin fans – known for disorderly conduct – rioted at the Orange Bowl in Miami in the small hours of 17th April, 1977. On this occasion the fans feared the tickets for a Zep show in Tampa would be sold out before the official on-sale time, 8.30 in the morning. The rioters broke seats, windows, lawn-mowers and loud-speakers. They vandalized offices and left a trail of debris behind them. Just after 4am the police arrived, to be followed by a SWAT (Special Weapons and Tactics) team. About 200 people threw a hail of rocks on the police, who opened up with teargas to disperse the crowd. One rioter was arrested for allegedly pulling a .357 Magnum revolver on a policeman.

In May 1979, Elton John played Leningrad for the first time. Around 2,500 Russian fans, starved of rock music, paid up to £75 each to buy black market tickets. After a 2½ hour show, many of them clearly felt worked up enough to surge to the front of the stage. Had it not been for the fact that many of the audience were specially selected as stolid servants of the state who remained in their seats, the crush would have no doubt been considerably worse. As it was, the aisles were swamped with cheering, stamping fans demanding an encore from Elton. The star obliged with a rendition of *Back In The USSR*. 'I didn't plan to sing that song,' he said, 'it just came to me.'

Too often in recent years, as at the Miami Orange Bowl, crowd control has broken down before the fans even get inside the auditorium. Concerts run like military operations can expect at times to have casualties more appropriate to a small war. The worst incident to date took place on the evening of 3rd December 1979, just before a gig by the Who at the Cincinnati Riverfront Coliseum. Over 18,000 tickets had been sold within 90 minutes of the box office opening. They were mostly for 'festival seating', which meant that the

Festivals seemed fun. A girl indulges her fantasies of freedom at the Isle of Wight Festival, August 1969, which drew 150,000 people to hear a bill topped by Bob Dylan.

earlier you got to the hall, the nearer you got to the front. By the early evening of the day of the concert, there were already some 8,000 fans waiting for admission. The show was scheduled to start at 8pm, but at seven o'clock the doors were still closed. Possibly because someone heard the band doing a sound check inside and thought the show had started, possibly also because of the size and impatience of the previously good-humoured crowd, a glass door was smashed and the fans swept into the hall. Before the show had even started, there were eleven people dead and eight injured.

Blame has since been directed at festival seating (which increases the gate while decreasing the need for ticket staff), and the lack of sufficient guards or police with large enough powers, at the tardiness of the hall or the band, and even at the fans themselves described as 'animals' by one editor. In an echo of every official criticism of rock'n'roll since the fifties, New York's deputy police chief, Gerald Kevins, accused the Who – along with Kiss, Led Zeppelin and Earth, Wind and Fire – of 'whipping the kids into a frenzy'.

Whatever the precise cause of the tragedy, it is only surprising that a similar tragedy had not happened before Cincinnati. Indeed, the Riverfront Coliseum itself had been the scene of two earlier 'serious crowd incidents', as *Time* magazine wrote, at a 1976 Elton

141

John concert and a 1977 Led Zeppelin concert. Pete Townshend thought the problem was the wrong sort of control. 'People in large numbers *need* controlling,' he admitted. 'They're like cattle.' But the question remains, as Townshend himself noted, whether fans are willing to be controlled.

Back in the sixties, the sense of the rock community on the West Coast was a powerful myth. But on the other hand, the history of Haight-Ashbury has already had to be rewritten to counterbalance the summer of love with an influx of weekend hippies, hard drugs and bad vibes. Things were never as rosy as they seemed, love was never as universal as it was imagined to be. The famous Woodstock Festival in August 1969, when half a million fans gathered in a field in upstate New York was rather less of a celebration of love and peace than most people assumed at the time and, like Monterey, rather more like a sordid story of rip-offs, near-disasters, mismanagement and bad acid. But, deluded or not, people spoke of 'Woodstock Nation' with conviction – they wanted to believe in the ability of people to organize their own lives, in the community of rock, in the shared commitment of performers and fans. Even the established press, amazed at the generally peaceful demeanour of 500,000 fans, could credit that this might just be, as Grace Slick had said on stage, 'a new dawn'.

The rude awakening came with Altamont, the free festival at a California speedway track, held on 6th December 1969, and organized by the Grateful Dead and the Rolling Stones as a sort of West Coast Woodstock. The promoter of the Stones' 1969 nationwide tour of America, John Ellsworth Jaymes, said: 'It's a Christmas and Hanukkah gift from the Stones and other groups to American youth.' In view of later events, Mr Jaymes was being a trifle starry-eyed. Early reports from Altamont were equally starry-eyed. 'The scene was very peaceful,' said the San Francisco *Examiner and Chronicle* as the event was just ending. 'The youthful auditors sat on the soil, smoked pot or drank wine, talked or slept – and listened.' 'We should be together,' trumpeted the headline, adding, 'and boy, were they together.' But the newspapers had not heard the news.

From the start, things went wrong. The show, originally scheduled to be held in the Golden Gate Park, had to be switched to the Altamont venue at the last minute, because of a disagreement about film rights. As a result, tens of thousands of fans got lost and the roads were blocked for miles around. As the music started (the first set was from Santana) things began to look bad among the 300,000 strong crowd.

- Hell's Angels battled with fans who tried to mount the stage. The Angels had been hired to keep the peace and they were paid with a few hundred dollars' worth of beer. As a result, they grew increasingly violent – perhaps in response to an increasingly worked-up audience. They knocked Jefferson Airplane's singer Marty Balin unconscious during a performance, but when the band stopped playing, tension in the crowd

Ants are better organized. An aerial view of the Altamont festival, 6th December, 1969, where the festival scene found some perspective.

grew worse and another Angel threatened to beat up Paul Kantner. Four of the 'peace-keeping force' beat up a drunk who had kicked one of their precious choppers; some others decided to punish a grossly fat young man who had removed all his clothes – offended by the sight, the Angels clubbed him to the ground. Things got so bad that the Grateful Dead decided not to play, but the Stones reckoned that they would cause even more trouble if they pulled out at this stage.

Jagger was brought face-to-face with the simmering violence as soon as he stepped from the Stones' helicopter. A young man leapt out of the crowd and hit him in the face. 'I hate you!' he was screaming; 'I'm gonna kill you!' Once on stage, Jagger went into his diabolic routine, prancing around for *Jumping Jack Flash* and *Sympathy For The Devil*. Meanwhile the Angels saw a young black called Meredith Hunter pull a gun and aim it at the stage (or so they testified at a

A Christmas and Hanukkah present from the Rolling Stones, the Altamont festival in December 1969 brought the Love Generation to a halt. With four deaths, three births and countless other trip-outs, ODs and injuries, first-aid teams ran out of essential medication.

subsequent trial). They clubbed him with pool cues, beat him with fists and chains and stabbed him five times in the back and once under his ear so that he bled to death. Hunter's gun was never found, but a court agreed it was 'justifiable homicide'. Justifiable or not, nobody seemed able or willing to stop the madness that seemed to take over Altamont.

Robert Santelli, in a book about rock festivals, points out that at Woodstock, for all its faults, the stage became a channel for messages, warnings, information and reassurance. At Altamont it was merely a stage. The Stones, scared to keep playing, at first appealed to the crowd. When that had no effect, they became even more scared to stop, playing for their lives as the rock 'community' shattered all around them. They were stars, the fans were fans – and that was that.

Within two days, the press had changed its tune about Altamont. Most of the fans there had already changed theirs. The *San Francisco Chronicle* headlined a front page piece, 'The Black Aftermath of Altamont'. While three babies were born during the event, three

other people besides Hunter died, and there was a host of serious injuries. Two people died when a car ploughed into their campfire at around midnight on the night after the concert, and another man was killed when he slid into the California Aqueduct Canal while on an acid trip. A man and a woman were hospitalized with severe head and internal injuries. Four medical teams at the site reported treating numerous people for overdoses and bad trips – an emergency supply of sedatives had to be flown in when the medical teams ran out. 'A sea of empty wine bottles and other refuse covered the speedway area...' said the *Chronicle*. 'Officers said several hundred cars were left at the scene, apparently broken down, out of gas or lost by their owners in the mass exodus ...' It would take a week to clean up the remains of this particular present for Christmas and Hanukkah.

As for the Hell's Angels security guards, Melvin Belli, the lawyer retained to represent the Stones said, 'They might have been a little too enthusiastic.' 'If Jesus had been there,' said Jagger, 'he would have been crucified.' Keith Richard commented lamely that 'lots of people were tired and a few tempers were frayed'. The Angels themselves defended their behaviour, saying that they had been hired to 'keep people off the stage'. 'I'm no peace-creep in any sense of the world,' said Sonny Barger, president of the

143

Oakland Chapter of the Angels, who provided the guards. 'If a man don't want to be my friend, I'm going to hurt him and he's going to hurt me.'

The violence and deaths at Altamont have made that festival part of the 'rock'n'roll frame of reference', while the Cincinnati deaths are all but forgotten. The reason of course is that no-one was surprised by Cincinnati – shocked, certainly, but not surprised. The deaths of those eleven unfortunate fans failed to impinge on the rock culture because, during the seventies, violence, whether pre-meditated or accidental, had become commonplace. Ten years earlier the deaths at Altamont were unexpected, brutal and not all accidental, producing both a collective revulsion and an endorsement of gratuitous violence that was to reverberate throughout rock for a decade.

The eighties saw the emergence of the most convincing and successful (if not the first) female Elvis impersonator in the androgynous shape of k.d. lang – lower case darling of the lesbian new country scene. At one time vast numbers of fans may have styled themselves on Elvis or the Beatles, Bob Dylan or Janis Joplin. They did not consider themselves lookalikes because the look was more or less universal. But care, attention and money were necessary to look like the glitter and glam stars of the past decades. Among David Bowie's or Madonna's fans, there have been coteries who assiduously cultivated the clothes, make-up, hairstyles and mannerisms of their idols. There were even successful lookalike bands – Bjorn Again's homage to Abba is a case in point.

In time, the process became institutionalized. Clubs held Bowie nights when fans tried their hardest to look like the man. BBC TV publicized a Deborah Harry lookalike contest (won by a receptionist from Newcastle-upon-Tyne); Alice Cooper even organized his own Alice lookalike competition (won by a Vietnam veteran on day release from a mental hospital).

Lookalikes even took to the professional or semi-professional stage. Today, there are dozens of Elvis impersonators – some who merely dress up like Elvis (including a Dr Reco H. Shane who, despite rhinestones and jet-black pudding basin hair, looks and sounds exactly like the Beverly Hills dentist that he is), some who look like Elvis (Malcolm Halsall from Scunthorpe, for example, who performs professionally under the name Rupert), some who change their names to Elvis, some who have plastic surgery to make themselves look like Elvis (professional impersonator Dennis Wise says he underwent surgery for over a year because 'I wanted to do something for

Elvis'). There has been at least one Jimi Hendrix impersonator (an old friend of his named Randy Hansen), and there have been several Mick Jagger impersonators (including, though he might not admit it, Bob Geldof). In the late seventies, a group of five necrophiliac performers billing themselves as 'Rock'n'Roll Heaven', underwent plastic surgery to make themselves look like Janis Joplin, Jim Morrison, Jim Croce and one male and one female Elvis. What is remarkable about all these people is not the lengths to which they have gone to impersonate dead (or living) stars, but the fact that audiences are often willing to recognize them as acceptable substitutes.

While some fans try and bridge the gap by physically copying their heroes, the increasing inability of rock stars and their fans to achieve a genuine intimacy has also led to violence by fans against performers who distance themselves on stage. In Germany, fans have learnt to throw cans at groups who displeased them. Toledo, Ohio, is known as the firework capital of rock'n'roll since fireworks are popular missiles at rock concerts in that city. In 1976, flying cans and bottles injured more than 50 people at an open-air Queen concert in London. The year before, a fan threw ketchup onto Elvin Bishop's jeans while he was performing in Florida and then broke a roadie's hand with his buckled belt. Lou Reed has been threatened with a knife on stage and in 1979, Cheap Trick's road manager, Kirk Dyer, was cut in the chest, ribs, arm and thigh when he tried to stop a knife-wielding fan from storming the stage at a Texas gig. In the same year, an Australian fan decided to pick a fight with Jerry Lee Lewis on stage. The two men fell against a monitor and Lewis broke several ribs, forcing him to cancel the rest of his tour. In one truly bizarre incident, the American group Wild Cherry were threatened with physical assault as they arrived for a performance. The threat was not, as one might imagine, intended to dissuade the group from playing but to *encourage* them. At the end of their set some of the group and their entourage were attacked anyway.

British punk groups (and some Americans), partly inspired by an antagonism towards the accepted ideas of stardom, cultivated violent abuse as a mode of performance. But punk was a style of dress and attitude almost before it was a type of rock'n'roll music, and more than most other styles, its fans were responsible for its existence in the first place.

It was composed of disparate strands. Out-of-work East End kids with no focus for their discontent, who only found that authority and other people's wealth were oppressive; art college students with a heady disregard for convention and a need for a style of their own; fans whose dreams of a passionate democracy of music had been trampled on by the lumbering mammoth of mid-seventies rock; experimentalists, anarchists and the ill-fitting rebels of a society in mid-collapse; kids who were having no fun, and found that even their anger had no outlet. 'Bored, denied, used, cheated, manipulated, ignored – this is what happens to the youth, the future of Britain,' wrote one London punk in one of the scores of fanzines that sprang up as

Rock'n'roll heaven: five singers who were surgically altered to resemble dead stars, 1978. Standing from the left are Elvis Presley (Erin Rhyne) and Elvis Presley (Jesse Bolt). Sitting from the left are Janis Joplin (Mona Caywood Moore), Jim Croce (Marc Hane Brouck) and Jim Morrison (Duke O'Connell).

Spot the difference Deborah Harry 'lookalikes' during a competition run by a British magazine in October 1979. The judges agreed that Ruth Merritt aged eighteen (top row, second right) was a ringer for Debbie.

an integral part of the punk scene. 'I'm seventeen-years-old and haven't got one qualification at all,' said another, proud to possess 'the most important asset . . . common sense.' 'In July 1976 I was knocking around with a few Bowie/Roxy freaks,' said a third. 'They were going to see Slaughter and the Dogs . . . also on the bill were the Buzzcocks and the Sex Pistols. It was exciting, raw, funny, I knew straight away it was for me. It was the first time I'd really got into anything.' The punks talked of energy, spontaneity, a life without rules, a life with 'nobody to answer to, nobody to satisfy, nobody to call "sir",' as Danny Baker, co-founder of celebrated punk fanzine *Sniffin' Glue*, put it, before he found true street cred advertising soap powder and chocolate bars on British TV. Split a T-shirt, hold the rent together with a safety pin and, bingo, a fashion. Rave about a band, find a photocopier, and *voilà*, a magazine.

Picking up on the New York scene, some people adopted music which had for a long time been called 'punk' because it manifested the same youthful disregard for convention, skill and morality suggested by the word's earlier meaning – the young, homosexual companion of a male tramp. The fetishistic clothing of the increasingly evident sexual fringe was taken up because it, too, pointed to experimentation, youthful sexual licence and a desire to shock.

It all gelled around the music: anger, frustration, rebellion, experimentation and delight focused on the sound and sight of groups of often incompetent musi-

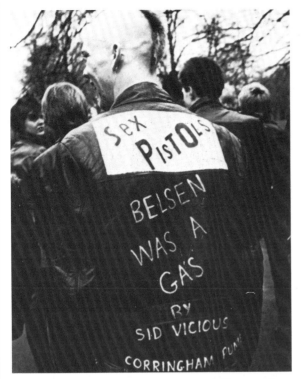

Remember me this way. The 1980 Sid Vicious Memorial Demonstration on the first anniversary of his death. Stars get the fans they deserve – or is it the other way round?

fucking sick of you fucking Californians driving your fucking Cadillacs! You're so fucking bored, you don't know what to fucking do!' Instead of simply negating stardom, the band had become anti-stars, with a massive anti-following of anti-fans. They were out of context, and their punk violence was a sham.

One way of avoiding the problems of confronting fans on stage is of course not to appear on stage at all. That was the solution the Beatles hit upon when, by 1966, they began to see their performances as meaningless and potentially dangerous ritual appearances. They retreated into the studio, never to perform live again. Since then, many star rock groups have spent extended periods avoiding live performance. But at the time the Beatles retired, the step was sufficiently risky to convince many people that it meant the end of the group's career. At around the same time, Bob Dylan took an enforced eighteen month break from performing and recording, following his near-fatal motor cycle crash. Most people assumed that nobody could ever come back after eighteen months out of the public eye. The effect of these retreats was, however, quite the reverse of most predictions. Both Dylan and the Beatles continued to be even more successful recording artists.

When Dylan returned to live performance in the seventies, he seemed to have acquired an extra-ordinary popularity. His first 'come-back' tour, eight years after the crash, attracted six million ticket applications from American fans alone – ten applications for every seat available. Similarly, Bruce Springsteen's 1981 European tour was a complete sell-out, after a five year gap and a disastrous tour in 1975 preceded by a risible media hype. But then Springsteen is one of the few present-day superstars who does seem to comprehend the importance of the star-fan relationship.

But his attitude was all but submerged from 1966, until the punks insisted on bringing it back ten years later. In the intervening decade, confronted by the barrier of the stars' physical absence and by the mysterious depths of songs no longer designed for live performance, fans frequently adopted a sort of code-breaking mentality. To learn the secret language of Bob Dylan and the Beatles would somehow compensate for not being able to see them perform. One would at least be hearing their *authentic* voices. Superstars like the Beatles and Dylan, no doubt fuelled by artistic pretensions and large amounts of halluginogenic drugs, were only too happy to oblige.

Secret messages – hidden in stereo tracking or run-off tracks or disguised in cover artwork – were all the vogue for a while. By late 1969, it was even possible for an elaborate hoax about secret messages to gain credence across the world. An American student publication, *Rat Magazine*, printed an alarming and arcane article in its issue of 29th October, 'proving' that Paul McCartney had died and the fact had been covered up. 'Knowing that perhaps the ruse couldn't last, the Beatles have hinted at the truth in every successive album,' the article said. 'On the *Sgt. Pepper*

cians playing as if their lives depended on it, but not really caring. It didn't matter what the music was like – because it was the music that had created, in Johnny Rotten's words, 'the entire superband system' and which, accordingly, stood in the way of rock'n'roll touching its audiences. If you were a punk fan, you felt you could become a punk musician.

Spitting (or gobbing), hurling insults and sharp objects, or merely sneering and snarling were as important a part of late seventies' punk performances as playing. As if to demonstrate their contempt for stardom, groups like the Sex Pistols or the Damned turned abuse and violence on their audiences, and the punk fans, who understood what was going on, retaliated by fighting, clawing each other or throwing cans and bottles.

Too often, however, punk groups found themselves gobbing against the wind. In becoming stars, (albeit small-scale ones), they would often have to face audiences who came specially to witness the spectacle of violence. Critic Richard Cromelin of the *Los Angeles Times* panned the Damned on the 1977 tour of the US for not being 'as rude and obnoxious as advertised'. The day after the Cromelin review appeared, the Damned took the stage at an LA club under a hail of ice cubes, bottles and coins. Drummer Rat Scabies threw his drumsticks at the audience, challenging them to a fight. Bassist Captain Sensible took off all his clothes (a nurse's dress and tights) and paraded round the stage. The band's manager joined them on stage to shout 'I'm

Diabolical wizard, proto-punk or plain murderous con? Charles Manson believed the Beatles were sending him messages in songs. His lawyers tried to call John Lennon as a defence witness for his trial on murder charges (23rd April, 1971).

album centrefold (*sic.* – it's actually on the cover), only Paul faces away from the camera . . . On the *Magical Mystery Tour* insert, only Paul wears a black rose . . . *Revolution No. 9* on the double album contains the phrase "I buried Paul" when played backwards . . . *Abbey Road* shows the Beatles walking in single file. The first two, John and Ringo, wear mourning clothes, "Paul" is barefoot and dressed for burial, George follows in the work clothes of an English grave-digger.'

In no time at all, the clues mounted: the juxtaposition of the two final tracks on *Revolver*, *Got To Get You Into My Life* and *Tomorrow Never Knows*, clearly pointed to McCartney's death in a car crash (*Tomorrow* was loosely based on Tim Leary's interpretation of *The Tibetan Book of the Dead*). *Sgt. Pepper* contained a picture of a fat man waving (an Eastern death symbol, said the secret agents), a four-stringed guitar (clearly an electric bass) outlined in flowers and Paul with his back turned. On *Sgt. Pepper* Paul is shown wearing an arm-band with the initials O.P.D. – said to be London police terminology meaning 'officially pronounced dead', in fact standing for nothing more sinister than Ontario Police Department. *Magical Mystery Tour's* walrus was supposed to be a Viking death symbol. One photograph of McCartney in the 'M.M.T.' booklet shows him seated above a sign that says 'I Was'. The

White Album was littered with secret messages hidden in the tracks – things like 'Miss him, miss him' and 'Turn me on dead, man'. Then, of course, there was the Volkswagen pictured on the cover of *Abbey Road*. Its number plate read, in part, 281F, or, the afficionados pronounced, he'd be *28 if* he was still alive.

Even a sound analyst from the University of Miami got into the act by announcing that scientific evidence proved that Paul's voice had changed more than it was humanly possible since the first Beatles' records. Others discovered a more direct route to the 'truth'. Gazing long enough at the cover of *Magical Mystery Tour* a sufficiently stoned fan might detect a seven figure telephone number picked out in the stars that made the 'Beatles' (I came up with 832–7135). Most of those who undertook this exercise, (and many did, ringing up to try and contact the ghost of Paul McCartney), found themselves connected to the hapless industrial editor of a national British newspaper, but the 'Paul is dead' story itself took a long time to die. McCartney's only comment was to say that he hadn't heard of his own death, but then he was 'always the last person to know of anything in the Beatles'.

The success of this hoax demonstrated just how loony fans can be. But there have been worse examples. Most tragically was the case of the Tate-LaBianca killings in 1969, when the psychotic petty criminal and failed song-writer Charles Manson deluded himself and his Californian followers into believing that the Beatles' White Album contained confirmation of his lunatic neo-Nazi theories. Having predicted a bloody race war from which he and his followers ('the Family') would emerge as survivors and leaders, Manson interpreted several songs on the White Album, (*Blackbird*, *Piggies*, *Revolution 1*, *Revolution 9* and, most notoriously, *Helter Skelter*), as support for his fantastic visions. 'The Beatles are telling it like it is' he used to say to the Family. 'Helter Skelter' became Manson's name for the race war. Convinced that the conflict needed a little encouragement (and, presumably, imagining that he had the tacit backing of the Beatles), he ordered Family members to commit a series of brutal murders (including that of movie actress Sharon Tate and her house party). To help throw blame onto black militants, Manson instructed his assassins to daub slogans like 'Death to pigs', 'Pig' and 'Helter Skelter' around the murder sites in the victims' blood.

For the Beatles themselves, even this particularly gruesome association was no more than an embarrassment. Despite a much-publicized but somewhat half-hearted attempt to call John Lennon as a witness for the defence at Manson's trial, it barely impinged on their lives.

Even when fans actually pursue stars after-hours, the result is usually little more than a mild irritation. They hang around the stars' houses, or outside recording studios, hotels and stage doors, but usually they will settle for a glimpse or an autograph. For some stars, even such relatively harmless displays of interest and affection are more than they would wish to handle. 'Imagine sitting in a house like this, nice as it

Daily Mail

Archbishop prays as millions join last, silent tribute to John Lennon

HE FINA AREWEL

THE Sun

ursday, December 11, 1980   12p

TODAY'S TV: PAGES 14 and 15

STARTS TODAY A super Sun exclusive on superstar Lennon

THE WILD WAYS OF JOKER JOHN

TODAY'S FASCINATING EPISODE — CENTRE PAGES

Newsweek

THE INTERNATIONAL NEWSMAGAZINE   December 22, 1980

John Lennon 1940-1980

Number 51

WHY DID HE MURDER MY DADDY?

From COL ALLEN in New York

HEARTBROKEN Yoko Ono told last night how she explained John Lennon's death to their five-year-old son, Sean.

The bewildered little boy had asked her: Why was my daddy killed? She spoke out only minutes before the former Beatle was secretly cremated.

Lennon was gunned down by 25-year-old Mark Chapman in New York on Tuesday.

In an

Yoko's sad talk

```
PRESS 12    2345 HRS    12-8-80    20 PCT
1 W.72 ST. . REPORT OF A MAN SHOT.
VICTIM REMOVED TO ROOSEVELT HOSP.
NOTHING FURTHER AT THIS TIME.
OPER UNIT- PO VAN ARSDALE
```

Left: The first police teletype report of a shooting on New York's West 72nd Street. The victim turned out to be John Lennon.
Below: Bagged for the last time. John and Yoko had appeared publicly in bags during their 'political' period in the early seventies. In a final irony, John Lennon's body was removed for cremation in a bag, 10th December, 1980.

Left: Mark Chapman, handcuffed and hidden by a blanket, is led away to face charges for the murder of John Lennon.

is,' said Barry Gibb of the Bee Gees during the height of their popularity, 'and not being able to go outside because of all those people going past.' 'It's like living in a goldfish bowl,' he said, echoing the star's eternal lament.

Once the illusions have been put on the market, it is no easy matter to withdraw them from sale. For star and fan alike, these illusions are often their most precious possessions – the means of achievement and success for one, the dream of achievement and success for the other. When Mark Chapman killed John Lennon, Lennon had just re-emerged from five years' retirement. He had tried to be an ordinary resident of New York City, made a point of being part of the street scene, chatting to people openly, even autographing an album, a few days before he died, for the man who would shoot him. He may have got away with the pose of Ordinary Joe under other circumstances, but not with a new album in the charts. That made him a star again and reminded the public that he had once been a

Beatle. To try and be an ordinary, home-loving, bread-baking husband and father *and* an ex-Beatle was a supreme exercise in cake-eating and having. To do that in public through the medium of press and broadcast interviews, releasing records celebrating his ordinariness and his successful passage through the dark night of Beatleness, was an affront to a fan like Chapman who virtually worshipped Lennon.

The consensus among many commentators on the circumstances of the Lennon shooting was that Chapman thought he was destroying a symbol, not killing a human being. This is a comforting thought, perhaps, but entirely wrong. Chapman knew he was killing a man – the man that he was not. But he was also murdering himself, or at least that part of himself that had made the journey with Lennon from stardom towards an attempted ordinariness. 'I don't believe in God . . . I don't believe in Beatles,' Lennon had sung. In the ten years that followed, Lennon's rough edges were planed down and he re-emerged, with Yoko, on the *Double Fantasy* album as a complacent homebody, but still a star. If he had kept his passion or lost his popularity, things might have been different. As it was, the 1980 version of John Lennon measured for Mark Chapman his own failure. Lennon was privileged enough to *want* to be ordinary. Chapman could never accept such an ambition for his idol, any more than he could come to terms with his own in-

ability to be extraordinary.

After the shooting, the BBC interviewed some people on the streets of Liverpool. One of them said that Lennon should never have left his home town. It had been a kind of betrayal, and his death a kind of punishment. When the Beatles moved to London in the sixties, their local fans in the north west held a demonstration against them. London meant stardom, meant separation, and the local kids who had breathed life into the Mersey scene knew that it was they who would be left behind. One of the group's earliest fans recalled to Liverpudlian writer Mike Evans how they felt the night Bob Wooler, the Cavern's DJ, announced that *Please, Please Me* had reached Number One. 'It was awful, because the reaction was the opposite to what they expected. Everyone was stunned. That was the end of it as far as we were concerned.'

There is an ironic postscript to the Chapman story. The killer's autographed copy of *Double Fantasy* was left outside the Dakota building after Lennon had been shot. It was propped against the wall at the spot where Chapman had been standing, reading *Catcher In The Rye*, while he waited for John and Yoko to come home on the night of 8th December, 1980. A fan picked it up and handed it in to the police. They returned it to the finder, who at once became the possessor of one of rock's most treasured relics. From the jail cell where he is now serving twenty years, Chapman announced his intention to sue for the album's recovery. His aim, said his lawyer, was to auction the album and give the proceeds to the American hand-gun control lobby.

I know what it's like to be dead. Fans mourn John Lennon outside the Dakota Building in New York, where he lived and was shot by one of their number.

BLINDED BY THE LIGHT

In 1956, an American Pentecostalist minister named Albert Carter condemned rock'n'roll as irreligious. 'The effect of rock and roll on young people,' said the minister, 'is to turn them into devil worshippers; to stimulate self-expression through sex; to provoke lawlessness; impair nervous stability and destroy the sanctity of marriage. It is an evil influence on the youth of our country.' While most teenagers might have answered, 'Right on!', the first flush of rock'n'roll resulted in moral panic – an outburst of fervent condemnation which ran from Reverend Carter's diatribe through the censorship of songs and performers to the elevation of an American payola investigation in 1959 to the status of national crisis.

The rockers themselves were deeply affected by all this. Many of them came from religious backgrounds from among the black or poor white communities; Elvis, for instance, never cast off the yoke of belief that supports Southern fundamentalist Christianity. He acknowledged his debt to God as a matter of course; it was more significant by its casual acceptance than any debt he might have thought he owed to human beings, his fans or the democratic system. Under attack for his lewd performances, Elvis would appear in public as a humble, god-fearing boy. He survived the moral outrage of the time because he thought he could challenge God on His own ground. Others, however, were less certain of their righteousness.

Confused by the significance of what he was doing and condemned for marrying his thirteen-year-old cousin, Jerry Lee Lewis was forced into temporary retirement. Rock'n'roll, he has always said, will send him to hell. 'I *know* the right way,' he said. 'I was raised a good Christian. But I couldn't make it.' Despite his conviction that Jesus Christ is not inclined to do 'a whole lotta shakin'', Jerry himself (like Elvis, a member of the evangelical Assembly of God), is unable to break himself of the habit. Riding the conflict has required a vast consumption of booze ('I used to have to drink a fifth of tequila to sober up and do my shows,' he once said), and a variety of drugs. As a result, Lewis's career has been marked by violent swings of mood and catastrophic incident. In 1979, 'strung out on pills . . . like a wild Comanche', he was pulled off stage at Baton Rouge by his cousin, TV and radio evangelist, the Rev. Jimmy Swaggart. Jimmy took him home, poured all his whisky and pills away and looked after him for a week. 'I guess it saved my

life,' said the old reprobate – a reformed character, at least until the next time.

Little Richard Penniman became a gospel student following that 'vision' on an aeroplane over Australia in 1958. ('It was at the time they sent the satellite up,' he said, 'and I was on tour with Eddie Cochran, Gene Vincent, and it was a fantastic, monstrous tour.' They couldn't, as the song goes, get much higher.) Perhaps becoming a preacher was just like joining another branch of show business, but the lure of rock'n'roll for this most flamboyant of the early black rockers was too great. He found the perfect excuse – rock'n'roll was to be the way he could 'teach love, because music is the universal language'. The Reverend Carter can't have approved, but Little Richard was not the only rocker to try and square the circle.

British rock'n'rollers were also prone to the call of God in those early days, though generally in a more quiescent manner. Brian Locking, who had backed Terry Dene before replacing Jet Harris in the Shadows, became a Jehovah's Witness, like Dene, in 1963. Hank Marvin, also from the Shadows, waited until 1973 before joining the same sect. Marvin, a father of six, seems to have been something of an exception – a successful performer who came to religion out of a positive sense of wonderment. 'I'd started to question the amazing things in nature that couldn't happen by chance,' he explained. 'I felt there really must be a creator and decided to get involved.'

The best-known convert of all in early British rock'n'roll remains Cliff Richard, who became a committed Baptist in the early sixties. Ironically, in Cliff's second film – *Expresso Bongo* (1959) – he played an innocent pop star whose manager devised the crafty strategy of having him present himself as a god-fearing, mom-loving boy in order to make the transition from teen-rave to star performer. The strategy, of course, had already been demonstrated in real life by Elvis Presley. Cliff, however, discovered a well-spring of sincerity which has enabled him to be actively involved in the evangelical movement, while periodically reviving his reputation as a raunchy rocker. When questioned as to how he can sing rock'n'roll and still support moralistic and ultraconservative organizations like the Festival of Light (anti-abortion, anti-indecency, pro-hanging and so on), Cliff resorts to a philosophy of pop values, innocent love and good, clean fun. Claiming to have remained celibate since 1965, Cliff is the perfect example of a performer who has reconciled one of rock'n'roll's central conflicts by learning how to be in two minds at once.

Ham with cheese. Cliff Richard, God's other son, accepts a gift of dairy produce from Miss Teenage State of Victoria, 19th July, 1960, on behalf of charity.

The conflict, of course, is between rock'n'roll's spirit-elevating impact and its crudely physical form and sexual symbolism. Rock'n'roll does not make you fuck, but it might make you want to fuck, or even feel like you already have. Repressive religious morality cannot tolerate anything that suggests that spiritual pleasure can be the result of physical stimulation.

The attacks on rock's irreligiosity and alleged immorality have continued through the years. In 1966, John Lennon told journalist Maureen Cleave of the London *Evening Standard* that 'Christianity will go. It will vanish and shrink. I needn't argue about that. I'm right and I will be proved right. We're more popular than Jesus now. Jesus was all right but his disciples were thick and ordinary.' This display of bravado was probably occasioned by no more than Lennon's increasing antagonism to the Beatles' 'mop top' image. As later commentators have pointed out, it was, in part, an accurate assessment – in the popularity stakes Jesus at that time was probably fourth or fifth behind Karl Marx, Mao Tse Tung and the Beatles (maybe Mohammed or Buddha or Elvis could also have given Him a run for His money). But Lennon was speaking in a Christian country and did his case no good by an ignorant comment about Christ's disciples. Inevitably a fuss ensued. It was worst in America where the extreme right of politics had already discovered the Beatles had to be communist atheists. It was only too easy for many people to believe that Lennon had advocated Beatlism as a state religion or that he had

154

claimed that Ringo Starr was the son of God.

It all added fuel to the fire of such men as the Rev. David Noebel from Billy Hargis's Christian Crusade. 'In the excitatory state that the Beatles place these youngsters into,' the Rev. David somewhat inelegantly pronounced, 'these young people will do anything they are told to do . . . One day, when the revolution is ripe, the Communists could put the Beatles on TV and could mass hypnotize American youth. This scares the wits out of me.' To the followers of David Noebel and his ilk, the day of ripeness seemed to be drawing nearer. Radio stations across the Southern states organized 'Beatles bonfires' to burn the group's records and ephemera. At first Brian Epstein and then Lennon himself were obliged to make some sort of apology. The fuss died down, but the group's image never quite recovered its middle American appeal.

Anti-rock sentiment has never disappeared among some evangelical Christians. At the end of the seventies, two 'born again' Minneapolis brothers, Steve and Jim Peters, began a career for themselves in this area. As ordained ministers, the brothers (in their mid-twenties when their crusade began), took as their text the warning that 'listening to rock music will be harmful to your spiritual, emotional and mental health'. In a little over a year, the brothers reckoned to have burnt and otherwise destroyed more than half a million dollars' worth of records, tapes and memorabilia associated with performers as diverse as Led Zeppelin and John Denver, Kiss and Linda Ronstadt (not forget-

Which one's Cliff? Evangelist Billy Graham recruits Cliff Richard (right) to the cause, at Graham's London rally, 16th June, 1966.

ting the dear old Beatles). The brothers' act featured a lecture, cunningly entitled 'What the Devil's Wrong with Rock Music?', in which they make some farcical claims, including that Mick Jagger is a 'proud and practising' homosexual, Barry Manilow is evil, Janis Joplin would have died of venereal disease if the drugs hadn't got her first, an album by the Alan Parsons Project features on its cover the veiled faces of girls with syphilitic sores, John Denver intends to become God, Kiss is an acronym for 'Kids In the Service of Satan', and the Eagles' *Hotel California* is about Satanism. Most of this is on the same level as earlier claims of extreme rightists about the Beatles. ('Norwegian wood is British teenagers' slang for marijuana' said the John Birch Society's rock spokesman, Gary Allen, about one song title; *Strawberry Fields*, he said, referred to the practice of planting marijuana in strawberry fields

because, according to Allen, the plants looked alike.)

Predictably, the Peters' paranoid version of rock'n'roll is replete with secret messages. The boys' mother, Josephine, first discovered such messages in a Beach Boys album brought home by a third brother. 'I sensed it wasn't Christian,' she said, and went on to describe how the family got rid of such Satanic instruments as the television set. 'The life-styles, lyrics, intentions and album covers of many of the rock stars,' said Steve Peters before each burning, 'are perverse, immoral, profane and unscriptural.'

It's fair to say that rock'n'roll has always stepped outside the boundaries of the established Christian churches. It is, after all, a music that espouses rebellion and eschews the order so necessary to official religion. But it has the energy, faith and abandon of less orthodox religious experiences. Theologically inclined propagandists who detect the dangers of mass hys-

Happiness is a hot disc. After Lennon remarked that the Beatles were 'more popular than Jesus', during summer 1967 Beatle burnings – like this one organized by station WAYX in Georgia – were repeated across America.

MAHARISHI'S FLYING CIRCUS

156

teria in rock performances are only observing a genuine emotional power from an external point of view. Rock'n'roll, at its best, has always been a spiritual music with roots in devotional forms (black gospel music, for example), as well as music celebrating secular ecstasy.

Two important things happened to rock in the sixties to transform the music's spiritual nature. The first was the tremendous success of large numbers of musicians who found that their power on stage was not, after all, matched by the ability to survive off it. The second was the education of a generation into a philosophy of 'love', inspired at first by the western world's infatuation with permissiveness and liberalism and fuelled by the apparently mystical revelations of LSD.

By 1967, the Beatles had stopped touring, there was growing and destructive over-indulgence among the members, Brian Epstein was being increasingly suicidal (he made his first, unsuccessful attempt in September 1966), in fact the group seemed on the verge of complete collapse. George Harrison reacted particularly strongly to the group's personal failure. Late in 1966, George and his wife Patti went to India, for George to study the sitar with one of its leading exponents, Indian musician Ravi Shankar. George's musical ambitions had already led him to experiment with the sitar in 1965. The ostensibly pastoral and mystic orient exercised a strong pull on many young westerners in the sixties, and for George Harrison, swamped in the mire of the Beatles' confusions, the sitar was more than just a novel instrument with an unusual sound – it was a repository of faith, spiritual awareness and beauty. It pointed to a way out. Ravi Shankar introduced Patti and George to his guru, Tat Baba, and the couple – who had already flirted with acid-inspired mysticism – became more and more attracted to the oriental view of life.

Back in England, word reached Patti about the Maharishi Mahesh Yogi, an Indian guru with a marketable line in meditation – a mantra-based technique backed up by some simplified and easily assimilable Hindu philosophy. The Maharishi's system was known as Transcendental Meditation (TM). The guru himself giggled a lot, clutched flowers and claimed to be bringing the West some profound and spiritual message that its materialistic, militaristic culture had ignored. (TM turned out to be so deeply spiritual and pacifistic that it was subsequently adopted by the US Navy as part of basic training, while the Maharishi eventually formed an investment organisation called The Age of Enlightenment Company.)

Patti Harrison joined the Maharishi's Spiritual Regeneration Movement in 1967, while the Beatles themselves were too busy with *Sgt. Pepper* for much meditation. The seed was sown, however, and when news broke that the Maharishi would be visiting

Britain in the summer, all four mop-tops decided to give him a try. The Beatles met the yogi in August, 1967, at a lecture in the London Hilton Hotel and agreed to accompany him to a weekend retreat in Bangor, North Wales, for a further dose of spiritual castor oil. Accompanied by wives, girlfriends, Mick Jagger and Marianne Faithfull, the Fab Four journeyed by special train from London to Bangor. The press and fans were out in full strength. The stars were sent off with screams and popping flashbulbs, the whole scene seemed awash with flowers. Jagger sneered that it was all 'more like a circus than the beginning of a religious event', and Cynthia Lennon got left behind on the platform.

While they were still in Bangor with the Maharishi's 300 other students, the press reporters brought the Beatles the news of Brian Epstein's death. It was, without doubt, a shock. Whether it had been accident, suicide or murder, it could not, however, have been a surprise. Under the circumstances, the Maharishi's advice to 'be happy' (spoken, no doubt, with a giggle) was probably as much as they could have expected from anyone, but his presence did act as a buffer. Media coverage soon guaranteed the Maharishi a solid reputation as someone who mattered to the Beatles, and the group members sang his praises and lauded meditation to the skies.

Beach Boy Dennis Wilson was the next big-name rock star to discover the Maharishi, who was, by later 1967, touring the world with his somewhat banal message. 'I shook his hand, and all of a sudden I felt this weirdness, this presence, this guy had,' said Dennis, who would later say much the same thing about Charles Manson, before the latter was revealed to be a psychopathic killer. (Dennis knew Manson as 'the Wizard' and put him and the Family up in his house for a period, during which, according to an acquaintance, the Family ran up – and Dennis paid – the biggest gonorrhoea bill in history.) Nevertheless, the Beach Boys (Mike Love in particular) were sufficiently taken with the Maharishi to become involved in TM. Can they really have been attracted by the appalling predictability which he displayed the first time he spoke to Dennis Wilson? ' "Live your life to the fullest," ' remembered Dennis, 'was the first thing he ever said to me.'

The Beach Boys, like the Beatles, were in something of a mess. In 1964, their leading light, Brian Wilson, had had a nervous breakdown and had collapsed on a plane. 'I was run down mentally and emotionally because I was running around, jumping on jets from one city to another on one-night stands,' said Brian. He was also producing, writing, arranging, singing, planning and teaching, in a punishing schedule that allowed no time for relaxation. On the occasion of his crack-up he had only been in the air five minutes when he told Al Jardine he was no longer able to cope. 'I started crying,' Wilson recalled. 'I put a pillow over my face and began screaming and yelling, and I started telling people I wasn't getting off the plane ... The rubber band had stretched as far as it would go.'

157

Brian Wilson retired to his home where he continued to compose and produce, becoming increasingly eccentric over the next couple of years. He installed a sand-box in his dining room containing eight tons of sand so he could bury his feet in it while playing the piano. He experimented with LSD and other drugs and sought to investigate 'the mind-expanding possibilities of music and the mind-expanding possibilities of drugs'. He picked up on astrology and health-foods (even opening a shop called 'The Radiant Radish'); he picked up on numerology and the *I Ching*. He radically revised his sex life ('refrains from coming' was how his wife described it). He also managed (he has since said) to destroy the tapes of an entire Beach Boys album, to have been called *Smile*, because it 'was destroying me . . . it just wasn't my kind of music'. Rumour had it that he had actually burnt the tapes, as a result of an apparent delusion that some tracks on the theme of fire had caused some buildings in Los Angeles to burn down. It may be, of course, that the appearance of *Sgt. Pepper* in 1967 was the real reason why Brian shelved *Smile*. The Beatles' album certainly ruined his self-confidence and, although many tracks from *Smile* were eventually revamped, appearing on a variety of records, Brian never again displayed the sure touch of his early career.

The rest of the group moved further adrift from their main creative talent. They refused to put their name to his songs. Brian himself has said that his drug consumption in the mid-sixties was phenomenal. 'I'd bought a lot of hashish,' he recalled on one occasion. 'It was really a large purchase, perhaps $2,000 worth . . . and the music was getting so influenced by it . . . I mean, we had to lie on the floor with the microphone next to our mouths to do the vocals.' By 1967, the group were having immense business and legal problems with their record label, Capitol, as well as bitter internecine disputes. These generally revolved round the creative hub of Brian Wilson and concerned how close each of the others felt to him; brothers Dennis and Carl Wilson tended to line up against Brian's cousin, Mike Love and his old school friend, Al Jardine.

In 1967, TM seemed to be the glue that could prevent the imminent disintegration of the group. They embraced it wholeheartedly, at least for a time, following Dennis Wilson's conversion. Mike Love and Al Jardine became teachers of TM (Love remained closely involved), and even Carl Wilson endorsed the Maharishi's system. 'I meditate regularly,' he said. 'Bad things, or rather difficult things, affect me less. I find that it relaxes me very deeply and gives me energy. I recommend it highly.' If TM seemed like some new superdrug – tranquillizing, stimulating, non-addictive, cheap and safe – that was perfectly acceptable to rock stars who were, whether they knew it or not, still looking for the perfect high.

When assorted stars followed the Maharishi to his Indian hideaway at Rishikesh in early 1968, the guru

fad really began. Of course, not everyone wanted a guru. Mick Jagger had already condemned the Maharishi as a fraud during his stay at Bangor. Life in the Meditation Training Centre was not to everyone's taste, although it did allow them to escape the prying eyes of the press. The trainee meditators, including the Beatles, Mike Love, Donovan and Mia Farrow, had been booked in for three months: but Ringo and Maureen left after ten days, complaining that the Centre was rather like a holiday camp with too many flies, too much heat and too many spices in the food. Paul McCartney and Jane Asher found the whole episode tedious – although it gave McCartney time to write several songs. When they left Rishikesh, Paul told the press that while the Maharishi was 'a nice fellow', neither he nor Jane were 'going out with him any more'.

John and George held on until, as John later said, 'There was a big hullaballoo about his trying to get off with Mia Farrow and a few other women.' Even George felt uneasy and Lennon himself wrote *Sexy Sadie* (in which Sadie, who 'made a fool of everyone', was meant to be the Maharishi) for inclusion in the White Album. The yogi's technique, said Lennon, was just 'coloured water'. And yet religion and the yogi's style of leadership grew in popularity. 'Pop is the perfect religious vehicle,' said Donovan at the time, in a flower-power echo of Little Richard's earlier pronouncement. 'It's as if God had come down to earth and seen all the ugliness that was being created and chosen pop to be the great force for love and beauty.'

One could hardly miss the message of love, but the appeal of gurus and mystical faith generally for rock stars seems to have had far more precise foundations. They promised some sort of order and therefore some sort of control in the chaotic and unbalanced world of rock'n'roll, and they offered inspiration, energy, and not least, a justification for doing what some rock stars were increasingly doing mechanically, lackadaisically and without conviction. Even the doubting Lennon eventually found a guru of his own in Dr Arthur Janov, a psychiatrist who had developed primal therapy, a form of treatment which required its patients to scream their way through repressed experiences. Brian Wilson also settled for psychiatry in the seventies when he put himself temporarily in the hands of one Dr Eugene Landis, after flirting with several other faiths, including the guru cult of Subud, which he heard about from the Byrds' Jim McGuinn. This cult was founded by the Indonesian mystic Pak Subuh and promotes the concept of a universal church. (It also demanded of McGuinn that he change his name to Roger – Subuh's name had been changed on the advice of a passing beggar while he was still a child and the change apparently effected a miraculous improvement in the infant guru's health.)

The Who's Pete Townshend discovered the Persian Sufi mystic, Meher Baba, during the group's US tour in 1967, when he met some of the guru's followers in California. He spent a great deal of energy devising new rock strategies to define himself as a spiritual seeker, and was joined in this exercise by former member of the Faces, Ronnie Lane. As with most gurus, Meher Baba – whose motto was 'Don't worry, be happy' – seems to have been content to let his message work at a very subtle level. (He died in 1969, after a self-imposed silence of over 40 years.)

Townshend doesn't proselytize, despite creating works like *Tommy* and *The Seeker* which revolve round his appreciation of Baba's philosophy. In fact his attitude to Baba is distinctly pragmatic. At the beginning of 1972, he made the trek to India where he stayed with Baba's family and disciples, visiting Baba's tomb and kissing the holy ground. 'I felt like a speck of dust,' he said. 'It was fantastic.' Baba's followers stood round the tomb singing the guru's favourite song, *Begin The Beguine* and Pete Townshend felt deeply moved. It was not, he said, 'a flirtation with the Maharishi thing', but neither has it solved the manifest problems of being a rock star. It has given him some equanimity, however. 'Jaded and worldly' as he confesses to be, Townshend said in 1981 that 'this is where Baba wants me to be. The rock business is a lousy world but I've got to work through it.' Any excuse, as they say.

Sufi mystic, Meher Baba, averts eyes from his disciple, Pete Townshend. Baba's motto was 'Don't worry, be happy.' Townshend doesn't seem so sure.

Guitarists John McLaughlin and Carlos Santana found a spiritual mentor in the seventies in their own Hindu guru, Sri Chinmoy. McLaughlin (who was known as Mahavishnu) has since rejected Chinmoy but used to say that 'my music is an offering to the Supreme Being . . . God is the Supreme Musician, the soul of music and the spirit of music. I'm trying to reach him by allowing myself to become his instrument.' Devadip (Santana's spiritual title) told *Rolling Stone* in 1980 that his conversion followed directly on his rapid rise to stardom. 'I got slapped by reality,' he explained. 'Platinum albums in my house, drugs, food, flesh and all those kind of things, but I felt such an emptiness . . . I was not taking my time to acknowledge my inner body.' Nowadays, his inner body tells him that 'perfect perfection . . . is the goal. Being at absolute oneness with the creator.'

Former Spooky Tooth vocalist, keyboard player and songwriter, Gary Wright, was introduced to the teachings of his guru, Paramahansa Yogananda, by George Harrison. The result was, according to Wright, 'the complete re-channelling of my energies'. A bestselling album, *The Dream Weaver*, followed in the mid-seventies. During the recording, said Wright, 'for the first time I took real control,' which is an understandable ambition for someone who emerged from a band as inconsistent and badly organized as Spooky Tooth. After his conversion, Wright expressed the view that 'groups are psychologically obsolete . . . Ideally,' he said, 'if you're in a band it should be, "Well, fellows, let's function as a company. We're in here to make money." But it never happens, so someone's got to take charge.' No doubt, it has made his manager's job easier to have been told by Gary, 'Dee, you may be my business manager, but Paramahansa Yogananda is my spiritual manager.' Manager Dee Anthony was blunter but nearer the point when he said, 'I told him, "Don't spiritualize yourself out of the business." If hymns were hits I'd be managing Moses – right?'

In a relentless pursuit for spiritual well-being which had already taken him up a hill in Cornwall for several days and nights and over to the mountain retreat at Rishikesh, George Harrison himself moved on to His Divine Grace, Guru A. C. Bhaktivedanta Swami, founder of the International Society for Krishna Consciousness. George had become infatuated with Hinduism – giving up meat, drugs, drink and (almost) cigarettes. He meditated for hours on end and recorded devotional ditties like *My Sweet Lord* (which sold a million) and albums with weighty philosophical titles like *All Things Must Pass* and *Living In The Material World*. The former Beatle seemed to find a certain peace of mind in Krishna Consciousness; when he wasn't turning hymns into hits he performed hits as though they were hymns.

In 1969, the Swami was seen leaving London Airport in a Rolls Royce lent by John Lennon. By 1973, he was able to afford to buy a fleet of his own. George Harrison, meanwhile, produced records by the Swami's followers – a group of saffron-robed, shaven-headed monks of both sexes who habitually danced up and down major thoroughfares of big cities wherever their temples were situated, jingling bells and chanting 'Hare Krishna, Hare Krishna.' (Hence George's irreverent nickname – Harry Georgeson.) In 1971, this chant, produced on record by George and released over the name 'Hare Krishna Temple', became a top ten hit.

The next year, George bought an Elizabethan manor house and seventeen acres of ground just outside London as a religious headquarters for the sect. The 55-room mansion houses 63 sect members and cost £250,000. George also helped to buy a building for their London temple. By 1973, it was revealed in the press that the Hare Krishna organization in England was making £400,000 from the sale of incense. Their merchandizing company was known as the Spiritual Sky Scented Products Company.

George's religious fervour was soured by his split with Patti, and by a plagiarism suit which accused him of stealing the melody of *My Sweet Lord* from the old Chiffons' hit, *He's So Fine*. He was eventually found to be guilty of 'partly unconscious plagiarism' and had to pay damages of around £250,000. By the mid-seventies, the man who had once described himself as 'just the servant of the servant of the servant of the servant of Krishna' was finding it hard to cope with the realization that while his life might have belonged to 'the Lord Krishna', the Lord Krishna steadfastly refused to live it for him.

Keeping his options open, Carlos Santana lights a candle to his guru, Sri Chinmoy, while Jesus looks benevolently on.

I wanna hold your hands. George Harrison poses with Shiva in 1971.

The guru followers have rendered unto Caesar that which is Caesar's and unto their Lords . . . a prayer of thanks, perhaps, that they need no longer question what they are. The poor old superstars can feel so burdened by their position out front that they need a god or a guru to put themselves back in perspective. Sometimes, the burden may seem intolerable – or so dangerously attractive, that substantial compensation is needed to ease the 'sacrifice'. Repressive faiths may be the solution.

Cat Stevens converted to Islam, took the name Yusuf Islam, and retired from the mainstream music business, emerging occasionally to attack Salman Rushdie and others. Leading English folk-rockers, Richard and Linda Thompson, also converted to Islam, but continued to perform. Mike Heron (formerly with the Incredible String Band), disappeared into Scientology. Michael Schenker of UFO joined the Christian sect, the Children of God, as did Fleetwood Mac's Jeremy Spencer, who was last seen selling tracts on a street corner in London's West End, and confessing to his former sins as a godless rock star.

Some performers are drawn the other way. Led Zeppelin's Jimmy Page discovered Aleister Crowley,

Cat among the Muslims. Yusuf Islam – formerly Cat Stevens – marries a Turkish woman named Fawzia in a London Mosque, 7th September, 1979.

Led Zeppelin as a group have had a peculiarly tragic record of untimely death and severe accident associated with themselves and their entourage.

In 1976, Zep associate Keith Harwood died in mysterious circumstances; Keith Relf, formerly of the Yardbirds, which formed the nucleus of Zep, committed suicide; and the wife of Zep's road manager, Richard Cole, also died. In 1977, Robert Plant's five-year-old son Karac died of a virus infection while the group was touring America. The next year was relatively disaster free but in 1979, Philip Hale, a photographer friend of Jimmy Page's, died at one of Page's homes after ingesting too much morphine, cocaine and alcohol and, in 1980 – at another of Page's houses – John Bonham met his untimely end.

Graham Bond, one of Britain's finest R&B organists, was also fascinated by Aleister Crowley. (At one time he fronted a band called Magick.) In the seventies, lack of recognition seemed to compound an unfounded and paranoid belief that he was Crowley's bastard son. In 1974, the delusion got the better of him and he killed himself by throwing himself under a train 'while the balance of his mind was disturbed'. It took the police two days to identify the body.

For the most part, however, black magic, satanism and the occult are merely fertile sources of shock imagery for bands devoid of any superior resources with which to get themselves noticed. Like the similar crop of late-seventies groups employing the symbols and styles of Nazism, their goal is outrage for its own sake. It is an indication of how bankrupt much of rock'n'roll has become that it should so readily accept diabolical imagery as an acceptable, not to say familiar, part of 'entertainment'.

Another aspect of this creative bankruptcy has been the recent spread of 'Born Again' Christianity among the rock community. Bob Dylan was rock's most notable convert – along with many of the performers on his mid-seventies' 'Rolling Thunder' American tour. Born-Again Christians – now something like a startling 40 per cent of all Americans – include Roger McGuinn (in yet another conversion), Donna Summer, members of the group Kansas and many others. As a religious movement, born again Christianity is a hodge-podge of differing ideals and philosophies, encompassing views from the centre to the extreme right of the moral and social spectrum. What unites it is the sense of reaction, a feeling of having gone too far or far enough on the wrong road, a desire to turn back and try another route.

Bob Dylan is hardly a conservative in the traditional mould, however, nor was his conversion a sudden acquisition of spirituality. On the contrary, Dylan has always been one of rock's most spiritual and most challenging performers. But now he has channelled his spirituality into a safe bywater. The poetry and intensity of Dylan's work in the early sixties may have been secular and political in a fairly narrow way, but it was always infused with a humanism that was more than merely mechanistic. After his motor-cycle crash, he began to trace his cultural heritage which eventually led him to flirt with

the leading Satanist of his day, who claimed to practise 'magick'. Page was involved in an occult bookshop in London and even bought Crowley's old mansion, Boleskin House near Loch Ness, where, he says, strange things have been known to happen. Jimmy Page is loath to talk about his beliefs or 'involvement in magick' in any detail, merely hinting darkly at mysteries experienced and as yet unexperienced. He claims, too, not to be interested in making 'converts' to Crowley, whose ideas are attractive to him because, he says, they are aspects of 'the unknown'. Among those also associated with Crowley have been experimental film-maker Kenneth Anger (for whom Jimmy Page once wrote some soundtrack music) and Robert Beausoleil, one of the Manson gang, currently doing time for torturing and murdering musician Gary Hinman.

Despite the fact that Page is careful to say he 'takes precautions' with his 'magick', it was rumoured at the time of Led Zeppelin's retirement that one reason for their split was an uneasy feeling that Page's activities might have had something to do with John Bonham's death. This is patently absurd – Bonzo's death was the result of years of over-indulgence of one sort or another. On the other hand, Page's mysterious association with 'magick' is bound to lead to that kind of superstitious sensationalism. It is certainly true that

161

The Born-Again Christian nearly saved . . . Bob Dylan still on the edge of sanctity, during his 1978 world tour.

Judaism (the religion of his parents). Some critics have detected in his work an obsession with the Tarot, and, some time in the seventies, Dylan employed a 'psychic guide' to assist his passage.

Unlike John Lennon, whose evident spirituality was far more diffusely expressed, Dylan seems to have remained untouched by either left-wing politics or feminism in the seventies. Certainly, the break-up of his marriage and the ensuing messy battle for custody of the five children revealed Dylan as something of an old-style patriarch. In this light, Dylan's conversion makes a good deal of sense – especially when, in 1979, a friend of his revealed that 'he hasn't given up Judaism, he just discovered Jesus.' Indeed, while fans barracked him as he returned to the stage with a 'gospel' show, an organization called 'Jews for Jesus' gave him their blessing and Pat Boone – one of the first of the Christian pop singers – 'lent his support to the Dylan crusade', as a newspaper put it at the time.

If Dylan's Christianity meant anything, it was that all the conflicts and struggles that emerged in the sixties and were embodied in rock'n'roll had not been resolved. The Christianity didn't last and gave way to a series of menopausal stances including a brief flirtation with orthodox Judasim. In the end, only rock'n'roll seemed to last the course and this may not be so surprising since it remains the soundtrack of the peculiar confusions of our age – and more vital and self-regenerative than any born-again belief. Dylan
162

had once believed in rock'n'roll and, thereby, caused a furore among political radicals and the traditionalist folk community, but in 1977 he denied rock'n'roll thrice and told journalist Jonathan Cott: 'There's no more rock'n'roll, it's an imitation, we can forget about that; rock'n'roll has turned itself inside out – I never did do rock'n'roll.' He had believed in the here-and-now, then turned to 'life, but not this life'. He had believed in the power of feelings to move and music to make feelings happen. Then he denied emotion. He had said, 'The highest purpose of art is to inspire', and then went on to produce art which was so much a caricature of inspiration – patriarchal, sloganizing, sentimental drivel, for the most part – that even (perhaps especially) life-long fans booed him at performances which occupied the cosy niche of Lord-praising. But one thing saved him from being saved: rock's demotic urge. 'I have to play in front of people just to keep going,' he said, and turned away from the trite certainties of godliness.

The banality of most rock conversions is, without doubt, their single outstanding feature. For the most part, a reassuring smile or being taught a breathing exercise are enough finally to destroy the last vestiges of rationality clinging to the wasted skulls of rock stars. If you lead a life of such ineffable confusion as is generated by mass adulation, large-scale drug abuse and late nights, it is probably only to be expected that nothing but the simplest of things will hold any mystery.

Eric Clapton's conversion was effected backstage during the Blind Faith tour of the US in 1969. 'Two guys came to my dressing room,' he later told Steve Turner (himself a Christian). 'They were Christians and they said "Can we pray with you?" I mean, what do you do?"' Clapton got on his knees and prayed. The experience evidently made him 'feel much better' – something like 'the blinding light', he said. For some unexplained reason, he wanted to show the two men a poster of Jimi Hendrix but, when he unrolled it, there was a picture of Christ inside it which, he said, 'I had never seen in my life before.' The possibility that someone might have put it there without his knowledge doesn't seem to have occurred to him. At once, he became a devout Christian.

That this trite experience effected a conversion suggests that the need for faith was already there, waiting for a trigger. Whatever else religion was for Eric Clapton, it was clearly something bigger than him, something that could control events as he had discovered himself unable to do. But Clapton discovered that if faith can move mountains, it often fails with considerably smaller things, like people. One of them was himself – for whom love and heroin were destined to become far stronger influences on his life than faith. The others were George and Patti Harrison. When Clapton learned their relationship was breaking up, his faith was shaken. 'The fact that George had been into TM for so long yet couldn't keep his wife . . . I mean, his wife just didn't want to know,' said Clapton. 'All she wanted was for him to say "I love you" and all he was doing was meditating . . . It caused him

In the presence of the Lady: Eric Clapton with his former wife Patti Boyd Harrison in 1975.

to treat her bad. Although it wasn't Christianity, I can see Christianity in the same situation doing the same thing.' Once Clapton's heroin addiction was defeated and his career on the up, he and Patti finally got together. An embittered George now had *his* faith shaken, but Eric's found its pragmatic level. 'I still pray,' he told Turner, 'and I still see God in other people more than I see him in the sky or anything like that.'

Clapton did at least write and record one superb religious song – *Presence Of The Lord*. Perhaps for some, conversion is a sign of complacency and advancing age, rather than a symptom of continued struggle. Like most of the musics from which it has borrowed, rock has never accepted the 'civilised' distinction between spirituality and physicality. As such it cannot be acceptable to the puritan (of whatever denomination) but it can be, in the widest sense of the word, a religious music. It is only when it stops working that the need is felt to inject faith from the outside.

Perhaps the last word should come from the Reverend Joel Agnew, black-satin clad and dog-collared pastor of the First Church of Rock'n'Roll, based in Niles, California. His leather-jacketed and denim-clad congregation paid $2 each a time to worship and they numbered in the hundreds. The church planned to start its own record label, Behemoth. 'For thousands of years the devil has been getting the credit for Saturday night,' said Agnew in 1980. 'Rock'n'roll has always been a religion – an alternative to the bullshit.' While Bob Dylan's badly-received Christian album, *Saved*, lay about in unsold piles in the shops, the Rev. Agnew announced that *his* church's aim was 'to work towards the more perfect party'.

FAKING CARE
OF BUSINESS

The rock'n'roll business is probably no more corrupt than any other business, but it is extremely sensitive to allegations of malpractice. Its operations are entirely based on the idea that it is selling talent and popularity, which is why allegations of record hyping have always been greeted by dismay, denials or excuses. 'Sure, there was hype,' said the then president of Capitol Records, Voyle Gilmour, commenting on the breaking of the Beatles in America. 'But all the hype in the world isn't going to sell a bad product.'

Hyping can take many forms, but its ultimate aim is always to create exaggerated reputations for records and acts through expensive, elaborate advertising and promotional campaigns. In the late sixties, subtlety came to be all important; record companies supported magazines like *Rolling Stone* even though they sometimes criticized the industry, because such magazines had the necessary 'counter-cultural credibility'. In the same way, the industry brought in so-called 'company freaks' like Danny Fields at Elektra or Billy James at Columbia, whose very belief in the acts they hyped charmed away all suspicion of corruption. The record industry put on a counter-cultural face and annual sales went through the billion-dollar barrier. The companies held parties at which journalists, disc-jockeys and TV producers could mingle with the rock elite; the straight-laced accountants and cynical businessmen who ran the industry stayed at home; at Christmas time, they gave away tasteful little *objets d'art* instead of envelopes containing bank-notes. This sort of hype was so much more effective once rock had become established as the dominant area of the music market, stressing the values of artistry, integrity and youth identity rather than the more traditional values of earlier kinds of mass appeal music. In the fifties, things had been a little different. The major form of hype took an altogether less subtle form. Its name was payola.

Payola is a particular kind of corruption involving the payment by direct or devious means of disc jockeys and broadcasters for playing specific records. Not only is it intended as a form of promotion, generating extra record sales, but it also makes money directly in the form of royalty payments. Payola had been an established part of the music business, since the late nineteenth century when composers, publishers and song-pluggers would pay performers to feature their songs, employ them as 'consultants' or give them spurious song-writing or arranging credits. But in 1959, the music business was changing beyond all recognition. In that and the following year, Congress investigated the fixing of popular quiz shows on American television. Not only were the contests often fixed, but several music publishers were also kicking-back a percentage of their song royalties to quiz-show producers who had featured the publishers' songs on their programmes. There had already been murmurings from another Congressional committee about gangsters fixing juke-box plays, and from the Federal Communications Commission (FCC) and the music business trade papers about payola itself.

Most of the publishers concerned in the quiz show scandal were members of the American Society of Composers, Authors and Publishers (ASCAP), a licensing and royalty collecting agency that represented the old tin-pan-alley establishment of Hollywood and Broadway. But since 1940, ASCAP had been in deep rivalry with a new organization, Broadcast Music Incorporated (BMI), which represented much of the new rock'n'roll business and was specifically geared to dealing with the burgeoning community of radio DJs. So, as an issue of the trade paper *Variety* noted at the time, 'ASCAP songsmiths . . . take the credit for switching the spotlight from TV quiz rigging to disc jockey payola'.

The major record companies and radio networks came out of it relatively unscathed. The investigations had done them a service by focusing on rock'n'roll – a monopoly-breaking music that had been nurtured by independent record companies, was heard mainly on independent radio stations and was published by independent publishers. The payola scandal stifled the entrepreneurial spirit that had pushed Elvis Presley, Chuck Berry and Buddy Holly to the fore. Rock'n'roll became a dirty word among broadcasters. Radio playlists came under increased scrutiny and tighter control so that anything risqué, raucous or merely innovative would almost certainly be thrown out along with the records that might once have clearly been hyped. Of course, by 1959 many of the innovative companies were themselves turning to a safer, cleaner sort of teenage music than rock'n'roll had been in 1955 and 1956, but the payola investigations set a sort of legislative seal on the process: this was 1960, election year, and right-of-centre America was asserting itself once more.

Payola, of course, wasn't an invention of ASCAP, major companies or government agencies. The boss of one small record label admitted to paying out $2,000

Who's kidding? Elvis tries a novel method of slimming Colonel Parker's share. The bogus Colonel Tom set the tone for rock'n'roll personal management when he took Presley over in the mid-fifties.

165

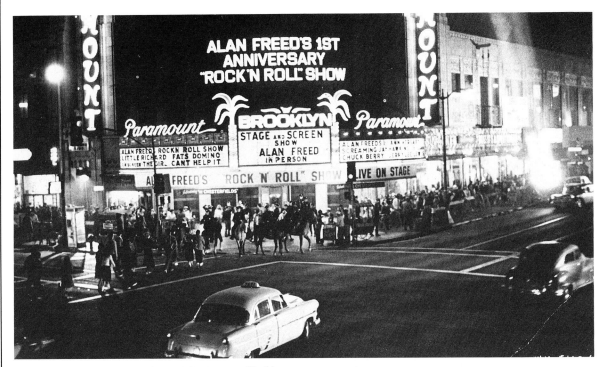

Alan Freed had been promoting mixed rock'n'roll package tours like this one from the early fifties – and ensuing riots brought him to the notice of the courts twice before the Payola scandal broke in 1959.

each month in payola and most of the DJs who lost their jobs confessed to accepting excessive amounts of cash or expensive gifts to play records. But for a small company, without the resources of the majors, payola was often the only way to get a disc-play and, in any case, the investigative dice were loaded.

A number of the FCC commissioners were themselves receiving bribes from major broadcasting companies – a fact which threw a new light on their threats to revoke the licences of over 5,000 smaller radio and TV companies under investigation. A counsel for the Congressional Committee investigating payola expressed views which were distinctly anti-rock. 'Suppose John Smith owns a record company,' he said, 'and then buys a broadcast station. Suppose he dumps its personnel and its good music format to push his own label, generally only rock'n'roll . . . Now, that's not in the public interest.'

The most tragic victim of the investigations was DJ Alan Freed, the man who claimed to have coined the expression 'rock and roll' back in 1952. Freed always promoted an 'authentic' version of rock'n'roll. He was not well liked by the powers that were, and over-enthusiastic response of fans at his concert promotions twice led to his arrest. Although a popular and successful figure, he always remained on the fringe of the entertainment industry. He certainly took payola in spite of earning a substantial salary and receiving money for public and film appearances and from concerts he promoted. He was given spurious writer's credits on several hits and he confessed to taking gifts 'if I've helped somebody . . .'. 'But,' he said, 'I

wouldn't take a dime to plug a record. I'd be a fool to; I'd be giving up control of my programme.' This by now familiar argument didn't stop him losing his job on a New York radio station – he sobbed as he announced his resignation over the air – nor did it prevent him being sacked from the *Big Beat* TV show. He was arrested for receiving $30,650 from six record companies, eventually receiving a six month suspended sentence and a $300 fine on a partial guilty plea. In 1964, he was indicted for evading the tax on this payola income and the next year he died drunk, broke and all but forgotten in a Florida hospital, aged 42.

Dick Clark, *American Bandstand's* clean-cut 'emcee', had no such problems. Clark owned or part-owned six music publishing companies, three record labels, one pressing plant, one record distributor and one management company. He owned sixteen songs as a publisher, most of which were 'free gifts'. Clark's network TV show was, of course, immensely influential in popularizing clean-cut Italianate pop idols. The show was aimed at a family audience and was specifically designed to launder rock'n'roll of its rebellious, arrogant, black and sexy image. It also brought in between $10–12 million a year in advertising revenue. When Clark was due to appear before the payola investigations, ABC told him that he would have to give up either *American Bandstand* or all of his other interests which conflicted with it. He chose to stay with the show, and at the hearing where he was star witness, the committee chairman told him, 'You're not the inventor of the system or even its architect. You're a product of it.' The chairman, who had himself been obliged to give up a 25 per cent share in a TV station,

166

Above: Payola roll blues. DJ Alan Freed arrives with his wife Inga at the New York District Attorney's office, 30th November, 1959. Implicated in the Payola scandal, Freed refused to testify before a Grand Jury. It marked the end of his career.

Below: Good guys wear white. 'American Bandstand's' Dick Clark shows his ring of confidence as he testifies that he never took Payola before the House Legislative Oversight Sub-Committee, 29th April, 1960. Clark gave up all his other interests rather than lose his position as host of 'American Bandstand'.

Rock jocks busted shock – Alan Freed (second right), programme director Mel Leeds (third right) and DJ Peter Tripp (fourth right) arrested in New York after being accused of commercial bribery by the Grand Jury investigating Payola, 10th May, 1960.

had a final testimonial to make. Clark, he said, was 'a fine young man'. When Alan Freed made his last, tearful, appearance on his (non-network) TV show, a young girl was heard to sob the teenagers' testimonial: 'They've taken away our father.'

If the 1959 payola scandal achieved anything of moment, it was to make sure that the next phase of musical innovation came from outside America and that many American musicians of originality with any sort of commitment to a genuine popular music were turned off rock'n'roll until 1964. The one thing it didn't do was put a stop to payola. Gifts and free records may have replaced direct cash payment, but in one area at least the gift-giving seems to have reached dramatic levels. They even labelled it 'drugola'. Certainly, in the mid-seventies, record company offices and studios were often the most reliable places to find an itinerant drug dealer if one was needed, and drug use is almost universal in rock today. One notorious recording studio was well-known in the seventies for debiting drug purchases to the accounts under the guise of 'gardening expenses'. 'In the advertising world, it's martini,' said one record producer in 1973, 'in the music world, it's cocaine.'

The record industry in Britain has long been less susceptible to classic payola than in the USA – largely because airplay is governed by the charts and these are compiled exclusively, if unreliably, from record sales. The energy of the British record business is thus centred on chart hyping. One easy and relatively undetectable way to guarantee airplay is to buy a record a chart position. With a few hundred pounds and a list of the 450 shops that now make sales returns to the market research organization which compiles the BBC charts, it is a matter of little more than leg-work to push a record into say, the bottom of the Top 40 or to nudge it from second place to number one. The effect is of course even better than with advertisements because once in the charts a single will sell on almost guaranteed airplay.

In fact 'shopping' (which is how the practice of buying records into the charts is known) is often considered too inefficient and obvious for successful chart hyping. Since a 1978 press investigation in the London *Sun* and *Daily Mirror*, which dealt with a number of well-known artists on the A&M label, it has become clear that one of the most popular techniques is now to offer 'favours' (free records) to dealers in return for entry in the sale diary which is used to compile the charts. This is particularly useful for hyping albums which might otherwise prove too expensive to buy into the charts. In return for recording a non-existent sale, the record dealer gets a free record of a different title. These come under the category of promotional albums for the record company, so there are no royalties to pay and the whole deal is very cheap to operate. There need be no secret shopping trips, no special agents and no disguising of intent – the ordinary record company reps. give 'favours' as a routine aspect of their work. In addition, it means that whatever

168

happens, more of the company's product gets around – so everybody, except for the deluded public and the performers and writers concerned, is happy.

Ironically, the most notorious British payola scandal to date focused on precisely the kind of music – traditional sentimental ballads – that hardly ever makes the pop charts but which can earn an awful lot in royalties from continued record play on light music programmes. The details were first revealed in 1971 by the *News of the World*.

The newspaper reported how orgies had been organized for BBC producers and disc-jockeys at a flat in Mayfair; how former singer Janie Jones had procured girls and arranged yet more orgies for radio figures; how a young female record plugger offered herself as an inducement along with free copies of the record she was handling and sealed envelopes containing used banknotes. All stirring stuff, despite the fact that nobody had ever heard of most of the people involved. Fifteen arrests were made but most were cleared of all charges. A loudly-trumpeted Scotland Yard investigation into chart-rigging followed on the newspaper exposé but without result. Accusations against singer Dorothy Squires were dismissed when she was shown to be entirely innocent of any involvement in the scandal. One freelance TV producer (who had already made a clean sweep of it before the exposé was published) was fined £100 for accepting £25 from one of Jones' associates to feature a group called Demon Fuzz (of all things) on his BBC show. Janie Jones herself was jailed for a few years for doing something immoral, which was an affront considering that all the men who were only too eager for her to do it got off scot free. And that was the end of that.

DJ Peter Myers, questioned at the time of the American scandal in 1959, commented that what was wrong with payola was 'the siphoning off of money in front of the artist's anticipated royalties'. Indeed, in all this wheeling and dealing, it's sometimes easy to forget that it is the performers and the public who prop up the whole edifice. The public at least has the illusion that it is getting what it wants, but performers often get precious little of anything. The standard argument is that without the industry pushing from behind, the artists would have no hope at all. 'Godammit,' says the archetypal music biz fat-cat, 'they ought to be proud that I think they're worthy hyping.' For many, proud is all they'll ever be.

In both the UK and the US, ripping off performers is virtually a music business institution. The musicians concerned too often accept it as just one more way in which they 'pay their dues'. In America particularly, black musicians have always been the most frequent victims of contractual rip-offs. The small record labels in the fifties – like Atlantic and Chess – were able to attract black artists because majors were often dilatory in paying royalties or giving composer credits.

If they don't actually falsify returns, or refuse to pay royalties, record companies (large and small, alike) often charge a contracted artist for studio time, hotel expenses, the cost of hiring instruments or vans – almost anything they can get away with. Under the terms of some contracts, the profits made by one record could be appropriated to pay for the next or any subsequent follow-up. Since much more care is invariably taken over follow-ups and since successful acts are supposed to make albums as soon as possible after hit singles, the resulting expenditure sometimes leads performers into a sort of debt-bondage.

In the fifties, Leonard Chess of the Chicago-based Chess Records (where Chuck Berry, Muddy Waters and numerous other R&B performers recorded), gained a reputation as a particularly exploitative record company boss. Chess – a Polish immigrant who started out running a number of downtown dives with his brother Phil – had an undeniable talent for money-making. His musical ear was more debatable. 'He knew nothing about it,' said Etta James, who went to Chess in 1960. If Chess was an astute businessman, it was an astuteness largely informed by venality. That he discovered many important performers and nurtured others cannot be doubted, but he never let musical sentiment interfere with his money-making drive.

Many companies in the fifties felt that the gift of a Cadillac or a new wardrobe of smart suits was enough to discharge their responsibilities to their artists. Atlantic Records' Jerry Wexler once defended such an attitude by saying of Leonard Chess's relationship with his artists, 'He recorded them – that's what's important.' Important it was and important it remains, but it didn't pay the bills.

In the early days, rock'n'roll performers were the 'white niggers' of the music business. The managers looked upon them as short-term talent and short-term investments. A typical rock'n'roll operation was run during the late fifties and early sixties by Irving Micahnik and Harry Balk in Detroit. These two managed Del Shannon and Johnny and the Hurricanes, among other less successful acts. They took 20 per cent of their artists' earnings and signed them to their own record label, Twirl, at the ludicrous royalty of $1\frac{1}{2}$ per cent, which was low even by the standards of the day. (Atlantic paid between three and five per cent.) Out of this royalty, artists often had to pay their own recording costs. Meanwhile, Twirl would lease its recordings to other companies at a rate of 8 per cent – giving Micahnik and Balk $6\frac{1}{2}$ per cent of every record sold to the public.

Businessmen could make a small fortune if one record hit, but there was no incentive to nurture a performer's career. Performers with hit records, meanwhile, could all too easily find themselves in debt as recording costs mounted for follow-ups and as they spent money on hotel accommodation, new equipment and all the accessories of stardom. Such performers might make money on live appearances (at least, until the concert circuit also became subject to grossly exploitative business operations), but it was rarely enough to cover the costs of the recordings and promotions that were considered necessary by the business as a whole to sustain a career.

Even performers who were regarded as long-term prospects, could become suspicious of the way their affairs were being handled. A well-known example is Norman Petty's dealings with Buddy Holly and the Crickets. Holly himself broke with manager-producer Petty in 1958, partly because he wanted to handle his own affairs and direct his own career and partly, so it seems, because of the arrangements Petty had imposed for the disposal of Holly and the Crickets' income. Petty seems to have had absolute control over almost all the money that Holly and the Crickets made. As a result, suspicion grew that he was withholding money that was not legitimately his. After splitting with Petty, Holly actually took legal action to try and recover money from his former manager – and in the end it was lack of cash that forced him to undertake his last fatal tour.

This case is complicated by the split between Holly and the Crickets and by Holly's death – more so by the way that all parties concerned seemed to rely on verbal agreements. Petty denies all accusations of malpractice and the surviving Crickets express few recriminations, noting Petty's crucial role in the development of their careers. But, after speaking with everybody involved (except, of course, Holly himself), Holly's biographer, John Goldrosen concludes: 'It is my own judgement that Holly and the Crickets probably never saw much of what was rightfully due to them. Though they may well have been paid all that was *legally* due them, in the entertainment business more than in any other industries [sic], what is fair and what is legal is [sic] often worlds apart.'

The music business changed quite dramatically in the wake of the Beatles. For one thing, many of the managers and new industry figures who emerged were little more than amateurs. Their motives for entering the world of rock'n'roll were often complicated by personal attachments to the performers with whom they dealt, or by private ambitions which went beyond the simple goal of money-making.

Brian Epstein, a masochistic homosexual, was sexually attracted to the Beatles (Lennon in particular). His liking for 'rough trade' was damaging in more than one sense. After his death, dark rumours circulated about the exact cause, which, it is said, had more to do with rubber masks and suffocation than overdose or suicide. At times during his life, he would disappear for days, eventually turning up bruised and blackened by one of his anonymous acquaintances. At other times, he would phase himself out of the daily struggle between his respectable middle-class background and his turbulent, guilt-ridden sexuality with the help of large quantities of sleeping pills. His was, inevitably, a desperation suffered in silence and remorse and he would go to almost any lengths to live out his fantasies and then to live them down. Spurned by Eric Burdon, with whom he had quite hopelessly fallen in love, he took LSD to 'get closer to Eric's mentality'. At home he would dress up in drag and sing songs – Lionel Bart accompanying him on the piano. In 1966, he was rushed to hospital suffering from an overdose and a

The Brian Epstein stable – from the left, four Beatles, Gerry and three Pacemakers, Brian Epstein, and two Dakotas on each side of Billy J. Kramer. Where are they now?

year later he died as the result of another.

No doubt, Epstein's sexual proclivities extended to a fondness for the paraphernalia of the torture chamber so beloved of masochists, and there is perhaps somebody who can say for certain how Epstein spent his lonely last weekend, but they're not telling. The chances are that another decline into the sado-masochistic twilight was followed by familiar dreadful recriminations, only this time – with the Beatles drifting from him, weekending in Bangor with a new, if short-lived, father-figure in the Maharishi Mahesh Yogi – on August 27th, 1967, he took one or two pills too many and escaped forever.

Perhaps it is no more than the traditional showbiz link with homosexuality, but a substantial number of rock's successful managers (especially those with British operations) are gay – a situation that seems to have been current since the first days of British rock'n'roll. No doubt, the sexual ambivalence of the male rock star's image – much remarked on since Elvis – has encouraged this trend. The managerial role itself combines power and benevolent paternalism in a way that echoes a distinctly male notion of sexuality.

Like Epstein, the Who's co-manager, Kit Lambert, was homosexual. Like Epstein, too, the very success of his wards seemed to leave him in an emotional vacuum, increasingly filled by drugs and casual sexual encounters.

Lambert began his career in film-making. He planned to make a film of a pop group with a fellow assistant director, Chris Stamp (brother of actor Terence). While casting round for a suitable subject, they came across the Who playing a gig at the Railway Hotel in the London suburb of Harrow, and took over their management.

170

Brian Epstein, clutching a Queen, *arrives at a press conference, 5th August, 1966, to apologize for John Lennon's 'blasphemy' about the Beatles and Jesus. Within just over a year Epstein would be dead.*

Lambert was soon indulging a taste for drugs which eventually began to take over his life. In Los Angeles, he was introduced to cocaine and a variety of other more-or-less exotic drugs and, while continuing to work with the Who, he rapidly became preoccupied with drug-taking. He evidently harboured an ambition to die young (his father, composer Constant

Lambert, had died of alcoholism at the age of 40). By the time the Who had actually achieved a level of success which guaranteed their independence and continued profitability, Lambert – whose inherited wealth, efforts and inspiration had been crucial to the band's survival – had effectively dropped out of the managerial picture. In 1972, he bought himself a small, decrepit palace in Venice. When not buying drugs, he spent much of his money on rebuilding the foundations of this property. He called himself Baron Lambert and, living in one room, he entertained himself by taking heroin and indulging in a succession of good-looking Italian boys. By 1976, his friends and family had made him a ward of court and he was persuaded to return from Italy to live at his mother's house in London, where they could keep an eye on him.

On 5th March, 1981, he returned home at 2.30 in the morning from an evening spent at a regular night-club haunt. The owner said he had been only a little drunk when he left, but added that Lambert was an habitual drug user who craved company and frequently lied to gain sympathy. 'I would describe him as paranoid,' said this man.

He arrived home penniless, claiming to his mother that he had been mugged and had had his wallet and keys stolen. However despite blackened eyes, the inquest found no sign of injuries beyond those 'consistent with the manner of his death'. At home he had fallen off a chair, dropped a cup of coffee and fallen over on his way to the bathroom. On leaving the bathroom, he had fallen downstairs and fractured his skull. He died in hospital three days later when his family agreed to switch off his life support machine. He was 45 years old. His blood, tested in hospital, had

The world's press waits for news outside Brian Epstein's house on 27th August, 1967. Epstein had been found dead in bed that morning but no details were released until later in the day. He had apparently overdosed on pills but a question mark still hangs over the precise cause of his death.

Finders and minders of the Who in the sixties. Chris Stamp (left) was the son of an East End tugboatman (and brother of actor Terence Stamp), while Kit Lambert (right) was the son of composer Constant Lambert, a product of public school and Oxford. No class distinction here.

contained significant levels of alcohol, heroin or morphine, and tuinal.

Whatever the private motives of men like Epstein and Lambert, the illusion they fostered about their professional relationships with their acts was one of mutual support. The model, of course, was Presley's manager, the self-styled 'Colonel' Tom Parker – a former carnival hustler and erstwhile manager of country singer Eddy Arnold.

Parker single-mindedly devoted his entrepreneurial efforts to Presley – or rather, to the Presley empire. The kindest argument is that such a relationship between performer and manager comes about because certain managers realize that only by nurturing a talent can it be brought to full flower – the implications being that such managers care for their performers, that the performers respect and trust their managers and that money only enters the relationship as the due reward for unique artistry. In fact, self-interest is more likely to be the true foundation of such management practice.

Much of the mystery about Elvis clears once you consider his relationship with Col. Parker. The measure of this relationship can be gained from the fact that, while Parker took 25 per cent of Elvis's earnings as a performer according to the terms of their first contract, by 1963, the two had signed a merchandizing deal in which Parker received 50 per cent of net earnings from the vast range of Presley souvenirs and memorabilia which still flood the market. Since his first studio sessions in 1954, Presley has sold around 300 million records and generated an estimated $5 billion worth of business, by far the greatest portion of

which derived from merchandizing, the apparently interminable series of lamentable Hollywood movies he made in the sixties and his later appearances in Las Vegas cabaret. All of these aspects of Presley's career reveal the hand of Col. Parker – ever concerned with where the most money could be made with the least fuss and bother. Parker's personal financial requirements became particularly extravagant during the seventies, when approaching his own seventies, he was doubtless concerned to get the most out of his remaining years. Parker's particular vice was gambling. 'Colonel Parker is the best customer you ever had at this hotel,' the general manager of Hilton Hotels Las Vegas International told the owners in 1972. 'He's good for at least one million dollars a year.' (Indeed, in 1973 Parker sold the complete Elvis catalogue to RCA for $5.4 million and a guarantee of $500,000 a year against royalties for seven years, just to raise some cash.) Before Hilton took over the hotel, Parker had signed Elvis to a five year exclusive deal at the International which paid a bare quarter of the going rate for an entertainer of Presley's stature. While Presley's earnings were severely limited by this deal, the hotel found itself in the remarkable position (for a Las Vegas establishment) of making vast profits from its live entertainment. In return, the Colonel was treated royally, given unlimited credit on the gambling tables and, on top of his cut of Presley's earnings, eventually received a $50,000 annual fee from Hilton Hotels for 'promotional services'.

Elvis Presley was not a clever man, and his extravagance was notorious. In spite of much outraged surprise at the diminished size of the Presley estate at the hands of Colonel Tom (which is the subject of a long-running legal wrangle, as yet unresolved), at least Parker had tried to guide Elvis from the start, even if it was sometimes into arenas unworthy of the King's talent.

Brian Epstein also thought that he had nothing but his clients' best interests at heart. But unlike Col. Tom, Epstein had four wilful and determined clients able to act with the assurance of their own collective strength. They grew away from Epstein and the evidence suggests that, in doing so, they found themselves ill-equipped to run their own affairs – ultimately almost breaking themselves in pursuit of the utopian fantasies epitomized by Apple, where money was lost hand-over-fist through mismanagement, idealism and plain stupidity.

Well-intentioned or not, Epstein actually left much to be desired as a businessman (possibly because *no-one* had had any experience of running this sort of business before). Like Colonel Parker, he became heavily involved in merchandizing and increasingly distant from any notion of his clients' developing talent. Parker, Epstein and their like were managers who saw their clients as long-term investments. Instead of taking a quick profit on a high turnover of short-lived acts, these managers stayed with their acts and 'nurtured' them. They may have been less than competent businessmen, but they knew (or rapidly became aware) that if successful rock performers could be an almost inexhaustible well of money, they could also dry up artistically in the process. In an attempt to

A picture speaks a thousand words: Colonel Parker, saving breath.

reconcile art and commerce, a new kind of manager was born.

'People see now that they can become millionaires by doing it right,' said Elliot Roberts who, through an interconnecting network of friendships, came to manage Crosby, Stills, Nash and Young, Joni Mitchell, Jackson Browne and the Eagles in the sixties, eventually founding Asylum Records with a young booking agent named David Geffen. Roberts' hip management style – 'doing the right thing by the artist' – is different from the approach of a Colonel Tom Parker because his idea of 'the right thing by the artist' is different. But in terms of artistry, independence or taste, the manager's prime concern remains the making of money – even if no longer just for himself. If that goal demands the contentment of performers, then contentment is what's offered – it may be a little harder to arrange than a Cadillac or a regular supply of heroin, but then it may actually keep the performer making records and concert appearances for a lot longer.

The long-term contracts which became standard industry practice in the sixties by no means satisfied all performers – even when they offered apparent security. The Beach Boys, for example, used to call Capitol Records – to whom they were signed – 'Captive Records' and tried to set up their own label, Brother Records. Other performers have found that low royalty rates – which might have seemed suitable for a new career being financed by a risk-taking man-

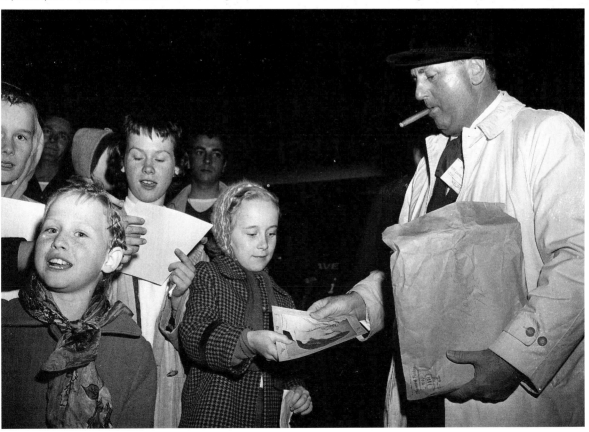

ager or record label – have allowed the business people to enrich themselves disproportionately after success has been achieved.

Some managers have gained reputations for intemperance, understandable in anyone involved in such a competitive arena as rock. In New Zealand, John Reid, the fiery Glaswegian who manages Elton John, once flattened two local journalists who had spoken disparagingly of Elton's sexual preferences. He spent three weeks in jail. On another occasion, he hit a San Francisco hotel doorman over the head with a cane. 'I've given him more than a black eye,' Reid said about Elton, displaying a certain fecklessness even in anger. Always prepared to lay blame wherever convenient, Reid fired two of his executives after Elton's record, *Ego*, failed to make the charts. Reid's 'workaholism' and his apparent lack of sentimental attachment ('I have Elton, family, friends, work,' he says, 'I can't give to a woman as well'), may well explain his temper.

Peter Grant, Led Zeppelin's manager, is a veritable whale of a man who worked as a wrestler for some time just to make money, and harboured an ambition to become an actor, even doubling for Robert Morley in films. In the fifties, he collected tickets at the 2 I's coffee bar in Soho and subsequently became a tour manager for Gene Vincent, Little Richard and Jerry Lee Lewis. Later he managed the New Vaudeville Band. The band were thrown out of Italy in 1967 after a row about fees – one member, Mick Wilsher, and their road manager, Richard Cole (a long-term associate of Grant's) were arrested. Grant threatened to sue, but the band were later accused by the Italian authorities of 'fraudulent insolvency' and 'unlawful appropriation'. Peter Grant became manager of Terry Reid and Jeff Beck in 1968, and then masterminded Led Zeppelin's meteoric rise through 1969 and 1970.

In 1973, following the unsolved theft of more than $200,000 in cash from a safe at the New York hotel where Zeppelin were staying, Grant pleaded guilty to a charge of harassment, resulting from an incident in which he seized a roll of film from a press photographer at the scene of the crime. In early 1978, Grant, Richard Cole, Led Zep's drummer John Bonham and one of their 'minders' (John Bindon) were found guilty of battering security guards during a backstage altercation at a Led Zep concert in Oakland, California. The four were sentenced to probation in their absence. 'I won't stand for people taking advantage of the group,' Grant used to say about Led Zeppelin – and, no doubt, he meant it.

Don Arden was a singer who worked as a compere on early rock'n'roll package shows in Britain. After compereing one of Gene Vincent's early tours, Arden decided to manage him. By the seventies, he was overseeing the career of one of the world's top-selling groups, the Electric Light Orchestra. His image is of an uncompromising businessman, but it is, he insists, *only* an image. 'That's the biggest joke of all,' says Arden, 'and everyone has fallen for it . . . In this business you've got to be tough and that kind of image
174

Peter Grant, the man behind Led Zeppelin, takes coffee (1977).

does come in useful.'

Indeed, Arden once prided himself on being one of the few real men left in an industry riddled with 'drug addicts, homosexuals and hangers on'. These days he describes himself as a 'pussycat', a man whose motto may well be his own comment that 'you don't succeed by being a softy'.

Sensational gossip is notoriously rife in the rock world, full of preposterous stories about people who send wheelchair catalogues to their enemies or who threaten to nail recalcitrant promoters' feet to the floor. Periodic rumours that certain rock'n'roll deaths have been the work of contract killers are backed up with little or no evidence. Yet death threats *are* made – and not always by warped fans. Elton John received several as a prelude to his retirement in 1976. He came close to leaving the business altogether at that time as a result, although he was also tired of the blind adulation of the public ('I could have read out the cricket scores,' he says, 'and still got a full house').

The fact is that rock stars are likely to suffer as much from legitimate business practice as they are from clearly criminal operations. Even the Beatles in their heyday discovered that it was easy to lose money in the labyrinthine complexities of the rock world. 'We didn't have anything in the bank really,' said John Lennon of the period after Brian Epstein's death. 'None of us did . . . When Klein heard me say that he came over right away. Now I've got lots more money than I ever had before. Allen got me more real money in the bank than I've ever had in the whole period.'

'One of the few real men left' in the music business, Don Arden, buried in flesh during his early days as a singer.

Allen Klein was one of the rock performer's attempts at a solution to the problem of being ripped off. He was a sharp New York accountant who made and saved the Beatles' millions in the two years during which he handled their affairs. His specialities were negotiating better deals with record companies and unearthing money they owed their performers through a studious investigation of company books. In 1965, he won $1.25 million in advance payments for the Rolling Stones. He became their manager for a time. Klein, who in his time has handled the affairs of Sam Cooke, Bobby Vinton, the Dave Clark Five and Jeff Beck, as well as the Beatles and the Stones, attempted an early coup when he bought a controlling interest in the Cameo-Parkway label and announced ambitious expansion plans which resulted in nothing except a reverse take-over of his own management company and a tenfold rise in the value of Cameo-Parkway shares until the American stock exchange suspended trading in them. In 1971, Klein was the focus of attention in Paul McCartney's suit to dissolve the Beatles' partnership. The judge pointed out that Klein's company, ABKCO, 'made grossly excessive claims for commission and . . . received commission grossly in excess of that specified in the appointment' (the specified figure was 20 per cent of all the Beatles' income generated under Klein's management). A New York court found him guilty of failing to make and file tax returns relating to employees' taxes at around the same time and, in 1979, he was found guilty of filing a false tax return for 1970, relating to the sale of $170,000 worth of promotional albums on the Apple label. He was fined $5,000 and served two months of a two-year suspended sentence. Clearly, Klein was not the shining knight he had once seemed.

When George Harrison was sued for plagiarism following the success of his song, *My Sweet Lord*, Allen Klein, who had lost control of the Beatles six years previously, bought the rights to *He's So Fine* (the song which Harrison had allegedly plagiarized), as soon as they became available. Three years later, the expected judgement was made that Harrison had indeed plagiarized the earlier song, albeit unconsciously. Noting Klein's ownership of the rights to *He's So Fine*, the judge declared damages against George of a little over half-a-million dollars – exactly the same amount, in fact, that Klein paid for the rights in the first place.

The vitriolic disputes between Lennon and McCartney which marked the last days of the Beatles as the group's assets were sold off and individual Beatles hurled abuse and law-suits at each other, were also marked by a choice of champions. John, Ringo and George plumped for a money man – the ubiquitous Klein. McCartney, however, chose Lee Eastman, Linda McCartney's father, and a respected New York lawyer. The lawyer and the accountant, together or apart, now stand as symbols of rock'n'roll.

Survival and success have become key words in rock'n'roll – and, although nobody can doubt the wisdom of performers wishing to control their own destinies, the end result often seems like a caricature of what rock'n'roll once hoped to be. Today's successful bands are probably more in control of their professional lives than ever before. But because success is measured in millions, they sometimes seem as soulless as any corporation turning a comparable profit. At the peak of their popularity, Kiss were grossing $130 million a year. The lion's share came from merchandizing Kiss comics, T-shirts, badges etc, all sporting the notorious SS slash symbol. Lead singer Gene Simmons (real name Klein but no relation) said proudly, 'Sure, we have regular meetings on merchandizing. I'm a good Jewish boy from Brooklyn and all four of us are members of the board. I don't have any respect for bands who get ripped off. Christianity and Disney have got nothing on us when it comes to merchandizing.'

Other sources of income include major investments. Abba (second biggest money-spinning industry in Sweden) got into the oil business when in 1977 they negotiated a barter deal with Rumania, exchanging records for part-payment in millions of dollars' worth of crude. In 1981 Paul McCartney and Yoko Ono got together behind closed doors to offer £25 million to

Allen Klein in 1966. Klein had a genius for getting unpaid royalties out of record companies for grateful rock star clients, including the Rolling Stones and Jeff Beck.

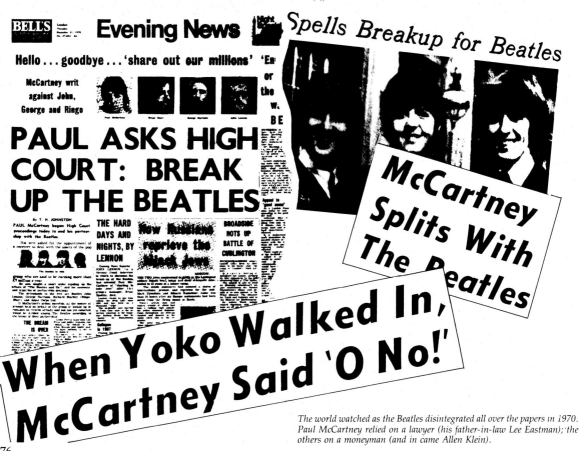

The world watched as the Beatles disintegrated all over the papers in 1970. Paul McCartney relied on a lawyer (his father-in-law Lee Eastman); the others on a moneyman (and in came Allen Klein).

Sign here and baby, you're a rich man. Allen Klein was brought in by John Lennon to help sort out the break-up of the Beatles. John and Yoko continued their association into the late seventies.

buy back the rights to all the early Beatles songs sold in 1969 to Lord Grade's ATV company.

'It's like a job,' said Freddie Mercury of his life fronting Queen. Queen was a planned operation from the start, because, said Freddie, they were never prepared to be 'out-of-work musicians'. Listening to him talking about Queen's 1980 tour of South America, one could easily imagine one was listening to a chairman's statement at a shareholders' meeting, full of references to 'new territory being opened up' and markets being conquered.

The late Freddie Mercury saw bands being geared to survive in the business: 'It's a growth process,' he said in 1980. 'I can't analyse every band, but take the Police – they're more geared up than we were ten years ago to taking this business, step by step, and finding a way through it.' The Police presented the perfect image of the modern rock group, from the tips of their dyed beach-boy blond hair to the toe-tapping rhythms bought but not paid for from fashionable reggae music. Somewhat too old to be punks and definitely too experienced to be fools, they incorporated only the largely uncontroversial aspects of the punk image into an entertainment form.

'Musically, the band is evolving at its own rate, and we're in control of that,' said Sting (real name Gordon Sumner), the band's chief appointed spokesman, pointing out at the time (also 1980) they were 'generating large amounts of money' and hence found themselves at the mercy of image-builders who, he said, were 'trying to soften the group to make it acceptable to even more people'. It was, perhaps, a trifle disingenuous, considering the values that the band readily admitted to. Drummer Stewart Copeland argued against punk's 'politically oriented' music, saying that 'I don't feel responsible for the ills of the world, and the only thing I'll go into battle for is my music.'

The result was a band run on the lines of a business venture. 'We're ambitious,' Sting said during a 1980 tour which set out to 'break new territory' in Mexico, Egypt, India, Thailand and Greece. 'We want power and I think occasionally you have to compromise yourself. The opportunities presented themselves and we took 'em. There's a very clear, very simple *gestalt* to the Police. There are three blond heads and that's it. That sells.'

One result of this heightened awareness of rock as commerce has been a number of dinosaurian battles between performers on the one hand and 'the business' on the other. The most notable of these to date was the case between Robert Stigwood and the Bee Gees. In 1980, the Bee Gees filed the largest lawsuit in showbiz history against their manager and the head of their record label, Robert Stigwood. They accused him of fraud, conflict of interest and unfair enrichment at their expense. The suit, for $125 million from Stigwood and his companies and $75 million from Polygram (the multinational conglomerate which owned Stigwood's label, RSO), cited 'grossly inadequate' contracts that Stigwood had made, apparently featuring royalty rates significantly below the industry norm, alleged that he registered their song copyrights in his name and pocketed money that was rightfully theirs. The Bee Gees, lest it be forgotten, had the biggest selling album of all time in *Saturday Night Fever*. Stigwood, on the other hand, has been no stranger to disaster in his chosen business.

Stigwood started in the entertainment business in Britain in 1961 managing actor-turned-singer, John Leyton, and singer-turned-film director, Mike Sarne, among others. Soon he was heavily involved in concert promotion. In 1965, the 29-year-old Australian put his company into liquidation having lost £15,000 on a cancelled Chuck Berry tour and £10,000 on a cancelled P. J. Proby tour. Proby was sacked because, according to Stigwood, he insisted on using his personal compere, Kim Fowley, who had still not received a work permit a week before the tour began. The promoter replaced Proby with Chuck Berry, only to find that 'contractual obligations' kept Berry from performing. At the liquidation, Robert Stigwood Associates owed a total of £39,000.

Stigwood worked for Brian Epstein for some time before moving into business on his own account with the Robert Stigwood Organization (RSO) and his own record label, Reaction. The deal he made with major acts like Cream and the Bee Gees reinforced his reputation as a cautious businessman. His public response to the Bee Gees' suit was to call it a 'cheap stunt'. But within weeks of this comment the group and their manager had achieved a reconciliation apparently as sweet as the split had been bitter.

If the enormous success achieved by rock'n'roll worldwide has to be celebrated for anything, it should be for providing us with the sweet irony of law's majesty and accountancy's order becoming entangled in a music that was described, barely twenty-five years ago, as lawless, anarchic and immoral. 'Money doesn't talk,' as Bob Dylan once sang, 'it swears.'

HEADLINE VIEWS

The rock'n'roll business is all about selling mass illusions – and for that you need the mass media. Consequently, the most effective hypes in rock have been those that turned rock'n'roll into news, not merely an entertainment for a specific audience, but a part of the general public consciousness. In some cases, incidents have been manufactured and the truth coloured by invention. This is not to say that every time rock'n'roll hits the headlines the event has been staged, or that the stories are themselves lies. Hype can just as easily be based on truth, because it is essentially a process of image building. Whatever materials come to hand are grist to its mill. The right image and the right approach are the keys to media interest. But, once aroused, the beast is often dangerously insatiable. If you give the non-rock press riots and rebelliousness, they crave more. The Rolling Stones found interest could soon turn to hostility.

The Stones were among the first rock groups to be deliberately hassled by the press – although they tended not to turn up drunk or drugged for interviews, and, for the most part, managed to keep a sensible division between their riotous public life and their quieter (but at times much seamier) private lives. That is until Brian Jones revealed his drug habits to two people he had met at a night-club. Ever eager for scandalous stories with which to assail its prurient readership, the *News of the World* ran the story of the conversation in the second part of their special series, 'Pop Stars and Drugs', in February 1967 and gained a libel suit from Mick Jagger for their pains.

At the Redlands trial in 1967, Jagger claimed that the paper had intentionally set out to discredit him in order to kill off his libel action. The paper admitted only that it had informed the police on the night of the Redlands' raid that drugs *might* be found at the house. That in itself was enough to inspire vociferous criticism – not least by the British 'quality' press. It was a matter of journalistic ethics – a newspaper should not act as a police informant, especially having failed to check its sources and with no intention of running a story on the matter. The ethics of newspaper coverage of rock'n'roll in general were never actually questioned and the traditional attitudes survive today as strong as ever: alternately celebrating the innocent joyousness of teenage music and condemning (usually with gleeful relish) the 'dangers' and 'immorality' of rock'n'roll.

The non-rock media can be extremely fickle – one moment courting you, the next condemning you, and after that ignoring you, exactly as they see the wishes of their readers, listeners and viewers. The Beatles first made the national press in the *Daily Mirror*, with a story of how John Lennon hit Bob Wooler at McCartney's twenty-first birthday party on 20th June, 1963. Wooler was a DJ at the Cavern club, and, like most other Merseyside music personalities, attended the party at Dinas Lane, Huyton, in Liverpool. As usual, Lennon – who later and rather disingenuously described Wooler as 'my best friend' – was drunk as a skunk. When Wooler insinuated that John and Brian Epstein were having an affair (common local gossip at the time), Lennon's macho working class upbringing took over.

'I was so high, I didn't realize what I was doing,' Lennon told the papers afterwards, adding that 'Bob is the last person in the world I would want to have a fight with.' In the end, Epstein intervened, driving the DJ to hospital and offering money and an apology on John's behalf – both of which were accepted. The press story treated the incident as the exceptional act of a drunken man, completely ignoring both Lennon's habitual drug-taking and drinking *and* the comments that caused the fracas. Even so, John Lennon's violence was scandal enough to arouse the interest of the press.

Soon, however, scandal gave way to praise: ballet critic Richard Buckle called the Beatles 'the best song-writers since Schubert', while music critic Tony Palmer went one better and called them the greatest composers 'since Beethoven'. As Lennon himself pointed out, there was, by that time, too much in the way of goodies and good times for anyone to risk the Beatles' wrath by raking up the muck. Swinging London had become the gravy train.

In time the swinging had to stop and the Beatles, increasingly tarnished with drugs, politics, religious heterodoxy and sex, became a freak show. The legal battles between McCartney and Lennon were gloated over; John and Yoko's 'political' activities – 'bed-ins', acorn-planting ceremonies, the 'War Is Over' campaign – were watched by the media with the wry amusement one affords a naughty child who has found a worthwhile, if naively pursued, hobby. When John and Yoko split up in 1974 and he ran off to Los Angeles with his Chinese secretary May Pang, the newspapers, once again, were interested only in his indiscretions. Visiting the Troubadour Club one night with Harry Nilsson, he became objectionably drunk,

The media gets the message. Andy Warhol (foreground) smiles benevolently at Deborah Harry, camping it up with Truman Capote at Warhol's Interview magazine party. Everyone should be famous for fifteen minutes, said Warhol and set about creating a magazine for people who are famous all the time.

heckled the Smothers Brothers who were trying to perform and paraded in the club with a sanitary towel fixed to his head. Lennon and Nilsson finally succeeded in getting themselves ejected and Lennon tried to attack a woman photographer recording the scene. The press lapped it up – perhaps out of their contempt for their earlier sycophancy during the Beatlemania period, the newspapers revelled in the vision of shoeless idols displaying their feet of clay. The nutty, noisy, happy, handsome, unbelievably brilliant, incredibly attractive, wonderful, wonderful Beatles were dead, said the supercilious media men and women; long live the next big thing.

Bob Geldof, considered by many to be one of the most articulate rock stars, was once, during his days with the Boomtown Rats, the next big thing himself. Finding himself on the sharp end of media attention, this former journalist began to object vociferously to the wrong kind of attention. In particular, he found the way the rock press treated his relationship with Paula Yates upsetting. 'They were really nasty about Paula,' he said 'They'd say "Geldof made an appearance with that ugly cow he calls his girlfriend" . . . or, "They're so boring, who do they think they are? The Rod and Britt of the new wave?" Jesus. You go somewhere with your girlfriend, and that's what happens.'

This outburst, made to the *Melody Maker*, seemed like a case of protesting too much, since neither Paula nor her swain were ever particularly shy of joint or individual publicity. Throughout most of 1978, the British press was lightly bombarded with stories of Geldof-Yates affair. In April 1978, Bob was making news with earnest declarations that, while living with Paula 'very happily', he had no inclination towards marriage. Geldof, it was widely reported, claimed that his three ambitions were 'to get rich, to get famous and to get laid'. By June, Paula was telling the *Daily Mail* that her eight-month relationship with Bob was 'a mad passionate affair'. 'I shall go mad before the end of the year if he doesn't marry me,' she announced breathlessly. Less than two weeks later, Bob and Paula announced their intention to get married – and so on. If that's not asking for it, I don't know what is.

In the end, Geldof claimed his self-confidence was shattered by all this coverage. He found he could not handle bad reviews and they were becoming more frequent. The Rats were associated with the general punk negative attitude to stardom, probably wrongly, but Geldof had put himself forward as a sort of spokesman for the new mood in rock while remaining unaware of the incompatibility of that mood and his role. Not surprisingly, members of the press wanted to deflate what was (even by his own admission) his overbearing ego. Geldof himself learnt (so he said) to keep a lower profile. 'No more riding around in limos,' he said in 1980. 'I won't do any more interviews unless I've actually got something to say.' Which of

course he found in 1984 with Live Aid, the benefit gig that brought him an honorary knighthood and, ultimately, a new career in breakfast TV.

Geldof at least has some control over his own movements and his own orientation. This is more than can be said of the Sex Pistols when they allowed Malcolm McLaren to take them over. McLaren's choice of Johnny Rotten to front the Sex Pistols and of Sid Vicious to replace Glen Matlock were entirely based on looks and attitude: musical ability did not even enter the picture. The Stones, the Beatles, Bob Geldof, even Bill Haley, had some musical substance behind the froth of media interest: the Pistols only had the froth.

Like the Stones, the Pistols soon learnt that the press expected them to be monstrous, and the group lived up to expectations. Every carelessly-worded complaint or angry response was turned by the press into a 'flood of four-letter words' or an act of 'vandalism'. To the traditionally intemperate popular newspapers, the Pistols were 'wreckers', 'hooligans' and 'degenerates'. A slight fracas at Heathrow Airport in which one of the group may or may not have been sick, became 'an uproar' in the London *Evening News*. 'They shocked and revolted passengers and airline staff as they vomited and spat their way to an Amsterdam flight,' said the paper. A similar vomiting incident at the London offices of A&M records (the Pistols' second label) was totally fabricated, according to the executive who signed the group to the label and then dismissed them a week later.

If the Pistols' manager, Malcolm McLaren, had decided that his group needed to break new boundaries of outrageousness, he failed to realize that the media like outrageousness to be contained and controllable: just an image, in fact. If Rotten spat and snarled on stage, threw chairs at amplifiers or – as he did on one occasion – ended a show by stripping punk fan Jordan, they were all outrages safely restricted to the stage itself. In October 1976, EMI – one of the giants of the record industry had no compunction about signing the group to a two-year contract for an advance of £40,000. (In fact, they beat their competition by drawing up the fastest contract in their history – it only took one day.) 'For me the Sex Pistols are a backlash against the "nice little band" syndrome,' said EMI's A&R man, Nick Mobbs, 'and the general stagnation of the music industry.' But the backlash could not be contained. The public fuss over the Pistols' first release, *Anarchy In The UK*, took off uncontrollably in the wake of the group's notorious appearance on Thames Television's 'Today' programme in December.

The Sex Pistols' interview took a course that was no doubt unplanned. The Pistols, who appeared as a last-minute replacement for another group who dropped out of the peak-hour, family news and chat show, were displaying their usual crass public face, and Bill Grundy, the presenter, was doing his best to show them at their worst. During the exchange, Grundy made an aside to some punk girls in the audience. 'I've always wanted to meet you,' simpered one of them, to which Bill Grundy replied, 'We'll meet afterwards, shall we?' One of the group remarked that

The real stars of the Sex Pistols' scenario. Malcolm McLaren impersonates Winston Churchill while Vivienne Westwood hangs onto a dream, 20th December, 1977.

make a statement in an attempt to defuse angry criticism from shareholders. By the beginning of January 1977, the group had been dropped by EMI – after receiving a total of £50,000 from the company.

Despite headlines detailing the Pistols' less savoury personal habits, *Anarchy In The UK* continued to sell (55,000 copies after only five radio plays). In March, A&M stepped in to sign the group in a staged ceremony outside the gates of Buckingham Palace (it was the year of the Queen's Silver Jubilee). A&M dropped the group within a week of handing over £75,000 in advance payments and having pressed but never released the group's second single, *God Save The Queen*. The Sex Pistols were rapidly becoming seen as a contagious disease. In April, the group played their first live concert since the 'Today' fiasco, before an invited audience at a cinema in Islington, London. 'The first number is dedicated to Bill Grundy and the Queen,' said Rotten, opening the Pistols' set. 'It goes, "Fuck You!"' Once more, the press were outraged.

Effectively unable to perform or get their records released as a result, the Pistols might then have fallen apart, had not Virgin Records stepped in, figuring, no doubt, to revitalize their ageing hippy image. *God Save The Queen* was released at the end of May 1977 and climbed to the top of the charts – despite the fact that the BBC refused to mention its name, let alone play it. The fuss continued – the Pistols were reduced to performing under assumed names to avoid bans. Johnny Rotten – the victim of physical and verbal assaults –

he considered Grundy 'a dirty old man'. Grundy, mindful of his live audience and with one eye on the studio clock, pushed them to their limit. 'You've got another five seconds,' he taunted. 'Say something outrageous.' To which one of the group replied in kind: 'You dirty fucker. What a fuckin' rotter.'

Of course there was an explosion of disgust in banner headlines. Grundy found himself suspended for two weeks and removed from the show to safer pastures elsewhere in the network for his part in the fiasco; but his career survived. Nevertheless, it was embarrassing to all concerned and potentially, if not actually, damaging to some people's careers. It certainly led to the cancellation of a number of Pistols' gigs and the eventual severing of the band's association with EMI (albeit for a very substantial 'golden handshake'). The facts that Malcolm McLaren had carefully cultivated the Pistols' outrageousness, Grundy goaded them on and encouraged their hostility and EMI had suggested that the programme feature the Pistols in the first place, all indicate that the interview was intended to work as hype, sealing their image as the latest and greatest 'group you love to hate'. But the media were beginning to discover that the Pistols did not respect anybody else's ground rules. Their response was to build the group into even bigger monsters than they intended to be. A planned tour was cancelled and the EMI packers refused to handle copies of the Pistols' single, *Anarchy In The UK*. At EMI's general meeting a few weeks later, the company chairman, John Read, felt constrained to

Melody Maker

MARCH 26, 1977   15p weekly   USA 75 cents

ROTTEN: ●**They've given us up through fear and business pressure. They've kicked us in the teeth. W mean what we say. A recor company is there to market records —not dictate terms** ●

FIRING OF PISTOLS —TURN TO PAGE 3

hired a bodyguard. Sid Vicious, who had joined in February 1977, became increasingly dependent on heroin. The band failed to write any new material and became tied up in McLaren's grandiose ideas for a feature film, originally to be entitled *Who Killed Bambi?* and to be directed by cult 'sexploitation' director, Russ Meyer. Internal disputes and bad press ensured that the film's backers would pull out – which of course they did in November 1977. Arguments amongst the group members and between Johnny Rotten and McLaren continued unabated. The American tour early in 1978 was greeted with bad reviews, audience hostility and a menacing atmosphere of simmering violence. After a gig in San Francisco, Rotten walked out he confessed in New York that he had 'hated it in the Sex Pistols' all along. McLaren and the other three continued gamely but, by 1978, even the press had become bored with their increasingly futile antics. Gradually the whole Pistols operation ground to a halt, probably because, as Oscar Wilde once wrote, 'There is only one thing worse than being talked about, and that is not being talked about.'

The media, of course, like to control everything. If they must be part of the hype, they want it to be on their own terms. Their periodic investigations into corruption sometimes seem less courageous investigation than sour grapes. But it takes a very clever hustler – or a great deal of expense in bribes – to ensure that they

Whose round is it, anyway? Johnny Rotten (left) and Sid Vicious, accompanied by the habitual photographer, giving their drinks' order to a 'blue-bottle', in Kensington, London, October 1977. The Pistols attracted attention wherever they went.

toe the line. In fact, most groups these days tend to restrict their contact with reporters to communications issued from behind those brick walls known as publicists, press agents or public relations officers.

At the simplest level, publicists are the source of the basic information that daily floods into the offices of newspapers, magazines, radio and TV stations. They supply photographs and sometimes autograph them in the star's name, and they act as 'gatekeepers', arranging interviews and promotional events and selecting which journalists will be allowed access to which stars.

Publicists create and sustain images, so they tend to have a strange grasp of truth and reality. Creating an image is a sort of Frankenstein process in which a performer can all too easily become a monster inhabiting a misty no-man's-land somewhere between truth and fiction. Elton John's bisexuality (although widely discussed by industry and media people), remained a furtively-whispered rumour, until, that is, Elton himself spoke of it in 1976 at the time of his first retirement from live performance. 'I would have said something all along if someone had asked me,' he told an interviewer who had actually had the temerity to broach the subject. This just confirms the idea that the public relations image was independent of the person whom

183

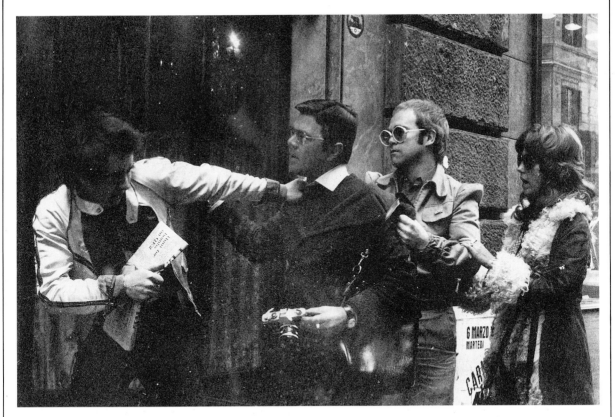

it was intended to represent.

There are a number of different approaches to image-building, any and all of which are at the disposal of the publicist. The simplest is the straightforward lie, in which performer, publicist or both offer the media unvarnished falsehoods. 'Kit Lambert used to brief us before we went into interviews about what to say,' Pete Townshend recalled, 'sometimes to be as objectionable, arrogant and nasty to reporters as possible. And oh, those outrageous lies we told: I remember telling Jonathan Aitken, "I have got four cars, a Lincoln Continental, a Jag XK150, a Cortina and a London taxi", and all I had was an old banger.' According to their early hype, the Who were 'a band with built-in hate', they were 'a new form of crime'. 'We didn't want any boy-next-door image,' said the group's co-manager, Chris Stamp.

In rock, it seems, there is sometimes such a thing as bad publicity. MGM's efforts in late 1967 to hype several groups from Boston as successors to the Liverpool and San Francisco groups, went strangely awry. Within a matter of weeks of MGM arriving in Boston with contracts in one hand and press releases in the other, *Newsweek* ran a lengthy piece on 'the Bosstown Sound'. An alleged quote from one local fan set the tone of the hype: 'They're Thomas Wolfe in sound,' she supposedly said of one group, 'with words that make you gloomy but always gladder.'

But by the middle of 1968, articles in *Vogue*, *The*

When in Rome ... Tempers flare as Elton John (second right) and an associate tangle with an unwelcome Italian photographer, 13th April, 1973.

Village Voice, *Time*, *Jazz and Pop*, *Rolling Stone* and *The Wall Street Journal* (this last accurately titled 'Selling a New Sound'), were noticeably critical. Jon Landau asked in *Rolling Stone* whether 'there is anything lying beneath the hype' and answered himself in the negative. *The Wall Street Journal* seemed content to let the hype speak for itself. Quoting the then head of MGM Records, Mort Nasatir, it reported on the most heavily backed of the Boston groups, Ultimate Spinach (yes!). 'Some of this music is so intellectual,' said Nasatir, 'that it is a little like the poet T. S. Eliot with his seven layers of ambiguity in each line'.

No group could live up to this sort of hype, and Ultimate Spinach were no exception to the rule. Despite the fact that the record trade papers continued to hype the success of the Boston sound, it was born a very lame duck. The groups were just not good enough, they were signed up too early in their careers and they never built up the kind of local fan following that could sustain them. All this was important at a time when live performance, musicianship, skilful lyric writing and the appearance of seriousness were at a premium in the kind of market into which MGM and their fellow labels were attempting to plug. You could fake a group like the Monkees, as Don Kirshner did with the Archies – a group of cartoon characters – but not the Grateful Dead.

Jon Landau, whose position as reviews editor of

Rolling Stone was influential enough to inspire his description as 'dean of rock critics', was himself indirectly responsible for another and similar classic hype. Having seen Bruce Springsteen in 1974, he wrote a piece about the performer for the Boston *Real Paper* in which he made the exaggerated and tendentious claim, 'I saw rock'n'roll future and its name is Bruce Springsteen.' Columbia Records (Springsteen's label) picked up on this outrageous but timely comment. Until Landau's review, CBS had been thinking about dropping Springsteen – despite critical acclaim, his first two albums had not sold well enough to recoup their huge initial investment. They decided to continue backing their performer. Landau was brought in to rescue Springsteen's new album from a mire of production difficulties and a campaign was planned. It opened with a number of full-page magazine ads quoting Landau's review prominently and at length. 'The future of rock'n'roll' became the best-known misquoted phrase in rock music.

In what is effectively an official biography of Bruce Springsteen, Dave Marsh argued that the subsequent build-up was not so much hype as 'auto-hype' – self-generated publicity triggered by fans in prominent positions on leading journals. This suggestion seems remarkably naive, even if one accepts that critical admiration for Springsteen grew rapidly by word-of-mouth. The co-ordination of the release of *Born To Run* in 1975 with the appearance of major features on the performer in the *New York Times* and in *Time* and *Newsweek* cannot be explained away by such simple-minded reliance on critical approbation.

In fact, interest in Springsteen seems to have followed on from interest in Columbia's promotional effort itself. The company spent an estimated $250,000 on pushing *Born To Run*. Without the already expressed approval of Landau and his fellow rock journalists, Columbia would doubtless have felt the expenditure unjustified. It was not the critics' approval that made Springsteen newsworthy, but the financial backing he was being given. *Newsweek* was particularly impressed and decided to carry a feature on 'the making of a rock star'. Springsteen's manager, Mike Appel, was meanwhile refusing all magazine interviews except those tied to cover features. *Time* was trying not to be caught out by *Newsweek*. And so an actual hype was born.

In Britain, the hype became almost feverish. Springsteen's first-ever performance there (in 1975) was heralded by the appearance of starkly dramatic black and white posters over London shouting out that 'At last London is ready for Bruce Springsteen'. Anybody who was anybody was invited to the show, and many accepted. After all, the future of rock'n'roll wasn't just going to breeze into town, play three chords and leave. The hype generated enormous expectations which were bound to be disappointed – even by a rock'n'roller as outstanding as Springsteen. Springsteen and his band were particularly affected by the excessiveness of the hype in Britain and the mini tour passed in an atmosphere of some gloom. Bruce was unhappy at having to perform the impossible task of living up to an impossible reputation (he even took to tearing Springsteen posters off walls in London).

Despite all this, the hype seemed to work. Bruce Springsteen was rapidly becoming, in theory at least, a very wealthy man. Unfortunately, his deal with Appel became increasingly a subject of conflict (Springsteen confessed to not having read his contracts with sufficient care). In July 1976, the writs started flying and for almost a year Bruce was effectively banned from recording (although he continued to play live). However his career hardly suffered and the break with Appel finally cemented Springsteen's business relationship with the man who had started it all – Jon Landau.

Another classic hype was perpetrated in Britain. This one was a disastrous failure. Brinsley Schwarz was a band formed in 1970 from the remains of Kippington Lodge, a BBC radio house band. They signed a management contract with a company called Famepushers whose intention was to launch them with a record released through Liberty/UA, a concert at the Fillmore East and a film of that concert. The idea was that each enterprise would both help pay for and promote the others. It was a complicated financial manoeuvre which absolutely depended on getting the right publicity.

Famepushers chartered a plane to carry rock and

Kissing Cousins. Pete Townshend gets close to Binkie Baker, husband of rock journalist and media personality, Anne Nightingale, at a promotional party for Ian Hunter.

non-rock reporters from Britain to the New York gig. But things went terribly astray. The three British members of the band (Brinsley Schwarz, Nick Lowe and Bob Andrews) had difficulty in getting visas into America, and eventually arrived tired, hassled and well below form. Meanwhile, the press plane flew in ten hours late after a delay at London and an enforced stopover at Shannon. The journalists arrived hotfoot and drunk at the Fillmore to find a nearly full house and no seats booked for them. The few that got in missed most of Brinsley Schwarz's woefully inadequate set. Reporters from the national press discovered a couple of celebrities in the crowd who were of more interest to them than some unknown rock group. And, to cap it all, the Famepushers' film crew were refused admission to the concert hall.

When it was all over, it had cost Famepushers more than £20,000 plus room service – the drinks bill for one hotel room alone came to £300. Those journalists who did not totally ignore the event wrote scathing reviews of the hype or dismissive reviews of the band. Despite the fact that the album heralded by the hype was the band's best-ever seller, the Brinsleys retired for some months to reconsider their position, eventually re-emerging as kings of the pub-rock circuit. It wasn't until six years later that the group's split-up freed Nick Lowe to become a successful new wave producer and solo performer and Brinsley Schwarz and Bob Andrews to win recognition as members of Graham Parker's backing band, the Rumour. At least two of the people associated with Famepushers went on to greater things, however – Dai Davies as a publicist, agent and the original manager of the Stranglers, and Dave Robinson as one of the founders of Stiff Records.

The fourth estate – down but not out. Smiling all the while, two of Rod Stewart's associates debag journalist Simon Kinnersley at a party for Rod, London, 1980.

Governments tend to be very sensitive about the control of broadcasting. For example, in the sixties, the British government outlawed the offshore 'pirate' radio stations that sprang up just outside Britain's coastal waters, despite the fact that most of these displayed a non-controversiality guaranteed by their dependence on payola and record company advertising. A more subtle process overtook America's 'alternative' FM stations in the seventies.

With an eye to both their advertisers and their FCC licences, FM stations were all too eager to discipline or sack any DJs who displayed too radical or too controversial an approach to broadcasting. In particular, the FCC pressured FM stations on the question of drug lyrics or allegedly obscene song references. This was part of a Nixonian tendency which embraced vice-president Spiro Agnew, the then chairman of the FCC; the head of MGM records at the time, Mike Curb, who, in 1970, announced very publicly that his label had terminated the contracts of 'eighteen groups . . . that are associated with hard drugs'; and a variety of unsavoury right-wing groups, including the John Birch Society and the Ku Klux Klan (who, in 1970, bombed a community radio station in Houston).

In Britain, the BBC claims never to actually *ban* records, merely to refuse to play them. The distinction

186

is too fine to be visible. The BBC (and the commercial broadcasting authority, the IBA) have 'refused to play' a long list of songs in which references to drugs, sex or distasteful politics have been noted. These include the Beatles' *Sgt Pepper* track, *A Day In The Life*, X-Ray Spex's *O Bondage, Up Yours!* and Paul McCartney's *Give Ireland Back To The Irish*. Despite revelling in the most lurid sexist imagery, some record companies have been quick to clamp down on 'unsavoury' sleeves too. One Beatles compilation album cover design depicted the boys as blood-stained butchers. It was banned. The Rolling Stones' original cover for *Beggars Banquet* showed a picture of a graffiti-laden urinal wall. It was banned. EMI refused to distribute John and Yoko's *Two Virgins* which depicted the couple naked on the front. Other albums featuring a little too much of the naked body (Hendrix's *Electric Ladyland*, for example, and an album by a group named Boxer called *Below The Belt*) have been withdrawn from display or 'censored' by prudish shops. Virgin Records was taken to court in December 1977 over the Sex Pistols' album *Never Mind The Bollocks . . . Here's The Sex Pistols* on the grounds of indecent display, following a complaint about a poster advertising the album in a Nottingham shop window. The case was dismissed but many records shops took to concealing the album all the same.

The most famous cases of broadcast bans involve Elvis, the Stones (again) and the Doors on the Ed Sullivan TV show. Elvis, of course, was filmed only from the waist up. The Stones were required to alter the words of *Let's Spend The Night Together* to 'let's spend some time together' – and acceded. Jim Morrison, asked to sing an alternative line to 'Baby, we can't get much higher' in the song *Light My Fire*, caused much consternation when he actually sang the original during the show after agreeing to censor himself at a rehearsal.

The rock press might seem to be a better place to seek rock's radical vision but in truth it's no less reliable than radio or TV on the patronage of record companies and concert promoters – patronage that takes the form of advertising, the supply of records and concert tickets and the provision of information and access to performers. It also takes the less direct form of subsidy to journalists through the supply of promotional records. Most of the time this subtle patronage encourages self-censorship by the rock press. Not wishing to offend the industry, criticisms are toned down and touchy subjects are often ignored completely. But threats to withdraw support and the actual withdrawal of support are by no means unknown, while patronage is often made explicit to the point of bribery. A magazine may be offered an exclusive interview in return for a favourable review, or ads may be placed on condition that they are backed by editorial. Many rock journalists are also part-time DJs, record company publicists or A&R people. The forms of bribery are many – job opportunities, exclusive stories, freebies – and even include offers of cash payments. 'I maintained my illusions about the value-free purity of rock,' critic Richard Goldstein wrote in *New York* magazine, 'until the day in 1969 when my agent informed me that a large music publisher would pay me $25,000 for three presentations on the state of popular music. It was understood that I would favour this company's artists in my reviews.'

But beyond this formal sort of bribery there is a more insidious informal process helping to diffuse criticism in which rock journalists are seduced by the glamour of their vocation. Promotional parties are where most of the stardust rubs off. Usually they are relatively routine occasions, at which the assembled hacks, publicists and general parasitic riff-raff get routinely drunk. At one end-of-tour party thrown by Rod Stewart at London's Embassy Club in December 1980, the unfortunate rock music critic of the *Daily Mail* was debagged by two of Stewart's henchmen. Journalist Simon Kinnersley, also involved in the *Sounds* libel suit, found himself set upon as if in jest, and unceremoniously divested of his trousers. It appeared that the writer had been less than flattering in his review of Stewart's gigs – so Rod's over-zealous associates turfed the unfortunate ex-public school journalist out into the street in his underpants. It may not sound too glamorous – but it *was* in Mayfair.

At the vertiginous, self-congratulatory heights of superstardom, glamour is often synonymous with excess. The end of Wings' 1976 tour of America was celebrated by a party on the estate of the silent comedy star Harold Lloyd. The pool was drained to provide a disco floor. There was entertainment from a chamber orchestra playing Beatles' songs, the cast of the Broadway musical *The Wiz*, the Los Angeles Ballet and comedian John Belushi (the high point of whose act was an insulting impersonation of Joe Cocker). An estimated 400 guests – including Bob Dylan, Elton John, Cher and Natalie Cole – cavorted into the night at a cost to the Wings tour budget of some $200 per person.

In 1981, Deborah Harry's record company arranged a party to celebrate the release of her solo album, *Koo Koo*, at the ultra-exclusive women's health club in London, the Sanctuary. The 400 guests desported themselves amidst the jungle foliage eating their way through mountains of seafood and drinking themselves silly. By the end of the evening there was so much food left that the guests (many of whom could afford to buy their own fishmongers) were wrapping up crabs, lobsters and prawns and taking them home. At an earlier seafood do for Harry's group, Blondie, the guests of honour arrived in a specially hired US Army tank!

The single most important aspect of these events is, of course, their prestige value. In some cases, record companies will arrange a plush event for a performer whose prestige value is more important than his or her popularity might suggest. Most performers are greatly impressed by a company's willingness to spend money on them. Hype they may be, but they certainly work towards general goodwill, improved artist relations and a good image for the industry. And, of course, a good time is usually had by all – so that the hype itself is clouded in the mists of mellow booziness and made to seem of little significance.

The surprising thing is that occasionally (very occasionally, it's true) rock journalists balk at the whole process. They are not, it then seems, fawning sycophants but merely people with a blind eye to turn on the machinations of the record industry. Sometimes the layer of comfortable privilege that isolates them from the world outside of recording studios, concert-halls and plush hotels is pierced, and they rally (or think they are rallying) to the defence of rock'n'roll.

For all its faults, the punk movement did pierce a few layers of privilege and open a few blind eyes. The rock press as a whole was made aware of what can only be called the glaring inhumanity of the industry's star system – a system which had reached Hollywood Golden Age proportions and was being more or less uncritically supported by the vast body of rock journalists occupied in their own versions of being 'on the make'. Suddenly, negativity was all the rage. New writers (and some old ones in disguise) emerged calling themselves 'Savage' and 'Suck' and so on. Sudden conversions to the dole queue ethos became all the rage. For a time, rock journalism acquired a social conscience. Political issues were vigorously discussed and even the record industry came in for some overdue criticism. For example, the British division of RCA

Records flew 200 assorted rock biz persons and journalists to Amsterdam for two days in September 1980, so that they could (at an estimated cost of £50,000) spend some time in a luxury hotel and between breakfast, lunch, dinner and drinks, visit a gig by RCA band Sad Cafe and the unveiling of Sad Cafe's new album. On that occasion, the British rock press wasn't slow to point out that not only had Sad Cafe previously sued RCA for allegedly failing to support them adequately, but that the company was, at the time of the trip, a week away from sacking 21 employees in a recession-inspired cut-back designed to save money. But such radical posturing could hardly survive, let alone flourish, given the cosy relationship between the rock press and the record industry. History could have shown the punk-era journalists how expert the record industry is at undermining the independence of writers.

In May 1973, 140 rock journalists gathered in Memphis for the 'First Annual National Association of Rock Writers' Convention'. Most came from America, two or three from Britain. They were there, it may be assumed, to assay the common problems of the rock writer. Among the questions discussed were the low rates of pay, the rock writer's lack of negotiating strength, and the difficulties of dealing with conservative publishers and a fickle record industry. In four days, the writers held a number of sessions at which the arguments ranged far and wide. Richard Meltzer suggested, not entirely in jest, that record companies should pay for reviews. Greg Shaw of *Phonograph*

188

Beggars can be choosers. To mark the release of their album, Beggars Banquet, *the Rolling Stones threw a launch party (complete with boar's head) and several 'custard' pies, 6th December, 1968. Aristocratic guest, Lord Harlech – former escort of Jackie Kennedy – wiped foam from his face and beamed: 'An absolutely topping party.' Presumably, dream topping.*

Record Magazine, which was funded by United Artists, argued that there were too many complaints about writing fees. 'I'm a fan,' he pronounced with disarming candour, 'not a writer.'

The discussions went on through the convention. Meanwhile the assembled rock journalists took notes on pads provided by MCA Records, their evenings were spent popping in and out of hospitality rooms run by MCA, Blue Thumb, London, Stax and Polydor, or maybe they were out to dinner with executives from CBS, Mercury, A&M or Motown, who were all present. Perhaps they just reflected on the fact that the whole event had been sponsored by Stax Records and organized by Stax's publicist who, not entirely coincidentally, was trying to break the British band, Skin Alley, into the States. The cost of the convention was estimated by one writer at $40,000 – a figure confirmed by one of the others present, who commented that it was quite reasonable compared to a recent one-night promotional event for Jefferson Airplane's RCA-sponsored Grunt label, which had cost $100,000. The writers made no decision of any significance except to call themselves by the grandiloquent title, 'Rock Writers of the World'. They never met as an organization again, Skin Alley never took off in the States, but the partying continues.

THE END OF MUSIC AS WE KNOW IT

The 1980s was the decade that discovered style - or so the legend has it. Before the eighties, there was nothing but a big platform boot and flared-trouser shaped hole called the seventies, the paisley patterned sixties and the fifties where the quest for style had begun. Before that came the War, dinosaurs and Julius Caesar.

In truth, the eighties was the decade that made style itself into a commodity sold in the mass market, not just an attribute of other commodities. In the sixties and seventies, people grew their hair long; in the eighties, they bought hair extensions. In the fifties and sixties, people wore jeans; in the eighties they wore the label on a pair of jeans. Where once they might have managed their time or organized their persons, in the eighties people invested in time-managers or personal organizers.

Rock'n'roll, too, was reduced to a production-line commodity. Style was no longer something a performer or a writer or a group had - it was something they captured in a sound sampler or bought as a preset patch on a Yamaha synthesizer. And when they couldn't buy a style, they borrowed someone else's.

At the limit of the process, as the nineties started to toddle, came Natalie Cole's ghoulish but prize-winning duet with her dead dad on *Unforgettable* - an unforgiveable techno-*trompe d'oreille* in which Natalie's voice was grafted on to some old but laundered Nat King Cole tracks for no apparent reason other than to demonstrate that technology presents no barrier to complete lack of originality. Elektra - the label concerned - had once been a hotbed of new ideas and new sounds. Now it was reduced to a form of grave-robbing.

Already by 1984, Chris Blackwell, co-founder and owner of Island Records (a British Elektra and one of the great artistic and commercial success stories of rock's creative past) could be heard complaining that there were no longer 'any record companies in the real sense of the word'. 'We're all in the fashion business,' said Blackwell, who went on to sell his company in 1989 to the global PolyGram empire - making multi-millionaires of himself and the already seriously successful U2, Island's biggest act at the time, who famously netted a profit of £70 million in the financial year 1987/88. 'You used to be able to sell records purely on music and musicianship,' Blackwell said.

Kurt Cobain, probably the only real rock'n'roll hero of the 1990s, spent his three years of fame trying to avoid it. He finally succeeded some time between 5th and 8th April 1994 by blowing his head off with a shotgun.

'Now it's packaging, media, television and video.'

Look at Madonna - a Marilyn Monroe image, blue-movie poses, and underwear courtesy of Fredericks of Hollywood and Trashy Lingerie, her music is the least interesting thing about her; her mouth is there to be looked at not listened to, her twin muses are fellatio and cunnilingus. But she doesn't do sex, she simulates it - an absolute triumph of culture over nature, just like nouvelle cuisine and health clubs. She even put her name to a book called *Sex*, consisting of photographs of her in provocative poses and mathematically complex couplings and triplings. And just to let us know she was no dumb broad, she would call one of her first singles 'Like A Virgin' (1984) and her 1990 world tour 'Blonde Ambition'. Her own blonde hair, as *Q Magazine's* Adrian Deevoy once noted, has black roots like her music.

The truth is that Madonna is not the rock'n'roll synthesis reworked, but a completely self-conscious pot-pourri of symbols and signifiers - nine parts clothes and make-up to one part music. And yet Madonna Louise Ciccone has been, arguably, the most successful *rock* performer of the decade, with a string of hits from 1983 onwards and a record of chart successes topped only by the Beatles and Elvis Presley. Lyrically explicit, with a stage show of unashamed vulgarity, Madonna has presented herself as a sort of sexual predator - bold enough to enjoy group sex, bondage or a little light spanking but always in command. Feminists have been divided by this image into those who see her as little more than a female pornographer and those who see her as an archetypal strong woman, promoting guilt-free female sexuality and damned successful at it, too.

She has, of course, turned all her fans into voyeurs, but what has irritated critics is the 'who cares?' attitude - so modern, so in touch with the street, so fascinating. She unleashed a flood of 'wannabees' (as in 'I wanna be Madonna'), who adored her sassiness, her nonchalance, her millions of dollars, her 'Boy Toy' belt-buckle, her apparent ability to straddle the sexual divide and still get her man, the ease with which she seems to change identities with her clothes, and above all her ordinariness. No Kim Basinger or Michelle Pfeiffer (despite collagen injections to enlarge her lips), Madonna was the girl next door - a perfect rock icon for the eighties.

While her route to stardom has been conventional enough - dance school, disco backing group, NY rock group, club reputation, signing to Warner Brothers - continued success has ultimately relied on movies and videos, on the self-conscious creation of image and the

191

clever exploitation of wardrobe, make-up and props (among which you can include her egregious underwear, her male dancers, and the Frida Kahlo paintings on her wall). Her image does not represent her as a creature of unattainable fantasy, but as a woman constantly re-inventing herself through play and fashion: rich or free and, latterly, both.

In videos accompanying single releases like 'Material Girl' and 'Like A Prayer' she played erotic scenes with tongue in cheek. In her 1991 documentary movie, called *Truth or Dare* in the US and *In Bed With Madonna* elsewhere, she watches two of her male dancers kissing, simulates fellatio on the neck of a bottle, is reprimanded by her father for seemingly masturbating on stage and ends up in bed with seven men. In the adult-rated *Body Of Evidence* (1992), promoted as 'an erotic thriller', she is shown loving her partner to death. None of this is particularly new or shocking, but two things make it different from past examples of sexual explicitness or self-styled 'erotic politicians' like Hendrix or Bowie, Jane Fonda or Grace Jones, Jim Morrison or the Tubes. One is the relentlessness with which the image is promoted - it is Madonna, that's all Madonna is. The other is the presentation of an unusual (not to say deviant) sexuality as fun, a sort of dormitory game among friends.

Ask Madonna what the truth is and she'll tell you she's sexual and spiritual, keen to reveal all to the cameras but not to let them 'in the room when I was fucking', wants to be taken seriously but despises people who take themselves seriously. 'You only have to have half a brain in your head to see I'm quite often making fun of myself. I mean, how obvious can I be?'

Well, obvious enough to sanction two titles for the 1991 tour documentary, the original and suggestive *Truth Or Dare* and the subtle-as-a-flying-mallet *In Bed With Madonna*. Her former lover, the sexually adventurous Warren Beatty, once observed that Madonna lives on camera. Mind you, Beatty could have taught Madonna a thing or two when it comes to self-publicity, and exhibitionism is a common complaint in rock'n'roll. But it's true that exhibitionism dominates eighties' rock, and Madonna dominates the exhibitionists. The camera made Madonna, not her music, and she has returned the compliment by making her life into a movie. Now, according to her publicity machine, she is 'the most famous woman in the world', a fitting star for her own life story.

'The hard thing for people to take is that there isn't someone playing the part of my life in the movie 50 years after I'm dead,' she told *Q Magazine*. 'I'm doing it myself. No-one has ever done this before.' Madonna's female fans are self-generated clones – to be like the image is to become it. And in a world of images, Madonna's sexual acrobatics are sterile and quite safe.

We have all become voyeurs and exhibitionists. In the eighties, videos and films mattered more than singles, probably more than most things – whether it was Madonna jerking off, Jane Fonda jerking up and down, or Freddy Krueger just jerking. The point is under-

Below: Blondes have more fun by themselves – Madonna makes out on the 'Blonde Ambition' tour. Right: Madonna models 'clothes' designed by the fashion world's favourite funny little Frenchman, Jean-Paul Gaultier, in 1992. But turn back to page 65 and find out that there's nothing new under the sun.

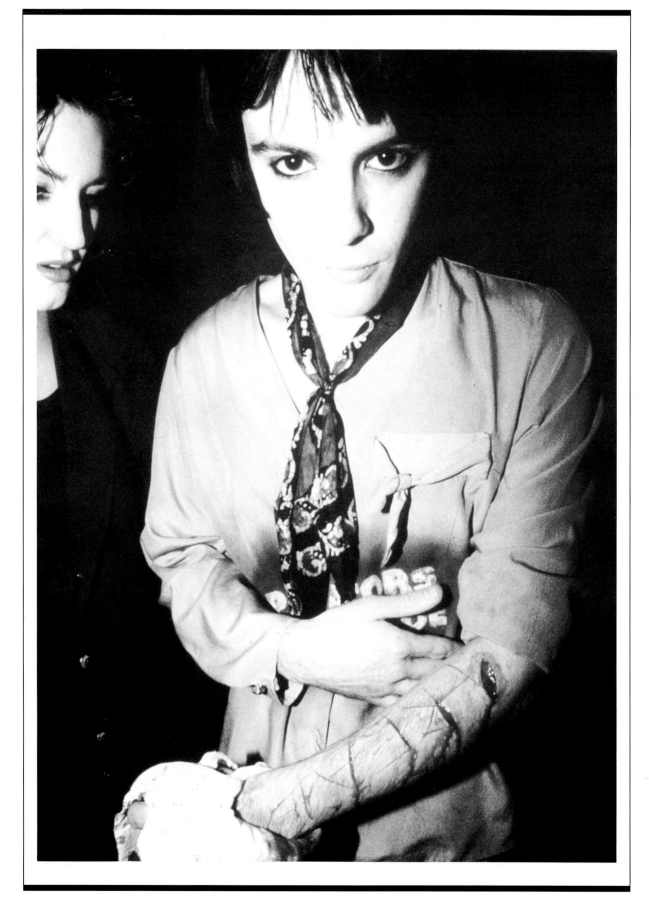

lined by the remarkable success of Michael Jackson in the mid-eighties. Perhaps, the most important thing about Jackson is not that his records sold by the bucketful producing almost as many record-breaking statistics as records and making him the first performer ever to receive more than $100 million a year, but that they were marketed by means of some of the most expensive rock videos ever made, like $7 million for ten minutes of *Thriller* (1982). His live shows would then reproduce these videos in exact detail and, heaping irony upon irony, fans at the back of the huge stadiums he performed in would watch him on enormous video screens hung above the stages. By comparison to the rock music of the eighties, the movies and videos of the decade had wit, verve, passion and, often, originality in abundance.

In fact, the single most important characteristic of the rock music of the eighties was its almost total lack of originality. Even punk – once hailed as the radical renewal of rock's cutting edge – was being recycled fifteen years later. In 1991, Richie Edwards of Manic Street Preachers reacted to accusations of lack of originality by carving '4 Real' into his forearm with a razor blade. The wound required 17 stitches and pictures of it were used as promotional material for the group. The second most important thing about it was its complete fragmentation into different markets. There was punk, rock, house, thrash, hip-hop, rap, death metal, new folk, old folk, roots, popular opera and world music (which covered everything else). Vinyl faded away, the single collapsed, CDs started a repackaging panic. Film soundtracks and TV adverts dreamt up by the greying rock generation now running Madison Avenue gave the hits of the past a new lease of life, sometimes in note-for-note recreations, sometimes in their original form. The search for the new Beatles gave way to the search for the next niche market.

Getting played on MTV, launched in 1981 and boasting 54.5 million subscribers ten years later, became the acme of a music marketing department's ambitions (at least, until Sir Bob Geldof's 1984 'Live Aid' concert lifted benefit gigs into outer orbit and paved the way for a series of global marketing opportunities with street cred like 'Farm Aid', 'Farm Aid 2', 'Human Rights Now!', 'Mandela Day' and 'The Simple Truth'). Today MTV can choose from over 8,000 different music videos compared to fewer than 600 in 1981. For MTV's tenth anniversary in 1991, New York's *Village Voice* newspaper came up with a memo from the very same Island Records mentioned above instructing staff to use speed-dialing buttons on their office phones to unbalance the ballot on the station's 'Dial MTV' segment in favour of a Drivin-n-Cryin video.

The power of video and TV is not just to sell music but to put the fragmented rock scene back together again under a seamless veneer of dissolves, freeze frames and special effects. According to *TV Guide* in the US (probably the highest circulation journal in the world), MTV 'shaped fashion, defined a youth culture and just may even have saved an entire industry'. Sounds just like the Beatles.

Look at Prince, an ersatz mixture of sixties psychedelia, funk and peace and love symbols. He's drawn comparisons with Smokey Robinson, Sly Stone, George Clinton (no relation), James Brown, Jimi Hendrix, David Bowie, Mick Jagger and Aerosmith's Steve Tyler. He has been, according to his fans and critics alike, the only figure in the eighties music scene to be close to genius. But his genius really consists of a light touch with histrionics and a bargain-basement approach to clothes, stage sets, lyrics and musical styles. Made for video!

If the very beginning of his career was in a more-or-less conventional soul-funk mould with a streak of glam rock thrown in, he soon adopted an entirely theatrical devotion to erotic themes. Early on, he cultivated sexual and racial ambiguity and a Bowiesque attachment to costume. He was interesting because he subverted racist stereotypes by playing up an apparent effeminacy and by adopting, musically and lyrically, a white idiom (so much so that many younger fans refused to believe he actually was black – a refusal made all the more natural by Prince's own habit of telling interviewers that, at different times, he had a half black, half Italian father; an all black father and an Italian mother; or just some very mixed genes). It was all cleverly contrived.

In the early eighties, he appeared on Dick Clark's vintage show *American Bandstand* and adopted an interview style which replaced Dylan's obliqueness and the Sex Pistols' vitriol with dumb insolence. This was not the legendary Prince shyness but a calculated piece of image-management. 'Before we went on we were sitting in the green room and Prince hatched this idea not to say anything,' band guitarist Dez Dickerson remembered. 'He said: "If he asks you anything just shake your head, don't talk".'

The idea was always simply to break out of the black music ghetto – to follow Chuck Berry and Hendrix into the big white world of pop stardom. For Prince Rogers Nelson this meant selecting the appropriate styles, themes and treatments. He moved on from the conventional black metaphorical approach to sex and became explicit; he introduced classic rock guitar elements, show-biz glitz and white bandsmanship into his music and his stage act, he learned the central importance of image and the presentation of image through TV, film and video.

The basis of the Prince image was from the outset rooted in performance. And the performances, inspired by Prince's own songs, were manipulations of his collaborators. In 'I Wanna Be Your Lover' from the second album, *Prince* (1979), he played a desperate man – he wants to be lover, sister and mother, 'the only one you come for'! And this was acted out on stage – a physical correspondence to Prince's lyrical attempts at creating an erotic family in a polymorphously perverse world. It didn't always work.

The best a man can get? Richie Edwards of Manic Street Preachers rolls ups his sleeves for a really close shave. This attempt at beating the punks at their own game required 17 stitches and was used in promotional material.

195

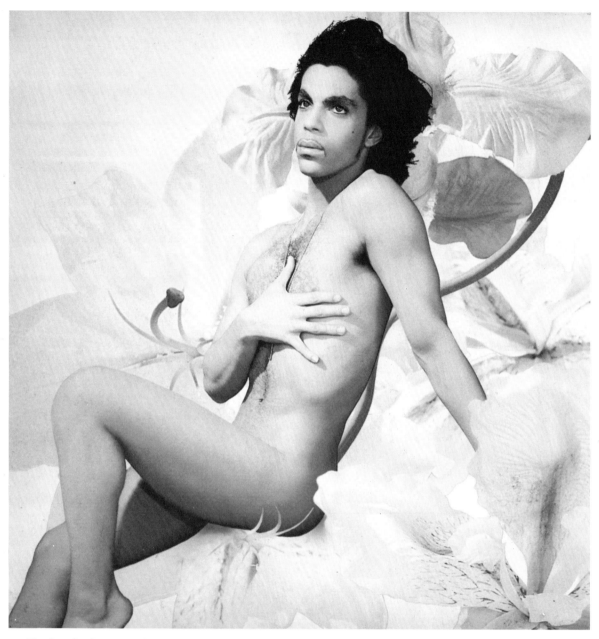

Small but perfectly formed: Prince shows himself to be just a hot-house flower on the cover of his mega-selling 'LoveSexy' album.

The band's first casualty was blonde keyboardist Gayle Chapman, in early 1980. Perhaps she found it too much to simulate intimacy with Prince during the finale of their set when His Royal Badness went into 'I Wanna Be Your Lover'. 'I know that she had some conflicts,' Dez Dickerson told Prince's unauthorized biographer, Dave Hill. 'She loved it, but she didn't love it.' Perhaps she didn't like the acting out of passion – or perhaps she liked it too much. During a hometown gig in Minneapolis, Prince is said to have French-kissed Gayle Chapman in the middle of a performance of 'Head'. In the end, she left the band and found religion, while other women in the Prince entourage have accepted his largesse and become star protegées with

his material or his production skills.

Also in 1980, Prince released his most controversial album to date. *Dirty Mind* was described by *Rolling Stone* as Rabelaisian. In songs like 'Do It All Night', 'Head' and 'Sister', Prince makes short (well, not that short) work of sex, oral sex and incestuous sex. His lyrics verge on a pornographic explicitness: vaginal lubrication and male ejaculation are not just alluded to. He claims the songs are based on actual incidents in his life, like 'Bambi' on *Prince* in which our hero declares his passion for a lesbian.

Sexual confusion and sexual explicitness are both elements of the Prince persona and they have enabled him to win an audience that incorporates adolescent females and older male funk and soul fans, both black and white. He has only gone so far in challenging stereotypes – far enough to construct himself in the image of his audiences' acceptable fantasies. They remain somehow bloodless. An extraordinary trick – made possible by the shadow-play of video and film which have elaborated and advertised the image.

Prince's crossover didn't happen until 1983 when MTV promoted '1999' and 'Little Red Corvette' and His Royal Badness's career rapidly became focused on a sequence of brilliant film and video pastiches which rarely distinguished between concert performance, video fantasy and uncertain narrative – *Purple Rain* (1984), *Under a Cherry Moon* (1986), *Sign 'O' the Times* (1987), *Lovesexy* (1988), *Graffiti Bridge* (1990), and of course *Batman* (1989) (the sound track of Prince's own version of dark fetishistic movie gothickery).

Crossing over into the mass pop market depended absolutely on Prince's ability to create himself as a plastic figure - a screen on which those acceptable fantasies could be projected – and a manipulator. The remarkable thing is not that he got away with it, but that he's been so single-minded. He has a Rolls Royce like John Lennon, but open a cabinet inside his car and you'd probably come face to face with a fax machine, rather than a fully equipped mini-bar with a little drawer for the dope.

Prince has been a one-man music industry, writing for, producing and nurturing the careers of a score of other performers – mostly young women. Even during 1991 which saw a slump in his career, he still appeared in the list of Top 40 highest grossing entertainers published by the US rich people's house mag, *Forbes*. His managers are reported to have said at the time: 'There are a variety of ways he can generate income by sitting still and doing nothing.' That, of course, is a definition of capitalism.

An illuminating aside on Prince's career is offered by a comparison between him and Rick James – once heralded as the future of funk, who might have been where Prince is today if he had been more in tune with the eighties' ethos of success and less in love with rock'n'roll's dream of excess.

James had already established himself on the black music scene as the eighties' began, with an act owing something to George Clinton's comic-book funk, something to Bob Marley's rasta pride and something to fast and flashy white rock. But Prince, who opened for James on a string of US East Coast dates in 1980, took the flashiness one stage further and buried his music's roots beneath layers of image. Prince understood what James seems to have missed – that image and the symbols and labels which carry it were the key to success in a consumer age. It was a masterly piece of marketing and it led Prince – in 1992 – to the biggest recording and publishing deal of all time, making him the crossover king of rock'n'roll: selling the recording and song publishing rights on six albums to Warner Brothers Records and Warner Chappel Music for an estimated \$100 million.

As Prince rose irresistibly, so his rival Rick James sank. It is difficult to say just how upsetting it was for James when Prince lined up James' girlfriend Denise Matthews to appear in the stage show as Vagina in an imaginatively named girl-group, the Hookers. No doubt drug-dependency fuelled Rick James' paranoia, but by the mid-eighties he had begun to demonise Prince – railing against his betrayal of black culture and calling him 'a mentally disturbed young man [who] sings songs about oral sex and incest'.

The Hookers became Vanity 6 with Denise Matthews as Vanity, while James hit bottom in 1991 after emerging from yet another bout of institutionalization when he and his then girlfriend, fresh-faced Tanya Anne Hijazi, were jailed for tying up a woman at James' Hollywood Hills home, burning her with a crack pipe and a hot butcher's knife and forcing her to perform oral sex on Hijazi. There is something so poetic about this Star Is Born scenario and so angled that it is irresistible to conclude that it's actually drawn from the lyrics of an unpublished song by Prince.

Crack (a form of smokeable cocaine) had the definitive name for an eighties drug, evoking images of sexuality, sado-masochism, speed and decay. But the real eighties drug was fantasy – notwithstanding the flood of narcotics and stimulants that threatened to inundate the West. Cocaine, cheap heroin and designer drugs like Ecstacy (or E, the street name for MMDA, a sixties era hallucinogenic whose full chemical name is methoxymethylene-dioxyamphetamine) were certainly easily available and widely used, but this was – even more obviously – the decade of role-play games, survival adventures, and virtual reality.

The world was being transformed before our very eyes into a Disneyland version of itself. Eventually, the process became sufficiently widespread to attract the interest of academics who promptly gave it its very own difficult-to-understand label. But even before 'postmodernism' was on everybody's lips, it became the modus vivendi of rock'n'roll. The generation of performers which emerged in the eighties was, for the first time, aware of all the arguments about rock'n'roll – the promise of rare wealth and hedonistic indulgence, the dangers of excess, the need for popular roots, the perils of financial exploitation. These performers made career choices as much as they made music. They plundered the past for images, attitudes, and material out of which to build self-conscious facsimiles of rock stardom: they were like Elvis impersonators, but they based their acts on moods and moments not individuals.

Chrissie Hynde's Pretenders, for example, came together as a result of Hynde's overwhelming determination to be a rock'n'roll star. The Ohio born singer-guitarist pursued this ambition to the point of obsession. Moving to London in the early seventies, she set out on the road to rock'n'roll fame. The route involved meeting, sleeping with, and then becoming, a journalist on *New Musical Express*, then the UK's leading rock magazine.

Through *NME*, Hynde got to know the hungrier

Chrissie Hynde gets in on the sex act: she is the 'S' to Vivienne Westwood's 'E' and Jordan's 'X'.

as Patti Smith's it was also as entertaining as Suzi Quatro's – and it was as visceral as both. The Pretenders were, perhaps, the first postmodern group – pretenders in both senses of the word.

Of their first few singles, two were Ray Davies songs previously recorded by the Kinks – 'Stop Your Sobbing' (1979) and 'Everynight I Just Can't Go To Sleep' (1981). The Kinks seem a curious influence – at least until you remember the dandy image (and the song called 'Dandy'), the sexual ambiguity of 'Lola', the deep and reactionary romanticism of Ray Davies, and the band's dismissive approach to the record industry. The Kinks were, after all, 'New Romantics' – the prototypes of New Pop, pure because they were outside the mainstream. It can hardly have been a surprise that Hynde started an affair with Ray Davies in 1981 which resulted in the birth of a daughter. Seeing The Kinks back home during the era of the British Invasion had, after all, been a key experience (perhaps one should say seminal). Better to fuck with an influence than simply dress up like it.

But the Pretenders was an ill-starred group. They were surrounded by death as though the illusion of rock'n'roll had become so strong that dying was the only way reality could make itself felt. Pressures of touring and Hynde's own dominating personality soon caused an irreparable rift to appear between her and Farndon. She moved out into a Covent Garden tenement occupied by Kevin Sparrow: a Keith Richard lookalike and junkie. Sparrow overdosed on Christmas Day, 1979, three weeks before the Pretenders made number one with their third single, 'Brass In Pocket'.

The problem was that nobody knew who to thank for their success. Sure, the critics had been kind and Chrissie Hynde did have a certain insolent charm, but The Pretenders had been massively hyped. In August 1980, WEA was fingered by the UK's leading investigative TV programme of the time, 'World In Action', in an exposé of chart-rigging and record industry malpractice. It was particularly embarrassing for WEA's managing director, John Fruin, who was also chairman of the industry watchdog, the British Phonographic Industry (BPI). He denied the allegations – which covered releases by Elvis Costello, Dusty Springfield, Gary Numan and Rod Stewart as well as the Pretenders – but left WEA a few weeks after the TV broadcast.

'We worked like mad to push them up the charts,' Fruin said later about the Pretenders, but the success of 'Brass In Pocket' and the first album, both here and in the US, surprised almost everybody.

Soon, the group had become completely immersed in the rock lifestyle – or, at least, in some version of it. Hynde – no mean abuser herself who once drank herself into a Memphis jail – has described guitarist Honeyman-Scott as 'a drug fiend', a speed-freak when they met and a heroin addict by the time success came. But he was less of a problem than bassist Pete Farndon who, according to Hynde, 'was one of those unfortunate people who saw a picture of himself in the paper and thought that was him.' Farndon 'had been taking

half of the UK's music establishment – in particular, Sex Pistols' svengalis Malcolm McLaren and Vivienne Westwood. You might say she put herself about a bit – and you might say it paid off, despite some negative reactions.There followed a series of romantic or professional liaisons with the likes of Nick Lowe (bass-player, songwriter and producer), Chris Spedding (guitarist, arranger and producer) and Tony Secunda (whose pioneering sixties PR moves for the Move led to the then British Prime Minister, Harold Wilson, suing for libel). Eventually, she hit it off with two former public school boys from the West Country town of Hereford, Pete Farndon and James Honeyman-Scott, slept with Farndon and gave birth to the Pretenders.

The Pretenders were driven by Hynde's consuming passion for rock'n'roll stardom and informed by a deep appreciation of rock culture, but it was as though the band played out a series of set-piece recreations – dioramas – of what they thought rock should be. Today, kids call them 'bland', but in 1981 they seemed to represent a never-before-possible synthesis. Chrissie Hynde was not the first woman to lead a rock group, but if her rock consciousness was as intellectual* smack for a long long time,' Hynde recalled, 'and his behaviour was completely erratic.' He became impossible to work with, increasingly heavy-handed in his playing, losing the tempo in live performance, sometimes passing out completely, fighting backstage and apparently hitting Ray Davies on one occasion. The other Pretenders refused to work with him and in June, 1982, he was unceremoniously booted out of the band.

In many ways, Farndon was the most tragic character in the Pretenders. He cultivated a wasted look and a rebel image, complete with earrings, quiff and leathers. No doubt, his relationship with Hynde had been a source of pain and confusion, but the greatest irony was that just when he might have been expected to climax his unhappy life with a spectacular death, blond, blue-eyed James Honeyman-Scott stole the limelight and, following a typical night out fuelled by liberal doses of drink, cocaine, heroin and whatever else came to hand, died in his sleep just two days after Farndon's sacking.

It took Farndon almost another year to die. His body was discovered by his wife in the bath of the couple's home in Kensington, London, on 14th April, 1983. He had drowned under the malign influence of heroin and cocaine. He was not yet 30. 'The guy blew it,' said Hynde, with a singular lack of sentimentality. 'He shot up a speed-ball and drowned in the bath. It's not really my idea of a beautiful rock'n'roll image – the tattooed arm hanging out of the tub, turning blue with a syringe stuck in it. But that's what it came to in the end.'

Chrissie went on to greater things: in the late eighties she adopted the pose of a militant vegetarian and eco-freak, embraced a variety of politically correct causes and became something of a habituée of the right-on benefit scene. She attracted widespread criticism (and many plaudits) for *appearing* to advocate the firebombing of McDonald's hamburger bars in 1989 during a press conference to launch a Greenpeace album, and slightly less attention for campaigning against Michael Jackson's notorious $15 million deal to advertise Pepsi Cola. (Coke got Tina Turner to do their ads during the soft drink wars, but Chrissie didn't write a song asking how much she got for her soul.) McDonald's, according to Hynde, 'is fucking disgusting'. Her vegetarian campaigning will continue, she has promised. 'It's got to be dealt with and I'll deal with it if no-one else will. Because I want to die for something.' Farndon may have left this world with less than the acceptable amount of style, but for pointlessness it's hard to choose between him in his bath and Chrissie Hynde on her high horse.

There have been other drug and drink troubles over the last few years, among new and old performers alike. Culture Club's Boy George (real name George O'Dowd) was pulled only just alive from the wreckage of a short but spectacular career as smack-happy androgyne with a disingenuous line in chat-show banter on how he preferred tea to sex. Former Velvet Underground associate, Nico, died in 1988 after suffering a heart attack while cycling in Ibiza. She was

still on a methadone rehabilitation course and long term heroin addiction had coarsened her features and fattened her until she had become unrecognizable as the person once described as 'the most beautiful woman in the world'.

In 1991, Perry Farrell, the former lead singer of US group, Jane's Addiction, was arrested on drugs charges in Santa Monica while Shane MacGowan, the lead singer of Ireland's Pogues, was sacked by the band for alcohol-related unreliability and Shaun Ryder of Manchester's scallydelia band, Happy Mondays, was revealed as a heroin addict since his teenage years.

Subsequently, rumours persisted in circulating to the effect that these three or any two of them would get together in some sort of drug-crazed supergroup (the rat-arsed pack?), although the idea may have been a narcotic nightmare. (In 1990, the fun-loving Ryder had to be dissuaded from posing for a magazine feature with a roll of bacofoil, intended to illustrate an item essential to his lifestyle.) In 1992, MacGowan – who had once hoarsely denounced the imprisonment of the Birmingham Six on trumped up charges of conspiracy to bomb and had been banned from British radio and TV for his trouble – bounced back with an unlikely Christmas song, a version of Louis Armstrong's sentimental 1968 hit 'Wonderful World' recorded with little known mega-cult-superstar Nick Cave.

Martin Hannett, who once called himself Martin

199

Zero, and who could well have been the single most important figure in the fertile music scene that developed in Manchester in the UK during the eighties, died of a heart attack at 42 after years of drug and drink abuse. Hannett had produced the Buzzcocks, Joy Division, New Order, the Stone Roses and Happy Mondays and worked with U2, Magazine, and Orchestral Manoeuvres In The Dark, among others.

Thin Lizzy's wild man, Phil Lynott, black, Irish and would-be star of the movie life of Jimi Hendrix, struggled for respectability and married the daughter of Brit TV personality Leslie Crowther in a much hyped show-biz wedding, but lost the battle and OD'ed ignominiously on Christmas Day, in 1985. David Ruffin, lead singer of the Temptations, OD'ed in Philadelphia at the age of 50. Def Leppard's lead guitarist, Steve Clark, died in London at 30 from a fatal mixture of

drugs and booze after a long and unsuccessful struggle against alcoholism. Thirty-eight year old Johnny Thunders, from the New York Dolls and the Heartbreakers, OD'ed in New Orleans, living life in the fast lane to the end. The Small Faces' Steve Marriott burnt to death in his country home in England at 44, a demise probably hastened by Marriott's propensity for dope. But, despite all that, and the deaths and disgraces still to come, the Pretenders somehow closed the book. Farndon and Honeyman-Scott may have died the last real rock'n'roll deaths.

On the street, the drugs may help to blot out pain and despair, but for the rock'n'rollers they became gewgaws. The 18th century poet and visionary William Blake had once written memorably about the road of excess leading to the palace of wisdom. Excess, of course, implied depth and in the eighties wisdom was shallow and widespread – a palace of varieties, a shopping mall megastore.

Even untimely death, which had once been such a startling punctuator of daily life, lost its special mean-

Doubling as a case history for orthodontists, ex-Pogue Shane MacGowan bares his tooth to the press at the 1994 Brit Awards before joining Van Morrison on stage for a gaping version of 'Gloria'.

The burnt-out remains of Steve Marriott's house in East Anglia. The former Small Face was killed in the fire in 1993 which was thought to have been caused by him smoking in bed.

ing. The shock with which we heard about John Kennedy or Jimi Hendrix would never be repeated – not even when Nirvana's drug-soaked front-man, Kurt Cobain, took the unusual step of blowing a hole in his own head with a shotgun sometime in the first week of April, 1994. Death had become commonplace, notwithstanding the arrival of a new killer on the scene – AIDS, which has afflicted many entertainers and artists and a few rock performers (notably Level 42's guitarist Alan Murphy in 1989 and Queen's Freddie Mercury in 1992). Today, the four Apocalyptic horsemen – disease, war, starvation and disaster – are subject to routine sightings. Cobain's death was mourned by fans in the US – even mimicked by a sad 28-year-old called Daniel Kasper – for whom Nirvana had been the first real home-grown rebel rockers to hit the big time since Gene Vincent or the young Bob Dylan. The rest of the world shrugged its shoulders and tut-tutted: another rock star death; more newspaper-shifting column inches of gristly details and futile speculation on why rich young things should want to kill themselves while the rest of us cling so tenaciously to life; 50,000 Nirvana albums sold in the US alone in two days after the news broke. Seen it, been there, done that, bought the tee-shirt.

In fact, our culture learnt to celebrate death in film, video game and music. It was, after all, just part of the postmodern mix: an image (or set of images) for the poseur and fashion victim. The most vital strand of

rock throughout the eighties was once again heavy metal: only this time transmuted into extreme forms, thrash, speed and death metal, whose very names suggest impotence and negation.

Bands like Megadeth, Slayer, Metallica, Anthrax, Mötley Crüe, Napalm Death, Venom, Nuclear Assault and Suicidal Tendencies specialised in grim faced posing, tight leather trousers, long, lank greasy hair, metal studs, and lyrics soaked in death, destruction, rape, pain. They represent a genuine underground, for the most part ignored by the mainstream music press and a cause of embarrassment to the rock establishment.

At its best, metal is an expression of the rebel energy that has always given rock'n'roll its power and authentic sense of creative challenge. But – let's face it – most of it is amateur macho posturing, schoolboy nasty, loud and stupid. You can tell what the music's like by what its fans use as mood-altering substances – and for metal fans it's mostly Carlsberg Special Brew and vodka.

The new breed of metal is dominated by Metallica, formed by Danish drummer Lars Ulrich and guitarist/vocalist James Hetfield in 1981. Thrash apocrypha tells of how Ulrich first met Motorhead's Lemmy – the godfather of metal music – in a hotel room in California and threw up over his carpet thanks to too much vodka. This is how metal bands behave – for them road fever goes on forever, inspired by waves upon waves of predecessors – role models like Led Zeppelin, Black Sabbath, Motorhead, Iron Maiden, Saxon, Def Leppard, and the Tygers of Pan Tang – the inheritors of classic cock-rock, acid rock and punk, play acting the parts of hard men, evil bastards, satanists.

Death metal, we're told, was invented by a band called Venom emerging out of the decaying industrial north east of England. Their lead singer calls himself Cronos, the father of Zeus who ate his own children. His real name is Conrad Lant and his theory is that death metal is nastiness brought bang up to date. Black Sabbath and former lead-Sabb, Ozzy Osbourne, come in for a lot of criticism: 'Death metal,' says Cronos, 'is basically saying things that Sabbath didn't have the balls to say. We are the Evil Dead to their Hammer horror. Ripping, slashing, maiming, tearing throats out – it's all there.'

Of course, this is ugly stuff, but then it's the ugliness that metal fans demand. The varieties are quite subtle as represented on album sleeves and in song lyrics – some bands go for sacrificing virgins, some for drinking blood, some go for leprosy or other forms of pestilence; some bands go for Nazi imagery or visions of political terror, some for nuclear explosions, mutilation, sadism, bodily functions or raising the dead. Personally, I doubt that any of the atrocities infecting the contemporary world have anything to do with any variety of heavy metal group, but it certainly upsets some people. In 1984, a lawsuit (thrown out of the California Supreme Court) tried to blame a teenage boy's suicide on the Ozzy Osbourne song 'Suicide Solution'. And, in 1988, Mötley Crüe won a coveted reprimand from the National Coalition of Television Violence in the US after a 12-year-old boy from Florida set his legs alight while copying a Crüe video.

Hidden messages on albums gripped the consciousness of American fundamentalists in the eighties, and charges similar to the Osbourne case were brought against Judas Priest in 1990, when the band was eventually cleared of accusations that the recording of 'satanic' messages backwards on their albums had caused the suicide of two fans. Even self-declared Christian groups like U2 and Stryper were condemned by some fanatical anti-rock groups. Rock still has the power to offend, it seems – even though that offensiveness may be so contrived as to be laughable.

'You don't go knocking on people's doors flogging Satan like the bloody Mormons,' says Venom's Cronos. 'My criteria for if a song's good or not is that I play it to me mam and dad. If they say, "Son, it's fucking disgusting," then I know it's alright.'

The irony is that heavy metal has also created one of the most successful rock groups of the nineties – Guns N'Roses, who adopted the tattoos, the codpieces, the leather and denim, the long hair, the sexism, the cigarettes and the booze, but not quite all the menace of their predecessors. Sure, they say 'fuck' a lot and drink Jack Daniels like Keith Richard used to, they

make a lot of noise about killing family pets and taking so many drugs, their best-selling 1987 album was called *Appetite For Destruction* and their songs get banned for offensive lyrics. But this is a group with its eye firmly on the main chance – and doing a whole lot better than previous contenders for the title of 'world's most outrageous rock band' like the Beastie Boys and Sigue-Sigue Sputnik (don't tell me you've forgotten them already!).

G N'R have tried – unsuccessfully – to get publications wanting interviews to sign over all rights in the published material to the band itself. They like to keep control of their image – so much so that singer W Axl Rose (real name, Bill Bailey – no kidding!) leapt from a stage in St. Louis in 1991 when he spotted a fan taking unauthorized pictures. After the scuffle, Rose stormed off the concert stage. Result: a riot tally of 60 injuries and 16 arrests, $200,000-worth of damage, two years probation for Waxl and a fine of $50,000 to be donated to St. Louis child abuse charities. According to his lawyer (speaking after the trial in 1992), Axl 'feels badly about his image in St. Louis.' This hasn't, of course, removed the words 'Fuck you, St. Louis!' from the liner notes to their *Use Your Illusion I* and *II* albums.

Axl, as if you hadn't realized, is the angry young man of the band – 'I'm very sensitive and emotional,' he says. His publicity in '86 and '87 focused on a professed habit of killing small dogs (after this story had been repeated in several newspapers, it was revealed as a joke – although, we are reliably informed, Axl did once shoot a pig; but only to eat). These days, Rose's anger consists mainly of badmouthing fans, journalists and record companies. He sports a pierced nipple and a penchant for ripping out the fixtures of hotel rooms.

Guitarist Slash (real name Saul Hudson), meanwhile, is the dissolute member of the band: born in Stoke-on-Trent in the UK from a mixed race background and raised in LA, his father designed album sleeves and his mother designed theatre and movie costumes. He wears his dark curly hair long and it often covers his face. Naked to the waist, he's the one who drinks, takes drugs and smokes to excess. 'Ozzie Osborne is someone I can relate to,' he says revealingly. 'His life is so rock'n'roll oriented. He doesn't have anything else. That's the way I feel.' This is the same Ozzie Osbourne, incidentally, who in late 1989 was arrested on charges that he had threatened to kill his wife and manager Sharon (daughter of legendary rock manager Don Arden), 'intending her to fear that the threat would be carried out.' Sharon later dropped the charges, after local magistrates had insisted that Ozzie attend to his drink problem at a rehabilitation centre.

The last of the silly names in Guns N' Roses belonged to Izzy Straddlin, who was the group's cynic until he was sacked in 1992 for getting up Waxl's nose. Being born Jeffrey Dean is clearly enough to turn anyone cynical but not enough to keep you in work. 'I expressed my feelings to Axl Rose,' said Strugglin, 'and

Axl Rose (it's an anagram – geddit?) felt bad about his image in St Louis – but at this MTV party he's feeling something different.

Axl Rose being arrested by US Customs Agents acting on behalf of prosecutors in St Louis, at Kennedy Airport, New York, on 12th July 1992. He was wanted on charges stemming from the outbreak of violence at a St Louis concert the previous year.

the very next night, on MTV, I saw that I was going to be replaced by the guy from Jane's Addiction. So,' concluded Waddlin, 'I took that as an indication that I'd really pissed Axl off.' Piddlin's main claim to fame is that he was once charged with 'interfering with cabin crew duties' after pissing outside the toilet in a plane.

Then, of course, there are the bass player and drummer who, not sporting silly names, are obviously disposable – in fact, the group's original drummer was sacked by the band in 1990, with no noticeable effect. According to Slash, 'Steven is about as rock'n'roll a personality as you can get. All he lived for was sex, drugs and rock'n'roll – in that order. Maybe drugs, sex and rock'n'roll. Then it was drugs and rock'n'roll. Then it was just drugs.'

The problem with all this is that, true or false, it's an obvious self-conscious contrivance, based on a simplistic view of rock. Guns N'Roses have created a new form of teenybop, a wilful parody for young fans – who can know no better – presented as the real thing; a cartoon version of debauchery. The band justifies itself by claiming that nothing of any importance has happened in rock, until they came along, since the Sex Pistols. But what they take from the Pistols (apart from a perfumed version of their name) is an approach to marketing. In every other way – musically, visually,

204

and lyrically – they're less interesting than the Pistols and, once you get over the punk association, Guns N'Roses is simply a pastiche of sixties and seventies hard rock, not nearly as amusing as Spinal Tap.

These days even the clean groups – teeny faves New Kids on the Block (the highest earning entertainers of the early nineties, according to *Forbes* magazine) – like to put in a pinch of hellfire. In 1991, New Kid Donnie Wahlberg even stole a march on G N' R by setting fire to a Louisville, Kentucky, hotel corridor with a bottle of vodka as fuel.

It may be kind of sad to be reduced to that, but it may be worse to be Nirvana who, starting out as punk pastiche rapidly descended into a mind-numbingly awful parody of thirty years of rock. In 1992, with only two albums under their belt – the blandly-titled *Bleach* and *Nevermind* – Nirvana had already managed to recapitulate a generation's music through PR image alone. They became the kings of grunge: a musical style self-consciously described as a punk-metal synthesis, but no less accurately a version of what rock music *ought* to sound like.

Before listening to a note actually played by the band, we can read all about lead singer Kurt Cobain's musical upbringing in numberless profiles – Beatles as a baby, Led Zeppelin, Kiss and Black Sabbath (not necessarily in that order) as a pre-teen, Sex Pistols as an adolescent, the Pixies, REM and a whole pile of indie groups as a grown-up. Look at the pictures – one minute they look like Grand Funk Railroad, the next

Getting in on the act – police identification mug shots of Donnie Wahlberg of New Kids on The Block, after he was arrested for setting fire to a hotel carpet with a bottle of vodka in March 1991.

they're Elvis Costello and the Attractions. Kurt, we're told, is like John Lennon, 'using his music to scream out an unhappy childhood'.

You just know what kind of a noise this band will make. Even their name is borrowed (from one of the most underrated of all sixties psychedelic groups), chosen after considering in turn Ed, Ted and Fred, Skid Row, and Fecal Matter – any one of which would have been equally unimaginative but more original. It probably doesn't help that the group comes from Seattle in the North Western United States – a city which combines cleanliness with cleanliness and which is known as the home of the Boeing Corporation and the richest man in America, the nerds' nerd: Bill Gates, co-founder and president of Microsoft.

So what makes Nirvana and the Seattle sound so exciting that *Nevermind* went triple platinum in weeks? Well, they all had unhappy childhoods and came from broken homes (and broken working-class homes at that), and serious critical opinion holds that they therefore represent the lost generation of 'post-boom' kids who have nothing to look forward to but unemployment, global warming, nasty wars and endless reruns of 'Cheers'. Others remind you that Seattle was also Jimi Hendrix's hometown and observe that Paul Revere and the Raiders, the Ventures and the Kings-

men all came from the region. The Kingsmen's grinding 'Louie, Louie' is often described as 'the original grunge classic'.

But Hendrix had to leave Seattle to make it, and most analyses of the Seattle music scene point to its isolation and small-town atmosphere as key ingredients in the growth of a vigorous indie scene. Grunge itself is a marketing concept – a cartoon version of punk packaged for a generation of musical tourists. Smash hits, like Nirvana's cynical "Smells Like Teen Spirit", are not the stuff of rebellion – but they can look and sound like it. The producer of this track, the monosyllabic Butch Vig, accidentally put his finger on it when he observed that, in his music, Kurt Cobain 'doesn't necessarily know what he wants, but he's pissed. . . . I don't know exactly what "Teen Spirit" means, but you know it means *something*, and it's as intense as hell.'

Cobain, of course, didn't want 'to be a fucking spokesman', but worried about 'the average seventeen-year-old punk-rock kid . . . calling me a sellout.' Back on Seattle's unemployment line, the no future

205

generation might with justice have called him worse than that – it rhymes with 'arrogant, self-obsessed, stupid banker'. But they seem on the contrary to have loved him and snapped up the band's third album, *In Utero*, despite its mood-setting lyric: 'Teenage angst has paid off well, now I'm bored and old'. What do you do when you spit in their faces and they come back for more? Harassed by press speculation that he was a junkie, and having fathered a daughter by his bride of several months – Courtney Love of (as *Rolling Stone* had it) 'fiery, neo-feminist band Hole' – Cobain decided to tell all to the *Los Angeles Times*. Well, not quite all . . .

Yes, said the bespectacled punk poet, he had dabbled with heroin ('once or twice a year') and, yes, he had developed a 'little' methadone habit, but he had nothing good to say about drugs and – besides – he had really bad tummy trouble which could easily be mistaken for being on heroin (or 'slam dancing with Mr. Brownstone', as Nirvana's label mates, G N'R, colourfully put it). This may, of course, have explained Kurt's propensity to scream: not an unhappy childhood at all, just troubled bowels. In any case, said constipated Kurt, 'My attitude has changed. . . . Holding my baby is the best drug in the world. I don't want my daughter to grow up with people telling her that her parents were junkies.' (For male rock stars birth seems to lead to an inevitable descent into toe-curling sentimentality, as if they – the rock fathers that is – were the only ones ever to have experienced the wonders of parenthood. Cobain followed Lennon, Springsteen, even Elvis, in this, even illustrating Nirvana's 1993 album, *In Utero*, with an ultrasound photograph of his unborn child.)

But junkie is what he was – and one of the greats. Perhaps it was that and an evidently stormy relationship with Courtney that gave Nirvana its edge. Kurt and Court (a sort of sophomore Sid'n'Nancy) stumbled from overdose to overdose, all the while engaged in histrionic fights. The police had to be called to the Cobain residence twice – in July 1993 and March 1994 – to take away Kurt's collection of guns, and Kurt himself threatened suicide on at least one occasion, observing in an interview that 'I felt so different and so crazy that people just left me alone . . . I always felt that they would vote me Most Likely to Kill Everyone at a High School Dance . . . I got to the point where I've fantasised about it, but I'd have always opted for killing myself first.'

With a head full of images from splatter movies and Stephen King novels, punk attitudes and the doom-laden lyrics of premier lost-generation bands like Joy Division (whose lead singer, Ian Curtis, also killed himself), Cobain was evidently fixated on adolescent fantasies, magnified by success, adulation, smack, downers and alcohol. Clearly Kurt and Court

had little opportunity to work through these problems, what with this being a modern marriage and both of them having careers to look after. Was Courtney having an affair? Is she the predatory bisexual of popular myth, or merely a disappointed Julian Cope fan (yes, Courtney was a Teardrop Explodes groupie in the eighties)?

After Nirvana stopped touring regularly in 1992, Kurt became more and more dependent on heroin and less and less satisfied with stardom. Suicide seems to have been a family trait – three uncles had died by their own hands – and whatever troubles he imagined he had just looked darker and darker. With the junkie's propensity for self-delusion, Kurt announced to the world in late 1993 that he was recovered, 'excited about touring again . . . totally optimistic'. But, as it always is for junkies, the reality was harsher. Performances – which had seemed to offer hope – became increasingly confrontational and disappointing. Overwhelmed by a sense of futility, joylessness and impotence, Kurt sunk further into the mire of hopelessness on which he and Nirvana had built their careers. Part way through a European tour in early March 1994, Kurt overdosed in Rome on champagne, sleeping pills (Roipnol), and a children's anaesthetic. It would have been an elegant way to die, but Courtney raised the alarm and Kurt's comatose body was delivered into hospital care. His record company – Geffen – strained its collective imagination to come up with an excuse to explain their star's vanishing act: 'Fatigue and severe influenza' must have pipped a bad stomach ache to the post.

But no sooner had Kurt recovered enough to fly back to the US and check in to a California drug clinic, than he disappeared. On April 2nd, his mother, Wendy O'Connor, filed a missing persons report. Six days later, an electrician working in the 11-acre grounds of the Cobains' Seattle home found his body in the upper loft of a garage, a shot gun wound to the face and an oddly formal suicide note a few feet away. Just when he died remains a mystery: medical evidence indicates April 5th, after taking enough heroin and tranquillisers to kill a lesser junkie, but two friends claim to have spoken to Kurt on April 6th. On April 7th, Courtney Love evidently overdosed and was arrested on drugs charges hundreds of miles away in LA, although Geffen Records allegedly said she was in London on April 8th when the body was found. 'After Rome,' she said later, 'I just couldn't take it.'

A memorial vigil in Seattle on April 10th attracted 10,000 Cobain fans who listened enthralled to a tape of Courtney Love reading out the supposed contents of Kurt's suicide note, complete with interjections. 'He left a note for you,' said Courtney, 'It's more like a letter to the editor.' The sign-off – 'Peace, Love, Empathy – Kurt Cobain' – seemed both stilted and inappropriate. Did it really need a surname? Perhaps it did, lest we confuse him with the other Kurt – you know, the one who didn't collect guns, who stayed with his family through love, and whose empathy for others sustained his art.

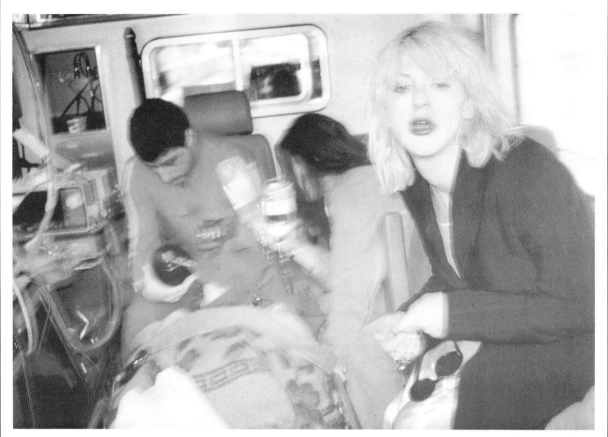

Above: Courtney Love accompanying the comatose Kurt Cobain to a hospital in Rome in March 1994. Her quick thinking saved his life that time.

'Sometimes I feel as if I should have to punch a time clock before I walk on stage . . .', wrote this Kurt. 'I haven't felt the excitement of listening to, as well as creating, music along with really writing something for too many years. I feel guilty beyond words about these things – for example when we're backstage and the lights go out and the manic roar of the crowd begins, it doesn't affect me the way it did for Freddie Mercury who seemed to relish the love and adoration of the crowd.' Quoting from Neil Young's song 'Out Of The Blue (Hey Hey My My)', Cobain wrote: 'It's better to burn out than fade away.'

Cue Courtney: 'This is not fucking true!' Amid audible tears the tape recording called Kurt 'an asshole' and urged the crowd to call him an asshole too. Ten thousand voices shouted as one to an empty stage: 'Asshole.' Kurt's mom told the press that she had warned her son against 'joining that stupid club' whose other members rode rock stardom to an early death. But it was the only club that would let the poor sap in. Bored witless, drugged crazy, half in love with easeful death, self-destruction is both the ultimate self-gratification and the ultimate self-denial. Cobain may have been a dyed-in-the wool rebel, for which his fans – reared on poseurs, AOR pap and rock dinosaurs – were clearly grateful, but he was rebelling against himself.

Left: Kurt with baby Frances Bean. His genuine devotion to her led to more than one abortive attempt at detoxification.

In the fifties, rock's offence was its relationship with black culture. The white music establishment ripped off black performers and black styles and were condemned on the one hand for lack of discernment and on the other for lack of authenticity. By the eighties, white performers were at last able to rip off black music with no shame. Often, they came right out and proclaimed it – New Kids on the Block, Vanilla Ice; proud to be pale. This was the ultimate racist victory – the black thing had become the white thing. The New Kids management team was itself black; having failed to create a winning post-Jackson 5 group with black performers, it succeeded with a white version of the same formula. Understandable then that Michael Jackson, the most successful of all the Jackson siblings, who had been raised from childhood under the glare of publicity to become the best selling black performer of all time, was rumoured to undergo cosmetic surgery to make his facial features whiter (although he claims it is in fact due to a skin condition that causes lightning of the natural pigmentation). Even Prince, as we've noted, was equivocal about his blackness, but then it was enough to believe that Prince wiped the skin colour off with his make-up.

Jackson, of course, has long seen himself as something of a freak – which is exactly what he is. His attempt to purchase the skeleton of 'Elephant Man'

Lost generation's leader finds his place in Nirvana

Grunge king Kurt Cobain's death was far from unexpected, report **Roger Tredre** and **Ed Vulliam**

TIMES · 10 APRIL 1994

WORLD NEWS

Grunge king unable to deal with stardom

Robert Sandall charts rock music tragedy

SELECT
POP BABYLON
JUNE 1994
DYKE-IL-LIKE! THE NEW LESBIAN COOL · BJÖRK · ERASURE
MUSIC MAGAZINE OF THE YEAR

"I hate myself and I want to die"

Q
The modern guide to music and more
SWEET!
EXCLUSIVE INTERVIEW

WHY KURT COBAIN HAD TO DIE

NIRVANA'S KURT BLOWS HEAD OFF

ROCK STAR KURT IN SHOTGUN SUICIDE

Nirvana
Kurt Cobain, father of grunge rock, shoots himself

WORLD PICTURE EXCLUSIVE
Daddy's gone: Cobain's daughter Frances cries at home

Grunge rock idol wanted to burn out not fade away

GLOBE
Hebd
15F

KURT COBAIN
MOURIR A 27 ANS
NIRVANA STORY
DOSSIER p. 44

REPRISE?
L'espoir américain
expertise p. 22

GROSSOUVRE
La dernière nuit
du chasseur p. 6

grunge rock.

WIFE SNIPS HAIR FROM BODY OF TRAGIC KURT

Grunge rock idol wanted to burn out not fade away

END OF A LI

THE STUPID CLUB
(founder: Brian Jones, 1969)
Latest recruit: Kurt Cobain

Shotgun suicide of rock singer
by MARGARET HALL

Wife fury at suicide star Kurt
by ANDY COULSON

Troubled singer Kurt Cobain

I'll hunt you down in Hell, Kurt!
Nirvana wife's shocking vow

THE WIFE of suicide Nirvana star Kurt Cobain made a chilling vow after he came close to death from his drugs overdose in Rome.

EXCLUSIVE by DOMINIC MOHAN

I LOVE YOU: Cobain left wife and daughter a suic

1977. Associate members (film division) include James

NIRVANA STAR FEARED DEAD
From ALLAN HALL in New York

A MAN feared to be Nirvana lead singer Kurt Cobain has been found dead at the singer's home.

DRUG-addict rock singer Kurt Cobain has committed suicide,

John Merrick for $500,000 from a London hospital for his private collection suggests a disturbing sort of identification, although he (or at least his office) has frequently vigorously denounced the plethora of rumours and half-truths that he seems to attract like flies. He was a loner, and therefore gay. He was petrified of illness and therefore slept in an air-conditioned capsule. His best friend was a monkey, which must have made him a nut. Gossip reached fever pitch in 1984. Jackson told *Rolling Stone* magazine that he lived 'just like a haemophiliac who can't afford to be scratched in any way', while the US TV show 'Saturday Night Live' lampooned him in macho conversation with a Liberace lampoon, and tabloids reported he was having an affair with Boy George.

Left: Kurt Cobain's death was the most notable in rock since John Lennon's assassination in 1980. Below: Kurt Cobain's body is removed from his house in Seattle to the Medical Examiner's van prior to post-mortem, on 8th April 1994.

Jackson appears to have been driven so far that refutation was demanded. A press conference was called on 5 September 1992, but Jackson failed to show and, for once, left the performance to someone else – his personal manager Frank Dileo. Dileo read out an angry statement that was somehow undermined by Jackson's absence.

'It saddens me that many may actually believe the present flurry of false accusations,' Dileo read, 'To this end, and I do mean END – NO! I've never taken hormones to maintain my high voice. NO! I've never had my cheekbones altered in any way. NO! I've never had cosmetic surgery on my eyes. YES! One day in the future I plan to get married and have a family. Any statements to the contrary are simply untrue.'

This is all somewhat disingenuous. Jackson had already had plastic surgery on his nose three times when this statement was made, his hair had been straightened so often that it had to be curled to get any

body into it, and he went on to have so many more nips and tucks on his face – including a dimple in his chin – that *The National Enquirer* (and *The Daily Mirror* in the UK) were able to print a telephoto lens picture of him which claimed to show a third hole in his nose. (Jackson immediately launched injunctions against the papers for this breach of privacy.) A nice story has a mutual friend tell Diana Ross that Michael is trying to rebuild his face to look like her. Ross is aghast. 'I look like that?' she shrieks.

'I guess you can say that it hurts to be me,' Jackson once said, demonstrating the kind of self-pity that only the very rich can afford. Whether he believes his pain arises from his blackness or his success is impossible to say. It's clear that he doesn't believe it to be a human condition, more a mark of Cain. It's equally clear that, musical popularity apart, Jackson lost touch with his audiences and *their* reality years ago – even though, it appears, he may have been touching his audiences (or a few of them) in other ways for a long while.

By the late eighties, Jackson had become a self-caricature. Discarding family, producer Quincy Jones and the black culture which had nurtured him, his music went from good (with the humungous bestseller *Thriller*) to bad (with the half humungous *Bad*) and then to a planned joint project with Madonna which eventually emerged, sans Madonna, as the undisciplined hotch-potch of an album called *Dangerous*. Madonna, keen as ever in pursuit of a cheap innuendo, accused Jackson of being too uptight; she wanted to remodel the plastic wacko, put him in touch with some gay dancers, help him out of the closet. In the event, *Dangerous* turned out to be tame – all cash and no cachet – and Jacko embarked on a world tour designed, it seems, to re-establish himself as a rebel performer. Calling it the *Dangerous Tour* turned out to be prophetic – the tour to be more dangerous than the singer could have imagined. Of course, the leathers and studs were never the stuff of risk and rebellion – Jackson's crotch clutching act had always been neutered by his resolute self-promotion as Peter Pan, the youngest member of his family, the childlike one, the one whose LA mansion was called Neverland. Except, of course, Peter Pan *is* dangerous: in the sexual universe where rock music lives the moral order is transformed, and it was no good Jackson trying to pretend that he was sexless off-stage while he grabbed his adult crotch on stage.

And then in August 1993, just as the tour was building up a good head of steam in Moscow, Malaya and other famed centres of repression, somebody said the unsayable; 13 year old Jordan Chandler (one of Wacko's newer friends) and his parents in LA accused Michael Jackson of taking little boys into his bed. The curious thing is they just had to say it and practically everybody believed it – except of course good old Liz

Taylor, dripping in costume jewels and sentimentality (which were all no doubt genuine) who rushed to Michael's side as he retreated from live appearances and distressed fans behind the psychic battlements of medical confessionals: first came the disabling migraines, then the mental anguish, and finally the addiction to pain killers, requiring sequestration in an expensive private clinic somewhere far from the telephoto lenses.

The whole affair is sordid in direct proportion to the amount of money at stake. Jackson's earnings are phenomenal, his accusers stood to make millions from legal actions, tour promoters have had to cancel sellout concerts around the world. Jackson sponsor Pepsi Cola was faced with an embarrassing PR fiasco: they couldn't drop Jackson at the first whiff of paedophilia lest they tainted themselves by association and were also seen as confirming mere accusations already dismissed by that very model of moral rectitude and legal probity, the LA Police Department. But they couldn't continue to support him financially when the accusation was so severe and so plausible. Pepsi was rescued by the addiction to pain-killers – it let the company off the hook and allowed it to drop Jackson for an altogether less troublesome reason – but Jackson himself was still in deep doo-doo.

The Jackson camp could do little; it was well-known that Michael hosted slumber parties for sub-teen boys and this has been acknowledged. But once the bandwagon of accusation started rolling, nobody could stop it. Servants at the Neverland ranch, parents of Jacko's small companions, showbiz commentators, practically anybody with a mouth all came out and pointed fingers at Michael. But if, as many of them said, they had all known about it for years, then the implication is shattering: because Michael Jackson was rich and famous his eccentricities could be treated as just that. If Wacko said his slumber parties were innocent horseplay, that was good enough for the armies of hangers on who depended on him: innocent horseplay was what it was (nudge nudge). The fact that Jackson was 35 could be quietly ignored – after all, he paid the wages.

As long as no one complained did it really matter what he did when the video was over and the pyjama bottoms slipped a little. He was special. 'If it's a 35 year old paedophile, then it's obvious why he's sleeping with little boys,' said Jackson's private-eye, Anthony Pellicano, 'but if it's Michael Jackson, it doesn't mean anything.' For the most part, people willingly suspended disbelief about what Michael Jackson did. And these, according to the allegations filed by lawyers acting for Jordan Chandler, are some of the things he was doing:

'Defendant Michael Jackson orally copulating plaintiff, defendant Michael Jackson masturbating plaintiff, defendant Michael Jackson eating semen of plaintiff and having plaintiff fondle and manipulate the breasts and nipples of defendant Michael Jackson while defendant Michael Jackson would masturbate.'

It is perhaps not surprising in the event that Jackson's lawyers counselled settling out of court – something which the Chandler family finally agreed to do

The Phantom of Never-Never Land – Michael Jackson arrives at Nice Airport with Jordy Chandler's sister (Jordy was also in the limo at the time) after the Monaco World Music Awards in May 1993. At the time people simply noted that he looked weird – within months they were alleging something a lot more sinister.

213

Left: Did he or didn't he? The tabloid press used this photograph as 'evidence' in speculation about whether Jacko had had cosmetic sugery. Opposite: Michael Jackson's trial by tabloid.

once the settlement had reached eight digits.

The psychology of all this is very disagreeable – and what it reveals about the American family, quite disturbing: parents who have happily delivered their children into the disturbed fantasy world of Michael Jackson just because he was a star; others who have seen Jackson's waning star as the opportunity to turn a profit from their children's exploitation; and – last but not least – Jackson's own parents who seem prepared to accept moral failure as a price worth paying for spectacular success.

The cast of characters is truly bizarre: Michael Jack-

son himself; his Svengali-like father, Joseph (who is said to have asked for $150,000 to appear on TV to defend his son); the supportive brothers; Jacko's look-like sister LaToya who claimed at a midnight press conference in Tel Aviv to have harboured the dark secret that her brother was a child-molester for years; the Hogarthian lawyers and agents; the hardboiled private eye, Anthony Pellicano, hired to defend Jackson; the suits at Pepsi Cola; the (by now) only half-innocent children accusing the host of a hundred slumber parties; and – in the margins as always – everyone's friend, Liz Taylor, looking bemused while she waits, no doubt, for some unkinder critic than me to describe her as fag hag. This is the worst of rock'n'roll combined with the worst of Hollywood, a mediocre melodrama with a rehashed and half-hearted Faustian plot-line, with no rhythm and a sentimental old melody. If you thought it was the plot of a video, frankly you'd leave it on the shelf. Unfortunately, it's all too real. The result: children sacrificed on the altars of greed, ambition and a pathological desire for celebrity. In this context, if in no other, Michael Jackson is one of the children.

All of these things had become matters of supreme indifference in the eighties, except to those who love their soap opera with real people. Even then, how could anyone take John Lennon seriously when there was Julian doing an impression that could easily get him a walk-on part in a sequel to the Blues Brothers? Doesn't he look just like his father, and sings like him too! As far as rock'n'roll is concerned, they used to say 'it's what's in the groove that counts', and that's still true about Lennon.

There was, of course, a Golden Age of rock, and like all golden ages it combined vast creative potential with destructiveness and despair in equal measure. Nothing comes free, after all. Re-packaged in the ubiquitous CD-boxed set, the Golden Age survives. The wrinklies of rock are still strutting their stuff. Neil Young and Lou Reed have been making records and live appearances into the nineties (some of their output being actually better than anything they'd done in the sixties). Bob Dylan undertook his most extensive tour ever in the eighties. Even the Grateful Dead re-emerged older, fatter and greyer but still selling out Madison Square Gardens nine times over in 1991. The Rolling Stones were also touring – and still getting banned (their original 1984 'She Was Hot' video was too 'raunchy' even for MTV). By the beginning of the nineties, the Stones had signed a multi-million dollar three album deal with Virgin Records, and Chuck Berry had celebrated his 60th birthday with a show stage managed by Keith Richards. And the surviving Beatles talked about getting back together again, and again.... and again....

There was, of course, something profoundly different about the activity of rock's great survivors once they had proved themselves, and accepted the role time had cast them in. They were established - part of a global process whose stability lay in its capacity for constant renewal and reinvention. It may be exciting, but it would never be new or innocent again. To recapture some of that sense of novelty, a few performers looked further afield for inspiration than the clubs of London, New York or Berlin. New technology worked for some, a return to old values and older music for others. The turbulent global events of the previous years stimulated some performers – others created themselves as events in their own right.

Take the Pink Floyd affair, which demonstrated that giganticism in rock is far from dead. The remnants of the band, which had split acrimoniously in 1984, suddenly started breaking rock records again at the end of the decade. Dave Gilmour and Nick Mason had revived Pink Floyd in 1987, amid legal wrangles with the estranged Roger Waters about copyright and the title to the name. This Floyd made a worldwide best-selling album, *A Momentary Lapse Of Reason*, and

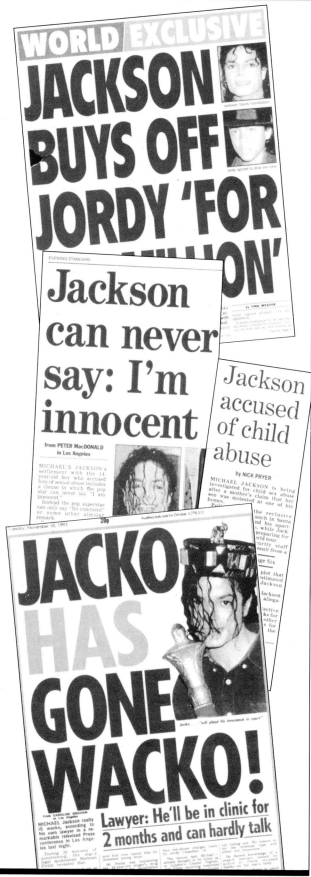

WHAM! GEORGE IS HIT FOR £3m

by PAUL CHESTON
and DAVID TAYLOR

ROCK superstar George Michael today failed in his multi-million-pound High Court bid to break away from recording giants Sony.

The defeat leaves a serious question mark over his future singing career.

Britain's most successful singer of the 1980s has threatened to never record again for Sony if he was to lose the case.

But after 74 days of complex legal argument Mr Justice Jonathan

Rock superstar loses court case

Parker threw out the star's claims that the contract he signed in 1988 — which could tie him to the label until 2003 — was a restraint of trade and unenforceable.

The 30-year-old singer, in a dark blue jacket and white open-necked shirt, with a red Aids awareness ribbon on his right lapel and his distinctive tinted glasses and designer stubble, sat poker-faced at the front of the court to hear the five-minute summation of the judgment.

Behind him the court benches were packed to overflowing with lawyers, press, hordes of fans, biting their nails in anticipation, and downcast members of his own family and friends.

Michael left court refusing to comment immediately about his singing future or the expected £3 million legal bill.

His counsel Mark Cran said he would be appealing against the ruling. The singer was due to hold a press conference to read a short prepared statement this afternoon.

His parents Jack and Lesley Panayiotou, also wearing Aids awareness ribbons, left court without comment.

The 270-page written judgment was issued in hardback after the hearing

Continued on Page 2 Col 6

George Michael arrives at court today to learn of his defeat. He will appeal.

Picture: NICK CORNISH

The press had a field-day when George Michael took on the music industry giant Sony over his contract, accusing them of 'artistic slavery'. While ripples from the outcome (he lost but was intending to appeal) still spread outwards, journalists were more interested in what he was wearing and how many minders were needed to push through the crowd of fans outside the court.

---

embarked on a tour which would take in 200 shows and more than 4 million people over a two-year period. The tour culminated in a spectacular satellite TV broadcast of a live show from a floating football pitch-sized stage in Venice. This was truly an event of world stature which, according to many commentators, was very nearly a disaster in its own right, as small mountains of rubbish, inadequate food and facilities and the sheer volume of noise, created a number of hazards which could easily have damaged the already shaky

Venetian environment. Gilmour blamed the city authorities and routine corruption; others observed that the Floyd had something to do with it.

Then, as if by way of a riposte, Roger Waters staged the Floyd album *The Wall* in Berlin a decade after the album's release. The $8.5 million event was designed to launch the Memorial Fund for Disaster Relief set up by the World War II hero and founder of the Cheshire Homes for Disabled People, Leonard Cheshire, in the wake of disasters like Chernobyl, the Armenian earthquake disaster and Hurricane Gilbert. It featured two helicopters, a 100-piece army band from the Soviet Union, 250,000 punters in the Potsdamer Platz, and appearances by Waters, Bryan Adams, Jerry Hall, Rick Danko, Levon Helm, Joni Mitchell, Van Morrison, Sinead O'Connor, Cyndi

Lauper, Albert Finney, Marianne Faithfull, Tim Curry and Ute Lemper. Luckily for Waters, the Potsdamer Platz is no jewel like Venice, and most of the infamous Berlin Wall had already been rubbished in any case. Otherwise, it's difficult to decide which of the events presented a more pointless spectacle.

Along with mature middle age came more domestic worries. Most of the oldsters had their own kids now. Having given their kids some really silly names in the sixties, you might have thought what happened to them subsequently was a matter of supreme indifference. But no! Serafina Watts, Zak Starkey, Jade Jagger, Zowie Bowie, China Slick, Dweezil, Ahmet Rodin, Moon Unit and Diva Zappa, Fifi Trixibelle, Peaches and Pixie Geldof and Cher's kids (would you believe Elijah Blue and Chastity?), are as loved and worried about as any children. In fact, these days the headlines are likely to be made by the antics of Mick and Ronnie's now celebrity daughters.

When it came to the media, however, rock grew up and asserted itself. When Elton John sued *The Sun* newspaper over allegations that he had been involved with rent boys at parties run by rock manager Billy Gaff, it wasn't the sexual scandal that upset him. Elton was always open about his bisexuality (at least, since his 1976 interview in *Rolling Stone*) and in any case sexual morality was less of a battleground in the eighties – it may have taken AIDS to break it, but the mould had definitely been shattered. What disturbed Elton more was the simple fact that the newspaper had lied and that their story was a fabrication. Suing *The Sun* was the act of a responsible member of society confronted by the excesses of tabloid press – Elton, after all, was a friend of royalty, Andy and Fergie went to his parties when they were still going to parties together.

The Sun story was a pot pourri of bondage, three in a bed, four in a bed, tattoos, leather trousers, spiky haired punks, and cocaine, based on the testimony of a former rent boy called Stephen Hardy who went under the pseudonym of Graham X and later confessed to making up the whole thing. When Elton consulted Mick Jagger, Jagger recalled his own experiences with the *News Of The World* and advised against suing. 'They can say I'm an old fat sod, they can say I'm an untalented bastard, they can call me a poof, but they mustn't lie about me because I'm going to fight,' said Elton. 'And I'm determined to be a winner.'

The Sun had made one fatal mistake in giving a precise date for some of the alleged sex parties. Elton could prove without doubt that he was 3,000 miles away from Billy Gaff's house in New York at the time. It wasn't until 12th December, 1988 – after Elton John had lodged 17 libel suits against *The Sun* and Stephen Hardy had long ago recanted – that the tabloid-weary from lying about Elton, obtaining photographs of the British Royals by shady means, and hounding TV star Russell Harty as he lay in hospital dying of AIDS – published a front-page apology under the banner headline 'SORRY ELTON' and agreed to pay £1 million in libel damages plus costs. By this time, Elton had already eked out his royalties with £14.8 million raised

in a Sotheby's auction of personal effects, stage props, and artworks collected over the years. Money was not the issue.

In the same way, Australian soap star and pop singer, Jason Donovan, would later successfully sue style magazine, *The Face*, not because an article on outing implied that he was gay, but because it implied that he had lied and pretended to be heterosexual. But if any kind of consensual relationship was quite acceptable, the implication of compulsion was enough to cause prurient minds to flutter. The public was amused by Rod Stewart's parade of young wives and girlfriends, but growing old disgracefully had its limits – as Bill Wyman and Mandy Smith found out.

There were, it emerged, hidden depths to Wyman – who had always seemed rather too old and too settled for the wild life. He came out as a Tory voter and in his autobiography, *Stone Alone*, confessed to 278 sexual encounters by 1965. As you might imagine, Bill likes to keep records. He started 'going out with' Mandy – a young woman just old enough at 13 to be his granddaughter. It was 1984; he was 47. By the time his book came out in 1990, Bill was admitting, rather shyly, to notching up four figures on the old tummy banana.

At 14, Mandy was on the contraceptive pill and in the papers all the time. At 15, she was posing topless for cheesecake photos. At 16, she told the *News of the World* that it was all over with Bill. 'My mother approved of my relationship with Bill,' she said, 'it was an unusual one.' At 17, she and Bill got married, with her mother Patsy's blessing. At 19, Mandy was admitted to hospital after her weight had fallen from 132 lbs to just 77 lbs. At 20, the happy couple split up after apparently managing to spend just five nights of wedded bliss together. With the tabloid press still yapping at their heels, Bill went back to his first loves: Gary 'US' Bonds, astronomy, keeping computer records on his group's progress and playing the electric bass. He was 55. It had been either the greatest publicity stunt of a career marked by a surprising lack of publicity or evidence that even a Rolling Stone can suffer from the male menopause.

By the time she was 21, Mandy had been diagnosed, at different times, as suffering from anorexia, AIDS, Addison's disease, candida and 'premenstrual syndrome'. She had become Bill Wyman's wasted middle age and all she had to show for it was a £530,000 divorce settlement (including the house in North London) and a figure that Gloria Vanderbilt would have killed for. She had asked for £5 million and, failing to get it, she announced in the newspapers that she was considering having her former hubby banged up for doing to her when she was 14 what she seems to have failed to do to Bill when he was dangerously close to pension age.

Recovering, she made the rounds of TV chat shows, with her loving mother in tow, looking like a blonde skeleton by Vidal Sassoon, blaming her decline on premature contraception. 'I noticed nothing wrong with Mandy when she was 14,' said Bill. But then he wouldn't have, would he? The postscript to this family saga was bizarre: Mandy's mother Patsy married Bill's son

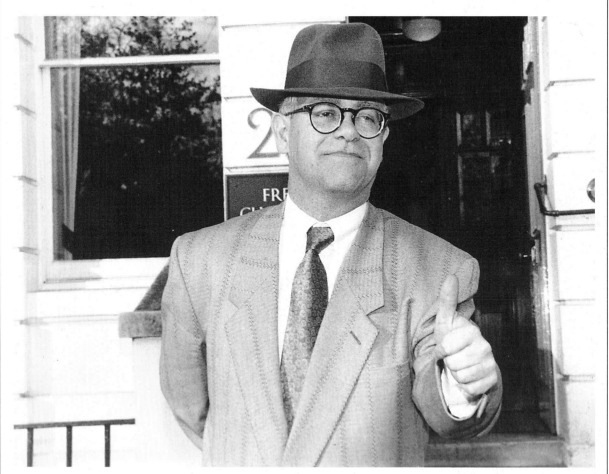

'Sorry Elton': Elton John emerges from his lawyers £1,000,000 richer on 13th December 1988 after The Sun agreed to settle out of court in his libel action against them. The Judge, who was to pass judgement on the case in court the next day, described the deal as 'distasteful'.

Stephen in 1993 while Bill himself married American dress designer Suzanne Accosta – at 33 she could probably be counted an older woman in Bill's canon. The tangled relationships thereby established would tax even the most assiduous genealogist, as Bill's ex-mother-in-law became – at the flourish of a pen on the register – his new daughter-in-law. Neighbours refer to the new Smith/Wyman household as 'the House of Dolls'.

If decades have colours, the eighties were the colour of money. Everybody became respectable, believed in Reaganomics and Thatcherism, and lapped up shallow fantasies of furfilment which masked an increasingly sordid and desperate reality. Caring and social concern were sold by the kilo, stuck on trucks and shipped out to Ethiopia or somewhere else a long way away, there to satsify the designer conscience of a generation. When you had enough of caring, you could buy rebellion, too. But if you didn't want to buy

Saturday night's all right for fighting … Elton John in slag drag. Elton John has never been image-shy but has successfully defended himself against lies told about him in the press.

rebellion you could invest in the product instead. Record collecting (which incorporates the obsessive hoarding of all kinds of promotional material and printed ephemera associated with popular music and is the modern equivalent of train spotting) has become a growth industry, with regular sales organised by all the major auction houses including Sotheby's and Christie's.

It was a time of illusion. And its passing was marked by the death of Freddie Mercury in the way that John Lennon's death marked the passing of an earlier time. For much of the eighties, Freddie Mercury partied like there was no tomorrow. The tales of his lavishly staged orgies are legion: dwarves handing round cocaine on silver platters, a naked woman emerging from a tub of raw calves' liver, sex, drugs and rock'n'roll. Like a scenario from one of Queen's more outrageous videos.

Mercury lived for sex – he said it himself – and his life epitomised that complete hedonism that becomes, through the play of surreal imagination, almost an art form in itself. He was, of course, a leftover from the seventies, when excess was the order of the day, and a camp survivor; but his time straddled a transition from the Blakean sense of excess – a getting of wisdom – to the Wall Street version – a buying of goodies. Queen, too, was a band whose music was increasingly

219

QUEEN STAR GOES PUBLIC AND CALLS ON FANS TO JOIN FIGHT AGAINST DISEASE

GLORY DAYS: Mercury the ultimate showman on stage with Queen

I've got AIDS, says Freddie Mercury

GAUNT: The public's latest glimpse of the ailing star in September

dominated by 'production values', and by the opportunities it offered for stunningly over-the-top but completely pointless extravagance. The group had long ago given up the simple ideals of musicianship and relevance.

Rock stars often have the liberty of living out their fantasies, and often it kills them. For Lennon, the fantasy had been to become an ordinary guy. With Mercury, it was licentiousness on a grand scale. Their deaths were not tragedies in the accepted sense - there was no inevitability about them. But somehow they point to the changes that overtook rock. Conspiracy theorists claim that Lennon's murder may have been a CIA plot to prevent his return to political activity. Even

Freddie Mercury fighting fit in Rio, January 1985. By the end of November, 1991 he was dead.

if this is true (and one has to remember just how influential Lennon's political activity was in its day), his killer remains an ordinary fan whose everyday world intruded violently into Lennon's exclusive reality. Mercury's fantasy, by contrast, was to be isolated from the everyday, to live an illusion of total freedom in his private Babylon and to pursue, through promiscuity the dream of a perfect sexual consumerism. He didn't appear to understand the risks, and fame, wealth and isolation cultivated an illusion of untouchability. When his illness was diagnosed as AIDS, he retreated into almost total seclusion, unable to let the world know until two days before he died.

As mournful and wretched a picture as this presents, it is somehow a perfect metaphor for all that's wrong in rock'n'roll.

PARTYING LIKE IT'S 1999

As the 1990s progressed, rock's established superstars visibly outlived the illusion of omnipotence and eternal youth. Rod Stewart – mullet-haired godfather of the 90s 'lad culture' – found the glove was on the other fist when Rachel Hunter, the latest of his seemingly interchangeable blonde wives, jilted *him*, for a change. After packing her bags and leaving, the twenty-something Ms Hunter complained that Rod the stud, now nearing his mid-fifties, lavished more attention on his model train set than on her – and, like all true 'lads', was most at home with his cronies down the pub.

Jumping Jack Flash himself – the eternally prancing Mick Jagger – was threatened with divorce in 1996. Jerry Hall, then in her forties, recruited the services of Princess Diana's divorce lawyer, Anthony Julius, on the grounds of Mick's serial infidelity. Making love to dispel the matrimonial war, the Jaggers seemed reconciled by the birth of their fourth child, Gabriel Luke Beauregard Jagger (dubbed 'the Kiss and Make up Baby' by UK tabloids) in December 1997.

Cricket-playing member of the MCC or not, however, a Rolling Stone is no servant to monogamy. By early 1999 reports that 56-year-old Jagger had left the Brazilian underwear model Luciana Morad (28, with sultry looks vaguely redolent of the young Bianca) with child finally spurred Jerry towards the divorce courts. Mindful of protecting his estimated £150 million fortune, the establishment's favourite rock-'n'roller was hit again in the pocketbook when a DNA test established that Ms. Morad's baby son, Lucas, was definitely his offspring. When a New York court arbitrated in Luciana's request for child maintainance to be paid at a cool $35,000 per month, Jagger – who previously avoided revealing the extent of his wealth even to his ex-wife – heard the court examiner utter words no corporate businessman wants to hear: 'Show me the money!'

Of the younger generation of superstars, boy-band progenitor turned blue-eyed soul singer George Michael was no stranger to litigation – having lost a London High Court action against his record label, Sony, in October 1992. By the late nineties, speculation as to the Anglo-Greek singer's reputed bisexuality was commonplace. UK tabloids reported his heartbreak when faced with the death of a close male friend, and how he coped by smoking large amounts of marijuana. (The songsmith later assured the public that 'the songs that I wrote when I was with women were really about women. And the songs that I've written since have been fairly obviously about men.') It was, perhaps, more of an eye-opener in his newly adopted homeland when the singer was forcibly 'outed' in the rudest manner possible.

On the evening of 7 April 1998, Beverly Hills police officer Marcelo Rodriguez arrested 34-year-old Michael after witnessing him masturbating in the public toilets of a local park. (Paradoxically defined as 'committing a homosexual act alone' – which, as commentators have noted, would make George a very gifted boy indeed.) In a subsequent TV interview with *CNN*, the unrepentant vocalist was gung-ho enough to claim that 'I feel stupid and I feel reckless and weak for having allowed my sexuality to be exposed this way. But I don't feel any shame whatsoever.'

Michael was fined $810 and sentenced to 80 hours of community service. With admirable cheek, he chose not to duck his lavatorial misconduct but to satirise it in the promotional video for his single release 'Outside'. However, this subversion of misfortune met with objections from officer Rodriguez, who had, he claimed, been slandered by the singer himself and by the video parody of the event. Michael had claimed entrapment, and that, according to a legal spokeswoman for Rodriguez, 'the cop came on to him'. For these hurtful insinuations Rodriguez announced in September 1999 that he was suing for a total of 'at least $10 million'. The claim was dismissed within six months, on the basis of an individual's constitutional right of free expression. With sleight of hand, George Michael had survived a seedy little episode to paint himself as an almost heroic outlaw figure – dancing defiantly in a public toilet.

However controversial such minor scandals seemed, they were pallid compared with the media outpourings that predated them by a few months. Diana, Princess of Wales was perhaps the closest figure to a rock star that Britain's House of Windsor had admitted within its stuffy environs – albeit a cleanly-produced, adult-orientated rock star. A personal friend of George Michael and other mainstream stars, she had become so ubiquitous a figure in the world media that it seemed grimly appropriate she should die a celebrity's death. When, on the night of 31 August 1997, she, her boyfriend Dodi Al-Fayed and driver Henri Paul (allegedly high on booze and prescription drugs) were killed after a high-velocity ride through the centre of Paris, all the elements were in place: sex, fame, speed, violence. The 'global village' was stunned – as were many of the British public, who, in their confusion,

---

'People like us like people like us.' Part of the popularity of Oasis stemmed from how the British 'lad culture' identified with their behaviour. Vocalist Liam Gallagher played the role of pub boor to a 't'.

223

The Mirror

GEORGE'S SHAME

FALLEN HERO: Pop superstar George is alleged to have played 'footsie' with officer

- **He lured undercover vice cop into park toilet**
- **He dropped trousers to perform lewd sex act**
- **He played footsie with officer under cubicle wall**
- **He wept in handcuffs after he was arrested**

SHAMED George Michael wept "uncontrollably" when he was arrested after luring an undercover cop into a public toilet for gay sex, it was revealed last night.

Pop superstar George, 34, played "footsie" with the officer while he sat in the next cubicle and performed an indecent act, it was claimed.

The multi-millionaire bachelor was then arrested and handcuffed and taken in tears to Beverly Hills police station.

The incident occurred in the Will Rogers Memorial Park near George's Los Angeles home.

Cops had been patrolling the park after complaints from nearby residents about

EXCLUSIVE

By ANDY LINES
US Editor

improper behaviour. An officer said: "Michael made eye contact with our undercover officer.

"He motioned for the officer to enter the toilets. Michael went in first and the officer followed him.

"They both sat in separate adjoining cubicles and Michael started to play 'footsie' with the officer under the partition.

"The officer then left his cubicle and looked round the corner and saw Michael committing an indecent act.

"He then formally arrested him. As he did so, Michael

started to cry. He was very upset."

The officer had no idea he had arrested one of the world's most famous singers.

George, wearing torn jeans, a denim shirt and a baseball cap, was booked for disorderly conduct under his real name, Georgios Panayiotou.

But he was released three hours after his arrest and given $500 bail to appear at Beverly Hills Municipal Court on May 5.

A report will be sent to the Beverly Hills City Attorney, who will decide if the case will go to court.

Last night George was staying at the Los Angeles mansion of gay record producer David Geffen.

● **CAUGHT RED-HANDED: PAGES 2 & 3**   ● **THE WHAM SHAM: PAGES 4 & 5** blamed the news media for her death, while imagining some kind of kinship with the woman whose existence they were only aware of via the newspapers or TV.

Diana – an immensely wealthy woman who took time out from her playgirl lifestyle to work as a figurehead for various charities – was regarded briefly as a latter-day saint. As the mourning that followed her death reached near-hysteria, it was considered not only apt but essential that the state funeral service of the only populist royal should feature a tribute that carried some resonance for the crowds who regarded her as 'the People's Princess'.

Enter Elton John – all-round entertainer and personal friend of the princess. The last time Diana and Elton were photographed in public together had been at the funeral of murdered fashion designer Gianni Versace, where she was seen placing a reassuring arm around the tearful pianist. It was time for Elton to repay the favour, to serenade his dead friend and to reassure the masses that 'their Diana' was sent off in a manner she would have understood.

'Candle In The Wind', in its original 1973 version, was an effectively schmaltzy tribute to Marilyn Monroe, a woman who lived a tempestuously insecure life. Stripped of its 1970s guitar licks, reduced to a plodding, barely existent piano melody, it became a maudlin lament that awkwardly replaced 'Goodbye Norma Jean' with 'Goodbye England's Rose'. In its own way, however, the British establishment allowing its performance in Westminster Abbey was a perverse triumph of pop-culture: a half-baked cover version of an old chart hit, performed by a flamboyantly theatrical former cocaine addict, and treated with sombre seriousness.

Not everyone saw it like that. Keith Richards – free from heroin for two decades, but still a walking testament to hedonistic living – acted for all the world as if the Rolling Stones were still the young demi-monde of yesteryear, rather than the merchandising business of today. Rock'n'roll, he explained, was nothing to do with acting as a funeral accompanist for the Royal Family, nor 'writing songs for dead blondes'. Pop music's pantomime dame found his remarks too provocative to ignore. 'He's so pathetic, poor thing,' bitched Sir Elton (for, as surely as night followed day, Elton John was knighted for his role as what the *Observer* called 'the Vera Lynn of the nineties'). 'It's like a monkey with arthritis, trying to go onstage and look young.' In his opinion, the Stones should have ditched poor old Keef years ago – suggesting that this conglomerate of late middle-aged businessmen strip itself of its last asset of credibility.

However, in this world of post-Band Aid/post-Diana superstars, Elton would unconsciously prove that he was the epitome of decadence. At London High Court hearings that ran from the autumn of 2000 through to April 2001, a negligence suit against one Andrew Haydon, the former managing director of John Reid Enterprises (JREL), and PriceWaterhouse-Coopers, the accountants who looked after Sir Elton's finances, was enlivened by the participation of John Reid himself.

The manager who guided Elton to an olympian level of success, Reid was retrospectively candid about their sexual relationship back in the days when his protégé was less openly gay than ostentatious. Against a background of mutual alcohol and cocaine problems came admissions of equally conspicuous, if less hazardous, consumption. Elton, who described he and Reid's 'somewhat lavish lifestyle', did his best to account for total spending of £30,000,000 over one twenty-month period. 'I have no one to leave the money to', he explained, with only a touch of defensiveness. 'I'm a single man. I like spending my money.' Indeed, in spending £293,000 on flowers during that period, tame old Sir Elton attained a level of aesthetic decadence matched by few others in rock'n'roll's Babylonian history. (The court found against Elton John, who was left with costs of several million pounds. The loss of control over his finances was attributed by the defence to his 'aversion to men in suits . . . badgering him to take on board lots of boring details'.)

Of all the nineties performers who sought to reinvent themselves as iconic figures, few were as unpredictable or as erratic as Sinead O'Connor. Still best known for a striking 1990 cover of Prince's 'Nothing Compares 2 U', her career owes more to headlines than hit records. From outspoken survivor of child abuse to evangelistic hash smoker (cannabis is a wonderful substance, she has said, and selling dope is an admirable profession), the crop-headed Irishwoman's greatest moment of notoriety occurred during 1992. Appearing on satirical US TV show *Saturday Night Live*, she aired her disapproval of the Catholic Church's dogmatic stance on birth control by burning a photo of Pope John Paul II.

The gesture hit the headlines, but its impact on the American public only became clear shortly after. At a tribute concert celebrating Bob Dylan's 30 years in the music business most of the audience booed and cat-called Sinead till she left the stage. The only reassuring words came from host Kris Kristofferson, murmuring, 'Don't let the bastards get you down,' while all other 1960s luminaries who once railed against the established order – including Dylan himself – remained conspicuously silent.

Perhaps incongruously – or perhaps not, in a life ruled by haphazard 'truth-seeking' – Sinead O'Connor was later ordained as a female priest by an unorthodox Catholic sect called the Tridentine Church. Mother Bernadette Mary, as she became known to her congregation, even took it upon herself to save one of rock-'n'roll's more unconventionally spiritual figures. Shane MacGowan – formerly of the Pogues, many times a drunk, composer of melancholic classics 'Fairytale Of New York' and 'Rainy Night In Soho' – is one of the most remarkable lyricists of the last 15 years of the twentieth century. This status (not to say his very existence) was threatened when MacGowan added heroin to the general alcoholic-chemical mix that keeps his mind free of mundane earthly matters. Shortly after a friend of the singer's was found dead from an OD at his north London flat, Mother Bernadette Mary decided it was her duty to alert the cops – who kicked down the door and busted MacGowan for possession in November 1999.

So the war of words started. According to the officers who raided his flat, MacGowan was found semi-comatose. Not so, said Shane: 'I was sitting on the sofa having a G[in] and T[onic] and watching a Sam Peckinpah movie.' The young man who died at the house the previous May, 25-year-old Robbie O'Neil, had snorted four times the lethal dose of smack in the apparent belief it was cocaine – the autopsy revealed no heroin in his system before the overdose, suggesting he was inexperienced in its use. But MacGowan, who slept through O'Neil's fatal OD, claimed to have scolded his lodger for using hard drugs. 'I use heroin only very occasionally', spoke the professional Irishman. 'To be honest, I prefer poitin [Irish moonshine] to heroin, and poitin is illegal' – as if heroin was not.

In a recent interview with *NME*, MacGowan had spoken of casual heroin use in a matter-of-fact 'I know what I'm doing' tone. Ominously, however, recent years had also seen the smack-related death of MacGowan camp follower Bryan Ging at the singer's previous north London address, in May 1995. Acquaintance with the least user-friendly recreational drug (at its deadliest mixed with booze) was clearly becoming a liability. As a casual user whose main problem was a general lack of sobriety, MacGowan escaped a possession charge by checking into London's Priory rehabilitation centre for treatment.

His second drying-out period ended after only two weeks, however, after he broke the clinic's 'no alcohol' rule. In spring 2001, a series of solo gigs at a bar in Dublin saw the familiar spectacle of a man too untogether to walk far but still managing to sing. But the lifelong dalliance with dissipation – and the occasional cheek-to-cheek dance with death – are part of the excesses that MacGowan wears like protective armour. His slurring, incapable persona has been described as 'a way of dealing with people who he just doesn't want to deal with' by his friend Bono of U2, who insists, 'Shane is more together than people imagine.' Veering happily from crisis to crisis, MacGowan is perhaps more aware of his mortality than his legend lets on. If he holds himself together long enough to live another decade, he may yet have the last laugh on many of his detractors (if not on the Reaper himself).

The War On Drugs in the USA – simultaneously the most prohibitive and the most drug-ridden western nation – continued to throw up anomalies. Over the last decade of the century prominent press coverage was given to stars busted for marijuana – an offence which in several European countries no longer even carries the penalty of a police caution. Former Van Halen singer Dave Lee Roth, country legend (and legendary pot-head) Willie Nelson, even mainstream diva Whitney Houston – all were caught in possession of substantial quantities of the weed, with legal penalties hanging over their heads until some nameless factor (presumably fame) persuaded the courts to treat them relatively leniently. In several states of the Land Of The Free, however, there are everyday members of the public serving life sentences for cultivating a few cannabis plants.

Ms. Houston's apprehension with an ounce of grass in her bag, at Hawaii's Keahole-Kona Airport in January 2000, seemed to grant her the street-cool of the new wave of young r 'n' b singers. (Kellis, for example, happily admits to smoking 'blunts' – big cigars stuffed with powerful weed – everywhere she goes.) But it also threw the spotlight on a more intense use of chemicals. Ms. Houston's erratic behaviour over the ensuing months included forgetting her lyrics before an Academy Awards performance, no-show at a tribute to Arista Records founder Clive Davis, and an interview with *Jane* magazine where she was described as 'extremely unfocused … [with] trouble keeping her eyes open … singing and playing an imaginary piano'. While her dreaminess might suggest she was smoking weed in Bob Marley proportions, drug tests scheduled for October 2000, to determine if she would face charges for the Hawaii bust, provided the incentive to clean up a long-term cocaine habit.

Bizarrely, it was her husband, r 'n' b vocalist Bobby Brown, who purportedly proved her saviour. When Brown – whose overtly sexual 'lurver man' act led to a 1993 performance ban in Georgia – was arrested in August 1996 for crashing Whitney's Porsche into a Florida street sign, his blood tests indicated twice the legal alcohol limit and traces of illicit drugs. Sentenced one year later, 'Bad Boy Bobby Brown' received 30 days in a rehab centre, one year's probation, suspension of his driving licence, 100 hours of community service, and to participate in anti-drug ads on TV – for which few celebrity drug users volunteer without legal compulsion. Subsequent to Whitney's arrest, he was extradited to Florida for violation of probation after testing positive for cocaine. Released from jail after two months, in July 2000, the fading star of 'new jack swing' decided his superstar wife had slid far enough into hedonist oblivion. According to reports of Whitney's 'detox hell' in the *National Enquirer*, on his return home he threw out any drugs he could find and forced her into sobriety the hard way. Reportedly, 'Whitney was battling panic attacks, her stomach was heaving, she couldn't sleep and her nose was constantly running' – testament to the thin grey line between psychological and physical addiction cocaine can sometimes cross.

Newly free from drugs, Whitney Houston may be on her way back to being r 'n' b's Ms. Squeaky Clean. At a party hosted by basketball star Magic Johnson in January 2001, however, husband and saviour Bobby Brown embarrassed her by taking the stage to give an impromptu, off-key performance. Sober or not, Bad Boy Bobby and his angry, screaming wife were asked to leave by the humourless host who failed to appreciate that, hey, that's showbiz, after all.

On the so-called 'alternative rock' scene (where, post-Nirvana and Pearl Jam, the commercial rewards were pretty similar to those of the mainstream), the drug culture's other hardy perennial still had hold. On 16 June 1994 Kristin Pfaff, 27-year-old bass player with Courtney Love's Hole, was found dead in her bath with a syringe stuck in her arm. She OD'd two months after Love's husband Kurt Cobain had shot up to calm himself before committing suicide by shotgun. Her death was attributed to the Seattle scene, where, according to one local user-dealer, 'Heroin is easier to get than any other drug' and where smack-related deaths increased by 60 per cent in the year prior to Cobain's and Pfaff's self-destruction. But such parochial causes were belied by nineties heroin chic, and the return of a fashionable 'heroin consciousness'.

Kim Deal, bassist with grunge godparents the Pixies and the Breeders, then leader of the Amps, observed of nouveau junkies: 'They blow on themselves and shit their pants, and look like death all the time. There's nothing more boring than a heroin addict ... These people can't even leave their neighbourhood, can't cross state lines, in case they stray from their main supplier. That ain't radical, that ain't rock'n'roll.' But this was the lifestyle of her twin sister and fellow Breeder, Kelley Deal, who was arrested on 30 November 1994 for receiving four grams of heroin via courier mail. The FBI had reputedly been watching her Dayton, Ohio home for several weeks. Kelley's musical career was immediately hit when her gig as producer of new band Star 69 was cancelled due to her forthcoming trial, and the Breeders ceased playing together indefinitely.

She had a long history of heroin use which, according to her sister Kim, stretched back to 1981, when, at age 20, her heart had to be shocked back to life 'just like in the fucking *Pulp Fiction* scene'. According to Kim: 'She totally didn't want to go [to rehab] ... we put her in the car and took her to the airport. She had no choice. She was a hostage at that time.' But the Deal sisters seem to have a capacity for survival (Kim claims to have indulged in every illegal substance, while avoiding addiction), and Kelley adhered rigorously to her Twelve Step Programme – continuing her career with a new band called the Kelley Deal 6000, whose first songs she wrote in rehab.

But the renewed vogue continued for what the late Grateful Dead guitarist Jerry Garcia (a junkie in later life) described as the 'great comforter'. In October 1995 Richard Shannon Hoon, 28-year-old singer for the Grateful Dead-influenced Blind Melon, comforted himself accidentally to death. He left behind a baby daughter. On 12 July 1996 touring Smashing Pumpkins drummer Jimmy Chamberlain and keyboard player Jonathan Melvoin, a young father who had been with the band less than a year, scored heroin on New York's Lower East Side before returning to their hotel room. Both passed out after taking the drug. In the morning, Chamberlain awoke but Melvoin had slipped straight from the arms of Morpheus into those of Death. NYPD confirmed that the lethally pure brand of heroin that killed him – known as red rum ('murder' backwards) – had become 'the product of choice' for local addicts. As any junkie knows, the closer to death the greater the high.

Billy Idol, the former Generation X pop-punk star who moved to Hollywood to live out the rock'n'roll cliché, engaged in further hackneyed behaviour by becoming a heroin addict. Two publicly admitted

Diva does dope: Whitney Houston's marijuana bust in Hawaii brought to the surface a long-term cocaine habit. Cleaned up and back in control, she reputedly owes her recovery to her loveable recidivist husband.

overdoses ensued, one in the mid-nineties and one at the beginning of the decade when Idol's heart stopped and he had to be revived by paramedics. The rock world's heart did not miss a beat – but more notice was taken when Hollywood Essex boy Dave Gahan, vocalist of Depeche Mode, had an equally close brush with the Grim Reaper.

Depeche Mode sailed away from their plip-plop electropop sound of the early eighties towards darker waters when Vince Clarke, later of Erasure, was replaced as songwriter by Martin Gore. After the platinum success of their *Violator* album, the band became perhaps the most incongruous stadium-rock act – with nary a crotch-slung guitar between them. And Dave Gahan reinvented himself as a 'proper' rock star. 'I actually consciously thought,' recalled Gahan, 'there's nobody willing to go the whole way to do this ... So I created a monster. And I made the mistake of thinking that meaning it meant you had to take yourself to the very depths of hell.'

In the early hours of 28 May 1996 an unidentified woman called the West Hollywood sheriff's department from Dave Gahan's room at the Sunset Marquis Hotel in Beverly Hills. When police and paramedics broke down the door at her bidding, they found the British singer unconscious in the bath. Drug paraphernalia and a large amount of mixed heroin and cocaine suggested he had shot up a lethal 'speedball'. Technically, he was dead – it was two minutes before the medical team were able to revive his heartbeat. 'The first thing I remember hearing was a paramedic in the background saying, "I think we lost him" … I woke up and I was handcuffed to a cop and he was reading me my rights.' But, typically, King Heroin still ruled the roost for a while.

'I came out of jail and I got straight back into it', admits Gahan. 'I remember Amanda [de Cadanet, British actress] came round to visit me at the Marquis, and her face said it all. She could see I was fucked up again, and tears were welling up in her eyes. When she left it was like she was saying goodbye … I just couldn't do this to people any more. I didn't want my son to grow up and wonder why his dad died or killed himself. So I picked up the phone. For the first time in the couple of years that I'd been in and out of detox, I picked up the phone and said, "I need help, I wanna get clean."' Gahan successfully completed the recovery programme at the Los Angeles Exodus Centre – previously flunked by Richard Shannon Hoon and Kurt Cobain. As mouthpiece and masthead for Martin Gore's songs of existential angst, he belatedly realised his life came down to a straight option of existence or non-existence: 'So that's the choice. The minute I pick up again, I'm gone.' Dave Gahan has, as they say, chosen life – and is no less credible a figure for it.

As Bobby Gillespie, of indie-turned-dub-funk-rockers Primal Scream, sang: 'If you play with fire you're gonna get burnt / Some of my friends are gonna die young.' And Gillespie should know, his band's former rock'n'roll lifestyle sounding every bit as clichéd as those lyrics. In the mid-nineties, an American tour saw a bar fight in New Orleans in which one band member remained blissfully unaware he had been stabbed, so 'anaesthetised' was he. This, too, was Primal Scream's wake-up call. The return of heroin consciousness was parodied by US band the Dandy Warhols in their catchy 1998 hit 'Not If You Were The Last Junkie On Earth' – accompanied by a satirical video featuring dancing syringes and synchronised emergency ward gurneys. While touring the UK, Warhols vocalist Courtney Taylor commented with apparent surprise on how the band were taken to task by the British press for their louche attitude to drugs and general rock'n'roll decadence. 'We've never met an English band that isn't mind-bogglingly fucked-up on drugs, alcohol and shitty sex', he insisted – though the drug of choice on the Britpop scene was not the soporific heroin. 'Most of those … British bands are doing way more coke and 16-year-old girls than we've ever done.'

One of the 1990s' most tragic losses, however, was caused not by narcotics but by a perverse accident. On 29 May 1997 folk-rock singer Jeff Buckley waded into the Memphis stretch of the Mississippi River, never to return. He had been sitting on the quayside with a

Dave Gahan of Depeche Mode being bailed from jail in LA, following a near fatal 'speedball' overdose of heroin and cocaine in 1996.

friend, playing songs on his acoustic guitar and listening to a ghetto-blaster. With apparently characteristic impulsiveness he decided to enter the water fully clothed. When a tugboat passed nearby, creating a large wave, Buckley vanished from view in the blink of an eye.

Concerns about Buckley's state of mind had recently been expressed by close associates. Way overdue on delivering the follow-up album to 1994's *Grace*, he had scrapped a number of recordings produced by former Television guitarist Tom Verlaine. In December 1996 he posted a cryptic message on his official website: 'I'm in the middle of some wild shit right now. Please be patient. I'm coming soon to a cardboard display case near you and I'll come out of my hole and will make bonfires out of ticket stubs this summer.' On 4 June Jeff Buckley's body was spotted by a passenger on a riverboat. He was pulled ashore at the bottom of Beale Street – Memphis's blues club area – and identified by his pierced navel and a T-shirt bearing the legend 'Altamont'. At 30, he was two years older than his father – semi-legendary blues and folk singer Tim Buckley, composer of 'Song to the Siren' – had been when he shot his own life away through the eye of a hypodermic needle. Buried at New York's Holy Trinity Church on 31 July, the younger Buckley was mourned by the likes of Elvis Costello, Marianne Faithfull – both of whom performed traditional ballads as tributes – and Patti Smith, who read aloud one of her poems.

One other major loss to American songwriting was narrowly averted the same week Jeff Buckley died. On 26 May, directly after his 56th birthday, Bob Dylan was admitted to a hospital near his home ranch in Malibu, California, undergoing severe chest pains. After initial fears that he was suffering a heart attack, he was diagnosed as having an infection of the sac surrounding the heart, known as histoplasmosis. As one of the primary sources of infection is chicken dust, the origin of Dylan's sickness was nothing more rock'n'roll than the life of a gentleman farmer. However, his eventual recovery ('I thought I was going to see Elvis real soon', quipped the one-time voice of a generation, recalling his 1980s song 'I Went to See the Gypsy' about how the two legends once met in real life) precipitated a renaissance in his career. The following year saw the release of 'Time Out of Mind', featuring the first new songs released by Dylan in the best part of a decade – and his best lyrics for easily twice that length of time.

Stranger shades of the past came rolling back when a rambling 14-page communication was posted on the Internet by A. J. Weberman, former head (and sole member) of the Bob Dylan Liberation Front in the sixties. With times a-changin' as they do, his attention focused on his former subject's son Jakob, young frontman of the band the Wallflowers. Jakob Dylan was, Weberman libellously claimed, a heroin addict, and the Wallflowers' lyrics were full of coded references to the drug. 'Somebody's got to get him straight', the cryptologist-stalker selflessly contended. 'Obviously his father can't or won't do it, so that task falls on me, the father of all children.' More paranoic than ever, Weberman, who clearly sees himself as having been locked in a war of wills with Dylan senior,

Buckley: debut success

Rock star vanishes after walk into river

claims also to have found references to himself stalking the Dylan home in 1970-71 in a Wallflowers lyric.

The dark side of stardom manifests itself on both sides of the Atlantic. In May 2000 the relocated Madonna, now living in Kensington, central London, was approached by young British fan Jonathan Sanders, attempting to take an unauthorised photograph. On hand to protect Ms Ciccone's privacy was Guy Ritchie, her fiancée and director of gangland comedies *Lock, Stock and Two Smoking Barrels* and *Snatch* (the latter title not, apparently, inspired by the content of Madonna's *Sex* book). When questioned by police as to why he punched and kicked Sanders, the Brit film luminary complained, 'He's a nutter who has been following us for months' – as evidenced by at least one previous photo of Ciccone being approached by her fan. An aggrieved Sanders demurred, but was reported to admit, 'I suppose I am a bit obsessed and some people would call me a stalker. But I don't think I am. I have been a fan for ten years. She means everything to me.'

(Madonna consolidated her arrival into British high society with a traditional wedding to Ritchie, a son of the landed gentry, on 22 December, 2000, at the vast Skibo Castle in Scotland. Attendant members of the British establishment included Conservative politician Michael Portillo, in the midst of a schizoid transformation from right-wing Thatcherite to 'outed' gay social libertarian. His friendship with Ms. Ciccone and spouse may have been a factor in his doomed attempt to win the leadership of the moribund Tories as the sex, drugs and rock'n'roll candidate.)

Elfin Icelandic chanteuse Bjork was subjected to the most terrifying form of long-distance fan adulation. In September 1996 Miami police contacted their London counterparts to warn of an explosive package sent by one Ricardo Lopez, a 21-year-old pest control officer who had recently committed suicide by shooting himself through the mouth. Recording the last hours of his life on videotape, the transatlantic stalker was seen preparing the device while muttering about the star whose posters adorned his walls. 'I am obsessed with Bjork,' he said to camera. 'Her relationship is unacceptable.'

Said relationship was between the single mother and metal-toothed jungle music producer/DJ Goldie – whose mixed-race origins were disapproved of by the psychotic Lopez. Scotland Yard Anti-Terrorist Squad intercepted the package before it could arrive at Bjork's management company, and found it contained a hollowed-out book filled with sulphuric acid, primed to explode in the singer's face on opening. Bjork, who relocated to Spain to record her next album after the incident, confirmed that the madness celebrity can attract 'had a really extreme and deep effect on me. You're doing a job that could get your kid killed, and that's some strange thing to get your head around. It's like, should I just get another job?' After she returned to her native Iceland, in 1998, a disturbed Spanish fan who had been trailing her for some while broke into Bjork's mother's house. He stayed long enough to steal some food and take a nap in bed, before leaving a threatening message for the singer. 'Maybe I should stop releasing my music', she later reflected aloud, understandably distressed. 'Before I was 26, my motto was to never let anyone else hear my music. Maybe I should return to that attitude.'

In the early hours of 30 December 1999 George Harrison, 56-year-old former Beatle, transcendental meditationalist and film producer, was asleep in the mansion house bedroom of his 37-acre home, in Henley in Oxfordshire. At 3.30 a.m he was woken by his wife, who heard the sound of breaking glass. Downstairs, he was confronted by a young man with a mop of wild blond hair -- armed with a knife, and a lance taken from a statue of St. George and the dragon in Harrison's observatory. He quickly became hysterical, shouting, 'You get down here – you know what it is!' In an idiosyncratic move, Harrison began a loud

chant of 'Hare Krishna' to confuse his unwelcome visitor. However, something other than a spiritual boost was clearly required: both men went hand-to-hand, but the unarmed Harrison was continually stabbed in a fit of rage.

As the knife was plunged into his chest, the mild-mannered guitarist felt his chest deflate: 'I could feel the strength drain from me … I believed I had been fatally stabbed.' George Harrison may have become the Beatles' secondary iconic figure if not for the intervention of his wife Olivia, a petite Mexican-American. Bravely, she flew at the intruder, splitting his head with a poker. But when he counterattacked, her wounded husband's attempts to defend her sent all three sprawling into a pile of meditation cushions – now stained, like much of the furnishing, blood red. 51-year-old Olivia gained the upper hand by bringing down the base of a lamp on the man's dishevelled head two or three times. He was dazed, but still conscious. 'Don't stop, hit him harder', pleaded George, his survival instinct overriding any old pacifist dogma.

When the disturbed attacker was able to rise to his feet, grabbing the cord of the lamp and flailing at her head, Olivia, exhausted, terrified and injured, finally turned to run for help. For once, the cavalry came. The police, telephoned before she ventured downstairs, arrived in time to save the traumatised Harrisons. Her husband, the main target of the attack, had ten stab wounds, and had to be taken to London for surgery on a collapsed lung. At one point, the knife had entered half an inch away from his heart.

When placed under arrest, the battered would-be assassin told the police: 'You should have heard the spooky things he [Harrison] was saying as he was going.' Seemingly, he found George's Krishna chants almost as frightening as the ex-Beatle found the murderous attack itself. 'I should have got the bastard better', said Michael Abram, 34, who believed that Harrison was 'an alien from hell', and that the Beatles were a witchcraft cult 'flying around on broomsticks'.

In many ways, Abram is a disturbed soul-mate of Mark Chapman – the pathetic obsessive who blew John Lennon away in NYC almost exactly nineteen years earlier, on 8 December 1980. (Chapman's first application for parole was turned down in October 2000 – the same month Lennon would have had his 60th birthday. In his application, he claimed deep regret for his actions – but in terms that suggested he saw John and Yoko as ciphers in his own personal tragedy, rather than two lives destroyed or damaged by himself. Abram, for his part, seems contrite for what he has done, but clearly remains a danger unless closely supervised and medicated.) But whereas Lennon's assassin lived out a private fantasy wherein the nonentity would eclipse the fame of the idol he was stalking (if only for one moment), paranoid schizophrenic Abram's inner world was one of exaggerated fear and delusion. He spent his days at home in a high-rise flat reading *The Bible*, studying the prophecies of Nostradamus and interpreting the 'hidden messages' in rock lyrics. (With the classically twisted logic of schizophrenia, 'Let It Be' translated as 'Hell' [L], 'Extra

FREE TODAY

IT'S PARTY TIME!

16-page guide to London's millennium weekend

PLUS 5-day TV listings

Mansion intruder attacks star

BEATLE GEORGE STABBED

Protection fails: George Harrison and his wife Olivia are both in hospital today after a knifeman beat the high security that surrounds their Friar Park estate

by JUSTIN DAVENPORT and NIGEL ROSSER

GEORGE HARRISON is in hospital with a stab wound today after grappling with an intruder armed with a knife.

The former Beatle and his wife Olivia tackled the assailant after they awoke and confronted him in the living-room of their multi-million pound house near Henley-on-Thames. Police said Harrison, 56, who was stabbed once in the chest, managed to fight off the intruder with a heavy implement and subdue him before staff called police. The

Private Beatle: Page 3   Price of fame: Pages 4 & 5

couple were "deeply traumatised" by their ordeal, said staff at the Royal Berkshire Hospital in Reading today. Harrison suffered a puncture wound to the chest while his wife was treated for cuts and bruises caused as she tried to stop the attack on her husband.

Mark Gritten, chief executive of the Royal Berkshire and Battle Hospital NHS Trust, said the stab wound did not puncture Harrison's lung. "It's not severe, he did not require surgery," he added. "Obviously as you would expect they are deeply traumatised, but they are recovering and feel much better. They are fine and comfortable and

deeply appreciate the thoughts and sentiments they have received from around the world. Mrs Harrison is suffering superficial injuries. She is in a little pain and discomfort. She's been by the bedside of Mr Harrison, who is suffering from superficial injuries and a stab wound to the chest."

Police were called to Harrison's high-security home, Friar Park, at 3.30am where they found the guitarist and his wife, who is in her early fifties. Harrison's elderly mother was asleep in the mansion at the time.

Officers arrested a 33-year-old man from Liverpool on suspicion of attempted murder. He was treated at the John Radcliffe II Hospital in Oxford for superficial wounds, but released into police custody at 8.30am. A blood-covered knife was found on the floor of the living room. A blue holdall believed to belong to the man was later discovered hidden behind wooden fencing panels and thick foliage in a garden directly opposite the main entrance to the Harrisons' home.

A Thames Valley police spokesman said detectives **Continued on Page 2 Col 2**

Fiasco as Dome tickets for thousands miss the post

THE GALA opening night for the Millennium Dome tomorrow has turned into a fiasco with a bitter row over the failure to deliver security passes to thousands of guests.

The Government-sponsored builder of the Dome at Greenwich has sacked the company handling tickets for 10,500 guests because, with only one day to go, many are still waiting for their invitations.

by STEWART PAYNE

But to add to the embarrassment, the man whose company is blamed for the chaos, Mike Lockett, is also project director for both the opening night celebration and the Big Time Millennium Eve party beside the Thames.

The Evening Standard has discovered that the

New Millennium Experience Company, builers and operator of the £758 million Dome, became so alarmed at the backlog in issuing security passes that it removed Mr Lockett's company, Live Productions Ltd, from its contract on Christmas Eve and took over the ticket administration.

Today NMEC staff were involved in a race **Continued on Page 7 Col 4**

Terrestrial' [ET], 'I've given you TB' [ITB].)

Native of a rundown section of the Beatles' very own Liverpool, Abram travelled down by train from Merseyside specifically to commit the attack. Ultimately, he would be found innocent of attempted murder on grounds of insanity – but sentenced to be confined indefinitely to mental institutions. Ironically, an examining psychiatrist expressed the opinion that Abram may not have felt able to carry out his mission unless he had heard his satanic enemy 'talking in tongues' – George's panicked chant of 'Hare Krishna'. Recovered from his injuries, but reluctant to return to his Oxfordshire mansion, Harrison and his wife were perturbed to find Abram's indefinite detention did not preclude his eventual release – with no compulsion for the authorities to notify them if such a decision were made. The emotional and physical trauma may also have been a catalyst for the return of the cancerous illness he seemed to have beaten in 1998. After earlier treatment for throat cancer, the ex-smoker had a malignant growth removed from one of his lungs in spring 2001 at the Mayo Clinic in Minnesota. Soon after, at the Oncology Institute of Southern Switzerland, it was confirmed that a brain tumour was threatening his life. On 29 November 2001, the ex-Beatle succumbed to the illness in Los Angeles. George Harrison was said to have accepted his fate with gentle stoicism. His reputed last words, ´Love one another´, seem like a quiet rebuke to the violence he himself had suffered, and to a world where a clash of cultures had exploded into war in Afghanistan.

Nine years of treatment had failed to diagnose Michael Abram's illness, his delusions blamed on heroin addiction. The patient had experimented with drugs from the age of 17 – including LSD, the hallucinogen John Lennon helped popularise, which can awaken latent schizophrenia – but heroin, while potentially lethal, has no hallucinogenic effect. Abram, it seems, was trying to medicate himself, to quiet his constant 'voices'. When rehabilitation freed him from his drug habit, the voices spoke louder. Drifting around town wearing a Walkman, he began listening to his mother's old Beatles records in 1999. It was a late-blooming obsession, meshing with his new personal crusades to save the world from drugs ('Did the Beatles take drugs?' he asked his mother) and 'witchcraft'. Ultimately, he reached the conclusion that: 'Paul McCartney's a witch but George Harrison is the boss' – in fact, earnest George was an invader from the heavens who Nostradamus predicted would destroy the earth. Abram now had the sanction of God Himself to kill the malevolent being he believed was controlling his mind. During November 1999, in the prelude to his attack on Harrison, Abram was charged with damaging advertising boards for the Cavern Club – the Liverpool venue where the young Beatles rose to fame.

Michael Abram's delusional fantasies were fed by the music of mainstream superstars: the Beatles; Bob Marley; U2; Madonna – who he believed was reading his thoughts; Oasis – self-professed contemporary heirs to the Beatles – who, he also believed, had written the song 'Wonderwall' specifically about him. In a

largely secular age, when madmen possess the strongest religious faith, the religion of celebrity attracts madness like a magnet.

The main strand of English rock music throughout the 1990s – in the wake of its introverted, dressed-down stateside contemporary, grunge – came under the ill-defined umbrella term of 'Britpop'. But what was so essentially British about this non-movement of casually dressed bands wasn't always so clear.

Decidedly defiant in his Englishness – despite being the son of first-generation Irish immigrants – Morrissey, former vocalist of remarkable 1980s Brit band the Smiths, courted adulation from a growing US audience and opprobrium from the UK music press in equal measures. In his former incarnation, the aggressively fey, gladioli-waving Morrissey was a witty chronicler of the Britain of his youth: composing monochrome kitchen-sink lyrics that took in everything from vegetarian disgust at the 'murderousness' of the British diet to the Moors Murders that blighted his native Manchester in the 1960s.

When he became a solo artist, a toughening of attitude reflected the late blooming of a burlier, beerier Morrissey, in songs such as the paean to sixties East End gangster Reggie Kray, 'The Last Of The Famous International Playboys'. At the time of promoting 1994's *Vauxhall and I* album, the man who once sang the line 'She's so rough and I'm so delicate' posed for the cover of Select magazine with a set of knuckle-dusters. (Two years later, enmity between the former rhythm section of the Smiths and Morrissey came to a head when drummer Mike Joyce successfully sued his ex-band leader for a higher proportion of performance royalties. The man once synonymous with adolescent hyper-sensitivity was blasted by the presiding judge as 'devious, truculent and unreliable'.) Of most concern to his former admirers, however, were the sentiments of 'Bengali in Platforms' – from the album *Viva Hate* – which satirised the stereotypical immigrant from the Indian subcontinent, keen to be assimilated: 'Shelve your western plans / Life is hard enough if you belong here.'

Morrissey continued to provoke the politically correct with comments such as 'I don't think black people and white people will ever really get on – is that a terrible thing to say?' Their discomfort briefly exploded in the aftermath of 1992's 'Madstock' debacle, when olde England's be-quiffed historian supported a reformation gig by Madness, the quirky ska/music-hall pop stars. On an open-air stage in north London's Finsbury Park, with a backdrop showing original late sixties/early seventies skinheads (inherently violent and intrinsically English, matching the singer's obsessions), Morrissey wrapped himself in the Union Jack flag as he sang. This, according to detractors, was a crypto-racist statement which brought bad karma down on his head – in the form of contemporary skinheads bombarding him with coins.

After a 1994 interview in *Select* where he opined that the neo-nazi British National Party should receive equal airtime on British TV (ostensibly to give them the democratic rights they claim to be denied),

Morrissey was seen to break entirely with the left-wing consensus that governs that most exploitative enclave of capitalism, the rock music industry. The Anti-Nazi League denounced him as 'highly irresponsible', while the editor of the *NME* agreed there would be no more coverage of Britpop's most awkward progenitor in its pages, turning a logical cartwheel on the subject of censorship: 'In an ideal world ... Freedom of speech should mean that everyone is entitled to their say. But this is far from being an ideal world ...'

In defence of 'The National Front Disco', the absolute *bête noir* of his enemies, Morrissey did at least feel moved to explain, 'The phenomenon of the National Front [a far-right party briefly popular in the seventies] interests me just like it interests anyone. Just as all manner of sexuality interests everyone. That doesn't necessarily mean you want to take part.'

Similar criticism was aimed (though less vociferously) at Crispian Mills, leader of psychedelic Krishna rockers Kula Shaker. Attacked for his remark that he saw 'no difference between killing a cow and killing a baby', the singer was faced with the standard 'Hitler was a vegetarian' riposte. While demonstrating that he had read a few books, his response was: 'Hitler and his whole gang weren't just a bunch of fucking psychos, they were also into magic and all that ... I love the swastika! It's a brilliant image, it symbolises peace and the sun and illumination – it's everywhere in India.'

Claims that his beloved starving Indians 'don't mind it [their poverty] as much as you'd think because they're in touch with their spiritual selves' revealed a smug naivety. He then flagellated himself in a long letter of apology to the *Independent on Sunday* newspaper, after they revealed his former membership of a band called the Objects Of Desire. Their particular sins were that they contained one member with far-right sympathies, and that the band had attended a conspiracy theory conference entitled Global Deception – featuring a handful of paranoid racists, alongside conspiracists of every stripe. The greatest taboo in rock'n'roll these days lies, it seems, not in extolling dangerous drugs but in holding eccentric opinions.

In such a pop-cultural climate, the role of cultural *agent provocateurs* was passed to the Manic Street Preachers. With an abrasive but confused blend of recycled punk rock, visual androgyny, social conservatism and cultural Stalinism, they were at least contrary enough to be a band with 'attitude'. At a Christmas performance in 1992, guitarist/vocalist Nicky Wire alluded to rumours that REM vocalist Michael Stipe had contracted Aids, by callously announcing, 'Let's hope that Michael Stipe goes the same way as Freddie Mercury pretty soon.' Forced to rationalise his remark, the young man whose band were destined to become mainstream stars insisted he had nothing personal against Stipe (who remains seemingly healthy and productive to the present day) – it was just his way of protesting against the stagnation of big-time American rock music.

Manics member Richey Edwards' bouts of self-mutilation appeared, however, to be more than an attempt to emulate Iggy Pop. When the androgynous guitarist was admitted to a clinic while suffering from nervous problems in August 1994, his disturbed mental state revealed his arm and chest slashing as a classic symptom of low self-esteem. The press release issued on behalf of the Manics stated that Richey was 'very ill at the moment and things have now developed to a point where the band – but more importantly Richey – have decided that he needs to seek professional psychiatric help to deal with what is basically a sickness'.

On 1 February 1995 the emotionally fragile young man went AWOL while leaving most of his personal belongings behind. He had not been located by the time his Vauxhall Cavalier car was found abandoned at a service station near the Severn Bridge, close to his native Wales, on the 14th. Despite myriad rumours, including a reported sighting in Goa, India, by the end of the year the investigating detective in the case aired his personal fears that the troubled performer was dead. (Edwards had left his passport behind when he disappeared, greatly reducing the likelihood of seeking anonymity in foreign climes.)

In August 1995, seven months after Richey went missing, the Manics announced they would be continuing as a three-piece. Nicky Wire and guitarist James Dean Bradfield were taking over the lyrical duties, and a royalties account would be kept open for their absent friend in the hope that he would eventually resurface. Bequeathed to his bandmates, the absentee had also left behind what are assumed to be his final lyrics – surfacing on the Manics' eventual next album, *Everything Must Go*. 'At the end of the day you can't feel grief because you don't know if he's dead', said Nicky Wire, challenging police pessimism. 'You feel anger, sympathy and sadness. The tragedy lies on a personal level. On a professional level, as a professional band, it doesn't really come into it ... It's the personal element that's the hardest to take.' Ironically, the process would gradually transform the Manic Street Preachers into a classic 'big pop' outfit, with portentous ballads like 'If You Tolerate This Then Your Children will be Next'.

The transitional period for Britpop had been the addition, to basic sixties r&b and post-seventies punk style, of the sub-genre known as 'baggy'. Originating in Manchester ('Madchester') in the late eighties, the MDMA (ecstasy)-influenced music of the Happy Mondays and the Stone Roses took these classic rock styles and married them to a meandering drum/dance beat. As the nineties wore on, and personal habits took hold, Shaun Ryder's drug-besotted Mondays remained the more prolific of the big two Madchester groups. (Later to be superceded by Ryder's follow-up band, Black Grape.)

The Stone Roses' eponymously-titled 1989 debut album, and their much lauded 1990 open-air concert at a remote venue called Spike Island, were followed by a five-year silence while the band was engaged in managerial and legal hassles, and the inordinately lengthy process of recording their second album – further delayed by much smoking of highly potent marijuana. Eventually dispensing with their management, the Roses had in mind a comeback of *Hammer of the Gods-*

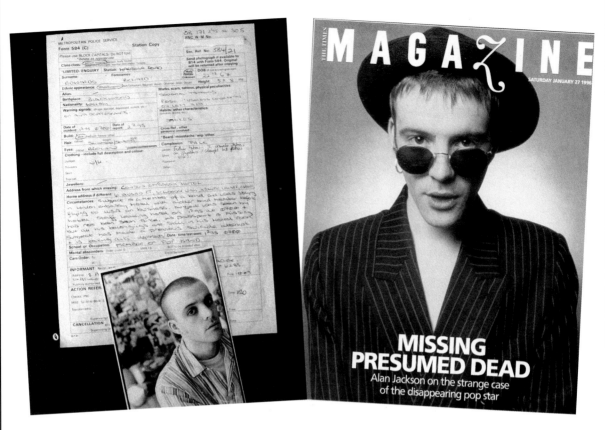

Richey Edwards (inset), missing Manic Street Preacher, and the police report on his disappearance. Like his acts of self-mutilation, his apparent suicide touched a chord with many emotionally vulnerable young fans.

proportions when they approached Led Zeppelin's former behemoth manager Peter Grant, encouraging him to put himself forward as their new manager. 'Who the hell do they think they are?' raved the man formerly feared throughout the rock'n'roll business. 'They wanted me to audition to see if I was suitable! I've never heard anything like it.' (It's not known if the big man's apoplexy at this outrage contributed to his death from a heart attack in November 1995.)

Modestly entitled *Second Coming*, when the album was eventually released it was generally received with disappointment, the consensus running that it really didn't add up to five years' worth of creativity. Following this, and the band's split in 1996, the mantle of Great Brit Hope in what singer Ian Brown described as 'the filthiest business in the universe' was passed on to other contenders. According to Brown, the rubber-limbed 'King Monkey', much of the internal friction that led to the split was generated by the difference between his drug of choice (weed) and that of ex-guitarist John Squire, founder of the Seahorses. 'On those tours there were two buses,' he elaborates, 'the cocaine bus and the non-cocaine bus. And if someone's on coke you can't work with them … I can't stand cocaine. It's the weakest thing you can do. There's no love, there's no soul.'

The main British contenders for the role of Next Big Thing were formed in the northern English town of Wigan at the tail-end of the 1980s. But it wasn't until 1997, with the release of 'Bitter Sweet Symphony' – and its much-parodied video showing lanky vocalist Richard Ashcroft striding determinedly down the street without swerving for passers-by ('try that in Glasgow', as one wag put it) – that their retrogressive 'classic rock' style came into its own. The Verve vacilated throughout their career between being Britpop's great hopes and missing their moment. Typical of their ability to snatch defeat from the jaws of success was Ashcroft's hospitalisation for acute dehydration in the midst of the 1994 Lollapalooza US band package tour – after knocking back trad rock-star quantities of brandy under a baking sun. As pressures mounted, emotionally vulnerable lead guitarist Nick McCabe left the group immediately after the release of their second album, *A Northern Soul*, in 1995, suffering from ever-deepening depression. (He was initially replaced by Bernard Butler, departed from nineties glam rockers Suede – who soon found his working relationship with Ashcroft paralleled a similiar ego-clash with Suede frontman Brett Anderson.) After his eventual return to the fold in 1996, when the Verve became a full-time band again, McCabe claimed, 'I've got a sense of whatever goes wrong doesn't really matter, 'cos I fell to the bottom and it wasn't so bad' – blaming his former disillusionment on 'too many drugs and not enough communication'.

The success of 'Bitter Sweet Symphony', just a few months after their reformation, promised that the Verve's time had come. Alas, with formidable timing, former Rolling Stones manager Allen Klein unleashed a lawsuit relating to the song's haunting orchestral string motif. In the manner of many eighties and nineties dance tracks, the Verve had fashioned the hookline from a looped sample from another record. While it wasn't a Stones track per se, the repetitive strings were taken from an instrumental version of Jagger/Richard's The Last Time recorded by original Stones manager Andrew Loog Oldham. Rights to the original song were now held by Klein, who quickly ensured the Verve never saw a penny in publishing royalties from their hit single.

Still, 'Bitter Sweet Symphony' was to find a second wind and massive exposure in the US, when its orchestral riff was llicensed for a Nike training shoes ad. Due to the plagiarism lawsuit, half of the $700,000 usage fee was divided between Jagger/Richard and publishers Abkco Music (Klein). The Verve made a point of publicly stating that their share would be divided between a children's charity and the British Red Cross Landmine Appeal, inviting their veteran compatriates to do the same. There was no personal response, but the Stones' office haughtily insisted that the band 'traditionally give substantial sums to charity, but they almost always do it privately'.

One last stab at major success came with 'The Drugs Don't Work' – a hauntingly retro song summoning up the ghosts of rock's great melancholics, and released on the same album, Urban Hymns as 'Bitter Sweet Symphony'. Derivative but powerful, it went straight to the peak of the British top ten in early September – only to be eclipsed, in terms of prominence and radioplay, by Middle England's lament, Candle In The Wind, one week later. In the midst of the surreal whirl of bigtime success (and litigation), Nick McCabe's personal fragility started to reassert itself. To no one's great surprise, the Verve imploded for good in April 1998 – after Urban Hymns had gone platinum on both sides of the Atlantic and won a Grammy award.

In the interim, two young bands who had been around for several years had stepped into the vacuum to redraw the template of British pop music. Blur were an almost clinical composite of Britpop styles past: mod suits (in their early days), self-conscious Ray Davies-type snapshots of how the band imagined British working-class life to be, mock-cockney accents. Their eventual rise coincided with that of a newer band from Manchester, both of whom were seen as twin heralds of a new 'British invasion' across the Atlantic. It was in the USA, on air at San Francisco's Live 105 Radio, that the frontmen of both bands made their first public appearance together: 'Alright, geezer?' chirped Blur vocalist Damon Albarn in post-baggy parlance. 'Nish, wanker,' sneered Liam Gallagher, cocksure frontman of Mancunian band Oasis.

Rivalry was already underway between the southern artschool boys and the working class northerners who fancied that their doggedly trad late sixties/early seventies sound with a pseudo-punk sneer would make them as big as their heroes, the Beatles. In commercial terms at least, Oasis's confidence would prove self-fulfilling.

Initially, the bands felt some degree of camaraderie born of being on the crest of a rising pop wave. Albarn was quoted as saying that Blur's 1995 Brit (UK music industry) Award for Best New Band should be shared with Oasis. Oasis guitarist/songwriter Noel Gallagher was initially friendlier to their rivals than his younger brother, urging band members to dance to Blur at the Brit Awards ceremony – though he later claimed to have been out of his mind on ecstasy. But it was Liam's characteristic leeriness that found an easy target in his contemporaries. At the same year's alternative to the Brits, the Brat Awards hosted by NME, he refused to be photographed alongside Blur, playing up his hardman image as he faced Albarn toe-to-toe: 'I'll tell ya. To your face. Your band's full of shit. Right. So I'm not going to do a photo with ya.' Elder brother Noel got in tune with his sibling in a later Observer interview: 'The bass player and the singer [Alex James and Albarn] – I hope the pair of them catch Aids and die because I fucking hate them two.' Two years later, at the 1997 Brits, when Oasis cleaned up for Best Album and most other categories, the entire band still felt moved to sing a parody of Blur's Kinks/Madness-inspired 'mockney' hit, Parklife – or 'Shitelife', as they retitled it.

The media-sponsored feud, which generated column inches as surely as someone exposing himself to the Queen, was exaggerated to the extent that the release of two singles on the same day – Blur's 'Country House' and Oasis's 'Roll With It', on 14 August 1995 – was presented as a battle of the bands. The elder Gallagher fed the press's trivial pursuit, claiming that Blur were 'a bunch of middle-class wankers trying to play hardball with a bunch of working-class heroes'. Tabloid opinion claimed this was a return to the classic rivalry of the northern Beatles and the southern Rolling Stones – though those two bands had remained personal friends, and, in Oasis's case, it was the tuneful northerners who were playing the bad-boy role.

Fervently believing his own publicity ('We're the best fucking band in the world!'), Liam Gallagher has consistently behaved in a manner that is less trad rock star than – in these egalitarian times, when cocaine use is no longer confined to the music business elite – local pub bore. En route to the band's first-ever overseas gig, in 1994, the singer, and the bassist Paul McGuigan, were handcuffed and locked in the brig of the ferry after becoming uncontrollably pissed on champagne and Jack Daniel's. Creation, their record label, explained that 'several of the band members have never been abroad before'. Once overseas tours had become a permanent fixture, the frontman could still see fit to walk out on the band 15 minutes before they were due to embark on a tour of the US. The ostensible reason was that he needed to find a permanent residence instead of living out of a suitcase – or, in Liam's own inimitable words, 'I don't give a fuck for any fucker. It's me who comes first!' By this time, such petulance was customary – and the tabloids were starting to

The new Beatles vs. the new Stones? According to one of the more cynical voices on the NME, *Oasis were as good as mid-'70s Wings while Blur's 'Country House' sounded like Bill Wyman's 'Je Suis un Rock Star.'*

hang onto every brattish utterance.

Liam's loutish behaviour at media watering hole the Groucho Club, smashing pool tables after an awards ceremony at London's Park Lane Hotel, suggested he'd taken the standard rock star route to being Superman for a night – born out by his arrest for possession of cocaine early the next morning. The decision of London's Metropolitan Police not to prosecute but to issue a formal caution was widely lauded as a victory for common sense. Ironically, apart from a few Colonel Blimps in Parliament and the press, the greatest unease about such leniency was that expressed by young rock fans – as *NME* pointed out, that previous summer the seasonal rock festivals had been blighted by the decision of some regional police forces to arrest and charge hapless fans for so much as rolling a joint. Still, Liam continued, in the Irish vernacular, to 'play the big bollocks'. He earned a further caution from the Met in May 1997, when he grabbed a cyclist by the shirt and pulled him along from the Mercedes he was travelling in. 'He's very boring really. We're sick to death of him', came the informal shrug from the police. But Liam is very impressed with himself. In March 1998, on tour in Brisbane, Australia, he headbutted a 21-year-old fan and broke his nose – for the offence of trying to take a photo. 'Now fuck off,' the *Mirror* tabloid reported him telling the bleeding young man. 'I'm Liam Gallagher, and the next time I'll glass

you!' An out-of-court settlement was eventually reached with the complainant, purportedly to the tune of £60,000. In contrast, and to his credit, Noel later described how he calmed a nervous young autograph-hunter who regarded him as a demi-god: 'We all shit in the same toilet. It's no big deal.'

Ian Brown, the ex-Stone Roses singer who once greeeted Oasis as his band's natural successors, had little doubt where such hollow arrogance originates from. 'It's like the days have been brought back where there is a separation between band and crowd, however much you say, "We're the people." If you've got coke up your nose, I'm sorry, but you're walking another way.' (In 1998, after the release of his well-received *Unfinished Monkey Business* album, Brown's supposedly more sensible marijuana (and alcohol) use did not stop him getting involved in a contretemps with an airline stewardess whose hands he reputedly threatened to cut off. In contrast to the authorities' tolerance of the younger Gallagher brother, Brown received a five-month sentence in Manchester's maximum security Strangeways prison for his piece of verbal nonsense – shouting, 'I didn't do it!' as he was led from court.

The elevation of the Gallagher brothers to rock's aristocracy was confirmed in February 1997. On Monday the 10th, Creation Records issued a press statement reading, 'Contrary to media speculation, Liam Gallagher will not be marrying Ms Patsy Kensit today.' When it happened, the vocalist's wedding to Kensit – already a veteran of rock-star marriages, having previously been hitched to a member of Big Audio

236

Dynamite and Jim Kerr, frontman of Simple Minds – was planned to avoid media intrusion, as indeed was big brother Noel's wedding to long-term girlfriend and publicist Meg Matthews the following Friday (Valentine's Day). As if to demonstrate the sibling connection, both brothers would officially separate from their wives within three and a half years, in September 2000 – Liam and Patsy granted a quick decree nisi on the grounds of the male partner's unreasonable behaviour, while the elder, rapidly maturing Noel stressed his wife Meg's difficulty in giving up the rock'n'roll lifestyle and settling down with him in the country as grounds for separation. (Once as notorious as his brother for powdered ennervation, Noel had casually but controversially remarked in 1995 that taking drugs was 'as normal as having a cup of tea'. The outraged response of Conservative Home Secretary Michael Howard, who labelled him a menace, was inverted by the 1997 election of a New Labour government, who invited the songwriter to a party at 10 Downing Street. As Gallagher later acknowledged, it was no more than a publicity stunt by rock fan Prime Minister Blair – who, in his Christian puritanism, is about as 'rock-'n'roll' as Cliff, rather than Keith Richard.)

That both wedding ceremonies were re-arranged as low-key registry office events indicates that, whether the Beatles comparisons were pertinent or not, rock stars and their girlfriends had not fallen under such an

intense media spotlight since the days of John and Yoko/Paul and Linda. As for the surviving members of the Beatles, they often seemed bemused by comparisons with the outfit who faithfully aped the sound of their late 1960s period: 'They think too much of themselves … they really mean nothing to me,' said Paul McCartney, dismissing Oasis as 'derivative'. George Harrison concurred: he found them 'not very interesting', and derided Liam as 'the silly one', asserting, as with Elton John and Keith Richards, that the band would be better off without him. Liam, characteristically, was in no mood to mince words. 'I still love George Harrison as a songwriter in the Beatles,' he insisted, 'but as a person I think he's a fucking nipple. And if I ever meet him I'll fucking tell him.'

Also of the 1960s generation, Keith Richards could not resist coming to the party. 'I've been pretty mean in my time, but these guys [the Gallaghers] are just obnoxious', sermonised Keef. More pertinent, perhaps, was the decadent old bluesman's opinion of their music: 'I don't hear anything there, it's all just retro to me.' Predictably, the target of this disaffection jumped right back out of his pram. 'All these old farts,' Liam declaimed on a BBC Radio One interview, 'I'll offer 'em out right here on radio. If they want to fight be at Primrose Hill Saturday morning at twelve o' clock. I will beat the fucking living daylight shit out of them, that goes for George, Jagger, Richards …'. Almost endearingly, he seemed to believe that, if the wrinkly rock stars did not respond to his schoolboy challenge, then he'd won the argument. (As a slightly wittier provocation, Oasis immediately announced they were

Mad for it: Patsy Kensit, veteran of rock marriages, with short-term husband Liam Gallagher of Oasis. Liam models the Lennon look and demonstrates the wit for which he is renowned with a two-fingered salute.

'I was a star the day I was born!' insists Liam Gallagher. Prophetic words, as he went through the 1990s as one of Britpop's biggest stars – while apparently no wiser than the day he was born.

to cover Jagger/Richards' 'Street Fighting Man'.)

The self-styled bad boy's penchant for violence was tested at a July 2000 gig in Nyon, Switzerland, when the band – minus an absent Noel, who recently said of Liam that if he 'wasn't me brother I'd have kicked him out of the band years ago' – left the stage in less than half an hour after being pelted with 'bottles, cans and coins', according to the band's PR – or water bags and pieces of rubbish, according to the concert's organisers, who claimed the band's walk-out was 'totally irrational and the result of a paranoid reaction'. The British Consulate and the local police were both contacted in order to ensure the band's safety – even when the cops decided the coast was clear, Oasis were afraid to leave until the audience, jeered at by Liam with leery contempt, had completely vacated the building.

It's perhaps ironic that rock'n'roll's ultimate nerdish outsider, Jarvis Cocker of Pulp – thirtysomething composer of pointed little vignettes of contemporary life, set to a basic seventies glam-punk backing – has been the most consistently inventive figure of the Britpop years. He is also more of a magnet for controversy than his image suggests. Pulp's tuneful satire on the ecstasy-rave generation, 'Sorted for Es and Whizz', created the inevitable headlines when it was released with a design showing how to make a paper 'wrap' for amphetamine sulphate. 'Ban This Sick Stunt' demanded the *Mirror*. (Shortsighted Cocker claimed to initially misread the headline as 'Ban This Thick Cunt'.) 'I don't want the sleeve to get in the way of this record being taken seriously because "Sorted" is not a pro-drugs song,' protested the singer. 'But it's been great publicity for us I suppose. The sleeve has had to be changed because they got the police involved.'

Such minor controversies were as nothing com-

pared to the deluge of bullshit Cocker brought down on his head after an impulsive moment at the March 1996 Brit Awards. With Pulp on the scheduled list of performers (performing their controversial drug song), the mildly drunk vocalist was obliged to sit and watch when Michael Jackson took the stage to perform his recent single, 'Earth Song'. As the immensely wealthy superstar, dressed in a white robe, agonised over the future of the earth, a contingent of would-be child stars in biblical fancy-dress beseeched him, 'What about us?' The messianic Jackson, arms thrown back in windmachine-swept cruciform, was clearly the only hope for the planet and for these poor children.

At this point Jarvis Cocker decided on impulse to re-take the stage. Inertly surveying the audience at first, he then turned his back, lifted the tails of his jacket, poked out his bottom and gave a little wriggle. Michael Jackson's stage act was given the bum's rush – in the most playful manner possible – and his management were not best pleased. Looking back on the spectacle he had interrupted, Cocker contended, 'It was in bad taste, given the allegations that have been brought towards him in the last year or whatever, having kids onstage. But the main thing was really this kind of Messiah figure, this idea that somehow by people touching the hem of his garment they'd be miraculously cured of all their ills.' After dashing gamely about the stage like some spindly silent comedy star, Jarvis Cocker was removed and detained in police custody overnight. He had, according to an unidentified complainant, posed a threat to the children on the stage: none of whom, as videotaped evidence of the event showed, he had so much as touched. Jackson himself was, going by reports, close to hysteria, professing himself 'shocked, saddened, upset, betrayed'.

By the time Cocker reported back to Kensington Police Station, on 11 March, the factions of young fans (mainly Jackson's) were outside in full force. The *Mirror* – his former persecutors, who had demanded Jarvis's own crucifixion by the music industry over 'Es and Whizz' – were now lionising him with a 'Jarvis is innocent' campaign. At the other end of the vocal battlefield were the little Jacko fans and the doting parents of the showbiz kids on the stage. Didn't 'madman Cocker' realise, they insisted, that he was putting their children at risk by storming the stage like that? And besides, even if no one was hurt, this wasn't just any two-bit act he was interrupting, it was *Michael Jackson*.

When the police finally confirmed that Jarvis did not, in fact, have any charges to answer, the Pulp artist gave a statement to the assembled press: 'As I've always said throughout this thing, I haven't got a personal vendetta against Michael Jackson. I think, y'know, he can dance. I mean, anybody who invents the moonwalk is alright by me … I just think … it would be good for him to get a bit of reality in his life, really.' But reality was off the menu for Jackson and his supporters. Despite the lingering allegations of child sex made by young Jordan Chandler and his family – bought off in a multi-million dollar out-of-court settlement, and therefore never legally resolved – in some starstruck quarters Jackson could be taken seriously as a potential saviour of children, simply because his performance deemed it to be so.

The unlikeliest 'yob' in rock music. Nerd laureate Jarvis Cocker, of Pulp, incurred a wave of hysteria when he dared to mock superstar Michael Jackson. Jackson will truly never live like common people.

The sordid leftovers of the early seventies British glam-rock era, which inspired the seedy bubblegum sound of Cocker's band Pulp, washed up another ugly scandal. On 18 November 1997, Gary Glitter (nee Paul Raven, nee Paul Gadd, the Elvis manque who hit lucky in the last ditch of glam) took his personal computer for servicing near his home in Bristol. For a long time, Glitter had been a selfconscious parody of his former gaudy glory, a footstomping fiftysomething in glitter-sequined suits and a gravity-defying quiff hairpiece to hide his baldness. The events that ensued would transform him in the public eye from rock'n'roll caricature to ugly grotesque. Instructed not to view his customer's private files, the technician alerted the police after his curiosity got the better of him. On his return to the store, Glitter was arrested for downloading hundreds of indecent images of young children – some of them photographed while enduring physical abuse.

The ageing trouper's career suffered few initial adverse effects. True, his scenes were excised from *Spiceworld*, the *Help!*-type fantasy film featuring pop's latest manufactured sensations, the Spice Girls, and (unsurprisingly) he was dropped from the BBC's *Children in Need* telethon appeal. But his 1997 Christmas tour went ahead as scheduled, its now traditional audience (of drunken students and ageing pop kids who remembered him from his 1970s heyday) tolerating what seemed, from press reports, to be

JACKO RAGES AT YOB COCKER

By MATTHEW WRIGHT

MICHAEL Jackson branded Pulp star Jarvis Cocker "disgusting and cowardly" yesterday following the singer's yobbish antics at the Brit Awards.

Cocker was arrested after crashing Jacko's star turn, allegedly knocking kids to the ground, giving V-signs and pretending to "moon" at the audience.

Yesterday, a spokesman for horrified Jacko said: "He feels sickened and angry.

Protest

little more than vague allegations against an eccentric entertainer. 'If people can queue up for Michael Jackson tickets,' ran a popular argument, 'then what's wrong with having a few laughs at old Gary Glitter?'

It took two years for Glitter to be brought to trial – doubtless because the downloading of child pornography from the Internet (seen by some as nothing more than 'thought-crime', however offensive the material) was difficult for the authorities to gauge in terms of seriousness. The case was further complicated when a woman came forward to say how, in 1980, nearly a decade after the faded star's heyday, she entered into a sexual relationship with Glitter when she was fourteen.

By the time the old glam-rocker came to trial, this illicit relationship (lasting, the complainant confirmed, over twelve years) resulted in eight charges of sexual assault and sodomy. The prosecution described how the paedophile entertainer persuaded the young girl to wear a child's white pants, vest and ankle socks to emphasise her immaturity. ('Gary Glitter's unmasking as a pervert in the Nineties was the Glitter Kid's equivalent of Altamont', lamented commentator Julie Burchill, reflecting acidly, 'could we ever have believed that a middle-aged man wearing make-up and a wig who blithely shrieked lyrics like "I'm the man who put the 'bang' in 'gang'!" at a bunch of hot-panted twelve-year olds was, in any way, shape or form, normal?')

Unwisely, however, the complainant had entered into a deal with the *News of the World* tabloid which earned her an advance of £10,000 rising to £25,000 upon the singer's conviction. Instructed by the judge that commercial interests had corrupted her evidence, the jury had no choice but to acquit Glitter of sex offences against an underage girl. (Cheers from diehard 'Glitter Kids' were heard in the public gallery.) The pornography charges carried no such ambiguity. The singer pleaded guilty to 54 counts of possessing indecent photographs of children under the age of sixteen, and, on 12 November 1999, was sentenced to four months in prison. (Any libertarian unease about Glitter being jailed for pushing buttons on his computer should, perhaps, be tempered by prosecution evidence that he sought out 'material of the sickest kind' – including images of a two-year-child being tortured.) He was released in January 2000, into a new millennium where the man who professed to have made 'more comebacks than Sinatra' no longer had a performing career, and special security arrangements had to be made to ensure his protection from the public. An impromptu press conference in London's Regent's Park was abandoned after Glitter told his lawyer, fishing for interview fees, that he could no longer go on. Looking shaken in shades and the outlandish wig he was allowed to wear in prison, it's not hard to imagine glam's clown-prince arriving to the sound of inmates taunting him with the intro to his hit 'I'm the Leader of the Gang (I Am)': '*Cooome on! Come on! …*'

Gary Glitter has subsequently attempted to leave his old life behind and live with his Cuban girlfriend, Yudenia Martinez, still in her twenties, in Havana – complicated by the Cuban authorities' reluctance to allow Britain to export her dirty old men to its impoverished shores. At last count, UK tabloids were quoting Yudenia's reluctance to grant the convicted paedophile access to her baby son (apparently the singer's own child).

More traditional rock'n'roll decadence was to be found on both sides of the Atlantic, in the couplings of leather-trousered rock stars and their TV personality girlfriends.

Pamela Anderson, the blonde, bountiful *Playboy* centrefold who found mainstream fame in the *Baywatch* beach-bunny series, was one half of a glamorous pairing with Motley Crue drummer Tommy Lee. As a part of a heavy metal band whose adherence to the sex, drugs and rock'n'roll lifestyle is comically self-parodic, Lee soon engaged his wife in activities that made prurient headlines worldwide.

Enamoured of the reflexive sexual activity that feels all the more dirty, all the more 'real', for being recorded, Lee celebrated his bagging of the *Baywatch* babe by making home-made porn movies. Excitement become embarassment, however, when a home video-cassette was 'found' by a building contractor working on their Malibu, CA home. Much of the footage was innocuous stuff – 'Pammy' and Tommy clowning around, shots of their home and pets – but it also contained explicit shots of a very aroused Lee joyously living out the fantasies of thousands of TV viewers. Pammy was no slouch herself: in one sequence, Tommy was seen at the wheel of their car while she simultaneously fellated him and one-handedly recorded the event on camcorder.

Though the Lees sued *Penthouse*, the recipients of the tape, for up to $10,000,000 in damages, the court found that grabs from the video were presented in a 'newsworthy' manner that made them acceptable. (Ironically, Pamela Anderson-Lee had recently opted out of a film commitment because she didn't want to appear in a nude scene.) Their marital privacy had apparently ended the moment they committed their sex life to videotape, and an attempt to stop the Internet Entertainment Group (IEG) from marketing the tape under the title *Pam and Tommy Lee: Hardcore and Uncensored*, was also unsuccessful. It has gone on to become the best-selling 'adult' (i.e. porn) tape on the market, with the eponymous stars making an agreement with IEG on an 'if you can't beat 'em, join 'em' basis. Meanwhile, Ms. Anderson-Lee and her previous metal-dude boyfriend, Bret Michaels of Poison, managed to prevent IEG from releasing an earlier celebrity skinflick of them making the beast with two backs.

By this time, the rock'n'roll lifestyle was taking its toll on the Anderson-Lee relationship. In an incident which smacks of the Roman Emperor/spoiled brat syndrome, a disagreement with his wife about having her family over for dinner culminated in Lee kicking her in the back several times as she held their baby son, Dylan. Though the physical damage was slight, the attack was enough to win Lee a 180-day jail term and a three-year probation period during which he would regularly be tested for drugs and alcohol.

Going even further, a ban upon entering venues or retail outlets that sold alcohol was instrumental in Lee leaving Motley Crue.

After separating as a result of the incident, Anderson and Lee got back together in 1999. (Ms. Anderson, the glamorous doormat, later admitted, 'I'm one of those people where it doesn't take a brick to fall on my head, just a building.') Lee's probation was extended by a further two years, however, in May 2000, when a seemingly vengeful Pammy ratted on bad boy Tommy for sharing a single glass of champagne with her on New Year's Eve, the dawn of the new millennium. Tommy Lee submitted again to the American puritanism that often persuades its opponents, such as himself, that happiness lies at the opposite pole of excess.

In the ensuing months, the newly single Pamela Anderson has experienced success with the TV show *VIP*, and earned the disapproval of veteran actress Joan Collins for dressing with 'all the taste and refinement of a hooker on holiday' at the 2001 Academy Awards. (Most male viewers felt the same way, but for them the comparison was strictly complimentary.) Tommy Lee, meanwhile, continues to grapple with problems, the latest being the June 2001 drowning of a four-year-old boy at his son's birthday party – a tragedy seemingly due to a momentary lapse of attention, rather than lifestyle excesses.

Another liaison between two factions of show business took on a much darker tone. Michael Hutchence, vocalist of hugely successful middle-of-the-road Australian rock act INXS, became seriously involved with kittenish TV presenter Paula Yates in 1994. Despite her flirtatious public persona, the peroxided mother of three – her daughters named Fifi Trixiebelle, Peaches Honeyblossom and Little Pixie – was best known as a devoted, monogamous mother and wife to former Boomtown Rats leader Bob Geldof (an honorary knight for the creation of 1985's massive Live Aid charity event).

The pugnacious Irishman was reputedly inconsolable when she walked out of the family home after a whirlwind tryst with Hutchence which began on Channel 4's *Big Breakfast* (where Yates interviewed the Australian star in the 'Paula's Boudoir' section of the show – sex occurring between them a mere half-hour later). They had first met eight years earlier, when Paula was one of the presenters of influential rock show *The Tube*. In adolescent fashion, she later admitted she kept a publicity photo of the singer on her refrigerator from that day on, much to Geldof's irritation. ('Bob would periodically deface it [the photo] with rude words', she later wrote. 'I'd just replace it and keep dreaming.') Though Paula later claimed she had already planned to leave the marital home, and that her affair with Hutchence merely coincided with it, Geldof was still reported to be moved to tears when he received her petition for divorce. In 1996 Paula gave birth to her fourth daughter, named, in by-now familiar fashion, Heavenly Hiraani Tiger Lily – but this time the father was Michael Hutchence.

While his biography, *Is That It?*, admits to the standard flirtations with booze and cocaine during his rock'n'roll years, Geldof was clearly too business-like, too family-minded, and, ultimately perhaps, too much of a control freak to let youthful indulgence turn into self-destructive habit. Hutchence was a different breed of animal altogether. As unremarkably bland as his band's output was, he played the role of the old-fashioned, leather-panted rock star to the hilt. 'The good, sensible rock'n'roll thing to do is to be completely drunk, take drugs and have sex all day', he was once quoted as saying. In a flash of the erudition which friends claimed belied the ordinariness of his music, he described himself as a 'Dionysian personality'. He had also taken the lead role in the 1986 Australian film *Dogs in Space*, about junkies living in a Melbourne squat – a world which, some claimed, he had at least some working knowledge of.

Suspicions of decadence were born out when a nanny reported Yates and Hutchence to the police in 1996, after finding a Smartie sweet tube filled with opium. (Opium, as the far less easily obtainable raw material of heroin, is considered a relative luxury.) The high-profile lovers argued that the drug had been planted in their house – convincingly enough, it seems, as the police agreed to drop possession charges. Still, it was a pivotal event in the deteriorating Yates-Geldof relationship, prompting her ex-husband to obtain temporary custody of the children as a matter of urgency. Thus began a battle of wills between the two factions, with Hutchence and Yates often vocally complaining, or even abusive, while a doubtless seething Geldof continued to keep his opinions to himself.

Reborn briefly as a social gadfly, Paula's sightings in London with her new man in tow grew ever more frequent. Perhaps inevitably, it also entailed run-ins with the Gallagher brothers – Liam claiming that 'sad' Paula, with her teasing jolly-hockeysticks manner, was coming on strong to him. At the November 1995 MTV Europe awards in Paris, Hutchence finally found occasion to have words with Oasis's resident mouth, the two of them intermittently engaging in taunts and back-offs until Liam managed to land a punch before being ejected.

Over a year later, when Hutchence tried to take the conciliatory approach by presenting Oasis with their Best Band award at the 1997 Brit Awards, rivalry was re-asserted by the elder brother. 'I'd just like to say that fucking has-beens,' sneered Noel, looking down his nose at the long-haired figure at the side of the stage, 'shouldn't be giving awards to gonna-bes!' Standing alone, Hutchence seemed humiliated and dejected by the mob-handed Mancs (though he later claimed to be honoured to have irked the young Brits so much). This did not, however, prepare anybody for the next act of the drama.

On 22 November 1997 Hutchence was found dead in his room at the Ritz Carlton Hotel in his hometown of Sydney, Australia. He was hanging by his belt from the self-closing mechanism of his door. Among his final possessions were found five types of prescription drugs, including the widely-used anti-depressant Prozac. Also lingering in his system were cocaine and

241

DAILY Mirror

HONESTY, QUALITY, EXCELLENCE

August daily sale 2,072,281 · 30p

MY ANGUISH AS OUR TWIN BABIES DIED
By TV Jerome
EXCLUSIVE INTERVIEW: PAGES 22 & 23

Thursday, September 26, 1996

EXCLUSIVE

RESTLESS: Tony Blair

BLAIR
'My mother's early death changed my life forever'

LABOUR leader Tony Blair told for the first time yesterday how the tragic death of his mother changed him forever.

He said that when his mother Hazel died of breast cancer in her fifties, his life "took on an urgency".

Mr Blair told Mary Riddell, the Daily Mirror's incisive new interviewer and columnist: "I was terribly close to my mother.

"She was a lovely person – not terribly interested in politics but just fundamentally decent.

Short

"She had an incurable form of cancer but somehow I never thought of her dying.

It happened when he was at Oxford University and her illness was kept from him while he took exams.

Mr Blair said: "She died before I met Cherie and before I reconciled myself to disappointment over one levels.

"For the first time I felt a consciousness that time is short.

"My life took on an urgency, which has probably never left it. I have a constant restlessness to do things."

INTERVIEW: PAGES 6 & 7

OPIUM AND PORN BUST AT PAULA'S HOME

Daily Mirror INVESTIGATES

COUPLE: Michael and Paula in Sydney, Australia, yesterday

By GARY JONES

DRUGS and steamy photographs showing Paula Yates and lover Michael Hutchence having sex were found in a sensational police raid on her home yesterday.

The drugs were believed to be opium. The sexually explicit snaps showed the couple taking part in wild romps. Police carried out an inch by inch search of the £500,000 house in London's exclusive Chelsea after arming themselves with a warrant.

They are thought to have found the drugs in the couple's bedroom. Later, plastic bags were taken away from the three-storey property. The raunchy pictures are also believed to have been seized.

Paula, 34, and INXS singer Hutchence, 36, are renowned for their no-holds-barred, high-speed lifestyle – seen here at home at the time.

Both are in Sydney, Australia, with their two-month-old daughter...

Turn to Page 5

DAILY STAR

OOH, AAH...No.1 NEWSPAPAAH

WEDNESDAY, NOVEMBER 26, 1997 · www.megastar.co.uk · 30p

MY BOOZE BENDERS WITH CHRIS By Zoe Ball · Centre Page

HUTCH'S DEATH NIGHT SEX SESSION

From KEVIN AIRS in SYDNEY

HANGED rock wildman Michael Hutchence had a last sex session in the hotel suite where he died. Police who examined his bed at the Ritz-Carlton in Sydney say they found evidence that the INXS frontman had a final fling. It has also been revealed that Aussie snap star Kym Wilson, pictured, was with the tragic singer until 4am.

TELL-TALE BEDROOM SECRETS · PAGES 4 AND 5

Sex, drugs and rock'n'roll stars: the lethal cocktail that ended in tragedy

Vikram Dodd

After two decades spent living in the public eye, the final act of Paula Yates had no audience. It was a tragic end to what was to the outside world a glamorous, if turbulent, life of sex, drugs and rock'n'roll stars.

Since 1982, pretty much everything she did had attracted headlines, often at her own behest. But the media maelstrom around Yates grew so much more intense after a chat in bed with the rock star Michael Hutchence.

She had interviewed the Australian frontman of the band INXS for Channel 4's Big Breakfast programme, made by a production company owned by her husband, Bob Geldof. With their legs entwined, the mutual attraction that would consume and destroy her marriage to Geldof was obvious to those watching.

Yates became famous as the front woman of The Tube, the groundbreaking Channel 4 music programme. She was hired for the job by Andrea Wonfor, the show's executive producer: "Everything changed after she met Michael Hutchence. She threw everything away and found nothing left after he died."

In 1982 Yates, then 22, burst on to television screens. With her blonde hair and low-cut, tight dresses, she came across as a wild child. The reality, says Ms Wonfor, was very different.

Restrained

Compared to the later stories of drugs and drink, her time at The Tube was relatively restrained as she soon became pregnant with her first child: "For the whole five years of the Tube, Paula was the bloody boring one. She'd go to bed at 9.30pm, when everyone else was in the bar, and be back up at 6.30am to take Fifi for a swim," Ms Wonfor remembers.

Yates began dating Geldof, the front-

drug-fuelled lifestyle: "That's when the spiral of decline started," the friend said.

The break-up with Geldof was acrimonious and detailed by the tabloids, with Yates' connivance. She went to the house they had shared in Chelsea and after shouting abuse at him, threw a rock through a window. Friends were authorised to leak details of the bitter wrangle, and Yates' financial straits as her debts on stage reached £100,000.

In May 1996 the divorce was granted and Geldof later won temporary custody of the children after a sweet tube containing opium was found at the home of Yates and Hutchence. They claimed it was planted.

If the fallout from her relationship with Geldof left Yates emotionally drained, the bizarre death of Hutchence as good as broke her. The singer was found hanging in a Sydney hotel room in November 1997 having consumed vodka, beer, champagne, cocaine, Prozac and other prescription drugs. Yates could never accept it was suicide. The couple had a daughter, Heavenly Hiraani Tiger Lily, who is now four years old. She described his death as like being "flung to the dogs", and tried to find comfort in Tiger Lily.

Yates branded Geldof "a killer" after it emerged Hutchence had hanged himself with a leather belt hours after pleading with the former Boomtown Rat over the custody of Yates' daughters with Geldof.

Yates later told an interviewer: "When Michael died I was tipped over the edge. I was beyond grief. I went completely mad.

"Now I'm starting, relatively, to think straight again. I live one day at a time, one hour at a time. What makes it all worthwhile is my children."

Rapid decline

Yates had to deal with more torment when it emerged that the man she thought was her father, the former Star...

242

a cocktail of alcoholic drinks, including champagne.

The circumstances surrounding the star's sordid end pointed to several possible courses. Conversations with the distraught Paula Yates revealed she had phoned him from London the day before to tell him she was unable to join him immediately in Australia. The couple had plans to emigrate in order to get away from press intrusion into their private lives, and to marry in Tahiti – although, redolent of the 'Princess Diana syndrome', Paula was happy to throw open her world to the media until she became worn down by the attention. Their plans had effectively been blocked by Bob Geldof, and a protracted custody battle over their three daughters. To try to resolve the situation, Hutchence phoned Geldof the next day to offer to fly his three daughters back to London first class on Christmas Eve to be with their father. But, classically, neither the adulterer nor the cuckold could see eye to eye.

Geldof later issued a press statement which read: 'In the wake of Michael's tragic death, I extend my sincere condolences and sympathy to Paula, Tiger, Michael's mother and father and all other members of his family. In these difficult circumstances,' he continued, 'I rely on the press to leave Paula and the children to the dignity of their own private grief.' Despite Geldof's cessation of hostilities (which, posthumously, would have been futile anyway), the Hutchence camp lost little time in going on the attack. 'I think it was the pressures about his child and Bob Geldof and all the escapades that went on in the last year', opined INXS manager Martha Troup of her artist's self-destruction. 'It just reached a climax. It was the culmination of everything, how he [Geldof] treated Paula, and how he was making his [Hutchence's] life miserable.'

This partisan view ignores how Geldof had to come to terms with being the injured party in the marriage, as well as watching from a distance as Hutchence indoctrinated his wife into the use of opiates. Photos of Paula reporting to the police station after the smartie tube incident show her looking 'elegantly wasted', to use the cliché, with huge shades and a thinning face – not so glamorous for her estranged husband, forced to entrust her with the care of his children.

In interviews with investigators Geldof confirmed their conversation had in fact, been a raging argument, with an exasperated Hutchence jeeringly referring to him as 'little man'. This exhibits petulance rather than depression. That Hutchence was, in fact, depressed, despite his cheerful manner when he spoke to Paula, is in no doubt – but this may have been more to do with chemical imbalance, the antidepressant downers and pick-me-up cocaine found in his bloodstream testifying that 'the drugs don't work' in the end. The absence of opium or heroin, the 'great comforters', indicates he had nothing to soothe his damaged pride with. The big rock star, used to indulging every whim, had a surly Irishman at the other end of the phone who would not let him have his own way. Michael Hutchence's suicide may have been no more than a little boy's violent temper tantrum.

Another view, reported in the press, was that Hutchence's death was the result of autoerotic arousal by asphyxiation gone wrong. This was dismissed by Paula Yates' lawyer Anthony Burton as 'scurrilous and grossly irresponsible speculation'. However, over the months that followed, Paula, having initially joined in the attack on her ex-husband, calling him 'a killer' for having wounded Michael's feelings, would sing a radically different song. In a TV documentary broadcast on Channel 4 in 1999, she continually stressed that 'Michael was a dangerous boy', given to sexual experimentation and recognising only the basic moral taboos. The inference from this, as she spelled out, was that, 'He could have done anything at any time, but the one thing he wouldn't have done was leave us,' and that misadventure remained the most logical explanation. Many commentators read this another way: the heartbroken Paula Yates needed to reassure both herself and – as she grew older – their daughter that the circumstances of their lives had no bearing on Michael's tragic end, and that he died happily in love with them both. (Certainly, the floral bouquet of a dozen red roses Hutchence sent back for Paula and her four daughters betrayed no finality in its attached message: 'To all my beautiful girls, all my love Michael.' Poignantly, however, it did not arrive until Paula was already on her way to Australia to arrange his funeral.) The mystery has not been satisfactorily resolved, and it is unlikely now that it ever will be.

In the aftermath of Hutchence's death, Paula Yates often found herself at war with the family of the man she had irrevocably changed her life for. On the day of the funeral she appeared to be on the verge of collapse. Seeking a bond with her lover's family, she was openly rejected by Hutchence's mother, Patricia Glassop, who pushed her away, angrily accusing, 'You killed him, you and all your problems! Now go back to where you belong.' It was reported that the bereaved mother believed Paula had introduced her little boy to sadomasochistic practices, although a great many people would place the responsibility the other way round.

Paula was also shocked to find that he had bequeathed her very little in his will, and that a £2 million trust fund for their daughter would not mature until her 25th birthday. (According to friends, in Hutchence's final weeks away from Yates he embarked on a crash-course of sexual flings with a number of young women.) Paula successfully fought to claim up to £400,000 of the singer's fortune to maintain her daughter and herself – as well as, most poignantly, to receive one third of the cremated singer's ashes, which she sewed into a pillow and slept with till the end of her days.

Her grief and bewilderment were compounded by further personal crises. In the month after her rock star lover's death, voluntary DNA tests conclusively proved – to her horror – rumours that her biological father was not, as she had thought, Jess Yates, an adulterous UK TV preacher who had brought her up as his own, but Hughie Green, oleaginous Canadian-born host of the TV show *Opportunity Knocks* who personified – perhaps even more than the pious Jess Yates – much of what was hollow about showbusiness celebrity. In 1998 Paula was found unconscious in a hotel room, half-naked, with a noose around her neck, in an apparent attempt to emulate Hutchence's death by hanging. She was booked in to a private clinic to recuperate. In October Geldof was granted full custody of his three children due to Paula's clear inability to cope. He made sure, nevertheless, that the custody order contained a clear provision for them to spend part of each school holiday with their mother.

Paula subsequently embarked on a number of affairs to try to fill the holes left by her deceased lover and ex-husband. Due to her circumstances, it was inevitable that many of these would be fellow addicts. Booked into the Priory rehabilitation centre in May 1999 – to recover from the addiction born out of hedonistic times, now just an escape from sad reality – she met the young reggae singer Finlay Quaye. With his known enthusiasm for cannabis, his habitual smoking and boozing had reached the stage where they were affecting his mental processes. (In one interview, he insisted that the spirit of Bob Marley had entered into the late Diana, Princess of Wales.) Himself the son of a heroin addict mother, who OD'd when he was 11, Quaye saw in Paula an unlikely figure 'to stop me smoking marijuana or drinking'. That summer she announced that her man had bought her a big Cartier engagement ring. Their relationship, however, scarcely survived another month.

Paula Yates retreated with her daughter to their home in Notting Hill, west London, engaged in sporadic attempts to revive her TV career and a continual struggle to fight her addiction. (According to one confidante, she was reduced at one point to having just £14 in the bank due to her recurring need for drugs.) Inside the house, promotional photos of her late lover decorated the walls as if Paula was a fan in mourning. In her fragile state, Paula feared more revelations about her private life in a book *Just a Man: The Real Michael Hutchence* written by Patricia Glassop and her daughter Tina, the mother and half-sister who had already tried to wrest custody of Tiger Lily from her. She asked her solicitor to obtain a copy of the proofs. On Saturday 16 September 2000 Paula and a young blonde – later identified as a 21-year-old heroin addict she befriended in the Priory – made numerous visits to a local convenience store to buy miniature bottles of vodka. This would be the former celebrity's last ever public appearance.

The next morning, Paula's friend Jo Fairley was alerted to a crisis by four-year-old Tiger Lily, who complained over the telephone, 'I can't wake up my mummy.' Ms Fairly gained access to their house with the help of the child standing on a chair. Upstairs, her worst fears were confirmed. Paula Yates – former rock chick par excellence and one of the more engaging personalities of light-entertainment TV – had become an unlikely casualty of 'heroin consciousness', choking to death on her own vomit. When police arrived they removed small quantities of heroin, barbiturates and cannabis from the scene. A coroner's inquest later confirmed that Paula, who had remained free from the 'great comforter' after being clinically treated for addiction, had accidentally administered more of the drug than her body could tolerate. (The overdose level was also lowered by mixing the drug with alcohol.)

'We are all so sad,' announced the press statement from a haggard and heartbroken Geldof – his choice of words a poignant echo of the condolences offered to those bereaved by his former rival and enemy. 'The loss for all the children is insupportable. It doesn't require much imagination to understand their pain. Please do nothing to add to that. Leave them with their loss and Paula with her dignity.'

On Saturday, 24 September 2000 the Live Aid generation of rock stars came to the Church of Saint Mary Magdalene at Davington Priory in Kent, site of the Geldofs' old marital home, to pay tribute to one of their own. Annie Lennox, Dave Stewart, Midge Ure, Paul Young, Martin Kemp of Spandau Ballet, rock video director Kevin Godley, and model Yasmin Le Bon were all in attendance. (As was a seemingly out-of-place Nick Cave, godfather to Tiger Lily. As one of rock's most uncompromisingly incisive songwriters, Cave had demonstrated the maturity of his recent, more contemplative performances in a vocal tribute to his friend Michael Hutchence at the fellow Australian's funeral.) Former *Tube* co-presenter Jools Holland (now veteran of the celebrated *Later*, British TV's broadest musical church), stripped of his cheeky chappy manner, strode mournfully to the piano to rock the congregation with 'Blue Skies' – accompanied by Bono of U2 on vocals: 'Blue skies, nothing but blue skies … from now on.' Saddest and most succinct was the card placed with the mass of tiger lilies covering Paula's coffin: 'To Mummy … I Love You', signed by each of her four daughters.

The keepers of the Hutchence flame, his mother and half-sister, have stressed an interest in gaining custody of Michael's little daughter, taking her half a world away from the half-sisters she has grown up with – an emotional wrench which would help nobody, according to the INXS man's bereaved father, Kell. Meanwhile, their son's former mortal enemy and their potential opponent, Bob Geldof, has committed himself to the welfare of Tiger Lily – the child who already bears a striking resemblance to her father. His unanswerable argument is that the child is best raised among her three half-sisters, with whom she finds the greatest sense of security.

In his musical heyday, Geldof was an entertaining though never more than minor figure, however much chart success he enjoyed at the time – his band, the Boomtown Rats, delivered a conventional r&b-pop style, only enlivened by lyricist Geldof's ability to turn their songs into something approaching sardonic short stories. In his own grief, and in his later struggle to give Tiger Lily the security of growing up with her half-sisters, the figure that Michael Hutchence sought to deride as a 'little man' was seen to stand head and shoulders above his contemporaries in the rock'n'roll circus.

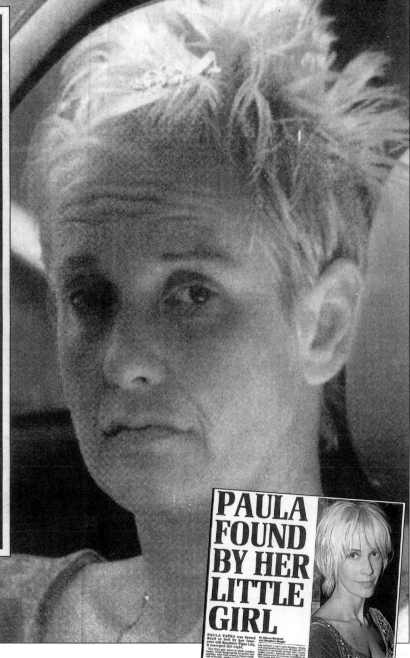

So sad but at least she's back with Michael

SUE CARROLL: PAGES 6&7

Paula: The pain is over

By RICHARD WALLACE

HER haunted gaze in this final picture reflects years of torment. But yesterday Paula Yates's anguish was ended . . by death.

The former wild child who became a lost soul was found by her four-year-old daughter Heavenly Hiraani Tiger Lily — sprawled across her bed, killed by a cocktail of drink and drugs.

Paula, 41-year-old mother of four, never recovered from the suicide of her lover, INXS rocker Michael Hutchence in 1997.

She had a nervous breakdown and months later tried to hang herself.

Lately, with her troubles spiralling out of control, the last traces of her image as a saucy, elfin faced rock chick vanished. She looked ravaged — and doomed.

Paula, who left Live Aid hero Bob Geldof for Hutchence, often talked of suicide. But police believe she died accidentally.

Ex-husband Geldof said: "We are all so sad. It doesn't require much imagination to understand the pain."

FULL STORY: PAGES 2,3,4,5,6,7,8&9

PAULA FOUND BY HER LITTLE GIRL

By Alison Boshoff and Stephen Wright

PAULA YATES was found dead in bed by her four-year-old daughter Tiger Lily, it emerged last night.

The tiny girl alone in their London home, tried desperately to rouse her mother, who had taken a lethal cocktail of heroin, vodka and barbiturates.

Then a dazed Tiger placed soft toys over Paula's body in an attempt to "make her better."

Caption: Paula Yates. Took a lethal cocktail of heroin, vodka and barbiturates

Turn to Page 8, Col. 1

BLACK RAGE
AND THE BLACK ARTS

Hip-hop was the most prominent form of black music throughout the 1990s – and by far the most controversial. Rap groups as different in their approach as Public Enemy, Niggaz With Attitude – who originated the 'gangsta' rap genre with their 1988 album *Straight Outta Compton* – and 2 Live Crew all cut imposing figures in their baseball caps, weird glasses, baggy trousers and enormous trainers.

Revenge was the *leitmotif* of much of their work. It found an opportunity for expression when, in 1992, four white policemen were acquitted by a local Californian court of the violent manhandling of a black motorist in Los Angeles – contrary to the evidence provided by an amateur video showing the motorist, Rodney King, being beaten up.

By the time of the subsequent LA riots, rap had already emerged as high-tech street poetry, with the music reduced to basic textures, rhythms, echoes and sounds. Lyrics were often doggerel – sometimes offensive doggerel in which sexism and racism were rampant: an indication of the misdirected anger of many black American men who, like their opposite numbers in the white racist camp, looked for easily identifiable targets for their hate and delivered an easy formula for provocation.

Public Enemy's Professor Griff – an associate of noted anti-semite Louis Farrakhan, head of the US-based black Nation of Islam movement – told the Moonie-owned *Washington Times* in June 1989 that Jews were responsible for 'the majority of wickedness that goes on across the globe'. When this inflammatory statement sparked the predictable furore, the band's lead rapper, Chuck D, announced that Griff had been fired. But after attacks by black organisations for knuckling under to a supposed white/Jewish conspiracy, Public Enemy appeared in Kansas City a few weeks later with Griff in the line-up, who confirmed the accuracy of the *Washington Times* quotes. Meanwhile, Public Enemy's record label, CBS, were preparing to release their third album, *Fear of a Black Planet*. (CBS's president at the time was the distinctly Jewish Walter Yetnikoff.)

Professor Griff was eventually fired from the band for calling a white rapper a 'Jew bastard', but the group continued to adhere to the Nation of Islam's distinctly stratified view of the US's 'racial war', and the dogmatic view that 'the White Man is the Devil'. As puritanical black Muslims, opposed to drugs and the criminal lifestyle, Public Enemy represented a polar opposite to their gangsta-rap contemporaries. When, at a 1991 concert in Hollywood, band spokesman and lyricist Chuck D addressed to the crowd about how he believed the white devil was conspiring to destroy black America, his words foreshadowed events that would soon take place in the rap community: 'We don't bring guns into our motherfuckin' community. We don't bring drugs into the country. There's an iron force of the establishment that's responsible for it and shit, and should be held accountable. Now – whenever they bring drugs in, guns in, give 'em to youngsters … anything could fuckin' happen! And it's happenin' right here in LA!' Their follow-up to *Fear Of A Black Planet, Apocalypse '91: The Empire Strikes Black* was a series of warnings to the black community about the behaviour of the gangsta groups. 'I'd like to express our deepest gratitude for the destruction of the inferior nigger race', intones the voice of an actor personifying the white devil. 'And I'm especially pleased to report that it's destroying itself without our help.'

Chuck D suggested that Islamic fundamentalism would provide no-nonsense answers to the black community's social problems. Specifically, he said that in the style of countries from Saudi Arabia to Sudan, convicted 'gang-bangers' would have their hands and feet cut off: 'It's not as heavy as people losing their lives in a hail of bullets … people haven't been programmed to feel as sympathetic about death as they feel about the severing of somebody's body part.'

Their sense of purpose and Islamic fervour were not always easy to maintain, however. Flavor Flav, who – with plated teeth and clock necklace – represented Public Enemy to many people, found it particularly hard to avoid gangsta-ish behaviour. In 1990 he was charged with assault on the mother of his children. In November 1993 he was charged with attempted murder, reckless endangerment and illegal possession of a gun. After a coke binge that left him wired, paranoid and awake for 72 hours, he had fired a shot at a neighbour he had convinced himself was sleeping with his girlfriend. (All charges were eventually dropped apart from gun possession, though the rapper was obliged to spend time detoxifying in the Betty Ford clinic.)

Rolling Stone, when reporting the highly visible event (Flav's arrest was filmed for the TV news), opined that Public Enemy's moral stance was now fatally weakened. Chuck D disagreed – blurring the lines between volition and manipulation by the white enemy, when he argued that Flav now had greater authority to tell black people 'don't be [i.e. don't

---

Heavy metal, epitomised by Marilyn Manson, appealed to alienated white youth in the manner that gangsta rap did to dispossessed blacks. Hip-hop and metal would cross-pollinate and cross the racial divide.

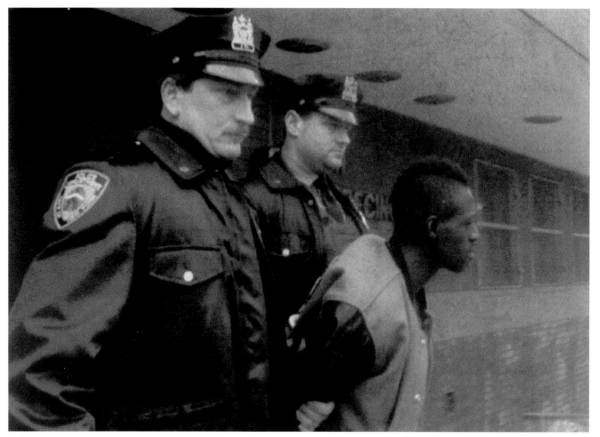

Rapper Flavor Flav of Public Enemy, William Drayton to his mother, is led out of the 44th Precinct in New York on 1st November 1993 after allegedly trying to shoot another man in a dispute over a woman.

choose to be] a victim'.

2 Live Crew were a very different proposition – 'porn-rap', as some derisively termed them. Leader Luther Campbell was arrested in Florida in 1990 on charges of obscenity after a nightclub appearance. Campbell was acquitted, barely three weeks after a record shop owner in the area had been *convicted* for selling copies of the Crew's album *Nasty as They Wanna Be*. The whole incident stimulated a growing and confused debate on censorship, which was led by the right-wing Washington group called the Parents' Music Resource Centre (PMRC).

The PMRC had been formed in 1985 by former Vice President (then Senator) Al Gore's wife Tipper and the then Treasury Secretary James Baker's wife Susan, along with nine other Washington wives. The inspiration for the group was a reference to masturbation that Tipper Gore found on the Prince album *Purple Rain* which she had bought for her eight-year-old daughter. The campaign soon discovered the richest seams of dirt were to be found in rap and metal music. The PMRC pushed for a ratings system for records, like that for movies, and provoked record companies into putting warning stickers on records which contained 'explicit lyrics'. A number of state legislatures in the US were

248

inspired to draft compulsory stickering laws. A Senate committee on the topic had five members with wives on the PMRC. Its hearings were better attended than those on the US budget or its defence policy.

The *Nasty as They Wanna Be* case created a curious alliance between the liberal wing of American politics (in particular, the American Civil Liberties Union) and rappers with a pornographic attitude towards sex. The ACLU believed that the PMRC, compulsory stickering and the case against Luther Campbell threatened freedom of speech, and this argument began to gain converts among politicians and constitutionalists as well as liberals. At the same time as Campbell's acquittal, for example, the Governor of Louisiana vetoed a compulsory stickering law on the grounds of unconstitutionality.

By this time, 2 Live Crew had already put out a cleaned-up version of 'Me So Horny' – the single from *Nasty* – in order to gain maximum MTV exposure. Sales of the album had been flagging when Campbell was arrested but soon took off again and rocketed to double platinum, while an anti-censorship rap released by Campbell as a result of the affair, 'Banned in the USA', (which used – with permission – Bruce Springsteen's 'Born In The USA' as its basic sampled track) went straight into the US top twenty. Though *Nasty as They Wanna Be* was the *cause celèbre*, the early nineties provided many instances of similarly nasty misogyny. (A group called FU2 released an overtly sadistic song with the words 'I'll drink champagne, she'll drink Ripple / scream when I put the safety pins through her nipples', which so appalled women employees of their label, MCA, that the record was pulled.) Luther Campbell would later be invited to attend a senate hearing on violence and misogyny in rap music, but would fail to attend due to more pressing engagements – principally, preparing his glossy magazine *Scandalous*, a multi-racial take on *Playboy* with three centrefolds per issue.

These less-than-sensitive attitudes were reflected by Niggaz With Attitude, whose songs – like 'To Kill a Hooker' and 'Findum, Fuckum And Flee' – also had a hard ideological edge. Former NWA-man, Ice Cube, the self-professed 'Nigga You Love To Hate', sneered at 'white bitches' in 'Cave Bitch', because they have 'no butt and no chest', threatened violence to Japanese and Koreans in 'Black Korea', and complained that his former band 'let a Jew break up my crew' – alluding to NWA's manager. Ice Cube was at least consistent, his wholesale adoption of the black separatist dogma of the Nation of Islam reflected in his attitude to the white race: 'White guys is all snakes – it's just that some are poisonous and some ain't.' According to the lyrics of his 'When I Get to Heaven': 'The same white man that threw me in the slammer / He bombed a church in Alabama / So if I cock the hammer, God

won't mind / If I have to kill the human swine.' His personal dogma of hate was no less tolerant towards white women (reportedly, at a gig in Salt Lake City he stared impassively and walked off when a nubile white well-wisher tried to get him in a clinch) or gays ('dicks up yo' ass is bad for your health' runs the Cube line on same-sex relations).

Fellow gangsta-rapper Ice-T, meanwhile, responded to charges that his film appearance in *New Jack City* glamorised crime (although the film is far more conventionally moralistic than gangsta rap itself), with the quip, 'Well, it is glamorous.' After the 1992 LA riots had unfolded to a rap beat, Ice-T said of it's first day, 'April 29th 1992 was the happiest day of my life. Anybody who says this uprising was ignorant is the stupidest muthafucka in the world.' Sound samples from the riots were also included in the 1992 debut album by one-time Ice Cube backing band Da Lench Mob, *Guerillas in the Mist*. Soon, the attitudinising began to spill over into real life.

Controversy had been precipitated in 1991 by the lyrics of rap-metal crossover band Body Count's 'Cop Killer'. The title alone was provocative enough, but the band were also fronted by Ice-T. The establishment backlash began. Police called for a boycott of Time-Warner, and Hollywood arch-conservative Charlton Heston interrupted a Time-Warner shareholders' meeting in Beverly Hills to quote from the manifestly anti-police lyrics. 'They let me know I'm not just a rapper', Ice-T later reflected. 'I am somebody they feel is a threat.' The company pulled the song and 'released'

'COP KILLER! / I know your family's grieving / but tonight we get even.' Despite the incendiary lyrics, Ice-T equates his most extreme material with pulp fiction. But no one ever went broke mythologising 'gangstas'.

Ice-T from book and cable TV deals. But the show was already on the road, and the icily-determined Mr. T was able to direct it better than most.

'It was black rage for white kids', he admitted candidly of the infamous Body Count track. 'The cops were just as angry we formed a South Central [LA] rock group as they were about the song.' He was already on the way to becoming a skilled manipulator of both his own image and the mass media. Ice-T may have helped originate the 'gangsta' template, but, like his hero Don King – the electric-haired black man who, before he became the USA's top boxing promoter, served time for kicking a criminal associate to death in a fight – he would move on to take America on its own mass-media terms: records, acting in movies, TV, even a collected book of his wit and wisdom (*The Ice Opinion*). But all these – even his purely sexual raps, which, profane as they were, were close to cartoonish absurdity – were given the hard edge of danger by a man keen to mythologise his own gangsta past. (Ice-T, an opportunist in pursuit of the white man's American Dream if ever there were one, now operates his own pornography outlet from the official Ice-T website.)

Contracted to host his own TV show, *Baadasss TV*, on Channel 4 in the UK, Ice-T dressed up like a 1970s pimp to introduce some of the kookier aspects of black culture. On the basis of 'Cop Killer', however, questions were asked in Parliament as to whether this infamous figure should be allowed to work in the country. Recognising the strength of their man's notoriety, the rapper's press office were less than diplomatic: 'Someone's just trying to ride Ice-T's dick.' Ice-T himself was refreshingly open about his appeal: 'it's a hardcore style – it ain't gangsta rap 'cos gangsters don't rap but a lot of it is based around talkin' shit, tellin' stories and spinnin' bullshit … sure, a lot of it is pulp fiction – cartoon shit that's way out there.'

Gangsta rap is the mirror image of the aggression inherent in a militant group like Public Enemy – but without any political objectives or ideals. 'Keepin' it real' became the catchword of the genre, reality equalling a narrow vision for the rapper (or narrator, so much of this material being one step removed from the artist's life) to claw his way out of the ghetto. The only options, if taken at face value, are dealing drugs or running 'hos' (whores). The Magnum pistol or semi-automatic rifle became as much a status symbol as ostentatious gold jewellery. Gangsta rap celebrated the law of the jungle – in its basic pessimism, almost a distorted reflection of its white conservative enemies who looked to their own weapons armouries for reassurance. 'I'm looking in the face of negativity, hatred, violence, nigger, bitch, ho', declaimed rapper KRS-One. 'If negativity comes with a .22, positivity comes with a .45. If negativity comes with a .45, positivity comes with an Uzi.'

So closely was gangsta rap associated with the criminal ghetto lifestyle that it soon became a question not simply of whether art was reflecting life, but whether art was reflected back in an ever-more distorted scenario out on the streets. Clearly, some representatives of African-American lobby groups thought so. Anti-gangsta protests by the National Political Caucus of Black Women (whose chairwoman unsuccessfully litigated against Snoop Doggy Dogg, on the basis of his 'offensive lyrics', shortly before he was due to stand trial for murder) led to LA's KACE radio banning the sub-genre from its airwaves. According to protesters, the music not only glorified violence against women but was exacerbating the gang activity and gunplay that were already taking place.

After a preview of his 1995 film *Clockers* – about a young black kid on a Brooklyn housing estate, used by his older buddies to carry crack – black film director Spike Lee said, 'I like rap. I just don't like gangsta rap … In America, to be a platinum artist now, you've gotta be charged with murder – you'll sell 5,000,000 albums. Because you're "real". You're "down". You're "hardcore".' Condemnation came from more reactionary quarters, too. In 1995, Republican presidential hopeful Bob Dole focused a campaign against the financing of 'anti-social' music by major corporations. The first significant casualty was Interscope Records, home of rap subsidiary Death Row Records and nihilist-industrial act Nine Inch Nails, which was dropped by Time-Warner.

With such absolutist arguments taking hold, the view that the music was a direct influence on modern society rather than a reflection of it became dominant, even among the artists themselves. 'Black kids shouldn't be pointing guns at one another,' emphasised Chuck D, detecting the influence of white supremacism even in the success of gangsta rap. 'They should be pointing them at the record company presidents. Then you'll see the shit stop.' His friend Ice Cube, conscious of being a 'war correspondent' who has described violence in great detail, observed, 'America is rooted in sex and violence, is founded on sex and violence. So how do you expect the citizens of America to differ when America is the teacher, the preacher, the killer … America made it cool to be violent. And that's why you have the kids and youngsters of America thinking like that.'

Ice-T played it both ways. In January 1994 he was one of 300 mourners at the funeral of Tyrone Thomas, a member of the South Central LA faction of the Bloods street-gang. Thomas had been blasted to death in a shoot-out with the rival Crips, not long after he had negotiated a truce between the two gangs. Ice-T was seen to be honouring a brother who had tried to do something for the 'hood, his send-off marked by the presence of local politicians. 'The capacity for violence in these kids is unimaginable,' stated the man who, in his youth, claimed to have seen '250lb dudes crying while loading guns' to avenge their dead 'homies'. He, at least, was putting all the killing into a context that made his lyrical statements more coherent.

Cuban-American rapper B-Real, of racially mixed, pothead rap group Cypress Hill, spoke of his time in East LA gangs as a kind of surrogate for the father who wasn't around. 'It showed me things that led to where I am,' he claimed – though one of the things it showed him was how close you come to death when a bullet passes through your lung. Even so, Cypress Hill took offence at the idea that their music promoted violence: 'By talking about it we try to let people know what really happens in the streets, hoping something gets done about it.' They contributed $10,000 to an amnesty initiative in the South Bronx called Goods for Guns, whereby unlicensed weapons could be exchanged for gift vouchers.

But despite Cypress Hill's claims, gangsta rap already had a history of connections with real-life violence. In the early 1990s the Geto Boys, from Houston, Texas, were regarded as bad news even by some hardcore rappers. Obsessed with violent death and deviant sex, they hold the distinction of being probably the only hip-hop group to rap about necrophilia. Menacing band member Scarface (later a solo artist) reckoned that, 'People should look forward to dying, 'cos it's probably the only thing in this world that's promised to you ... If I don't know anything else in the world, I know I'm gonna die.'

Another dimension was added to the extreme morbidity of their lyrics when lead rapper Bushwick Bill, a four-foot-six-inch dwarf, was hospitalised with a gunshot wound. After a binge on grain alcohol and painkillers he had experienced a psychotic episode at his girlfriend's apartment, insisting he wanted to die there and then. He threatened to throw her baby out of the window unless she shot him. Naturally she complied. Bushwick survived, but his right eye was obliterated. The hospital aftermath to this moment of madness is immortalised on the cover of the Geto Boys' second album, *We Can't Be Stopped*, which featured Scarface standing to the right of his severely injured 'homie'.

In March 1994 T-Bone of Da Lench Mob was charged with murder after being identified as the killer of a man shot dead in a bowling alley. Police reportedly confiscated rap lyrics from his home as evidence, along with his handguns. When acquitted in March 1995, he gave his perspective on the allegations: 'From day one, I have said it was a case of mistaken identity. I think [the LAPD] were going after rap and using me as a way to do it.'

That previous month his bandmate J-Dee was convicted of the murder by shooting of his girlfriend's flatmate, Scott Charles, nearly two years previously and received a total of 29 years. Unease was expressed by the editor of *Source*, LA's premier rap culture magazine: 'This case further legitimises white people's image that most black men are violent and dangerous ...' As paranoid as it is to lay every black-American defendant's convictions at the door of racial conspiracy, it's worth noting that the prosecutor cited Da Lench Mob's 1992 hit 'Who You Gonna Shoot Wit Dat?' as evidence, claiming the crime was a case of 'life imitating art'.

In November 1993 Snoop Doggy Dogg was indicted, under his real name of Calvin Broadus, for a murder in Los Angeles the previous August. The victim, Philip

Snoop Dogg's gangsta credentials were second to none: he was tried for murder; his friend Tupac was gunned down – and Snoop later dared to diss his old label, the infamous Death Row Records.

KICK THIS EVIL BASTARD OUT!

ANTI-HERO: Rap star Snoop glorifies drugs and cop killing

EXCLUSIVE
by **NIGEL PAULEY**

FURIOUS MPs last night called for evil gangster rapper Snoop Doggy Dogg to be booted out of Britain.

They demanded an inquiry into how the 23-year-old American star — on £625,000 bail in connection with a U.S. murder — was allowed into the country.

His songs glorify drugs and cop killing and are littered with swear words. His debut album DoggyStyle — at Number One in the US — has sold four million copies and contains 100 F-words.

Last night Tory MP Terry Dicks stormed: "We don't want a man involved in murder and advocating the use of drugs in Britain. He should be put on the first plane back."

And another Tory MP, Sir Rich-

Turn to Page 5

Woldermariam, was allegedly shot dead by the rapper's bodyguard, McKinley Lee (known as Malik), and Snoop Doggy Dogg was arrested when his jeep was identified as the assassin's vehicle. Under a peculiarity of Californian law, the rapper was held culpable for the killing, although, according to witnesses, there were another three unidentified figures sitting in the back seat. Snoop Doggy Dogg's bail was posted at $1,000,000.

'Snoop' – as he is known to admirers – claimed to have seen his first shooting at age 15, and soon after inflated his weekly income from $50 to $1000 by dealing in drugs. He had already been sentenced to one year's jail for cocaine possession with intent to supply

at age 18, before being discovered by ex-NWA member Dr Dre. He also claimed to have been instrumental in the LA riots of 1992, and to have helped sign the truce between the Crips and the Bloods that was later broken by the murder of Tyrone Thomas. Despite minor jailbird status, he denied any LA gang connection and professed to disapprove of the gang culture. On his raw, foul-mouthed debut album, *Doggy Style*, the fastest-selling American debut album up to that point in time, he recorded a track called 'Murder Was The Case' that imagines the dying consciousness of a drive-by victim. The rising rap star came under attack when he and Dre created an 18-minute video based around the song, for misguidedly cashing in on his own homicidal notoriety and prejudicing his chances at trial. Scheduled as a main-feature support, the short failed to find a cinema in LA that would accept it. As one unnamed theatre manager admitted, 'The idea of 2,000 fanatic Snoop fans in the theatre and 2,000 waiting outside was something we were nervous about.' The soundtrack album, however, went straight to the top of the *Billboard* charts, selling a million copies in its first week.

Snoop denied he was exploiting his infamy: 'The inspiration was the actual fact that death is happening every day on the streets in the ghetto. It's just situations that niggaz is faced with on the streets. You're faced with being shot. It's sayin' to stop the violence.' In fact, so opposed did he claim to be to black-on-black violence that he insisted his brothers in the 'hood should be put under martial law until the violence ends: 'When it's black-on-black crime, the authorities won't call the National Guard to stop that shit … The authorities don't care. It's two niggers for one. One dead, one in jail.' Nevertheless, while touring the UK on police bail, his first performances outside the US, he was met with the Daily Star's screaming tabloid headline, 'KICK THIS EVIL BASTARD OUT!' 'They got me twisted up,' protested Snoop, 'makin' mo'fuckers think I'm some crazy lunatic who you can't go up to an' speak to … they're gonna make any black man that's doing some good with himself an example … Michael Jackson never made a violent song in his life. Look how they've come at him.'

Opening Snoop Doggy Dogg's defence in November 1995, star attorney Johnnie Cochrane (former defender of O. J. Simpson) claimed that Philip Woldermariam had provoked the event that took his life by flashing signs related to the gang By Yerself Hustlers outside the Long Beach house where the rapper was staying while recording *Doggy Style*. Woldermariam, an alleged drug dealer, felt that Snoop had 'disrespected' him by flashing back a Crips handsign. The situation escalated until the local gangbanger held a gun to Snoop's head and began to beat him: 'My client was totally unarmed, ducking in the back seat. Why is he here? This is a self-defence case for everyone in that car.' As a curt answer, bodyguard Lee drew his gun and shot Woldermariam twice, who staggered off into an alley to bleed to death. As witnesses changed their story from one of directly gang-related violence to one of self-defence, the LA District Attorney suggested they had been intimidated. Nonetheless, Snoop Doggy Dogg was finally acquitted in 1996, along with his bodyguard – though he agreed to an out-of-court settlement with the family of the dead man, rumoured to be around $1,000,000.

Resuming his career, his next recording was an album entitled *Tha Doggfather* – which, unrepentant, continued to romanticise gangsterdom. 'A lot of people get gangsta and gang-banger confused', he insisted. 'Doin' something the gangsta way is stayin' in touch with your family, stayin' cool with the people and keepin' your business happening, but not being a gang-banger who is bangin' for a flag or for negative reasons: they're keeping the right things hardcore.' He also intended a joint American tour with his friend and supporter Tupac Shakur, another young performer who adhered to the 'righteousness' of the gangsta ethic, under the heading 'All Eyes On US'. But these particular plans would never be fulfilled.

Tupac Shakur was a star of the movie screen as well as the hip-hop scene, having made his movie debut as a doomed street kid in *Juice*. In November 1993 he was charged in New York alongside two friends with forcibly sodomising and sexually abusing a 21-year-old woman fan in a midtown hotel. Ironically, though Shakur's music and image were street-tough, he had recently defied the standard gangsta misogyny with 'Keep Ya Head Up', a rap paean to women. Although he pleaded not guilty, he still put a voguish amorality on display: 'We're just being who we are. It's beyond good and evil. It's a thug life.' Ironically, shortly before his sentencing, he received a further conviction for assaulting black film director Allen Hughes, for which he served 15 days. The young rap star had auditioned for a part in the Hughes brothers' *Menace II Society*, a crime movie reflecting the sensibilities of rap music, but had failed to get the part. In between these events, in November 1994 Tupac was held up at gunpoint outside Quad studios, a recording studio associated with Bad Boy Records luminary Sean 'Puffy' Combs in New York City. The robbery might have turned homicidal when he was shot several times at point blank range, but he was lucky to escape with no fatal injuries. (Rumour has it he lost one testicle due to a bullet wound.)

In December 1994 Shakur was convicted of sexual abuse, along with his road manager Charles Fuller, though they both escaped the charge of forcible sodomy, which potentially carried a much longer sentence. In February 1995 he was sentenced to between 18 months and four and a half years in prison. During sentencing he broke down in tears and made a verbal apology to the youth of America, while insisting, 'I've done nothing wrong. I feel no shame.' His fame and success had, he admitted, made him 'lose focus'. Out on bail during his appeal against conviction, he sat in on the murder trial of Snoop Doggy Dogg. ('He's my homeboy and a friend,' the Doggfather said of his supportive contemporary.)

Despite the huge international success of professed former petty criminal Coolio's 'Gangsta's Paradise' in 1995 (a big production number taking its structure and tune from Stevie Wonder's 'Pastime Paradise'), pointing a finger at the absurdity of black-on-black killings, gangsta rap gained a new level of infamy with the so-called 'rap wars'. It soon became a conventional wisdom that it was dangerous for East Coast rap performers to visit their West Coast rivals' territories. B-Real of Cypress Hill questioned this belief: 'We think it's a bunch of bullshit … The problem with that East Coast/West Coast shit is that the people are loving it, as far as people who are trying to destroy rap. Because, really, you get both coasts against each other and they're really gonna start pointing fingers with all this dissing – "see, look at that, they can't even get along amongst their own community".' As heartfelt as B-Real's sentiments may have been, they came from outside the black communities themselves – where factionalism really was reaching murderous proportions.

Tupac Shakur fed back into the paranoia he was doubtless suffering from when he gave an interview for *Vibe* magazine while awaiting sentencing on Rikers Island Prison in New York. His former friend Biggie Smalls (aka Notorious BIG) and his record label boss, Sean 'Puffy' Combs, had, Shakur contended, set him up for the East Coast shooting that nearly cost him his life. Both parties were aghast at the suggestion, particularly Smalls, who, despite pandering to the dominant gangsta image, seemed more of a gentle giant figure. But the flames of hate were fanned by Marion 'Suge' Knight, head of Death Row Records, who saw Combs as both a rival and an enemy and was only too happy to enter into a war of words between Death Row and Combs' own label, Bad Boy. Knight, who had been cultivating the troubled Tupac as a Death Row artist, eventually posted the rapper's $1.4 million bail on his early release from prison in November 1995, in return for his signature on the dotted line.

The hysteria was fanned further when a friend of Knight's, Jake Robles, was shot dead at a party at the Platinum House club in Atlanta, Georgia, in August 1995. Once again, Knight left no one who was willing to listen in any doubt as to who he saw as implicated in the crime. The attacks reached a new personal level when rumours began to circulate that Knight had been having an affair with Combs' former girlfriend, Misa Hylton, while Shakur had allegedly been sleeping with Biggie Smalls' ex-wife, singer Faith Evans. Both women denied the rumours, but, on a B-side release entitled 'Hit 'Em Up', which directly attacked Notorious BIG and the whole Bad Boy stable, Shakur charmlessly boasted, 'I fucked your bitch, so what?' It was later alleged that, at the 1996 Soul Train Awards, Tupac had pulled a gun on Biggie when they and their two entourages met for the last time. At a performance at the House of Blues in LA that spring, Tupac spoke on stage about the coastal rap wars, concluding, 'Fuck that peace shit!' before launching into his next number.

On 7 September 1996 Tupac Shakur and his Death Row entourage were heading clubwards after attending recently released ex-jailbird Mike Tyson's comeback fight in Las Vegas. At the head of the small convoy of vehicles, the car carrying Shakur and Knight was ambushed by a white Cadillac containing black gunmen. Twelve shots were fired, only one bullet grazing the entrepeneur but most of them hitting the rapper. Although he was in the habit of wearing a bulletproof vest, so convinced was he of the ill-will out on the streets, he had made an exception that evening that would cost him dear. Initially conscious though badly injured, Shakur was taken to a nearby hospital. He fought for life for six days. As complications set in, however, and his weakening condition was exacerbated by internal injuries, hip-hop's 25-year-old superstar started to go under. He died on 13 September 1996.

Not one of the people riding with Tupac that evening ever gave any formal description of his killers.

NYPD blues: Tupac Shakur under arrest in New York City for sexual abuse and forcible sodomy. Despite his chequered history, he has become a posthumous icon to urban black communities.

The only individual who offered to do so (fellow rap artist Kadafi, of the group Outlawz) stayed out of the way of the Las Vegas Police Department for so long it was assumed that he, as with apparently everyone else, was sticking to the street ethic of no cooperation with the cops. Before a warrant could go out to bring him in for questioning, he too was shot dead in what was believed to be a local neighbourhood incident.

Rumours that the target of the shooting was Knight rather than his protégé Tupac were enhanced by rumours of his gang affiliation. Always seen in public wearing at least one red item, – believed to mark the Blood's – Knight also had a ring bearing the legend 'MOB' which was widely believed to be an acronym for 'Member of Bloods'. In fact, not long after Tupac's murder he found himself in a great deal of trouble. One of the missing pieces of the jigsaw has long been believed to be the CCTV footage of the Death Row entourage, particularly Tupac, embroiled in an argument in the boxing arena foyer with a young black man named Orlando Anderson. After being struck by both Shakur and Knight, Anderson was asked by intervening police officers whether he wished to press charges, but declined (Anderson would later change his mind and file suit for 'mental and physical injuries'). The videotape of the incident was enough to have Suge Knight arrested for parole violation, on account of a pistol-whipping attack on young rapper Lynwood Stanley at Dr Dre's studio in 1992. In a further twist, one year after the shooting, Tupac's mother,

Afeni Shakur, took out a civil suit against Orlando Anderson for the 'wrongful death' of her son. Anderson, together with an accomplice, had been the Las Vegas Police Department's initial suspect in the shooting, with revenge as the likely motive. The accomplice was also claimed to be linked with a car impounded by the LAPD at the Californian end of the investigation. However, neither man was ever charged with the murder. Orlando Anderson continued to deniy affiliation with the Crips, and rumours that he had boasted of killing Tupac to his 'homies', but lived in fear of retribution. He was shot dead, aged 23, while Afeni Shakur was seeking to sue him in the civil courts, on 29 May, 1998 – one of three young men hit in a Compton shoot-out. As with Tupac, no one has ever been charged with his murder.

On 9 March 1997 Biggie Smalls became the latest victim of the machismo and paranoia of the hip-hop community. Once again there was a road ambush. He was travelling along a main strip in LA after leaving a party thrown by *Vibe* magazine. As recalled by Puffy Combs, who was travelling in the car behind him, 'There was a car that was parked on the side of the street and somebody began shooting from it.' Smalls, an obese young man whose mobility was further hindered by a broken leg, had zero chance of staying out of the line of fire. 'It was just such a shock, it all happened so quick,' said Combs. 'When I realised that he was dead, it just hurt.'

He later answered police questions on apparent discrepancies as to whether the assassin(s) stayed in their own car or approached the victim's vehicle (Combs claimed the former). 'When shots are being fired people are ducking down. There's not a lot that you're seeing. That's a reality. It's not like, "Ooh, let me see his face." I know I was there, 'cos I was ducking down in the car.' Like that of Tupac Shakur, the murder of Biggie Smalls remains unsolved – though the suggestion remains, as held likely by Combs, that he was murdered by gang members hyped on the mythical East Coast-West Coast war they imagined themselves to be a part of, and that Smalls was killed to supposedly 'avenge' his one-time friend Shakur.

On 23 March 1997 the Nation of Islam staged a rally in South Central LA attended by up to 50 members of the Crips and the Bloods, as well as Ice Cube. The subject was the urgent need for a cessation of hostilities in the so-called East-West war; the subtext was that it was a media invention, originating, according to Minister Tony Muhammad, with the entertainment media rather than inside the gangsta-rap culture itself. 'The spin doctors are trying to take the rap culture and do with it what they were not able to do with crack cocaine', he righteously proclaimed, believing that magazines such as The Source and Vibe were part of a conspiracy to destroy the culture that gave them their very existence.

Marion 'Suge' Knight served five years out of a possible nine-year prison sentence, most of it in Mule Creek State Prison, southern California. During his incarceration, the LAPD made it clear they were investigating claims that Knight set up Death Row Records on the back of a loan from a PCP (angel dust) dealer, and also named him as an ongoing suspect in the murder of Biggie Smalls. No charges or conclusive evidence were brought in either case, remaining hearsay and rumour – though retired white rapper Vanilla Ice's accusation that Knight once recovered a debt by dangling him off a balcony suggested the Death Row boss's business ingenuity knew few boundaries. ('I never preyed on the weak', was Knight's put-down retort to Vanilla Ice. 'I'm not a bully. I pick on my equals.' As for the drugs accusations, Knight claimed, 'I'm from the ghetto … I saw what drugs could do. I never sold nor used drug money to start this company.')

Ultimately, the Biggie accusations were later withdrawn – having been fed, perhaps, by Knight's assertion that he would never give up Biggie's killer to the cops even if he knew who he was. He later explained this to an interviewer in Mule Creek Prison as obeying the code of the street: 'We're not in heaven – this is the real world. Whoever did this, they know who they are and they have to live with themselves. I would never be a snitch.' As for the recurring rumours, Suge conceded, 'They were ready to let me out of prison till Biggie was shot, then they put the judgement on hold.' And the rumours would come back to haunt him when he least expected it.

Meanwhile, the career of Knight's one-time rival, Sean 'Puffy' Combs, went from strength to strength – whether as head of the r'n'b/soul-orientated hip-hop label Bad Boy, as owner of the Sean John fashion line (named, naturally, after Sean John Combs), or, under the name Puff Daddy, as the single biggest-selling artist in the history of the music. (His rap-soul tribute to Biggie Smalls, 'I'll Be Missing You', based on the

The most feared man in hip-hop: Death Row founder Marion 'Suge' Knight. In Las Vegas, September 1996, Knight committed the assault that sent him to prison. That same night, Tupac Shakur died in Knight's car.

Police's 'Every Step You Take', was a massive world-wide hit. Intriguingly, Biggie's mother, Violetta Wallace, claims the man who still refers to her son as his 'best friend' had never been anything closer than a business associate.) As one of the most visible figures of the hip-hop culture, however, his career has not avoided controversy.

In December 1998, he was ruled 50 per cent culpable, alongside co-promoter rapper Heavy D, for a disaster at a 1991 rap concert at the City University of New York – where, due to overcrowding and poor crowd control, nine young people were crushed to death. In 1995, he was arrested for threatening a man with a handgun after an argument in a Washington parking lot. (Combs surrendered himself to the FBI when a warrant was issued, but the case was quietly dropped.) In November 1997, a guest at the Ritz Carlton Hotel in Cleveland, Ohio was awakened by a loud noise from the next room, later finding a hole in the wall and a spent bullet on the floor. At the time, Puff Daddy and his entourage were partying next door. In 1999, after misgivings about a music video where Puffy played the part of a flogged and crucified Christ, he vented his anger on the producer. Steve Stoute filed a complaint stating that Combs and two associates beat him about the head and body with 'a glass champagne bottle, a chair and a telephone', allegedly breaking his jaw and arm. Bad Boy's head honcho was arrested for assault and criminal mischief, but the charge was reduced to harassment. He was made to pay a 'crime victim assistance fee' and attend a one-day anger management class.

But the incident that linked him to the gun culture that killed his protégé Biggie occurred on 27 December 1999, at the Club New York in Manhattan. In attendance with his glamorous girlfriend, Hispanic singer-actress Jennifer Lopez, and Bad Boy Records rapper Jamal Barrow, aka Shyne, Puffy was seen to get into an argument with a heavy-duty club member, who threw a wad of notes in his face as a mark of disrespect. (Hearsay at the subsequent trial claimed the local heavy was heard conferring with others about 'melting Puffy's cheddar' – ripping off his money.) Guns were pulled – a warning shot was fired into the ceiling, but three bystanders were also hit. 29-year-old Natanya Reuben was shot through the cheek; club bouncer Julius Jones, 27, and Robert Thompson, 39, were both hit in the shoulder. The bullet passed through Ms. Reubens' cheek and nose, fragments remaining lodged in her skull and at the top of her spine, reputedly causing seizures. Damningly, both she and Jones claimed to see Puff Daddy's arm raise and fire a black semi-automatic handgun in the split seconds before they were hit (Ms. Reuben claiming to see two bursts of gunfire).

After Puffy and his entourage fled the club, they were arrested in their host's Lincoln Navigator after jumping eleven red lights. Upon arrest, the most serious charges were faced by Shyne – including attempted murder. Combs, however, was accused of firing off the warning shot and faced an illegal firearm possession charge carrying a maximum fifteen-year sentence.

To compound his troubles, he was charged with attempting to bribe a witness – his driver complained he had been offered $50,000 and a diamond ring Jennifer Lopez gave to Puffy, as payment for claiming ownership of a discarded handgun. Puffy countered that his distress over seeing Jennifer under arrest in handcuffs had put him 'on a mission' to find who owned the gun. Countering this was police evidence that a dazed Ms. Lopez was apprehended walking away from the scene as her boyfriend, his driver and bodyguard were being cuffed. 'I'm going home', she allegedly told a police sergeant. 'It's not my gun.'

Testifying before a pre-trial grand jury early in January 2000, Puff Daddy earnestly pleaded his innocence: 'My father [an alleged drug dealer] … got killed through gunfire when I was three years old. My best friend [Biggie Smalls] got killed … I would never, never, never disrespect the life of my father or my best friend by owning or possessing a gun.'

Civil lawsuits relating to the case began to pile up: Julius Jones filed suit not only against Shyne (who, the public prosecutor would contend, was responsible for his injuries) but against Combs – though, as he was claiming damages of $700 million, it made more sense to go after an entrepeneur whose fortune was estimated at $400 million; Natanya Reuben was seeking $150 million; even the driver, Wardel Fenderson, filed for $3,000,000 in compensation for 'personal injuries' and 'intentional infliction of emotional distress'. (To cap all this, Public Enemy's Chuck D – the more socially responsible, if not outright reactionary, voice of rap – was filing a minimum $1,000,000 damages suit against Bad Boy for the sampling of his voice in the Notorious B.I.G.'s 'The Ten Crack Commandments', which shamelessly glorified crack dealing.) Puffy acknowledged that the total damages sought amounted to a cool 'billion dollars and change' – most of which depended upon his conviction. As his own hit record had put it, 'Mo' Money, Mo' Problems'.

Combs' trial began almost exactly a year later, in late January 2001. Just over two weeks later, on Valentine's Day, Puffy's spokesman made a PR announcement outside the courtroom that his paymaster's three-year relationship with Jennifer Lopez was now ended. Press and fan speculation as to whether she would take the witness stand had been intense, but Puffy stated that he still loved Jennifer too much to subject her to the ordeal – while, for his part, the public prosecutor delicately explained: 'I'm supposed to call the defendant's girlfriend? … I'm not a complete moron.' Combs has continued to state his undying love for Jennifer, but – riding high as she was with her hit album *J. Lo*, and a lead role in a hit film, *The Wedding Planner*, both of them topping their respective charts – she may just have had enough of living the 'gangsta life' at a remove.

As jury deliberation began, support for Combs came from a most unlikely quarter. 'Prison's not the place for Puffy', opined his old rival and enemy Suge Knight in Mule Creek. 'Prison could destroy this guy … I thank God that He made me a man who, if I'm incarcerated, I'm still gonna be the same person I am … by him being

LOPEZ AND LOVER IN GUN ARREST

CLUB FRACAS: Millionaire rap star Puff Daddy

From ANDY LINES in New York and JAMES SCOTT

SINGER Jennifer Lopez and rapper boyfriend Puff Daddy were arrested yesterday after a nightspot shooting.

The two stars fled after a man opened fire and hit three dancers at trendy Club NY in New York.

Lopez — voted the world's sexiest woman — and her millionaire lover leapt into a waiting limousine, which was stopped by police after jumping a red light.

Officers found a gun in the car and the pair were charged with illegal possession of a firearm.

Witnesses to the club fracas said Puff Daddy — real name Sean Combs who had a huge hit with I'll Be Missing You — had let loose with a weapon after the original burst of shots.

Rising rap star Shyne, 19, was also arrested at the club and charged with illegally having a gun. Puff Daddy gave him a £600,000 record contract but the two have fallen out.

Lopez, 30, and Puff Daddy, 29, were quizzed by police for more than 13 hours. A spokesman said: "They were in a car with two other people, which was stopped about 2:30am — 10 minutes after the shooting at Club NY.

"A gun was found in the car and none of the four had a licence. Officers stopped the car because it was

TURN TO PAGE 7

ARREST: Singer Lopez

Puff Daddy charged after 13-hour quiz

a small guy, there's probably gonna be guys trying to prey on him.' By such a show of concern, Knight gave an estimation of Puffy Combs as belittling as his implicit demolition of Vanilla Ice.

Ultimately, though the prosectuor had damned the trial as 'rampant with bribery, money, influence and witnesses changing their testimony', the jury were unimpressed by the opportunism of litigant witnesses. Further, five others with no apparent axe to grind all testified Puffy had not appeared to be carrying a gun, before or during the incident. Most unwavering in her account – and most contrary to the macho image of Puffy presented by both the prosecution and his entourage – was female bouncer Charise Myers. As the shooting started, she described how she protected the rap star with her own body: 'I fell on top of Mr. Combs and other people fell on top of me … He looked shocked', she said of his lack of composure as she led him from danger.

As Combs' defence lawyer, former O. J. Simpson/Snoop Dogg defender Johnnie Cochran had 'rapped', 'If it don't make sense, find for the defence', and, on 16 March 2001, the jury acquitted Sean Combs of all charges. 'I've changed, I've matured', the elated superstar told *Time* magazine. 'This whole thing has made me deeper … I thank God, I'm blessed I was able to find fine lawyers like mine.' (Blessed by an estimated $400 million, the cynic might add. Other black men on trial, or indeed poor whites, might not find themselves bestowed with such divine grace.) 'No more Puff Daddy – the first week in June we're gonna have a name change ceremony', he excitably told MTV. 'I'm rockin' with P. Diddy now – my man Biggie gave me that name.'

Jamal 'Shyne' Barrow wasn't quite so blessed, receiving ten years for reduced charges of assault, reckless endangerment and illegal possession of a gun. In him, at least, the New York City Police Department could be seen to punish the 'culture of violence' they had recently condemned in the hip-hop community. Now, after staying silent and aloof throughout proceedings, Shyne claimed to the *Village Voice* to have been abandoned by his label boss: 'There are no boundaries to what he would do to exonerate himself. I had the Bible in front of me, and I was just praying that he wouldn't continue to lie.' Indeed, both 'P. Diddy' and Shyne had kept pristine copies of the New Testament at their table during the trial – seemingly at odds with the lyrics of the eponymously-titled debut album, *Shyne*, like 'Spend Some Cheese': 'live for the moment / fuck atonement / explain to God when you see Him'.

Aware that insinuating Puffy's guilt made himself no more innocent, Shyne complained, 'As soon as we were indicted, he wanted to keep me away from him.' Claiming to have been 'inseparable' from his mentor when first signed to Bad Boy, the rapper noted how Puffy had claimed to be no closer to him than to any other Bad Boy artist, and accused Combs of trying to drop the *Shyne* album. Combs expressed his disappointment at the accusations, but stressed that, despite earlier protestations that he was a mere business acquaintance, he would always regard Shyne like 'a little brother'.

Meanwhile, Marion 'Suge' Knight prepared for release from prison on parole. During his sentence he had financed the restoration of a kindergarten playground and generally come on as the elder statesman of gangsta rap. Much hostility had come his way, however. His former protégé, Snoop Dogg (formerly Snoop *Doggy* Dogg), had recorded a rap entitled 'Death Row is Bitches', which appeared to blame his old label for the murder of Tupac Shakur: 'Niggaz put my nigga 2Pac in the mix … That nigga didn't know what he was getting into / Had him caught up in the middle / While you fuckin' with his revenues.' The recurring line, 'Yeah, if it's on it's on' (basically, 'If you want to fight, I'll fight you anytime') , seemed to throw down the gauntlet to Knight. Just over one year from the record's release, however, Suge Knight was ready to pick up from where he left off. 'Most of my artists like Snoop and others would have never left Death Row if I hadn't gone to jail', he reflected, with a quiet edge of paranoia. 'A lot of people had a lot to gain by me being away.' Press reports claimed that a nervous Snoop Doog was hiring extra security staff in anticipation of Knight telling him, 'It's on.' 'I have to trust in the Lord', insisted a less belligerent Snoop, continuing the gangsta tradition of falling back on The Bible when the 'thug life' no longer suits. 'I've been hearing Suge was getting out every month since he went in. What am I supposed to do? Go hide?'

For his own part, Knight was full of optimism. 'I still can tell what's hot on the streets', he claimed. 'Because, if you think about it, most of the slang off the streets comes from the brothers in jail.' As to his old rival at the head of Bad Boy Entertainment, Knight was dismissive of Combs' hold on the hip-hop market and, indeed, his luck in beating the weapons rap: 'Who is he a threat to? He's just acting a fool.'

Prior to his release (on 6th August 2001, after a short transfer to federal prison in Oregon), Knight aimed a blow below his rival's belt. Via the video subsidiary of Death Row, he announced his intention to release a cassette entitled *J-Lo Uncut: The Real Story*. Jennifer Lopez's lawyers moved fast. Hearing echoes of the Pamela Anderson and Tommy Lee sex-tape scam, she applied for an injunction against release in the Los Angeles Superior Court. (Confusingly, Ms. Lopez stated in her lawsuit that she was unaware of the existence of such a tape, while asserting, 'If the tape is, in fact, publicly displayed and disseminated, [the] plaintiff will suffer greatly in her occupation.') The motion was denied when Knight's representative announced his client did 'not possess a so-called "sex tape" involving Ms. Lopez and an ex-boyfriend', and that he had merely financed an unauthorised video-biography.

But if the Lopez tape was a mild diversion, Knight found accusations of involvement in the murder of Biggie Smalls more taxing. Back in late 1999, the LAPD had confirmed they were investigating a corrupt cop – one David Mack, serving a fourteen-year prison sentence for bank robbery – to trace any connections between him and Knight. Even though Mack himself was picked out of a photographic line-up by one of the two men travelling with Biggie on his fatal car ride, rapper Little Caesar and road manager Damien 'D-Rock' Butler, the *Los Angeles Times* reported he was suspected of hiring a contact named Amir Muhammad to carry out the hit on Knight's behalf.

In spring 2001, the theory resurfaced when its elements were tied together in a *Rolling Stone* article entitled 'The Murder of the Notorious B.I.G.' by Randall Sullivan. The author quoted former LAPD Detective Russell Poole's belief that a cell of police officers within the LAPD had been, audaciously, both affiliated to the Bloods street gang and working as hired security for Suge Knight at Death Row Records (Knight's own alleged association with the Compton Bloods being a very open secret). The vital link was a corrupt black policeman named Kevin Gaines who had died in a shoot-out. Gaines lived an ostentatious lifestyle, drove a Montero registered to a Death Row subsidiary, and, supposedly most crucial of all, had a relationship with Sharitha Knight, ex-wife of Death Row's founder. It was also stated as a proven fact that, since 1998 (during Suge Knight's incarceration), six black officers had been sacked from the force for moonlighting as Death Row security staff without permission.

The trouble with this seductive conspiracy theory was, it seems, that the journalist had overlooked its basic flaws: there was no evidence that David Mack had ever worked for Death Row, although he was known to have attended several of their parties; Kevin Gaines had intervened on behalf of Sharitha Knight after an alleged threat from her ex-husband, and was therefore disliked by Suge; the 'six black officers' were an overestimate – records proved only one cop had fallen foul of LAPD by working for Death Row, and even he had a departmental permit. Most crucially, however, the Biggie murder conspiracy was based on anecdotal evidence from career criminal Mark Hylland, on trial for more twenty counts of grand theft at the time of the article's publication. According to Sullivan's story, Hylland was 'with Mack and [his partner Rafael] Perez when they met with Suge Knight in the parking lot of a Denny's restaurant in Bellflower during early 1997'. The timeframe is based on the fact that Biggie was murdered in March '97, while the conspiratorial meeting allegedly took place that February. Suge Knight, however, had been held in prison since October 1996, on account of a further violation of his probation period (failing a drug test). At time of writing, the head of Death Row was considering his legal response to *Rolling Stone*.

In the UK, the smaller, more confined culture of urban mayhem failed to accommodate a 'gangsta rap' scene, though a few performers tried to buy into its shady charisma. Techno-dance band Mekon chose a particularly unusual rapper on their track 'Revenge of the Mekon' after a chance meeting with veteran Brit gangster 'Mad' Frankie Fraser at a north London bus-stop

Plastic 'gangsta': British r'n'b star Mark Morrison styled himself 'the Mack', after black-American pimps, but was ridiculed on receiving a year's imprisonment for failing to attend community service.

(the venue somehow lacking the dark stateside glamour). Fraser – now in his seventies, having spent more than half his life in prison – was recruited to read a section from his autobiography, *Mad Frank*, over Mekon's

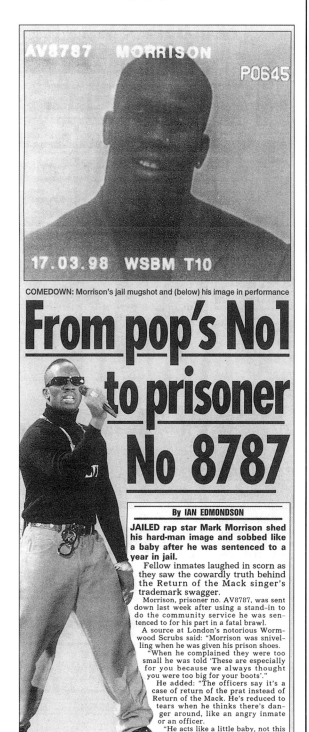

COMEDOWN: Morrison's jail mugshot and (below) his image in performance

From pop's No1 to prisoner No 8787

By IAN EDMONDSON

JAILED rap star Mark Morrison shed his hard-man image and sobbed like a baby after he was sentenced to a year in jail.

Fellow inmates laughed in scorn as they saw the cowardly truth behind the Return of the Mack singer's trademark swagger.

Morrison, prisoner no. AV8787, was sent down last week after using a stand-in to do the community service he was sentenced to for his part in a fatal brawl.

A source at London's notorious Wormwood Scrubs said: "Morrison was snivelling when he was given his prison shoes.

"When he complained they were too small he was told 'These are especially for you because we always thought you were too big for your boots'."

He added: "The officers say it's a case of return of the prat instead of Return of the Mack. He's reduced to tears when he thinks there's danger around, like an angry inmate or an officer.

"He acts like a little baby, not this LA gangster image he goes for."

259

backing. His status as the British media's most convivial criminal celebrity was reinforced when he appeared on an album by Tricky – a paranoid, reefer-mad, but innovative trip-hop artist. 'I used to be a in a straitjacket or just eat bread and water in a padded cell or Broadmoor [hospital for the criminally insane] or wherever and I used to be able to sing a song to myself', the ex-hood reflected on the importance of music. Frankie Fraser's former crimes, as an 'enforcer' for the infamous Richardson gang in the 1960s, included torture by dental extraction with pliers and electric shock. His mixture of old-fashioned charm and raging psychosis lent a vicarious 'dangerousness' to artists whose sensibilities would never allow them to participate in or withstand life's brutality in the way that he had.

In 1996 a young black R&B-soul singer reached the top of the UK charts with a song he performed with props such as handcuffs or a replica semi-automatic rifle. 'Return of the Mack', by Mark Morrison, took its terminology from the Afro-American underworld: a 'mack' being a pimp-cum-professional-hoodlum as immortalised in the books of Iceberg Slim, a former pimp himself, and the 1973 blaxploitation movie *The Mack*. Morrison claimed inspiration for his quarter-million selling tune came from time spent on remand for murder in his native Midlands town of Leicester. The charge arose from an incident outside a nightclub, when one of the singer's friends stabbed another young man to death. Morrison claimed he had being trying to stop the altercation's after three months on remand he was released, convicted only of 'violent disorder' and sentenced to community service.

In October 1996, shortly after the success of 'The Mack', Morrison was arrested after he and three friends were seen 'acting suspiciously' by police at an all-night convenience store in Notting Hill, west London. Despite the dubious rationale for the search (Morrison was suspected of stealing food, while a perusal of his wallet revealed about £1000 in cash for 'small purchases'), the singer was found in possession of an illegal electric stun gun. The police claimed he threatened a plain clothes officer with the weapon; Morrison claimed he was trying to throw the gun – kept strictly for self defence – away. The cops won out: he was sentenced to three months' imprisonment in May 1997, reportedly stamping his feet in anger as he was led away. 'Only God can judge me' were the first words spoken by an image-conscious Morrison on his release from Wormwood Scrubs Prison, surrounded by 'minders' dressed, like himself, in gangster suit and shades. *Only God Can Judge Me* was also the title of a self-important 'mini-album' released soon after, containing tedious recordings of crowds chanting Morrison's name and a reiterated tally of all his problems with the law. Self-mythologisation was the name of the game. 'There's no more real artist in England than Mark Morrison,' he told the *NME*, 'and it angers some people to see me, the naughty black boy, still strong, no matter what I've gone through … they're gonna have to kill me to stop me and maybe one day they will,' he announced, suggesting that the police

were on a mission to hound him to death.

The tabloids carried stories about Morrison being placed on the prison's hospital wing after a near nervous breakdown. Morrison countered by claiming that he was there at the insistence of the prison governor because 'they didn't want me leaving prison with a scar on my face, complaining that I wasn't protected enough'. The prisoners had, he claimed, 'showed me love. They were star-struck and it felt good to them having Mark Morrison, someone they respected, in the same position as them; someone who didn't appeal against his sentence but just got on with it like a man.' The UK's recidivist community had further opportunity to pay homage to him when Morrison was arrested for sending a look-alike to perform community service as part of the 1994 conviction for violent disorder. This time, he was sentenced to 12 months. Tabloid reports insisted that both he and his doting mother were reduced to tears in court. Back inside, he was again placed in the hospital wing, where he received a bizarre message from the man labelled 'Britain's most

Twisted firestarter: Keith Flint of the Prodigy looking like a Beano comic punk rocker. Despite their liking for controversy, the Prodigy were coy about the meaning of the chant 'Smack My Bitch Up'.

dangerous prisoner', long-term solitary con Charles Bronson. The prison hard man, presumably not one of Morrison's convict fan club, sent a self-penned gangsta rap lyric about the singer 'missing his mama's apple pie'. Since serving his sentence, the Mack has failed to return to prominence on the UK music scene.

The biggest controversy in British dance music at this time originated with a reputedly mild-mannered bunch called the Prodigy, whose singer, Essex boy Keith Flint, exhibited a manic punk persona straight out of a children's comic. Already notorious for 'Firestarter', a paean to pyromania, they hit the headlines even harder in 1997 with 'Smack My Bitch Up'. When the contentious title appeared on a plain black billboard around the UK, its lack of context caused a mild furore in Parliament: one MP branded it 'cruddy, sad and pathetic'. Answering the obvious accusation of violent misogyny, songwriter Liam Howlett claimed, 'It's just street slang, a phrase, it's not "smack your bitch up", it's "we're here just letting off energy".' In fact nobody in Britain seemed to recognise this particular 'street phrase'.

The Prodigy made no bones about going for controversy with the promotional video for the single. Based around a cocaine-snorting, random-coupling night in Soho, this mildly alluring little piece of porn ends with the 'shock' revelation that the video's antagonist, through whose eyes the viewer is seeing the softcore action, is a woman. An attempt to neutralise the thorny subject of gender exploitation – or just a sexual frisson to celebrate the fact that the video was never going to be shown on primetime TV anyway?

In the US, the outrage at the title was even stronger: the *Fat of the Land* album, where the offending track originated, was pulled from the shelves by the Wal Mart and K-Mart chains, on account of the offending track. More incongruously, objections came from reformed caucasian rap group the Beastie Boys – whose lyrics previously betrayed an attitude to the female gender that was locker-room at best. 'You know, a woman gets murdered in America every twenty minutes,' explained the Beasties' Adam Horovitz, 'every day, in domestic violence … So "Smack My Bitch Up" isn't that funny … And it may sound hypocritical of us to say that but okay, there you go.'

Hip-hop and gangsta rap were now the music of choice for a large proportion of white American youth. Even a Nation of Islam hardliner like Ice Cube had to concede where his bread and butter came from. 'I figure they [the white kids] need to hear the truth, too,' he rationalised. 'They've been subjected to a lot of lies about us, how we live, how things happen, things about our neighbourhood. And, shit, if we really wanna break this tradition, we not only have to start in our house, but we have to start in their house.'

Though holding up the militant rhetoric, Ice Cube had also been shrewd enough to take the Ice-T route to media infiltration. Starting with an acting role in John Singleton's socially concerned gangsta-rap film *Boyz 'N The Hood*, he moved to more standard Hollywood fare with *Trespass*, in which he and Ice-T played vil-

lainous black gangsters, set against frightened white heroes looking for hidden loot in a derelict tenement building. As an entertainer, the militant Ice Cube has learned to play the game while, like Ice-T, still keeping up the macho tradition of a cartoonish form of gangsta rap. (His part-time group, Westlife Connection, gave Cube the melodramatic title of 'the Gangsta', while his fellow members were referred to as 'the Killa' and 'the Dope Dealer'.)

Rap's similarity to heavy metal runs deeper than a simple love of shock. Both cultivate aggressive posturing as a statement of identity. Metal aspires to be the music of the white dispossessed, to distil their hate and hopelessness. Rap, rooted in the oppressed communities of urban black America, seeks to drown its community's oppressors in vitriol. Despite the racism and sexism, soon everybody wanted to be associated with rap – from Prince to death metallers Anthrax and white megastars Guns N' Roses. It was, after all, a sound that displayed more life than rock'n'roll had shown since the death of punk. Ice-T was among the first to see the inevitability of the rap-metal crossover, claiming to have formed his controversial rock band Body Count as a way of finding employment for five black rock musician friends. 'When you see the stuff like what I'm doing with Slayer,' he announced as the most brutally macho genres of popular music began to cross-pollinate, 'and turn around and watch what Onyx is doing and Wu-Tang Clan, you start seeing it's going to eventually happen.'

Wu-Tang Clan proved to be one of the most popular hip-hop crossover acts of all, starting with their debut album *Enter the Wu-Tang (36 Chambers)* which exploited the fixation with Shaolin kung-fu that lent the band its name. Individual members' names seem to emanate from some streetwise modern comic book: Genius, Golden Arms, The Rebels INS, Shallah Raekwan, U God, Ghostface Killah, Prince Rakeem. Lingering gangsta affectations were illustrated by Ghostface wearing a mask at early performances because of an outstanding arrest warrant.

The most notorious of their number, going by the quaint moniker Ol' Dirty Bastard, has maintained hip-hop traditions via continual trouble with the law: in the mid-nineties, he was charged with burglary after seriously injuring his back jumping from a third-floor apartment; in 1998-9 (when he eccentrically demanded to be known by his 'real' name of Big Baby Jesus), he was arrested for shoplifting, threatening his girlfriend, making 'terroristic threats' to nightclub security men, illegal possession of body armour (a bulletproof vest), possession of 20 vials of crack cocaine, driving without a licence, and the attempted murder of an NYPD officer. The latter charge came from an allegation that he fired at an undercover policeman who pulled over his Chevy truck. In November 1999 the rapper was sentenced to one year in a drug rehabilitation facility; at a subsequent hearing in NYC, relating to crack possession, he asked the female prosecutor if she found him 'horny' and whether she would agree to his being her 'sperm donor'. In September 2000 he was commended for his progress at the centre, and issued with 12 hour supervised passes in order to perform 'fellowship work'; in October he absconded from the facility. After a no-bail warrant was issued for his arrest, ODB made an audacious guest appearance at a November Wu-Tang Clan show in New York City, then promptly disappeared again. He was arrested again one week later, this time after being seen acting suspiciously in the car park of a McDonald's burger bar in South Philadelphia. According to the bureau chief of narcotics trials for the borough of Queens, once extradited back to NYC the luckless petty felon would be able to cop a plea bargain provided the police contacted 'all the other District Attorneys [Brooklyn and LA] to find out if some kind of package deal can be put together'. The following spring, ODB pleaded guilty, under his given name of Russell Jones, to criminal possession of a controlled substance – an offence which, even under a plea bargain, is likely to carry a punitive two-to-four-year sentence.

Meanwhile, Ol' Dirty Bastard's estranged band, the Wu-Tang Clan, draw ever closer to the eccentric white-boy terrain of metal, even recording with original Black Sabbath members Ozzy Osbourne and Tony Iommi. The generic crossover is as much a matter of content as musical style. The advent of bands like Gravediggaz – with the metal-ish band monikers of Dr. Strange, Grym Reaper and the Gatekeeper – took rap lyrics closer to the dark fantasies of black metal, in the sub-genre dubbed 'horrorcore'. Insane Clown Posse took a less gothic approach to plain old-fashioned outrage. White rappers in creepy clown make-up, redolent of serial killer John Wayne Gacy or Stephen King's *It*, ICP were rejected from the Disney corporation's Hollywood label on the basis of lyrical gems like, 'When your mom's done the dishes and silverware / I'll dry fuck her 'til I nut in my underwear!'

Attacked in the pages of *Spin* magazine for dragging hip-hop culture down to a nadir that gangsta rap supposedly never reached, the Clowns are American outrage merchants of the most old-fashioned kind. Happily admitting that they 'totally fucking suck', leader Violent J. makes telling comparisons in terms of their forebears: 'KISS spurting flames from their guitars! Alice Cooper chopping his own fucking head off! That's entertainment!' In their trash aesthetic, they have far less in common with Public Enemy than they do with the androgynous shockmeister who milks middle-American gullibility for all it's worth: 'we are the wickedest band in the world! I stamp Marilyn Manson in the balls and break his fucking legs!' runs the perverse acknowledgement of their kinship.

But the biggest – and perhaps unlikeliest – hip-hop star to emerge in the late nineties is a feisty, ill-tempered blue-collar boy from Detroit: close to the Michigan hometown of the Insane Clown Posse, with whom he has an ongoing feud. Discovered by Dr. Dre, he could be defined as the white Snoop Dogg to the power of ten. 'I don't like to get into the thing of "white rapper",' says Chuck D of the young 'cracka', 'because he's just a kid who's come up from the 'hood, and he's good. If you were blind you wouldn't be able

to tell.' Eminem is the logical conclusion to the popularity of gangsta rap with white kids. With the real name Marshall Mathers, he is a cold-eyed young crophead with a schizoid attitude to performance who mythologises himself in rap under his own name and that of his alter ego, Slim Shady, while performing under the title Eminem. Eminem approaches every aspect of his career as if it's a blood feud.

The aftermath of his first album, *The Slim Shady* LP, saw Mathers going head-to-head with his mother, Deborah Mathers-Briggs, after she objected the line 'I just found out my mom smokes more dope than I do' and others describing how she allegedly beat her son during her early years. It got the ball rolling on a seemingly endless round of litigation, the first of which was a legal action from his mother, claiming $10,000,000 compensation for what her attorney described as 'emotional distress including diminished self-esteem, humiliation, sleepless nights, harm to her credit rating, and even loss of her mobile phone'. Using his emotionally unstable young life as inspiration for his lyrics, Eminem conducts his personal life as a battlefield – and the dividing line between the two is arbitrary. (In his earlier years, the tough guy admits, he was emotionally vulnerable enough to attempt to kill himself with an OD of painkillers. The legend 'Slash Here' is tattooed on his right wrist.) His friend Fred Durst, of crude shock-rockers Limp Bizkit, claims, 'The more they say Eminem's stuff is terrible, the more he's gonna make his stuff ten times worse than that and they're gonna want it even more.'

The feud between Eminem and the Insane Clown Posse quickly built to a crescendo. 'Slim Anus', they called him; 'Damn right,' came his rhyming retort, 'I don't get fucked in mine like you flaming faggots'. Of all the gangsta rap influences he has absorbed, homophobic machismo is one of the most powerful, and has brought him the most disapproval. But it is little more than macho provocation, in the tradition of Cypress Hill, who showed their own intolerance to other peoples' lifestyles with a cry of 'Fuck all the fags and homos in San Francisco!' at a concert in that most cosmopolitan of cities. Eminem's own producer Dr. Dre mocked his former NWA partner Eazy E as a 'little faggot', before admitting that E's subsequent death from Aids (apparently contracted via heterosexual contact) was a wake-up call for himself and the black community.

Eminem's 'private' life is lived like some unrestrained white-trash soap opera. Catching his blonde wife Kimberley in an embrace with a barman at a place just outside of Detroit, he called them both out and began pistol-whipping the man. After he was released on $110,000 bail for assault with a dangerous weapon and carrying a concealed weapon, Kim Mathers felt moved to give her side of the story to a local paper: 'I don't think anybody in their right mind would cheat on a millionaire husband – especially with a nobody in a neighbourhood bar … I would also like to state, since my husband has no problem making me look like an unfaithful wife, that every time I see a picture of him with other women, or read that he's involved with groupies, I don't go and show up where he is, making a big scene and getting our faces all over the TV.'

Having already exhibited his love/hate relationship with Kim in raps entitled ''97Bonnie And Clyde' and 'Kim', and in the dedication 'Kim – Rot in Pieces' tattooed around his navel, Eminem's obsession was further demonstrated on the 2000 Up In Smoke tour, where he shared billing with Ice Cube, Dr. Dre and Snoop Dogg. Christening a blow-up sex doll 'Kim', he simulated sex and violence upon his inflatable wife. On one of these occasions, Kimberley was actually in attendance. Returning home drunk, she wrecked part of the house in a fit of depression then slashed her wrists. Fortunately, her concerned mother put out a 911 call and saved her. Marshall Mathers subsequently sued his wife for divorce; in return she sued him for $10,000,000, on account of distress caused by the song 'Kim', which, her attorney described as depicting, 'horrific domestic violence against the wife, resulting in her grisly murder', and his stage antics with the inflatable doll.

''97 Bonnie and Clyde', the first murder-rap songs where Eminem imagines killing his wife, is a black comedy in which he uses a child's voice to represent his own little daughter: 'Da-Da made a nice bed for mommy at the bottom of the lake / Here, you wanna help Da-Da tie a rope around this rock? [yeah!] / 'We'll tie it to her footsie then we'll roll her off the dock.' 'Kim' ups the intensity of the family psychodrama. Rapped as a dialogue between the messed-up lovers, Mathers played up his fear that Kim was about to leave him for a new husband and his small son. The solution, as ever, was homicidal: 'There's a four-year-old boy lyin' dead with a slit throat / in your living room / HA HA / What you think, I'm kiddin' you? / You loved him didn't you?' With its provocative sick humour, ''97 Bonne and Clyde' is the equal of anything Frank Zappa did with the early Mothers of Invention; 'Kim', with its escalating hysteria and violence, is a narrative worthy of Lou Reed at his most unflinchingly streetwise. Despite his obvious talent, what remains discomfiting about Eminem is that he fashioned these lyrics from his own domestic life, and his young daughter will grow up to realise how Da-Da publicly fantasised about making her complicit in Mommy's murder.

A controversial superstar since the success of *The Slim Shady* LP, Eminem is a son of the gangsta rap culture for whom life only becomes 'real' if played out against a garish media backdrop with police sirens for a soundtrack. With small-time criminal charges hovering over his head, Mathers kept up the stance of the fatalistic tough guy: 'Being taken from my money, being thrown in jail, none of that shit bothers me.' Despite the macho-nihilist posturing, however, some elements of his life came to a civilised resolution.

In February 2001, Deborah Mathers-Briggs (accused by Eminem, in 'Brain Damage', of using 'tar [heroin], liquor, cigarettes and speed' when she carried him) withdrew from litigating against her son. 'When I saw the attorney,' she claimed, 'he was to send Marshall a letter warning him to stop being so

demeaning …' The $10 million lawsuit, she claimed, was her lawyer's initiative, while she personally wished only that 'things could be different'. In March that same year, Marshall and Kim Mathers agreed a divorce settlement whereby he would buy her a new house for $475,000, while custody of their daughter would be shared. ('He [Mathers] feels it's only appropriate,' asserted Eminem's lawyer, 'because he's had this significant role in his daughter's upbringing to date, and that's going to be ongoing.' For his part, Mathers appears devoted to the child to an extent that transcends his anti-social attitudes.)

But the parallels between the provocation of gangsta rap and the playground nihilism of metal – drawn when Eminem and androgynous 'antichrist superstar' Marilyn Manson formed a mutual admiration society (despite Eminem's provocative comments about 'faggots', i.e. anyone he preceives as less manly than himself). In the single, 'The Way I Am', Mathers raps about the Columbine High School massacre of 1999 and similar tragedies: 'When a dude's getting bullied and shoots up his school / They blame it on Marilyn …' (Eminem and Marilyn Manson would later duet on the track for the soundtrack of the horror film *From Hell*.) Manson reciprocated the support: 'I think Eminem is going through it now. I'm not going to say gay-bashing is a good thing, but he's being funny on his record. I don't think he's sincerely trying to hurt gays. He's catching all this heat for it, and I think that's really dangerous' – though he also conceded, 'It's probably too complicated for his audience to try and understand.'

But some aspects were a little too complicated for fans and detractors alike. Already the subject of an action which tried to ban him from performing in Canada on account of 'public incitement of hatred', Eminem was controversially nominated for a 2001 Grammy Award for the best-selling Marshall Mathers LP. (On that album's 'The Real Slim Shady', he had already feigned indifference with the words: 'You think I give a damn about a Grammy? Half you critics can't stomach me, let alone stand me.') Prior to the event, the Gay and Lesbian Alliance Against Defamation (GLAAD) announced they would form picket lines, and criticised the organisers for granting 'a high-profile platform for Eminem's messages of violence'. The rapper himself was berated for offering a negative role model to an audience 'largely comprised of adolescent boys beginning to form their adult attitudes towards gays'.

Emblematic of the whole Eminem controversy were the lyrics quoted in GLAAD's press statement, 'Kill You' and 'Criminal': combining sardonic awareness of his own public image ('Oh, now he's raping his own mother / abusing a whore / snorting coke / and we gave him the *Rolling Stone* cover'), wilful provocation ('My words are like a dagger with a jagged edge / That'll stab you in the head / whether you're a fag or lez'), and pure absurdity ('That's Dre with an AK to his face / Don't make me kill him too and spray his brains all over the place' – Dr. Dre being his friend and mentor). That Mathers' role-play of blue-collar brutalism

was dredged up from the atavistic depths of his own psyche and out of a sense of malicious fun, each element inextricable from the other, was no reassurance to the politically sensitive.

'No artist – hip-hop or otherwise – is making music as fresh and exciting', acknowledged Anthony DeCurtis in *Rolling Stone*. 'Eminem has galvanised his young audience, crossed racial boundaries in ground-breaking ways and displayed a charismatic star power all too absent from the music scene in recent years.' But DeCurtis, as a member of the National Academy of Recording Arts Sciences (NARAS), declared he would not be voting for his album: 'For Eminem to walk out onto that stage to claim the Album of the Year prize would tell the world that the music business is perfectly comfortable with the gratuitious victimisation of gays and women.' (At Sheffield University in England, which has no equivalent to the First Amendment's right to free speech, the student union banned Eminem's records from campus and the student radio station, forbidding their members to review his records in the college paper or wear promotional t-shirts. There, at least, the white rapper's music had made a full-fledged transition into 'thought-crime'.)

The president of NARAS, Michael Greene, tried to have it both ways: 'You have kids whose whole job in life is to find ways to piss their parents off. I think Eminem has done a spectacular job pissing just about everybody off. We certainly don't condone the message, but it is a curious situation when probably the most repugnant recording is also, in some ways, the most remarkable.' By the time the event took place at the Staples Center in Los Angeles, on 21 February, Greene had hit on a method of deflecting some of the heat. As invited by the Academy, 'faggot'-baiting Eminem would duet with an unlikely partner: Sir Elton John, British pop's pantomime dame. GLAAD were understandably bemused. 'John has played an enormous role in educating the world about Aids and gay issues through his music and charitable work', acknowledged a spokeswoman, while stressing, 'GLAAD is appalled that John would share a stage with Eminem.' Despite his status as a former GLAAD award winner, however, Elton John went right ahead – with two Los Angeles SWAT team members in tow to supplement his bodyguards. (It's not known whether extra precautions were due to PC hostility, or simply a guard against the madness that surrounds celebrity.)

Sir Elton had effortlessly jumped aboard the credibility train. 'I think there is far more humour in the [*Marshall Mathers*] album than people think', he observed. 'It appeals to my English black sense of humour' – conveniently forgetting some of the humourless reactions to Eminem in his homeland, and that Mathers originated from the nation that made 'sick humour' into an industry. Written support also came from fellow Grammys performer Madonna, who (signing herself 'Mrs. Ritchie') argued, slightly incoherently, 'Since when is offensive language a reason for being unpopular? I find the language of George W. [Bush] much more offensive.' (Although a friend of British conservative politicians, Mrs. Ritchie had an

unspecified problem with their counterparts back home.) More pointedly, she noted, 'I like the fact that Eminem is brash and angry and politically incorrect … He's stirring things up, he's provoking a discussion, he's making people's blood boil. He's reflecting what's going on in society right now.'

At the end of their duet – on Eminem's remarkable hit 'Stan', a rap narrative in which, in trademark Eminem style, the deranged fan-narrator's girlfriend is found dead in the trunk of his car – old Elton gave the young iconoclast a brief congratulatory hug. 'Of course I'd heard of Elton John', commented Mathers afterward, feeding the impression that the duet was a committee decision. 'I didn't know he was gay. I didn't know anything about his personal life.' Unlikely as this sounds, it should be remembered that Em an' Elton were a distinctly odd couple – not least because it's unlikely Eminem ever cared about Elton John one way or the other, much less gave any thought to his sexuality. But that, the rapper insisted, was not a problem. 'I think it made a statement in itself saying that he understood where I was coming from', Eminem told Kurt Loder of MTV. 'If I didn't make a statement with Elton John tonight, I don't know what else to do.'

Indeed, Antony DeCurtis had described how Mathers became frustrated when he tried to explain how, when he 'dissed' people as 'faggots', he wasn't actually attacking homosexuals. This may be strictly true – but his jibes about anal sex showed how the application of the word 'faggot' to straights was intended as the grossest insult imaginable. The sentiments were an accurate reflection of his blue-collar origins, the vernacular was authentic, but no one could prettify his attitude.

In the wake of the Grammys, Eminem's subsequent world tour (on police bail, awaiting prosecution for the summer 2000 gun incidents) met the now inevitable controversy. This time, however, it looked like pure showbiz. In Manchester, England, a police inspector studied video evidence to determine whether the rapper had really taken ecstasy on stage. According to the Eminem camp, however, the only thing their man was popping was chewing gum, and a stage-led chant encouraging the audience to take drugs was supposedly ironic. (Eminem, it can be argued, has placed the subject of drug use within a stronger moral context than many of his politically-correct detractors – his binges on weed and MDMA were not evangelised as having any great benefits, being simply a means of getting 'fucked up'. Most coldly realistic, the rap 'My Fault' describes the narrator talking a young woman into taking magic mushrooms, then watching with horror as she has a bad trip and becomes suicidal.)

The contradictions between Eminem's nihilist bad-boy image and the demands of stardom and fatherhood seemed to reach a compromise in the courtroom. On 10 April, 2001, Judge Antonio Viviano sentenced him to two years probation for carrying a concealed weapon – relating to the pistol-whipping of the barman. On 28 June, he was sentenced to a further concurrent year's probation by Judge Denise Langford Morris at a circuit court in Pontiac, Michigan, for threatening Insane Clown Posse crew member Douglas Dail with a handgun. In both cases, he pleaded no contest.

'I had suggestions from the public on a wide range of ideas', noted Judge Langford Morris. 'I received letters that said I should wash your mouth out with soap, make you write a clean song, or sentence you to life in prison.' Instead, she took the more lenient route, replicating the list of restrictions already imposed in April: total abstinence from alcohol; random tests for controlled substances; anger-management counselling; prohibition from ownership or use of firearms – any violations of which make him liable to a five-year sentence in state prison. 'The world is watching you', the judge reminded the young man who courted notoriety. 'Don't misstep. Don't fall down … Now is the time for you to please stand up', she deadpanned, quoting 'The Real Slim Shady'.

Dressed in conservative suit and studious-looking rimless spectacles for the first sentencing, Eminem expressed apparent relief that Judge Viviano 'treated me like any other human being'. 'He's impressed with the sentence of probation he received', attorney Walter Pisczatowski assured Judge Langford Morris two months later, promising her his client had 'worked hard to stay out of trouble' ever since. As to whether Eminem, who rapped about his hallucinogenic intake and swigged from a bottle of Bacardi onstage, could stay clear of booze and drugs, his lawyer insisted it could be taken as read.

Tellingly, the white-trash street poet has become both a caricature and a commodity – and a children's commodity at that. Eminem action doll figures were initially marketed in spring 2001, aimed at the unfeasibly young section of his audience. Based around his tri-schizoid personae – Slim Shady, Marshall Mathers, Eminem – the most controversial figure featured the transgressive white rapper in his recent overblown stage persona, wearing a hockey mask and wielding a chainsaw. While a Woolworth's spokesperson explained their refusal to stock it in their toy department ('having it around a Barbie doll, for example, didn't feel right'), the splatter-movie imagery of the stage show, complete with execution by electric chair, failed to achieved the level of outrage once reached by its progenitor, shock-rocker Alice Cooper, in the early 1970s.

But the outrage, real or manufactured, continues. Emblematic of the desire to have it all ways, Eminem's records are released in 'clean' versions for radio play and for those fans too young (some of them pre-teen) to escape parental disapproval. In January 2001, a Madison, Wisconsin radio station played the unedited version of 'The Real Slim Shady' and was subsequently fined $7,000 by the Federal Communications Commission; that following May a station in Pueblo, Colorado was fined the same amount by the same commission for playing the edited version of the same song. Eminem, whose popularity seems in direct proportion to his controversiality, has become an exceptional case who receives little benefit of the doubt. It was left to Russell Simmons, co-founder of Def Jam Records, to complain, 'The hip-hop community – no, all of America – should be outraged at this blatant act of censorship on our brother Eminem.'

Not Thor, the Norse god of thunder, but Varg Vikernes of Burzum. Vikernes exceeded his pagan posturing by murdering his friend Euronymous in August 1993. Now serving 21 years, he has become a cult figure.

The question of freedom of speech did not test the Australians who protested against Eminem's July 2001 concerts in Sydney and Melbourne. Religious and conservative pressure groups, self-appointed representatives of the nation that descended from British convicts, insisted this was one little criminal they would not accept. 'I call him a preacher of hate', accused one religious leader; Prime Minister John Howard stepped into the fray, asserting that Eminem's lyrics 'demeaned women and encouraged violence', while Liberal Party politician Peter Slipper illiberally suggested, 'What someone should do is lock him up in a mental institution and throw away the key.' Whatever the probationary restrictions on his behaviour, there is no going back for Eminem. His career will continue to be defined as much by those who despise him as by his admirers.

In the early 1990s a new wave of metal bands were happy to confirm Christian fundamentalist accusations that they were earthly agents of the Dark One (unlike heavy metal progenitors Black Sabbath, and their unpretentious admission, 'The nearest we ever got to black magic was a box of chocolates.')

The label given to the first wave of satanic metallists was 'death metal', which encapsulated the moribidity of a form that jettisoned much of its rhythm 'n' blues heritage for a wailing, cacophonous celebration of death and violence. One Florida-based band actually took the name Deicide – 'the murder of God'. Their leader, wild-eyed/wild-haired Glen Benton, is a Bible Belt preacher's nightmare: inverted cross burnt into the middle of his forehead; glaring eyes made more intense by smoking vast quantities of weed. Dedicated to 'Lord Satan', he professed to loathe Christians.

Deicide's music consisted of wailing, sometimes unlistenable paeans to pain – as if the promise of a really bad time was enough to recruit someone to Devil worship. Their leader's regime of worship also included the torture and killing of small animals (mostly in his rural Florida habitat), which he boasted about in numerous interviews. Why Old Nick required such sacrifices is unclear, but Judgement Day almost came for Glen Benton on a European tour in 1992: after he received death threats from a fanatical group called the Animal Rights Militia, a bomb exploded at a Stockholm venue during a set by the support act (Gorefest, whose name very nearly became more apt than anticipated). Next, convinced their idol's satanic utterances called for action rather than nodding approval, a small group of high school-age fans styling themselves the 'Lords of Chaos' committed a rapidly

Pushing all the right buttons: blasphemy, sex, blood. Is it any wonder that Cradle of Filth – whose Desire *album cover is seen here – are the most popular band in black metal?*

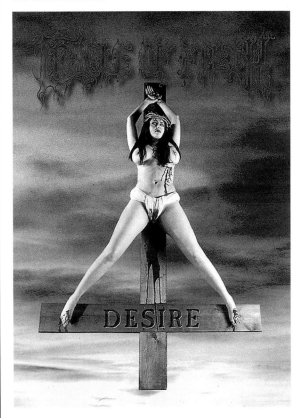

escalating series of crimes. Starting with arson attacks on a supermarket trailer, a Baptist church and a bird aviary they worked up to the shotgun murder of one of their schoolteachers. Arresting officers claimed the boys were planning to don cartoon-character costumes at Disneyland in order to shoot 'black tourists with silenced handguns'. Deicide would neither support nor condemn the kids when they were apprehended, and the whole thing might have been written off as a freak incident of teenage maladjustment – except that similar criminal campaigns were enacted in metal's new European heartlands over the next few years.

Deicide went on to plow a lonely furrow, upstaged in terms of outrage and controversy many times over. Glen Benton had pause for thought about his original pledge to commit suicide at 33, a plan perversely based on not wanting to live longer than the Christian Messiah he claims to despise. Having subsequently dismissed his plan as 'ridiculous', he is left to ponder how an antichrist deals with the onset of middle-age.

In northern Europe, particularly the chilly lands of Scandinavia, satanic metal music mutated into a new form. Slower than frenetic thrash metal, more coherent than the growled, slurred lyrics of death metal, black metal was so named in reflection of its content: 'black' in terms of bleak outlook and the 'black arts' of the occult. Black metal philosophy, such as it was, simplistically adhered to the forces of 'darkness' against 'light', with 'light' construed as any vaguely positive element of life, be it love, light-hearted frivolity or racial tolerance. In fact, several young bands at the heart of the Norwegian scene, collectively known as 'the Black Metal Circle', would engage in a criminal campaign similar in futility to that of the 'Lords of Chaos': mainly a series of arson attacks and acts of vandalism against Norwegian churches – several of them historically significant buildings – but sometimes escalating to murder.

On 10 August 1993 one of the Inner Circle, Euronymous (real name Oystein Aarseth) of the band Mayhem was murdered by black metal comrade Count Grishnackh (real name, ironically, Christian Vikernes) of Burzum. ('I actually had to knock the knife out, it was stuck in his skull,' an unconcerned Vikernes later recalled in court.) The murder had little to do with the Black Metal Circle's campaign of anti-Christian desecration. It seems instead to have been the outcome of bickering about money, and which of the two puny young men was the biggest, hardest satanist. Nevertheless, it instantly placed the Burzum leader among a misfit contingent of imprisoned Norwegian black metallists: Faust, the drummer of Emperor, was jailed for a lenient 14 years for the murder of a gay man who propositioned him in a park, while Fenriz, the drummer of Darkthrone, was sent down for his part in the arson campaign (boasting that the Black Metal Circle were 'music's answer to the IRA').

Black metal terrorism hit Britain in 1994, when the native band Necropolis copied the church-vandalism campaign of their Norse brethren. Covering their faces with black and white 'death paint', armed with swords, scythes and other medieval weapons, they lived out destructive fantasies in several churches and eight graveyards, at an estimated cost of £100,000. Brought to book in Tunbridge Wells, Kent, one of the bedrocks of British conservatism, they received harsher sentences than the Norwegians (who benefited from the liberalism they loudly despised) at two-and-a-half years apiece.

Given the brevity of Norwegian prison sentences, Fenriz was soon pounding the black metal beat again. In 1994, his band issued a press release about their album Transilvanian Hunger, whose nonsensical racist crux was that anyone who dared criticise the record should be 'patronized for their obviously Jewish behaviour'. Darkthrone, who had previously spoken about their mission to 'spread the glories of fascism', backslid with less than diabolical fervour when their burblings were perceived as neo-Nazi in tone. 'We were as shocked as anyone else', ran an aggrieved press release. 'None of our albums have ever contained any racism, fascism or Nazi slant at all.' The former iconoclasts of the Black Metal Circle hastily agreed to a commercial compromise whereby their UK distributors (Peaceville) would release the album without promoting or advertising it. (They were later dropped by the label.)

In the interim, the re-named 'Varg' Vikernes (Norwegian for wolf, ideologically preferable to his given 'Christian') had become a bizarre Scandinavian youth cult figure, partly on the grounds of his unapologetic neo-Nazism. Sentenced to 21 years (the maximum term under Norwegian law) for the murder of his friend Euronymous, he enjoyed the lenient prison conditions that allowed him to continue to compose on guitar and keyboard in his cell. Still recording as Burzum, his melancholic, dirge-like compositions, distributed by a handful of specialists, are said to reflect his Norse racial and cultural heritage. (Vikernes is no longer a satanist but has gone back to ancient Viking paganism, worshipping Odin and the other Norse Gods.) He also rejects the blues base that even the most ham-fisted metal musician starts from, dismissing the influence of Robert Johnson and his descendants as 'primitive, degenerate, subhuman … nigger music' like some old Bible Belt preacher. Hellhammer, the drummer of Mayhem (still extant despite the deaths of Euronymous and one other member named, sublimely, Dead) agreed: 'We don't like black people. Black metal is for white people.'

'You see the photos of these guys and they all look really tough and really scary', one British black metallist (who declined to be identified) told rock journalist Steven Wells. 'Most of them are these skinny little Norwegian guys who've never even seen more than a couple of black people in their lives … Take any one of these guys and put them in a Washington DC housing project at midnight on a Friday and we'll see just how much their satanism is going to protect them.'

By the late 1990s, however, the dying embers of the black metal murders still occasionally ignited. In July 1997 Jon Nodtveidt, vocalist of Dissection, was convicted, alongside a man claiming to lead something called the 'Misanthropic Luciferian Order', of murdering an Algerian immigrant in Oslo. Black metal had by then become a less fanatical, more theatrical staple of the underground rock scene (perhaps, as its enthusiasts contend, the only genuine underground rock music extant). Most prominent among the subculture were the British band Cradle of Filth – a quintet of leather-and-studs rockers complimenting their grinding Black Sabbath riffs and cacophonic wails with Hammer horror appeal. Their fan-club accoutrements include a wilfully provocative black T-shirt bearing the legend, 'Jesus is a Cunt'.

Demonstrating how easily shock-rock is absorbed into a fragmented marketplace, in 1998 the BBC invited the band to take the concerned mother of a 19-year-old fan along with them on a five day tour in France. ('He's driving me demented', testified fifty something Janet Robinson, 'with all these screaming noises.') With some degree of dissent within the band, Living with the Enemy filmed the worried mum in her best rock-chick clothes, arguing against the black metallists she believed were stealing her son's soul.

'Cradle of Filth are getting away with things that in the 1600s they would have been burned at the stake for', bemoaned Janet, who clearly saw the end of the witch trials as a retrograde step. 'I think that for every person who wears that T-shirt out on the streets, Cradle of Filth should be fined £10,000. And that nun on the front masturbating [on a separate design, 'Vestal Masturbation'] … that is horrible.' Despite her feeling that she was taking on the might of the Antichrist himself, gothic pixie vocalist Dani Devey seemed concerned that a fan's mother should not walk away with the wrong idea: 'Do you perform necrophilia?' asked Janet earnestly. 'I might shag me girlfriend when she's asleep,' conceded Devey. At the end of the BBC's film, Dani had a few quiet words offscreen with Janet before the worried mum returned to give her final verdict. Still dubious about their whole schtick, she managed to concede that the Filth were nice boys after all.

Cradle Of Filth still promoted old-fashioned bad-boy behaviour in public. At the 1998 Kerrang! magazine awards, they felt free to verbally abuse their award presenter, 'society' girl Tara Palmer-Tomkinson. At the end of that same year, they were put under arrest by the Vatican police in Rome on account of Devey wearing a sacrilegious T-shirt: not 'JC is a C', but the less provocative 'I Love Satan'. Though they initially held them at sub-machine gunpoint, the God squad let them go when it turned out they were just a wacky English rock band. Cradle of Filth's 'satanism' is fed by the imagery of classic gothic horror stories and movies, as any perusal of their lyrics or website shows. Their need to offend the pious seems to start from the premise of 'How would Count Dracula act if he was around today and brim-full of rock'n'roll attitude?' – all in the name of fun.

Back in the USA, the dark side of rock'n'roll can still reassure its audience that there's life in the worn-out old beast yet. In an era that seems to have seen everything, the urge to cause outrage reached back to the dark tail-end of the sixties for inspiration. Guns N' Roses, the late eighties'/early nineties' most successful recyclers of cock-rock clichés, hit the headlines with a track from an obscurely-titled covers album *The Spaghetti Incident?* The offending cut, 'Look at Your Game Girl', was a seemingly innocuous song which had in fact, been composed by hippie gang-leader turned life prisoner and self-styled philosopher, Charles Manson. In its original form, 'Look at Your Game' is a track from Lie, the album of Manson recordings released by 'the Family' to help fund their legal defence.

Negative publicity attracted the attention of a victims' rights group fronted by Patty Tate, sister of Sharon Tate, the pregnant Hollywood actress murdered by the Manson Family. Vocalist Axl Rose and his fellow bad boys capitulated immediately to criticism that they were seeking to profit from a convicted murderer's notoriety, sending a royalties cheque for $72,000 to the son of Voytek Frykowski, another victim murdered during the Tate massacre.

The belief that Manson is a wrongly imprisoned poet-rock star grew enormously in the USA as the millennium approached. Typical of this tendency is a rapper calling himself Evil Jared Hasselhoff of the Bloodhound Gang, one of rap-metal's 'sports-jock' outfits. Hasselhoff included Manson among his heroes: 'He didn't really kill anyone! Is it a crime to suggest that maybe someone should go and do it and maybe suggest where they should go and do it and when they should do it and give 'em a knife to go and do it with but not actually do it yourself? That's not a crime!'

In fact, while he was absent from the Tate massacre, the next evening Manson took his young followers to the house of Rosemary and Leno LeBianca, where he tied the couple up at gunpoint and sent his 'family' into the room to kill them. This is a crime, and it's called murder – as was Manson's shooting of ranch-hand 'Shorty' Shea.

Trent Reznor – the man who is effectively Nine Inch Nails – even recorded his powerful 1994 album The Descending Spiral at a makeshift studio at 10050 Cielo Drive, Beverly Hills, the house where Sharon Tate and her friends were butchered on 8 August 1969. The performer's claim that he was not initially aware of the history of his recording venue is difficult to swallow: 'We had one day to look for a place, and it was just the coolest house … And then, at the end of the night, I heard it was, like, *the house* … I wasn't thinking in terms of press or anything like that …' (Very soon after the recording of *The Downward Spiral*, 10050 Cielo Drive was purchased by a buyer who put a demolition order on the building, levelling it to dust. Rumour suggested the deal was set up on behalf of Roman Polanski, the film-director widower of Sharon Tate, now a legal exile in Paris.)

Famously, the Manson Family claimed (though their former leader denied it) to have studied the Beatles' *White Album* for 'messages', and splashed 'Piggy' on the walls in the victim's blood in reference to the track 'Piggies' from the album. Reznor was forced to concur that the same theme featured in his own compositions, but denied a deliberate link with Manson. ''Piggy' was written before I was even in California. And it wasn't, in my mind, in any way about the murders. "March of the Pigs" was formulated there, but not consciously about killing Sharon Tate. I guess I just used that word generically, as a metaphor for people I don't like … '

With Manson a more powerfully provocative figure than ever, musicians who jumped on the Family bandwagon included grunge band the Lemonheads, who featured his 'Your Home is Where You're Happy' on their debut – and, most overtly, a Florida industrial-metal band who christened themselves Marilyn Manson after two great American icons (Monroe and Charlie). The band also included an adaptation of Manson's song 'Mechanical Man', entitled 'My Monkey', on their debut album *Portrait of an American Family*. The album was recorded, in the aftermath of *The Descending Spiral*, at the Tate massacre house under

The Man That You Fear: cynical shock rocker Marilyn Manson has recycled middle-America's nightmares. Delusional beliefs that his stage shows were a front for sex rituals and murder were actively encouraged.

the auspices of Trent Reznor.

Despite their trendy nineties nihilism, Marilyn Manson presented an old-fashioned image. Eschewing the take-me-as-you-find-me ethos of grunge, they appeared as slap-painted glam-rock stars in the mold of *Ziggy Stardust*-era Bowie or early Alice Cooper, except that, in the Mansons' case, the androgyny was layered with hints of deviation that made bisexuality seem tame. (The band's frontman, a former resident of Florida, was inspired by his ambition to surpass the outrage of local porn-rap band 2 Live Crew.) As with Alice Cooper, the name was simultaneously that of the band and the artiste who fronted it (thin six-foot-six-inch Brian Warner to his mother).

The Mansons' policy of cultivated outrage earned the ire of Middle America and the rapt attention of her teenagers. A good few degrees smarter and more cynical than the death/black metal bands that preceded him, Marilyn himself was an ordained minister of the Church of Satan. While his conjuring with blasphemy and the occult could be relied upon to elicit sanctimonious outrage, his 'satanic church' was basically a misanthropic glee club that enjoyed going against the social grain. It would indulge in sacrilegious rituals, with a willing young woman as the naked, fleshly 'altar', but had no more belief in a corporeal Devil than in a blasphemed God. 'I'm a member of the Church of Satan,' confirmed Manson, 'and I'm still a member of St Paul's Catholic Church in Ohio, my main influence and something I've never officially left.' (The late Church of Satan founder, Anton LaVey, once described his brand of satanism as the next logical step after Catholic ritual.)

Allegations of what occurred at a Marilyn Manson concert reached surrealistic levels, as if entering a concert auditorium was to enter Hades itself. Anonymous signed affidavits and a telephone hot-line run by a conservative group called the Gulf Coast American Family Association claimed that the onstage orgy featured genuine rape, bestiality, coprophagia (eating of feces) and vomiting over fans, and that those animals not being sexually abused by Manson and his band (principally puppydogs and chickens) were sacrificed. Most incredibly, perhaps, the band were supposed to spend their concert revenue on maintaining a team called by Manson his 'private Santa Clauses', which selflessly distributed free marijuana and cocaine to the audience. Most disturbingly, according to one 'eyewitness' allegation, 'I witnessed Manson call for the virgin sacrifice, in which all the children in the concert arena are pushed forward by the crowd to be dedicated to Satan.' (As the singer himself put it, 'How can someone actually believe that I could be involved in something like that and I wouldn't be in prison?') One council member in the small town of Utica, New York State, confirmed she had received 'firsthand accounts that there are satanic altar calls, live homosexual acts on the stage, and he [Manson] would call up girls on the stage and do something vulgar with his fist'. The barbarians were at the gates of Middle America.

The band's cynical frontman professed himself flattered by the hysteria: 'I never dispel rumours,' he confirmed, 'because people can believe what they want.' Indeed, on the Internet new myths had been propagated by Manson's fans: how their hero had one rib removed so that he could perform oral sex on himself, and even how he was building up to a piéce de resistance, to be killed 'live' onstage.

Manson gave the audience as much calculated outrage as he could likely get away with, then let their imaginations and the rumour mill do the rest. He had twice been arrested for indecent exposure onstage (though charges were dropped), and one legendary instance of him fellating (or pretending to fellate) a musician onstage mutated into the legend that he gave Trent Reznor a full-on blowjob in public view. The owner of Squeeze, the Florida club where Marilyn Manson and the Spooky Kids (as they were then billed) debuted, confirmed this sleight-of-hand: 'It's an illusion. People see what they want to see … He [Manson] had a girl named Terry tied to the cross and semi-naked at a show here, and when everybody left, [they] were saying she was totally naked and her throat was cut.'

Eventually, however, the deliberate outrage got out of hand and became self-destructive. On the band's 'Dead to the World' tour to promote their second album, the pivotal *Antichrist Superstar*, kneejerk legislation was passed by several community councils to stop Marilyn Manson performing in their town. The state of Carolina simply offered the band $40,000 to go away. As many as 60 tour dates were threatened with bombing by bible-bashers worked up into a lather over all they had read and heard. 'We've lost 20 per cent of ticket sales across the board,' claimed band manager Tony Ciulla, 'from parents telling their kids not to see Marilyn Manson. And hotels – when they find out who we are – cancel our reservations.' In order to survive the unreal, media-fed madness that is modern America, Marilyn Manson half-conceded defeat by calling in high-powered attorney Paul Cambria, the man who ensured that Larry Flynt, controversial publisher of porn mag *Hustler*, remained under the constitutional protection of the First Amendment. 'We've put [town authorities] on notice that we're going to pursue all the remedies, damages – the works,' confirmed Cambria, cutting through all the myth-manipulation and getting down to business.

One of the few features of the 'Dead To The World' tour to escape condemnation by the Christian tendency was a parody of a Nuremberg rally. In black suit and tie, performing before a lightning symbol that resembled both the SS logo, and the streak painted across Bowie's face on the cover of *Aladdin Sane*, MM roused the crowd to fever pitch while appearing to read from – and eventually tear the pages from – *The Holy Bible*. Interestingly, the Mansons were not keen to export this part of the act wholesale for the European leg of the tour, and dropped the directly Hitlerian trap-

The disadvantages of being an Antichrist Superstar. After the appalling Columbine High School massacre of April 1999, where 15 died, the press found a ready scapegoat in Marilyn Manson.

Trenchcoat Mafioso:
EVERETT TRUE

BLOOD ON HIS HANDS?

After the Colorado school massacre, the world's media was quick to point the finger of blame at the killers' idol MARILYN MANSON. But can the 'God of F*' really be held responsible?**

IS Marilyn Manson really the most dangerous man in rock?

On April 20, the 110th anniversary of Adolf Hitler's birth, Eric Harris and Dylan Klebold, two Littleton, Colorado students went on a killing spree at Columbine High School which ended with 15 people dead, including themselves. One of the pair owned a KMFDM baseball cap (KMFDM are a German, Seattle-based goth-industrial group who deal in violent, misanthropic imagery and whose final album, "Adios", coincidentally came out the same day). Much more important to the self-righteous American and world-wide media, however, was the fact that both members of the now-infamous Trenchcoat Mafia were known to be fond of "cross-dressing, long-haired, tattooed Satanist" Marilyn Manson's records.

The Antichrist Superstar had struck again – or had he?

MANSON has long been the favourite scapegoat for certain sections of the US media. There are Christian websites on the Net dedicated to exposing the "Satanic menace of Marilyn Manson", and he's the number one nemesis of the American Family Association. (A favour he returns, incidentally, calling Christian America, "the biggest Satan of all".) The singer has been accused of inspiring fans to commit suicide, and legal bids have failed to ban his concerts.

After a 17-year-old Manson fan was accused of stabbing a 14-year-old girl in Texas in 1997, a local group held regular Manson "awareness seminars". Numerous colourful rumours abound about the "creepy, charismatic lord of disorder" – he was supposed to have masturbated a dog on video, simulated sex onstage (including one time where a six-year-old in a cage sang, while a naked girl cavorted nearby) and "worse". Manson's abuse and ritual humiliation of fans backstage are near legendary (in his autobiography, "The Long Hard Road Out Of Hell", he boasts of "examination" and strangulation techniques).

His stage show features arson, self-mutilation and crucified girls – at a recent Seattle show, he even tried to stage an elaborate hoax to have himself assassinated from the audience. His lyrics preach negativity, violence, disillusionment with modern-day society, with a self-

righteous, semi-ironic, "the world owes me a living" tone which only a child of America's pampered middle class could add. It's all play, of course – dark theatre. But do you think the guardians of morality in late-20th-century America – or even some of Manson's own fans – are aware of that? You've got to be joking.

BORN Brian Warner to a Vietnam vet in Canton, Ohio, in 1969, Marilyn likes to portray his past as being. . . hell. In his book, he claims he was abused by older boys, and he was nearly suffocated by an intruder in the family home when he was eight years old – leading to later problems with narcolepsy.

According to Manson, even before he was born, the odds were stacked against him: his dad was sprayed with Agent Orange, a defoliant known to have caused birth defects among soldiers' offspring, he also had to have his urethra enlarged because he couldn't piss properly and his fanatical Christian teachers constantly warned him against the imminent Apocalypse.

His formal introduction to sex was Grandpa Jack's collection of bestiality and enema mags. His way out of the situation was to listen to a lot of metal records – Judas Priest, Queensryche, Black Sabbath – and to start studying art (Manson claimed he was expelled from his religious school for stealing money out of girls' purses during prayer).

Shortly after Manson completed his education at Glenoak High School, his parents moved to southern Florida. He soon became embroiled in the local death-metal scene, and even began a fledgling career as a music journalist, reviewing shows in local magazines. By about 1990, Warner had hooked up with his future band-mates and – all of them taking the abridged names of serial killers as their new identities – started gigging.

FAR from being abashed by the controversy he excites from Christian organisations like the American Family Association, Manson positively encourages it. A master media manipulator, the singer is well aware that his fans revel in the distrust he generates among their parents' generation. In this, he is merely following the time-worn tradition of rock'n'roll – each generation has always sought

to alienate the previous, from Presley onwards, via the Rolling Stones, Sex Pistols and mid-Eighties rap groups. Manson has never, ever sought to discourage that antipathy. Until now, perhaps.

"I have been asked to comment by numerous news organisations on the Colorado school tragedy," a statement on his behalf the day after the killings read. "It's tragic and disgusting any time young people's lives are taken in an act of senseless violence. My condolences go out to the students and their families."

(This statement is actually an echo of a previous comment made when he was asked how he'd react if a fan were to do something "tragically stupid" after listening to his music: "If someone were to kill themselves or somebody else," Manson explained, "that would just go to show how ignorant people were raised.")

WHAT a wuss! You'd think The God Of F*** – the 6ft 6 transvestite who's never been shy of espousing his hatred for the outside world – would welcome a little blood shed by some of his followers. But no, it seems some things are beyond the pale, even for America's self-styled Most Evil Man. Or maybe it's just that the witch-hunt is threatening to hurt sales? (Witness also the way Manson changed his goth image circa 1996's "Antichrist Superstar" to that of an end-of-the-world glam rocker on last year's "Mechanical Animals", after the first tour was met by protests almost every step of the way.)

You see, when Manson is instructing his audience to salute him Nazi-style, or boasting about how he once tried to burn his girlfriend's house down with her in it ("The Long Hard Road Out Of Hell"), it's all just an ironic game – a pose.

"Kids today are so desensitised, it's almost impossible to shock them," he once said, before going all-out to try. When Manson's singing "AntiChrist Superstar" or "The Irresponsible Hate Anthem", however, he's being sarcastic – playing upon society's deepest fears in the way art has always sought to do. He's nothing but a shock-rocker, the Nineties version of Alice Cooper, David Bowie (who flirted with fascism a lot more heavily than Manson, truth be known) and Kiss. Clearly, his music has no bearing on real life – his followers are much too clever to take darkly ironic proclamations like "Kill God, Kill Mom & Dad, Kill Yourself" (a shortened version of a T-shirt slogan) and "I want to f*** you, Daddy" seriously. Right?

SO is Marilyn Manson the most dangerous, subversive man in rock, or simply an amoral, selfish prick who played too much Dungeons & Dragons at school, and got f***ed up by a rigorous Christian education? Right enough, the message he preaches is deeply misanthropic, but consider this.

The week after the Columbine High School tragedy occurred, both the National Rifle Association (the most vocal of all America's pro-gun lobbies – they've even appeared in court to overturn laws designed to stop criminals from buying guns) and Marilyn Manson were due to appear in Denver, mere miles away from Littleton. Marilyn Manson's show has been cancelled. The NRA conference hasn't.

One million American students are estimated to carry guns to school. You can buy a pipe bomb – similar to the ones killers Eric Harris and Dylan Klebold planted – for just $2 on the Net.

And it's a f*** of a lot easier to kill someone using a gun than using a record.

FROM ERIC HARRIS' SUICIDE NOTE

By now, it's over. If you are reading this, my mission is complete. I have finished revolutionising the neo-euphoric infliction of my internal terror.

Your children who have ridiculed me, who have chosen not to accept me, who have treated me like I am not worth their time are dead. THEY ARE DEAD.

Surely you will try to blame it on the clothes I wear, the music I listen to or the way I choose to present myself – but no. Do not hide behind my choices. You need to face the fact that this comes as a result of YOUR CHOICES.

Parents and teachers f*** you up. You have taught these kids to be gears (sic) and sheep. To think and act like those who came before them, to not accept what is different. YOU ARE IN THE WRONG. . .

pings for fear of misinterpretation – as if every scream-ing kid or condemnatory authority in the US really understood what they were saying. ('People assume that I'm stupid,' Manson complained. 'They think that I don't know that rock'n'roll is as fascist as Christianity.')

More controversies were in store for Manson. In spring 1999 a joint tour with Hole, the band fronted by Kurt Cobain's in-your-face widow Courtney Love, was quickly aborted. Opening to an audience of Manson fans largely uninterested in Hole, Love felt upstaged by Manson's outrageous antics. Pulling out of the tour, she sacked the group's management then sued them for subjecting the band to 'public ridicule' for booking them into the tour, as if she had had no inkling of the nature of the beast. 'I think that in a strange way I respect her,' said Manson, damning with very faint praise, 'because she's just so ridiculous and she's managed to make a career out of that.'

Within a short time, however, Marilyn Manson had bigger problems on their hands. On 20 April 1999, two young men – Eric Harris, 18, and Dylan Klebold, 17 – set off to their high school in Littleton, near Denver, Colorado. They had long planned this to be their final day of school, and, indeed, their final day of life. Alienated from the sports-loving, conventional, white-bread mainstream of an American high school, these two had found solace in a group known from their dress as the 'Trenchcoat Mafia'. Under their coats that day Harris and Klebold concealed a small arsenal of firearms and explosives. Fond of anti-mainstream music and esoterica collected from the Internet, they had long been taunted as geeks or, worse, as 'goths' by the school 'jocks'. With the boys adhering to what has become almost an American tradition of pupils inflict-ing a 'payback day' on their schools, the ensuing Columbine High School massacre was remarkable in the scale of its tragedy, rather than in the nature of what occurred. By the time a SWAT team stormed the school building (delaying their rescue operation for hours for fear of pipe-bomb boobytraps), 15 people lay dead – 12 of the killers' classmates, one teacher, and the boys themselves, who had shot each other in an act of shared suicide. The criterion for choosing victims had been arbitrary and childish: 'You're going to die if you are the wrong colour, wearing a hat or do blade sports,' one of the adolescent murderers gleefully told a schoolmate.

The two boys had lived out their fantasies on the Internet before enacting them in real life. The Trenchcoat Mafia website, accessed by kindred souls, had already made cryptic promises about 'Preparin' for the big April 20!! You'll all be sorry that day!' Significantly for the two young fantasists, the date was the 110th anniversary of Hitler's birth. Ironically, the main hate objects of these young wannabe-Nazis were the jocks who bullied them – robust, athletic types the Führer might have idealised as examples of Aryan manhood (apart from the few black kids who, ironical-ly, were also despised by outsiders Klebold and Harris). Eric Harris' final act before setting off for school that day was to post some lyrics from Seattle-

based industrial band KMFDM on the website. (20 April was also the release date of the band's final album, *Adios*, KMFDM having split that spring.) Voguishly misanthropic, the band's initials purported-ly stood for the German phrase *Kein Mitleid fur die Mehrheit*: 'no pity for the masses'. In the immediate aftermath of the tragedy, unaware of the pair's self-destruction, one of the 'regular kids' at the school told of how they 'sing Marilyn Manson songs and joke about killing people. They're into Nazis. They take pride in Hitler. They're really, really creepy.' That one phrase pushed the mass-media's buttons: they had an instant target who, it seemed, personified exactly what went wrong at Littleton that day.

Self-professed experts were quick to express their views. Dr Carl Raschke, professor of religious studies at the University of Denver, stated, 'It appears you have a bunch of kids who've been into black metal music – Marilyn Manson – who basically have apoca-lyptic fantasies and a heavy code of neo-Nazism.' Which all seems valid, until one considers that indus-trial-gothic rock superstar Manson had nothing to do with the black metal underground. Michigan Senator Dale Shugars had been studying the Manson phenom-enon, and had at least taken the trouble to attend a concert in his home state. 'We're having an alarming rate of killings in schools. I'd say that though they're not all to be blamed on a shock entertainer like Marilyn Manson, I think he promotes it and can be part of the blame.' In an uncomfortable coincidence, Manson was due to play a concert in the nearby Denver suburb of Morrison on 30 April. The Mayor of Denver demanded it be cancelled, and the band rea-sonably acceded.

Such reasoning may not seem so far-fetched in a land where defence attorneys tried to lay the blame for a 14-year-old boy shooting his teacher and two school-mates dead in Washington on grunge-rock band Pearl Jam's song 'Jeremy' which is itself based on a similar true-life tragedy. (The boy had actually been trauma-tised by the recent separation of his parents and the aftermath, in which his mother threatened to tie up her estranged husband and his girlfriend and shoot herself dead in front of them.) Similarly, after the horrific murder in 1995 of 15-year-old Elyse Marie Pahler in San Luis Obispo, California, by three disturbed teenagers, her parents attempted civil litigation against the perpetrators' favourite band, original death-metal group Slayer. Prosecutors at the trial of the young murderers claimed that Elyse had been chosen as a human sacrifice to 'earn a ticket to Hell', inspired by lyrics such as 'Virgin child now drained of life / Your soul cannot be free' from Slayer's 'Necrophiliac'.

Distressingly, the Pahlers' pursuit of Slayer has become a long-running saga which can only intensify their agony. Their civil suit against the band and Sony Records (distributor of their record label) finally came to court in December 2000, after the judicial and appeal process for each of the boys (all of whom pleaded guilty to murder and received 25-years-to-life) had been exhausted. Despite the parents' contention that Slayer's lyrics had instructed the young perpetrators how to 'stalk, rape, torture, murder and commit acts of necrophilia' on Elyse, the case was promptly thrown out by a judge who cited the First Amendment: 'There's not a legal position that could be taken that would make Slayer responsible for the girl's death. Where do you draw the line?'

But that was not the end. The family have appealed for the case to be heard by a higher court, and are currently seeking damages via a California business law that forbids the marketing to minors of 'harmful' and 'obscene' material. According to their argument, the PMRC's 'Parental Advisory' stickers merely acted as incentive for the young teenagers to obtain the band's albums. 'They don't care whether the violent, misogynistic message in these lyrics causes children to do harmful things', accused David Pahler of Slayer. 'They couldn't care less what their fans did to our daughter.' The Pahlers' personal loss and pain is immense, and can only be sympathised with. However, their campaign to achieve closure (to coin a cliché) by locating the killers' pathology in death-metal lyrics, with their crude gothic-horror imagery, can only serve to muddy the issue of personal responsibility.

In the aftermath of the Columbine massacre, fingers also briefly pointed at *The Basketball Diaries*, a film of 1997 starring Leonardo DiCaprio that was based on the autobiography of rock'n'roll junkie Jim Carroll, writer of the ultimate death-rock song, 'People Who Died'. The film contains a heroin dream-fantasy wherein the teenage anti-hero shoots dead his teacher and a number of classmates after producing a machine gun from under a long black leather trenchcoat. (Parents of children killed in a similar but smaller-scale school massacre to Columbine in Kentucky were already trying to sue the film's producers.)

But there was something especially hysterical in the rush to pillory Manson – implicit in a London *Daily Telegraph* headline entitled 'Violent sub-world fed by sadistic rock and films', which, though it was headed by a captioned picture of the performer, made no mention of him in its analysis of the boys' purported cultural influences. Other headlines placed the Antichrist

superstar at the heart of the cause of the carnage: 'Shock rocker who filled pair with a thrill to kill'; 'Rock king of evil the kids adore'; 'Killers worshipped rock freak Manson ("Evil is good" he says)'.

Ironically, the only voice that dismissed accusations against the star was that of one of the two deceased murderers: 'Your children who have ridiculed me,' raged Eric Harris in the suicide note posted on his website, 'who have chosen not to accept me … They are dead … Surely you will try to blame it on the clothes I wear, the music I listen to or the way I choose to present myself, but no. Do not hide behind my choices.' Typically, the murderer held his victims responsible for their own deaths, but he at least did not try to present rock lyrics or doggerel as justification for his acts.

Manson's considered response came in early June – entitled 'Columbine: Whose Fault Is It?' – on the Internet, and in *Rolling Stone*. Its rambling eloquence challenged a few of the more damning assumptions: 'America puts killers on the cover of *Time* magazine, giving them as much notoriety as our favourite movie stars', announced the performer who named his stage persona after Charles Manson. (Now claiming that this was a 'criticism' of the media's hypocrisy.) 'I remember hearing the initial reports from Littleton, that Harris and Klebold were wearing makeup and were dressed like Marilyn Manson … These two idiots weren't wearing makeup, and they weren't dressed like me or like goths. Since Middle America has not heard the music they did listen to (KMFDM and Rammstein, among others), the media picked something they thought was similar. Responsible journalists have reported with less publicity that Harris and Klebold were not Marilyn Manson fans – that they even disliked my music.' While this ignores the schoolmate's remark about the killers' favourite songs, which may have been a misconception, Manson went on to say that whether or not they were fans of himself or the industrial bands, music did not offer a rationale for the murders. Admitting that he had, after all, accepted the role of America's 'Antichrist', which made him a volunteer for scapegoating, Manson ended on the valid point that 'the National Rifle Association is far too powerful to take on, so most people choose Doom [the computer game, a genuine favourite of the killers], *The Basketball Diaries* or yours truly.'

In the aftermath of Columbine, Marilyn Manson has reconstituted himself as the elder statesman of shock-rock. Free to play with fire again, he warned in an Internet address of summer 20000 that 'for each critic or skeptical fan that casts harsh words of hatred or misunderstanding upon my change [of image, the latest variation on a theme], remember those words always come back … Sometimes with insults, sometimes with fists and sometimes with guns'. Earlier, he stated in *Rolling Stone* that 'guns exemplify man and his other limb that he wasn't born with, that he felt a need to create'. This would form part of the theme of his subsequent 'Guns, God and Government' tour, even though Manson stressed, while posing with a

MAC 10 submachine gun, that he was not enamoured of America's love affair with firearms at all. As for government, on the eve of the US presidential election in November 2000 he raised some eyebrows by attacking pragmatic liberal-cum-conservative Bill Clinton for 'fucking America in the ass with his communist cock'. His bitterness sprang, it seems, from Democratic Vice-President Al Gore's choice of a running mate in God-fearing Senator Joseph Leiberman, who was vocal in his attacks on Marilyn Manson as 'perhaps the sickest act ever promoted by a mainstream record company' (though, as they were signed by Trent Reznor's small subsidiary, Nothing Records, that was debatable). Offers to give his support to marginally victorious Republican candidate George W. Bush were politely declined by Bush's office, with some bemusement.

The release of Manson's *Holy Wood* album that same month saw business as usual. Controversy was caused by a Goya-esque cover painting of Manson as the crucified Christ, his face missing its lower jaw, which was rejected by two major retailers. 'The irony is that my point of the photo on the album was to show people that the crucifixion of Christ is, indeed, a very violent image,' said Manson, enjoying the game all over again. 'My jaw is missing as a symbol of this very kind of censorship … those offended by my album cover have successfully proven my point.' The corresponding tour saw the Antichrist himself dressed as the Pope, praying beneath huge pictures of Christ, Elvis Presley and Charles Manson – celebrating the 'worship and martyrdom of dead celebrities and criminals', according to Manson. 'There have been some protesters,' he mocked, 'but I have assured everyone that I am a good Catholic Republican.'

In the video of Nine Inch Nails' 'Starfuckers, Inc.', for which he was reunited with old friend Trent Reznor, Manson strolls in full female drag (rather than his usual android androgyny) through a bizarre carnival where a sideshow allows him to pitch baseballs at plates featuring the faces of rock stars like Billy Corgan of the Smashing Pumpkins, Fred Durst of Limp Bizkit, and even Marilyn himself. The vitriol reaches its peak when a portly, slap-painted, ageing prom queen is seen sitting atop a vat marked 'Waste'; this was perceived as an attack on both performers' former friend, Courtney Love. 'Manson said it best; "There's mean, and then this is just brutal," acknowledged Reznor.

Manson was more tolerant of the profane performers who had erupted over the last couple of years of the 20th century. As well as expressing support for the much-despised/much-idolised Eminem, he spoke of the possibility of shows with the masked nine-man oddity called Slipknot.

Slipknot, an obscurely-titled nine-piece band from Des Moines, Iowa, in the American Mid-West, mark the point where American rock music is not only produced for the benefit of a bunch of guys swearing loudly in a sports bar, it has *become* a bunch of guys swearing loudly in a sports bar. Disguised in a variety of grotesque Halloween-style masks – sinister Clown, the Devil, the Gimp from *Pulp Fiction*, Pig, Pinocchio, etc. – this semi-improvisational death metal band came on the scene as the next step beyond, or below, Insane Clown Posse. Renowned more for their extreme antics than their music, features of their performance have included beating themselves beyond the point of injury, setting fire to the stage, vomiting (jars of decomposing animal corpses reputedly kept on hand to aid the process), drinking their own urine and, if the audience gets really lucky, defecating and throwing their feces around the stage.

Slipknot's nihilistic behaviour onstage is an end in itself: 'If we could shoot you with a gun while we were playing, I would,' claims clown-faced drummer Shawn Crahan, whose concept created the band. 'We would blow up the stage and kill ourselves, if we could,' adds vocalist Corey Taylor. 'That's the only logical place we can go.' All of this 'if we could' qualification overlooks the fact that if Slipknot were the nihilist-madmen they pretend to be – rather than the even-tempered nice guys interviewers have claimed they are in person – they would need no one's permission to live out their most extreme impulses.

Their best-selling second album, *Slipknot*, is an apparent howl of pain from the terminally disaffected: 'Fuck it all, fuck this world, fuck everything that you stand for / Don't belong, don't exist, don't give a shit!' 'This pre-packaged angst is very popular,' noted Marilyn Manson, whose material – however meretricious it may sometimes seem – is at least possessed of content. 'They're angry about something, but they're not real clear why. Someone at their record company told them it was a smart thing to do.' Such profane inarticulacy might mean something, if the band were genuinely giving a voice to psychosis, or at least malcontentment. But, as Crahan concedes, he's a happy, well-adjusted family man with a wife and children who decided one day it would be a great idea to start a band – and an even better idea if they got noticed quickly. In the late 1960s and 1970s, Iggy Pop, as frontman of the Stooges, had pushed audience provocation and his own physical endurance to the very limit. It took him to the brink – hospitalisation, a final Stooges concert where the audience threw bottles at him, and a spell in a mental institution. In the early 21st century, bands like Slipknot are trading in behaviour which is more wilfully offensive but never quite as authentically extreme – and signifies nothing, apart from some perverse career move. rock'n'roll, which grows progressively less capable of shocking the mainstream with either form or content, is regurgitating itself. In the case of some of the grosser shock-rock bands, this is less of a metaphor than a literal description.

The all-singing, all-dancing, all-puking, all-defecating Slipknot. Along with cartoon rap bands like Insane Clown Posse and Gravediggaz, Slipknot's world is an insular carnival of excess.

BOYS AND GIRLS
COME OUT TO PLAY

As the 1990s gave way to the new millennium, some of the traditional boundaries were beginning to break down between rock music and its closest cousins. In the USA, the formerly racially segregated genres of hip-hop and heavy metal had begun to merge in a way that seemed unthinkable in the early 1980s; the thrash-metal and revivalist punk genres, too, once strictly the preserve of America's social outcasts, had been infiltrated by the type of laidback dudes who might once have played southern boogie. In the mainstream, the Fugees lit the way for a crossover between hip-hop, r&b, and the less familiar rhythms (to American ears) of Jamaican reggae.

In Britain, there was a more fundamental crossover, although large sectors of the market resisted it. Some artists had set out (in some cases, quite unselfconsciously) to break down the fences that separated the 'trivial' pop performer from 'serious' rock bands, hoping to earn credibility in both quarters. 'I don't think people should ever be ashamed to be incredibly pop and have loads of screaming fans, because it doesn't last forever,' testified Neil Tennant of electro-irony duo the Pet Shop Boys. 'The history of pop stars trying to become credible is littered with Kylie Minogues.'

The Australian bubblegum goddess who travelled from dreary TV soap opera *Neighbours* to pop stardom with eighties hit factory Stock/Aitken/Waterman, Kylie had become associated with the crossover project that may have incurred Tennant's displeasure. (Her supposed search for 'credibility' also took in a nineties album cover that had her looking stern in a pair of old-fashioned glasses: they only served to emphasise her alluring bone structure, and emphasise how spectacles were becoming a fashion accessory.)

Kylie made a bid for 'seriousness' in the the 1995 hit single 'Where the Wild Roses Grow' made with lugubrious songsmith Nick Cave and his band the Bad Seeds. In this folk/country-tinged tale of love and death, the obsessed male narrator, (Cave) bludgeoned in the head of his innocent, besotted female co-narrator, (Kylie) because 'all beauty must die'. Cave had previously recorded a covers album that included MOR standards like Tom Jones' 'Sleeping Anleah' and the Seekers' 'The Carnival Is Over', alongside more 'credible' rock, country and blues classics, and he had been fascinated by the effervescent young fellow Austalian for some time. When they first became acquainted, he persuaded her to appear with him at a

poetry reading where her most famous lyric, Stock/Aitken/Waterman's 'I Should Be So Lucky', was stripped of it's musical backing and recited as straight verse. 'When Nick first planted that seed,' she admitted, 'my first reaction was, "Have you lost your mind?"' Nevertheless, the frothy eighties anthem of wishful thinking underwent a further revision when, post-'Wild Roses', Minogue made a guest appearance with Cave at a concert in London's Royal Albert Hall, equipped with the confidence to sing 'I Should Be So Lucky' stripped of its SAW bounce. The Bad Seeds' melancholia emphasised the wistfulness, and possible defeat, inherent in the song's title.

On the tail of the sweetly unassuming pop star's collaboration with rock's chronicler of the lower depths, the Manic Street Preachers co-wrote her single 'Some Kind of Bliss', and provided a cover version of their own 'I Don't Need Anything'. (As pop-rock revisionists, the formerly furious Manics had also appeared on Christmas TV putting their hearts into a rendition of Wham's syrupy 'Last Christmas'.) When vocalist/guitarist James Dean Bradfield first met the 1980s bop-along queen, he played her an old Tamla Motown song with the compliment, 'This is how I've always heard you.'

The band's fascination with Kylie extended from way back into their cultural Stalinist period, when pop-culture figures were either praised as immortal icons or cursed as useless figures worthy only of death. Sweet little Kylie (as the TV sitcom *Men Behaving Badly* used to describe her) made the former category: unbeknownst to her, she had been sought out to provide backing vocals to the 1991 Manics song 'Little Baby Nothing' (which, several years later, she would cover). At this phase of their career, when the vulnerable Richey Edwards was still part of the line-up, and androgynous clothes and make-up adorned their adolescent features, Nicky Wire had actually been beaten up for wearing that most unmanly of fan accoutrements, a Kylie T-shirt.

'James Dean Bradfield, Nick Cave, I trust them,' Kylie enthused. 'I will just embrace them forever because they embraced my past ... I'm happy to bump into their world from time to time but not to pretend I'm in their world. I'm not, absolutely not.' Despite the appearance of being an innocent abroad, however, Kylie was still a Big Name in the UK, which meant her private life was as subject to speculation as that of any 'wild man of rock': 'Being rushed to hospital to have my stomach pumped: I wasn't even in the country for that one. Anorexia. Heroin. Bisexual, trisexual, XXX film star.' Typically, none of these stories have ever

On the cusp of leaving teenbop stardom and finding a solo career. Robbie Williams, once dismissed as a 'dancer from Take That', lived the dissipating rock'n'roll lifestyle without being a rock'n'roll star.

been verified. But there were still demarcation lines between the imagined misbehaviour of a 'pop star' and the antics of a 'rock star'.

The conflation of celebrity and pseudo-significance was epitomised in the Brit pop-rap band East 17. As innocuous purveyors of danceable pop music, much beloved of very young girls, the band deserved neither too much attention nor too much criticism. They did what they did well enough, and fulfilled an adolescent need. However, such is the distorting effect of celebrity that band lyricist and rapper Tony Mortimer took to speaking from a higher plane. He was extolled as a spiritual 'guru' figure by his white mock-'yo boy' bandmates: 'he's studied all sorts of books, Buddha, spiritualism, shotokan,' enthused goateed vocalist Brian Harvey, apparently unaware that shotokan is a school of martial art. Mortimer depicted himself as a kind of street-mystic. 'I've sold my soul to the devil on the mountain high,' he told fashion magazine *i-D*. 'I've dealt drugs, contemplating suicide every day. I think you have to in this world. [Whether the compulsion is to sell one's soul, deal drugs or contemplate suicide is unclear.] I've … smoked it, sniffed it, swallowed it. I try to give some wisdom back from someone that's been there, done everything and come back with the T-shirt.' Mystic Tony also confessed, 'I used to read [The Book Of] *Revelations* every night and smoke a joint' – his liking for mild hallucinogens and apocalyptic imagery suggesting he missed his true vocation in black metal.

East 17 had made their name with harmless pieces of pap like 'Everybody in the House of Love' and 'Stay Another Day', although the latter, ostensibly an unexceptional love song, was apparently inspired by the suicide of Mortimer's brother. Admired by early teen girls and middle-aged mothers alike, they were caught in an uneasy compromise between the po-faced 'streetwise' image they felt they had to maintain and being British teenybop darlings. (Even their name was an attempted romanticisation of their origins: Walthamstow, London E17, a pleasant district in the north-east of the capital with a mile-long street market and lower-middle class population, was described by them as a 'roughneck area'.) However, despite still boasting of his former drug use, Mortimer went on to show himself to be the polite suburban boy, giving up smoking weed because it was not allowed: 'You know it's going against the law, and I'm not gonna fight the system.'

East 17 were simply another cog in the minor British celebrity scene. Singer Brian Harvey's treatment by the tabloid press was a measure of this: lionised in the *Sunday Mirror* in 1995 as the man who supposedly saved *Eastenders* cast member Daniella Westbrook (then his girlfriend) from cocaine addiction, he was later treated as a penitent 'survivor' for admitting to having dabbled himself, then, after further admissions of drug-taking, vilified as a pariah in a manner which, at least temporarily, put paid to his career. (Despite initial optimism, Daniella Westbrook failed to bring her habit under control. She literally became the poster girl for an anti-drugs campaign after horrific photographs surfaced in 2000 of her face after her septum had been eroded by compulsive snorting that turned her nose

into one big skeletal hole.)

With a police caution for posession of marijuana already behind him, Harvey was to find that laddish boasts of narcotic indulgence were an option reserved only for 'proper' Britpop bands like Oasis. In a radio interview in January 1997, he touched on the subject of ecstasy, the streetname for the popular hallucinogen-amphetamine derivative MDMA. 'I've done pills myself, I done 12 one night, you know what I mean?' he bragged, as casually as if he was at a danceclub. 'If you bang one, you go out, you have a good night and if it brings out the better in someone, then really in the long run, it's a safe pill and it ain't doing you no harm.' Life was 'too short' not to try 'E', he opined.

Harvey's unbridled enthusiasm and choice of substance showed a lack of caution. Though cocaine and speed (in its strongest forms) had proven detrimental effects on physical and mental health, it was ecstasy that was the media's current interest. Since its popularisation on the late eighties acid-house scene, the 'dance drug', or 'hug drug' had become the chemical of choice for upwards of half a million regular users. But, as the drug became increasingly widespread, so the number of casualties grew. Ecstasy occasionally becomes lethal when a user's body – especially that of someone dancing manically under its influence – overheats, and their internal organs literally boil in their blood. (Though, in relative terms of the numbers of people using the drug in the late nineties, such fatalities were rare, they occurred at a regular rate of at least one or two every month.)

In 1996, a girl from Essex named Leah Betts sought to control her body's reaction to ecstasy at her eighteenth birthday party by drinking plenty of water, just as drugs advisory pamphlets suggested. Locked into the repetitious mindset that overtakes users (hence the appeal of house music), she continued drinking until she consumed well over two gallons of water, then fell into a fatal coma. Leah, like many of her MDMA-using peers, was far from the media stereotype of the 'drug taker'. She became the poster girl for an anti-drugs campaign that robbed the word 'ecstasy' of any spiritual or sexual connotations, reinforcing the view of the drug as a game of Russian roulette regularly played by British teenagers. (The rate of ecstasy use also began to stabilise around this time, then gradually to fall, as users and potential users found the drug's side-effects ever harder to ignore.)

It was in this climate that Brian Harvey's naive words were measured. Once the tabloid press got hold of them, their censorious reaction spread to Parliament. The Prime Minister was asked to comment, and the Parliamentary Drugs Misuse Group entered full hellfire-and-brimstone mode: 'It's quite likely youngsters will die by Harvey's words. Those who have resisted this drug may weaken.' The media outrage was overwhelming: 14 regional radio stations banned East 17's records, while Central TV dropped an interview with the band that was to be screened on a children's programme. The rest of the band, suddenly aware that street wisdom is not much of an asset when many of your fans have still to reach puberty, professed themselves aghast at Harvey's attitude. ('Brian Has Virtually Destroyed Us Say E17' ran the headline in *The Sun*.)

Harvey made a self-flagellating attempt to 'get with the programme'. 'It was really stupid of me to spout off,' he announced in a press statement. 'Now that I know more about the deadly dangers of ecstasy, I realise I was completely out of order and am horrified at the thought that anything I could have said could influence anyone. All I'd like to say now,' he sermonised, making a swift 180-degree turn, 'is never take ecstasy – it can kill you.' His admissions of snorting cocaine with Daniella Westbrook had never become such an issue, neither had the 'been there, done that' boasts of Tony Mortimer – or, indeed, Mortimer's bold assertion, just several weeks earlier, 'If someone takes an E they're increasing their love, and that can only be a good thing', which bandmate Harvey was commenting upon when he made his contentious remarks. But despite his words of contrition, he was served the next week with legal papers sacking him from the band. According to a spokesman for the group's label, London Records, 'Tony [Mortimer] felt that if somebody died over the weekend from taking E, he couldn't live with his conscience.'

Such are the hazards of teenypop bands, confused by a world in which 'proper' rock stars boast about their drug intake and still keep their jobs. In the spring of 2001, the media hypocrisy that rules the sanitised world of boy/girl bands bit twice: three male members of insipid teenypop act S Club 7 made the obligatory apology to their fans – 'We regret it very much. We know we have let a lot of people down …' – after being caught sharing a joint in a central London street; Myleene Klass, 22-year-old vocalist of manufactured pop band Hear'Say, was hit by flak for expressing the common opinion that cannabis should be legalised. (Only weeks before, another girl singer auditioning for the same TV pop group was raked over the coals for admitting she once smoked marijuana. Needless to say, she never made the final line-up.) In a booze and drugs-saturated Britain, the tabloid press manufactures headlines that only the most gullible are moved by – most people realising that scandals have to be created, papers have to sell, and that tabloid reporters have lifestyles (and, occasionally, cocaine habits) to support.

'Roughneck' Brian Harvey, who faced charges for assaulting two tabloid photographers soon after his own drugs scandal, is now a sadder, wiser man. As he acknowledges, 'It might as well have been me that gave Leah Betts the pill that killed her.' (Though the unfortunate Ms. Betts died in the year before the E17 'E' scandal.) However, his career may have survived that of multi-face(te)d band guru Tony Mortimer: in the late 1990s, Harvey and the two remaining members had one last hit, promoting their comeback with a radio interview where they got stoned on 'skunk weed'. As the truncated E17 fade into oblivion, Harvey – hair cropped and dyed blonde in the style of hardcore rapper Eminem, who he befriended in New York – now seems set for a 'grown-up' career as a modern r'n'b singer.

Take That, East 17's chart rivals, presented a more clean-cut image, somewhat like a soul-influenced, better-choreographed version of the Osmonds. The most popular member of the group among their predominantly female fans was Robbie Williams. While his bandmate Gary Barlow wrote all the songs, Williams was the singer of two of their biggest hits, 'Everything Changes' and 'Could it be Magic?'. On 17 July 1995, he caused a consternation not heard of since the height of Beatlemania when he announced he was leaving the group 'for my own piece of mind'. The success of Take That can be gauged by Williams' testimony that they had to don police uniforms as disguises to leave a record signing in Manchester, and, only part in joke, entered the centre of Rome in an armoured tank to make a path through the thousands of hysterical fans. When the news of Williams' departure broke, the national tabloids and teen mags received calls from distressed young girls. In Germany, a telephone helpline was set up after one apparently traumatised fan inflicted bodily-harm on herself. 'That is scary', confirmed Williams. 'I'm sat in Tunstall, and it's like a wake at my house because a big divorce has just gone on. And there's protest marches going on about it in Berlin. That is very, very weird. And I'm reading stuff with some girls going, "It's Robbie's fault that girl tried to commit suicide" and they started burning my pictures!'

The band's official press statement suggested that Williams' departure was as much a case of being pushed as of jumping: 'Robbie was unable to give us and the fans the long-term commitment we deserve. It was agreed by all five of us that the best thing to do was for him to leave the band to pursue a solo career.'

In just over six months the whole band would split, in February 1996. The 24-hour helpline services Childline and the Samaritans were put on alert and, for a short period, both helplines were jammed.

In fact, in Take That's insular, homogenised world Robbie Williams had long seemed wilfully out of place – cutting his hair spiky short and dyeing it dirty peroxide blond, and drunkenly socialising with rock bands, particularly Oasis. The *Daily Star* even ran a story suggesting his leaving the group was due to a drug problem, but salvos were immediately fired by the 21-year-old singer's lawyers. While hedonism may not have been the direct cause, Robbie was certainly earning a reputation as a party animal. 'How long can you go on saying you'd not got a girlfriend?' he later bemoaned, 'Yes, I am a eunuch! I am Robbie blond hair action man with a champagne bottle in one hand and a cigarette in the other. No genitalia, though.'

During a solo interview with the gay magazine *Attitude* (Take That never disavowed the gay section of their record-buying audience, despite their clean-cut image), Robbie had spoken bitterly of his colleagues: two fifths of the group (excluding his friend Mark Owen) were 'selfish, arrogant and thick', while unofficial leader Barlow was 'a clueless wanker'. Declining a security accompaniment in attending summer 1995's Glastonbury rock festival ('I think that was the straw that broke the camel's back,' he opined), he met up with a friend who in turn was a friend of Oasis's Gallagher brothers. 'I was a bit apprehensive at first,' he admitted, 'because you read all this stuff about Liam and Noel and the lads, and I was wondering how they were going to take me. But it was top. I walked in and Liam goes, "Take fucking what?" And that was it. I knew we'd have a laugh.' The laughter extended to the audience when Liam pulled Robbie onto the stage during the band's set where, wide-eyed, he went into an unselfconscious, ecstatic dance.

Beginning to live his life by the principle 'Just be a dick and people respect you more for it', when speaking backstage to a journalist from *Select* he went into caricature Gallagher-speak: 'I'm mad for it. I'm always mad for it. I can't find anyone that's mad for it with me. Are you mad for it?' The rumour soon spread that Robbie's first post-Take That gig was likely to be a 'Mancunian supergroup' – though the singer was actually from Stoke-on-Trent – with Noel Gallagher of Oasis and Mani, former bassist of the Stone Roses. Gallagher later had to contact *NME* to disabuse confused fans of the notion that he was writing Robbie's first solo single – which turned out to be a cover of George Michael's 'Freedom' – and that he was responsible for the singer's rift with Take That. With his new friendships, it seemed as if Robbie Williams was intent on tearing down the walls separating rock'n'roll and bubblegum pop.

Williams had developed a talent for genial self-deprecation that detracted from his image as a showbusiness brat. 'When I was sacked,' he later recalled with remarkable candour, 'I wasn't worried about any allegations about anything at all. They could say what they liked about me. Other than I was a flop in bed. Truth to God, I was shitting myself. I thought it would-

280

n't do me any good at all if someone came forward and said, "I had him in Germany and he was crap." The funny thing was, two people sold their story about me, one girl in Germany, one girl in Scotland, and they're the two people in the world that I've ever done good performances with!'

Williams would later engage in a two-year on-off relationship with Nicole Appleton of all-girl band All Saints, at one point being engaged to marry her. He began to live the life of a rock star, trading in his boyish naivety in order to enter the British showbusiness elite. In reality his was an inversion of the rock star career, living it all in reverse: months of drunken stupor, cocaine binges, doomed relationships, weight gain, spells in rehab – all before he managed to put the shadow of his former boy-band behind him and reinvent himself.

Various boy-bands – Boyzone, Westlife (absolutely no relations to Ice Cube's Westlife Connection), Five – tried to take on the mantle of Take That. But Take That's most prominent successors were to be the nineties' female answer to the Monkees, a group whose best-selling records were always secondary to the ingeniously marketed group identity.

The Spice Girls were formed by manager Simon Fuller in the mid-1990s, around the concept of matching disparate personalities. Like characters in a pre-adolescent girl's magazine, five young women were chosen from around the UK to personify an exaggerated persona: Posh Spice (Victoria Adams, a starved, fragile-looking brunette, more Home Counties middle-class than aristocratic); Scary Spice (Melanie Brown, or 'Mel B', a leggy young northern English Amazon of mixed race, less scary than scatty); Sporty Spice (Melanie Chisholm, or 'Mel C', casual, unpretentious, the girl-next-door for the sportswear age); Ginger Spice (Geri Halliwell, a bit risque, with hints of a mildly salacious past, who quit for a solo career in 1998), and Baby Spice (Emma Bunton, blonde ingenue).

From their hugely successful debut, the pop-rap 'Wanna-Be', through subsequent hit singles and albums, the essence of the Spices' success was the identification felt by their young audience. Though their motto, 'Girl Power', seems to have been dreamed up by manager Simon Fuller (and apparently taken from the title of a mid-nineties single by bottle-blonde girl duo Shampoo), he must have felt some surprise when his protegés decided to put it into practice and fire him with a multi-million pound pay-off.

From a young male point of view, the sense that the Spices were the type of young women he might run into in a bar after work made their relative lack of showbiz gloss and glamour appealing. ('We're not the best-looking girls in the world,' Victoria Adams later admitted with disarming modesty, 'we're not the best singers or dancers … ') An anonymous pop song like 'Giving You Everything' was given an edge of 'danger' by its promotional video, featuring the girls posing as wildcat women in the desert in a parody of the sex-and-violence exploitation movie *Faster Pussycat, Kill! Kill!*. (Veteran producer and music business legend Phil Spector quipped, at an awards ceremony, that

THE Sun

Tuesday, December 29, 1998   **28p**   **THOUGHT:** HE'S GOT A SPLITTING HEADACHE

ROBBIE'S XMAS BUST-UP

Drunk star passes out in hotel corridor after row with Nicole

Nicole . . Christmas row with star

By DOMINIC MOHAN and ANDREA BUSFIELD

EXCLUSIVE

THIS is pop hunk Robbie Williams lying drunk in a hotel corridor — after drowning his sorrows to forget a Christmas row with All Saints fiancée Nicole Appleton.

The millionaire star, with tooth-paste and shaving gel smeared in his hair by pranksters, passed out on a sofa after a booze binge.

He had earlier stunned guests by staggering into the hotel bar in the early hours of Boxing Day and telling drinkers about the bust-up.

One said: "Robbie was absolutely slaughtered when he turned up some time after midnight. He said he'd had a *Continued on Page Five*

---

watching a Spice Girls video was like watching a porn movie – only the music in porn movies was better.) In fact, by the time of the release of their own answer to *A Hard Day's Night* or *Help!*, the 1998 *Spiceworld*, satanic shock-rocker Marilyn Manson applauded the Spice Girls as the only other popular music act working on the same grandiose scale as him, creating their own personal universe.

Success on this scale was unlikely to last – but still,

the Spices managed to confound the critics who promised, in the words of the World War I generals, 'It'll all be over by Christmas.' Meanwhile, Posh Spice moved straight into the centre of the British public consciousness via her marriage to England football team player David Beckham, the couple then becoming 'Posh and Becks' to the tabloids. Endless coy conjecture about their sex lives created the apparent myth that David liked nothing better than a little mild transvestism,

281

THE EXPRESS on SATURDAY November 8 1997

MOVING ON: The band have promised fans they still have an exciting future ahead of them despite the shake-up

Spice Girls sack the manager who made them stars

AXED: Simon Fuller

BY ANTHONY MITCHELL

THE SPICE Girls sacked their manager on the day they were voted the best band in the world, it emerged last night.

Simon Fuller, 36, who catapulted the girls to fame, was dealt the blow as the band picked up their MTV award on Thursday in Holland.

Music industry sources believe the girls want to go it alone after raking in £4 million each during a punishing two-year schedule.

Fuller, who has a reputation as a tough businessman, paid tribute to the girls and blamed the split on a "parting of ways". He has netted £4 million from merchandising deals and the band's hits.

The break-up comes at a crucial time for the band, who launched their second album Spiceworld this week and start a world tour next year.

Julian Henry, a spokesman for Fuller's 19 Management, said: "We confirm that there is to be a parting of the ways between the Spice Girls and 19 Management.

"It's been great for us to be a part of the success of the girls over the last two years. This is very much the girls' idea and we wish them the very best of luck in the future."

Fuller is credited with promoting their five No. 1 hits: Wannabe, 2 Become 1, Mama, Say You'll Be There and Spice Up Your Life.

Mr Henry denied the decision had been a shock to the management company but admitted there was "an element of truth" to the claim that the move was made at the MTV ceremony.

"It's been talked about for a few days. It wasn't a big bombshell," he said. "Things come to an end naturally sometimes and the girls are going onwards and upwards.

"They are five very talented, successful, motivated women who knew what they want and Simon is a brilliant manager and the girls are now empowered to go on to new heights."

Fuller, who rarely speaks publicly, moulded the girls into a hugely successful act.

He also lined up lucrative spin-offs such as the girls' sponsorship deals with Walkers Crisps, Pepsi, Impulse deodorant and Polaroid cameras. Last night Fuller, who began his career as a talent spotter at Chrysalis Records, was enjoying a break from the hype surrounding one of the world's most successful bands.

The Spice Girls said in a statement: "We are hugely grateful to 19 Management but we feel in our hearts that this is the right decision for us.

"We would like our fans to know that we are positive and excited about the future."

It was unclear if they had signed up with a new team.

In the past 10 days the Spice Girls have launched the poppy appeal with Vera Lynn, and shared a photocall with Nelson Mandela and the Prince of Wales in South Africa.

Earlier yesterday it was revealed the Queen will be next in line to meet the band.

They are top of the bill for this year's Royal Variety Performance which will also feature singers Celine Dion and Shirley Bassey.

The Spice Girls will be presented to the Queen and the Duke of Edinburgh backstage at London's Victoria Palace Theatre on December 1.

The show, hosted by Des O'Connor will be seen on ITV the following Saturday.

'We feel in our hearts this is the right decision'

The Spice Girls siezed autonomy by sacking manager Simon Fuller, and by 2001, low record sales would prove that 'girl power' had burned out.

SPORTY ON THE BRINK

Mystery as she pulls out of tour

EXCLUSIVE by Ben Todd

THERE are renewed fears for Mel C's health this morning after she dramatically called off her British and Ireland tour with just three days notice.

The official reason for the postponement of the countrywide jaunt is that Mel C is suffering from a "throat infection".

But last night, a source claimed: "Mel is having a really difficult time. It doesn't matter who you are, whether you're rich or poor.

"The plain fact is that if you're depressed you are depressed. It's a very tough time for her."

Prozac

Last autumn, it emerged she'd been suffering from depression. As a result, she was taking Prozac, the powerful anti-depressant drug.

Speaking at the end of November, Mel admitted: "Yes, I have been depressed and I want to stand up to everyone and say, 'I am suffering from depression but it's all right to be depressed.'"

But it was not known exactly how serious the illness was - until now.

Earlier yesterday, Sporty called off her British tour, publicly blaming the throat problems. She had been due to kick off her solo jaunt on Sunday night in Belfast.

The 26-year-old singer issued a statement saying: "I was really looking forward to the tour and I'm sorry to have disappointed my fans but I have to follow doctor's orders and look forward to touring in May."

An announcement naming the exact rescheduled dates in May will follow in the next few weeks.

A spokesman for the singer added: "It's not thought to be serious but doctors have ordered her to rest her voice for the next month so that she does not cause any further damage."

Mel C, who is dating Dan Williams from band Tomcat, was due to play 11 dates beginning on Sunday and ending on February 11.

Last night, a spokesman for Sporty said: "We've spoken to Melanie today. She's in great spirits and had a lovely break over Christmas."

■ AS well as being a cover version, there is more than one reason why top house tune All I Do sounds familiar. The track, by Cleptomaniacs, is a cover of a Stevie Wonder classic and only got the go-ahead when Stevie heard it over the phone. On the original, backing vocals were supplied by none other than

---

on a motorway speeding charge. Victoria denied the accusation, as she also rubbished the more complimentary suggestion that Morton's attentions heralded her as 'the new Princess Diana'.

Minor scandal also focused on the life of Mel B. (Scary), the Spice Girl with the most aggressively sexual image. She entered into a showbiz marriage with black dancer Jimmy Gulzar, who worked as an employee of the group, but they were later estranged in an unedifying display of recrimination: no interest in sex, she accused, making insinuations that the press blew up into a question mark over her partner's sexual orientation; not true, he responded, she's simply become impossible to please in any way at all, sexual or otherwise. While their domestic problems became tabloid property, the Spice Girls' success was still measured by their ability to charm the public into thinking of them simultaneously as everyday 21st century girls and superstars. As Posh put it, 'at the end of the day, [selling] 40,000,000 albums can't be wrong, mate'.

However, the cult of everyday-person-as-major-celebrity they helped propagate started to leave them behind. *Forever*, the Spices' third album, failed to set the tills ringing in the way expected of a major recording act. In media interviews, a depressed Mel C. (Sporty) – already targeted by the press on account of her drinking binges and subject to apparently ill-founded speculation about her sexuality – claimed the girls were not going on tour to promote the album, and

---

borrowing his wife's leather thong to wear as a turn-on before making love.

The couple became a target for herd-mentality football fans, who found their celebrity partnership somehow offensive. ('We've got something in common!', Victoria told Sir Elton John on prime-time TV, because of the football crowd chant, 'Posh Spice takes it up the arse', which was the sort of verbal recognition he enjoyed from rival fans at Watford football club matches.) It reached its nadir when a few semi-retarded louts hollered at her that they hoped her child died of cancer. This show of hate was supposedly repayment for the sin of burdening Beckham's mind with family life, rather than the 'beautiful game'. Further spotlight fatigue came for the Beckhams when Victoria revealed to the press that the police had warned them of a plot to kidnap their baby son, Brooklyn. This was the first of a distressing series of events, which included doctored photos sent through the mail of Victoria and Brooklyn with apparent gunshot wounds to the head. Curiously, the couple's unauthorised biographer Andrew Morton – author of the mildly salacious bestseller *Diana: Her Story* – later accused 'Posh and Becks' of concocting the story of a deranged fan trying to grab their son as they went Christmas shopping at Harrods, to win sympathy for David when he appeared in court that their recent appearance at the MTV Europe Awards may have been their last time onstage together. At the end of 2000, the readers of Brit teenypop magazine *Smash Hits* reinforced her prognosis, voting the Spice Girls the winners in the worst group, worst album, worst single and worst video categories. In March 2001, Mel C insisted that she really had worked with the band for the last time. 'We were such a huge phenomenon, and there's not really anywhere else to go with that', she acknowledged with a tinge of regret. Her words were predictably countered by a band spokesperson the next day – claiming that, no matter how Ms. Chisholm felt, she was in fact still a member of the Spice Girls, although, coincidentally, they had no group plans for the rest of the year.

Meanwhile, as the Spice Girls slowly dissolved, their former member Geri Halliwell stepped up a gear on her unlikely solo career. Starved into the predominant emaciated female shape, tanned and toned, she became increasingly visible as a media 'fag hag' – celebrity accoutrement to a gay culture she was apparently not part of – and close confidante to the increasingly troubled Robbie Williams. Enjoying a minor hit with a 2001 cover of the Weather Girls' 'It's Raining Men', her performance at that summer's family-orientated Party in the [Hyde] Park pop festival made an audacious late attempt to capitalise on lipstick lesbian chic: the lithe Ms. Halliwell surrounded by six leggy brunette dancers who, unconvincingly, licked her armpits rather than her genitalia.

In his new role as rock showman and all-round variety-style entertainer, Robbie Williams could happily parody his own past by including one of Take That's updated Osmonds-style songs, 'Back For Good', in his live show, and turning it into a comical mock-punk thrash. (Gary Barlow, who had lately gone for the same born-again badboy appeal as his old bandmate, was finding it far harder to maintain a core post-Take That audience.) He blurred pop music's demarcation lines twice over by collaborating with ambient dance band the Orb on a track for a cover version tribute to the Bee Gees. ('We did *Top Of The Pops* with Take That,' recalled Alex Paterson of the Orb, 'and we were giving it the football chants and drinking brandy at eleven o' clock in the morning. He [Robbie] said that when he saw us doing that he wanted some of it.') He performed a live cover of the La's 'There She Goes', a favourite of Oasis' – combining Beatle-esque harmonies with lyrics by eccentric Britpop influence John Power, that allude to heroin use. He sampled the voguish soundtrack music of John Barry from the Bond movie *You Only Live Twice*, for incorporation into his 1998 hit 'Millennium'. A teaming-up with Kylie Minogue, post-modernism's favourite pop poppet, for the single 'Kids' seemed in retrospect inevitable. The support act for his autumn 2000 tour was scheduled to be Crispian Mills, late of nouveau psychedelicists Kula Shaker, who asserted that he 'couldn't think of anybody better' to launch his personal comeback with. He was even photographed, apparently a few drinks down the line, with his arms around former Sex Pistols Steve Jones and Paul Cook at a screening of the docu-

mentary about the Pistols' brief, iconoclastic history, *The Filth And The Fury*. (As nonplussed as Cook and Jones appear in the picture, it's hard to imagine them giving the time of day to, say, an ex-member of the Bay City Rollers back in 1977.)

The focus of Robbie Williams' material is life as lived by Robbie Williams, and his friends and enemies in show business ('Singlehandedly raising the economy / Ain't no chance the record company dropping me' runs one typically self-regarding couplet in 'Kids'). Inside this insular environment, he has grown up to become an all-round entertainer version of the rock stars he admires. This playing to both ends of the market has born valuable fruit. In early 1999, after the performer had been nominated for six Brit awards, his success began to wipe out dissent in the mainstream entertainment press. *Mirror* rock and pop journalist Matthew Wright, who had long mocked Williams as a ridiculous 'wanna-be', was forced to recant his heresy by virtue of readers' support for their idol (and possibly by populist editorial diktat). Under the heading, 'Dear Robbie, I'm So Very Sorry (For Everything!)', his *mea culpa* ran, 'I apologise to you, your family … and to music fans.'

Ironically, Williams' wooing of both markets seems to have alienated the first 'real' rock band he ever associated with. To Noel and Liam Gallagher of Oasis, Robbie Williams – or 'tubby-arsed Williams', to call him by their pet name – has long been a moving target for ridicule. (With an old-time variety artist's talent for ingratiation, Williams had acknowledged his own fluctuating weight to the V98 festival crowd – a 'real' rock audience – in Leeds by throwing them a bag of pies to throw right back at him, leading a chant of 'You fat bastard!' 'A woman came up to me in the pub the other day,' he related in an interview as if he was a working man's club comedian, '"Um, hello, me and my friends are having a bet over there that you're Robbie from Take That, but we think you're far too fat …" Straight away I went, "It's funny you should mention that actually, 'cos we were having a bet that you were a model, but we all think you're fucking ugly."')

Noel Gallagher clearly regarded his supposed former friend as a great pretender, calling him 'a fat dancer from Take That'. Williams provoked the situation further by sending a funeral wreath after the release of Oasis's lacklustre third album, the attached message reading, 'Heard the new album, RIP.' The torrent of abuse that flowed back was tediously inevitable. Williams tried to pull the plug on Oasis once and for all, particularly the surly Liam, in a pure showbiz touch befitting a man used to working with choreographers and fitness trainers. At the 2000 Brit Awards, he challenged the leeriest Gallagher to a charity boxing match for a 'purse' of £100,000 each. Panos Eliades, Lennox Lewis' promoter, and Lloyd Honeyghan, former British welterweight boxing champion, both agreed in principle to promote the bout, as long as both amateurs were brought up to fitness requirements and donated their individual purses to charity. British bookies placed Williams at two-to-one favourite.

Liam did not respond with his usual vociferousness. The joint mutterings from him and brother Noel

– that this was childish, that it wasn't what rock'n'roll was all about – gave the impression that one of rock's most obnoxious celebrities was trying to hide between a newly acquired shield of maturity. However, during an MTV interview several weeks later he returned to form: 'He's a fuckin' idiot for a start, right. Now, if he thinks for one minute that I'm gonna get into a boxing ring with him and give the money to charity … I don't believe in blood money', he rationalised, as if it were a major moral issue for him. 'Whenever I meet him, in a club or a disused railway line or anywhere, I'll break his nose for what he said to my brother [insulting the new album] … He'll get a slap when I bump into him, and that'll be the end of that.' Though it seemed as if both sides were making purely theatrical gestures – after all, there was more chance of both men passing insulting messages to each other via their bodyguards – the feud intensified over the following months.

The venue for the next instalment was at the Q magazine awards in London, November 2000. This time there was an added impetus to hostilities: following the collapse of Robbie's relationship with Nicole Appleton, she had, almost poetically, taken up with his Oasis rival. With the Gallagher and Williams parties sitting just a few tables away from each other (Nicole included among the former), as if the organisers were hoping for some impromptu drama, Liam accepted the Best Live Act Award on behalf of Oasis. 'This one's for Robbie,' he announced, looking down at his rival's

Celebrity soap opera: the tabloids had a field day with the feud between Robbie Williams and Liam Gallagher. Threats and challenges filled the air, but the bodyguards still didn't take a day off.

table. 'He stands for the letter Q.' Gallagher later explained his half-baked crack: 'Robbie Williams is a fat poof, man. "Q" is for "Big Queer". I don't mind gays at all, what I mind is gays who offer me out. I don't give a shit about who's gay, I'm a bit gay,' he dissembled, applying homosexuality as a form of abuse but not wanting to fall foul of political correctness. 'But with a fucking dick like that I'll rock his head off.'

Williams, the man who formerly offered to take his rival on in full view of the media, fell silent. His opponent was on a roll, however. Motioning to Williams' table, shouting over abuse, Liam found a particularly soft target when recent Robbie collaborator Kylie Minogue took the podium to present an award. 'Get your tits out, you lesbian, and write your own songs!' hollered the professed lover of gay people who – as Johnny Rotten once tried to remind him – has never written a single song in his life. Kylie did her best to ignore the 'witticisms', while Robbie stalked off to the balcony area in a silent rage, murmuring only, 'I fucking hate that twat.'

Robbie Williams' capitulation to Liam Gallagher personified one strand of showbusiness trying to claim pre-eminence over the other. Williams, the all-round entertainer, wanted to make a family event out of their spat, fighting by Marquess of Queensbury rules and using his dancer's suppleness to make an example of the loud-mouthed Manc. But Liam was playing by rock 'n' rules, where the leeriest mouth ultimately carries the day. 'He's been mouthing off about me,' he explained afterward, 'but when he's sitting in the same room he shuts his mouth … I'm not in the school playground anymore, I'm in real life. I'm a real man. Why didn't he get up there and offer me out for the £200,000

ROBBIE
In the blue corner, Williams is flanked by more "people" than a prize fighter

LIAM
He turns up, guns blazing, to pick up Best Live Act award for his "dead" band

Liam & Robbie: the full story

While Liam ranted, Robbie kept a dignified silence at last week's Q Awards. But behind the scenes he admitted he "hated" Liam and mocked him onstage the next night…

FOR A MOMENT AT THE Q awards last week, it looked like we might finally see the much-hyped fight between the wild man of rock and the king of pop take place. Robbie Williams bristled at Liam's taunts of "Queer" and "Fat boy", and looked seconds

away from launching himself at the Oasis star.
It was the first public confrontation for the feuding frontmen since their verbal spat began, after Noel Gallagher called Robbie "a fat dancer from Take That" in a *heat* interview, and Williams replied by

sending a wreath bearing the words, "Heard the new album, RIP".
The Gallaghers and Robbie were sat just tables apart at the awards. Liam picked up the Best Live Act Award with Oasis. He told guests, "This one's for Robbie. He stands for

the letter Q."
Later, Liam spelt out what he meant, telling *heat*, "Robbie Williams is a fat poof, man. 'Q' is for 'Big Queer'. I don't mind gays at all, what I mind is gays who offer me out. I don't give a shit about who's gay, I'm a bit gay, yes I am. Try being gay –

it's good! But with a fucking dick like that I'll rock his head off."
Publicly, at least, Robbie wasn't taking the bait. Collecting the award for Classic Songwriting moments later, Robbie stepped up to the mike with a flicker of a smile as the crowd

fight? I would have gone up there and battered his head all over the piano.'

'Real life', as experienced by Liam Gallagher since his early twenties, has consisted of a largely adulatory rock music industry, the protection of security staff, and awards events like the one at which he humiliated his erstwhile friend. Still, he knows the game well enough to know that in rock'n'roll tradition it's the *appearance* of possessing street smarts that has always counted, the *impression* of wildness, at which he beats the new boy hands down. At a live performance at London's Docklands Arena the following night, Williams made a perfunctory attempt to satirise Gallagher – 'So I thought, "What does Q stand for? Quite simply bigger than Oasis? ... Quite simply Nicky [Appleton] would prefer to sleep with Robbie every time?"' – but it sounded desperate. Particularly in the light of the subsequent announcement that Nicole Appleton was expecting Liam's child, and that the reputedly besotted pair were looking forward to parenthood.

(Their son Gene was born in early July 2001. He is Liam's third child, after his daughter Molly, conceived with singer Lisa Moorish in the first week of his marriage to Patsy Kensit, and his son with Ms. Kensit – the unfortunately-named Lennon, victim of the 'lad culture's' reverence toward the ex-Beatle and hippie-hypocrite. Gallagher celebrated the birth of his second son at a nearby London pub, allegedly playing to type by pushing a camera into a middle-aged photographer's face and bloodying his nose.)

Speculation about Williams' well-being continued apace in the media: he was being treated for the Hollywood disease of 'sex addiction'; his drink problem had returned. Certainly he did nothing to dispel this when he appeared at that autumn's MTV Europe awards – offering no further challenges to the ever-present Gallagher, but seeming on the verge of collapse. (Again, Williams blamed exhaustion, but one attendee claimed the singer had downed approximately 20 double measures of vodka – straining credulity, as the same basic volume of alcohol killed John Bonham of Led Zeppelin outright.) In the week that followed he meekly offered his best wishes for the future of his ex-girlfriend and her man, with no abusive response given in return. But the air of fragility that surrounds Robbie Williams is less evocative of rock'n'roll than it is of every showbiz performer who ever lived a life entirely within the industry's airless bubble, from Judy Garland on down. Reputedly weak and agitated, he entered the year 2001 in a state of sobriety – the latest episode of his recurring battle with cocaine. Like much of the pop music industry, and many binge drinkers, Williams has a fatal attraction toward the drug that provides exhilaration while hastening total burn-out. Also like much of the industry, he has nothing good to say about the chemical he has been only too willing to spend his money on. 'I wish they'd never invented it', he avows, sniffily. 'It makes you do anything to get it and you end up in horrible situations with horrible people.' His remedy was, in traditional rock'n'roll style, to pass the responsibility for his excesses on to other people: 'Anyone who does

The leeriest mouth wins the day: Liam Gallagher with his partner Nicole Appleton. The All Saints singer was formerly the girlfriend of Gallagher's humiliated rival, the visibly fragile Robbie Williams.

drugs on my tour gets the sack. So if I get drunk and ask anyone, they won't have any drugs.' With a modernised family entertainer ethos, and a background in a manufactured pop band, Robbie Williams has acquired all the trappings of the rock star. He may yet survive the industry's pace if he keeps reminding himself that, even at best, it's only rock'n'roll.

Meanwhile, as superstar performers bicker over which of them is the 'real' rock star, new forms of musical self-expression are found in the most esoteric quarters: in collaborations between country artists and folk-rockers; in recording studios where the dance-psychedelia hybrid called 'trip-hop' is created; even in the sonic experiments of the most obscure black metal bands. We live in an age where traditional rock'n'roll, with its voice/guitar/bass/drums line-up, is merely another strand of showbusiness, however much it protests otherwise. But its ambition should remain the same as it always has been: despite all the grand follies of vanity, excess, ego, and, occasionally, tragedy, the greatest effect any form of popular music can have is to create a momentary shiver down the listener's spine, and, for one moment, to touch upon emotions that remain otherwise inaccessible.

ACKNOWLEDGEMENTS

There are many thanks to be made, not least to the numerous writers and critics whose books, articles and interviews have provided me with invaluable insights and source-material. It is a measure of my indebtedness that I must forbear to mention each and every name and that I may omit one or two of the more general or less significant books or publications that I consulted while preparing this book. Space is just too limited to allow a comprehensive listing.

Among the periodicals I found most useful, I should like particularly to acknowledge *Rolling Stone*, the *New Musical Express, Melody Maker, Sounds, Crawdaddy, Creem* and *Circus* - these have been a fund of useful interviews and thought-provoking comment. It is appropriate that I should express my immense gratitude to the staff of the British Newspaper Library at Colindale and the *Daily Express* cuttings library in Fleet Street. Particularly helpful newspapers have been the London *Sunday Times*, the London *Observer*, the *Daily Mail*, the *News of the World*, the *Los Angeles Times* the *New York Times* and the *San Francisco Chronicle*. Specifically, I would also like to thank the following newspapers and magazines for their permission to reproduce cuttings from past issues: *The Sun*, the *Daily Mail*, the *Evening News*, the *Daily Mirror*, the *London Times*, the *Evening Standard*, the *New York Times*, the *New York Daily News*, the *Sunday People, Newsweek, Q, Select, Metal Hammer*, the *Sunday Telegraph*, the *Observer*, the *Sunday Times*, the *News of the World*, *Sunday Magazine, Globe Hebdo, Today*, the *Evening Standard*, the *Mirror*, the *Mail on Sunday, New Musical Express, Melody Maker*, the *Guardian, The Independent*, the *Daily Express, The Face, the Daily Star* and *Heat*.

Writing this book would have been considerably harder without the previously published work of the following authors and editors: Robert Santelli (Aquarius Rising); Steve Chapple and Rebee Garofalo (Rock'n'Roll is Here To Pay); Jerry Hopkins (The Rock Story, Elvis and Elvis: The Final Years); Jim Miller (ed. The Rolling Stone Illustrated History of Rock'n'Roll); Ellen Sanders (Trips); Tom Wolfe (The Electric KoolAid Acid Test); Michael Lydon (Rock Folk and Boogie Lightning); Jonathan Eisen (ed. The Age of Rock I and II and Twenty-Minute Fandangos and Forever Changes); Albert Goldman (Elvis); Simon Frith (The Sociology of Rock); David Dalton (Janis and The Rolling Stones - The First Twenty Years); Tony Sanchez (Up and Down With The Rolling Stones); Dave Marsh (Born To Run); Phil Hardy and Dave Laing (eds. The Encyclopedia of Rock); Steve Turner (Conversations With Eric Clapton); Hunter Davies (The Beatles); Philip Norman (Shout); Geoffrey Stokes (The Beatles); John Blake (All You Needed was Love); Fred and Judy Vermorel (The Sex Pistols); R. Serge Denisoff (The Sounds of Social Change); Bev Bevan (The Electric Light Orchestra); John Goldrosen (Buddy Holly); Ian Hoare (ed. The Soul Book); John Pidgeon (Rod Stewart and the Faces); Curtis Knight (Jimi Hendrix); Jenny Fabian and Johnny Byrne (Groupie); David Leaf (The Beach Boys and The Californian Myth); Michael Cable (The Pop Industry Inside Out); Greil Marcus (Mystery Train); Virginia Boston (Shockwave) and Tony Palmer (Born Under a Bad Sign).

It should go without saying that any mistakes, misconceptions and misjudgements included in this book are entirely my own responsibility - however, I should like to thank John Pidgeon, John Tobler, Phil Hardy, Dave Laing, Penny Valentine, Frances Kennett and Richard Barber, all of whom in various ways helped with the original research of this book. I would also like to thank Lisa Hardy, Sue Holland, Debbie Geller, Fran Pelzman, Thaddeus O'Sullivan, Bob Ughetti and Jonathan Read for their help in researching visual material. Thanks are also due to Barry Plummer, Terry Norman of London Express Features, John Halsall at LFI, Steven James of Flicks, Joe Canale at Wide World, Colin Crawford of Syndication International, Simon Crocker at The Kobal Collection, Tony Gale of Pictorial Press and Lynn Facey at Record Mirror for assistance with photographs. Special thanks are due to Jim Marshall for his co-operation in supplying his copyright photographs featured on pages 4, 36, 38 and 121, and to all the following who have supplied photographs elsewhere in the book: All Action, Alpha, Associated Press, John Beecher, Camera Press, Chet Flippo, Gamma, Bob Gruen, Dan Hardy, Famous, John Frost Newspapers, Keystone Press Agency, Scarlett Borg at *Kerrang*, Laurie Lewis, MPL Communications, No Limit Records, Nothing/Interscope Records – a Universal Music Company, Denis O'Regan, Polydor, Popperfoto, Neal Preston, Chuck Pulin, Retna, Rex Features, S.l.N., Shep Sherbell, Joseph Sia, Carter Smith, *Sounds*, Syndication International, Allen Tannenbaum, Virginia Turbett, UPI, Burk Uzzle, Virgin Records, WEA, Michael Weinstein, Valerie Wilmer and Michael Zagaris. It has not been possible in all cases to trace the copyright sources, and my publishers would be glad to hear from any such unacknowledged copyright holders.

I would also like to express my gratitude to Harvey Weinig, Alice Morey and Sue Cochrane for specialist assistance; to John Parker for support; to Robin Allen for his design; to Sandra Wake and Terry Porter at Plexus; and, especially, to my editor Nicky Adamson, without whom …

I must add Richard Woodcock to the list of people whose help has been invaluable. Like the others, however, he should in no way be held responsible for the contents of the book. I toyed with the idea of changing the dedication - on the grounds that while a disturbing number of friends had absented themselves from my life since the first edition, those who remain deserve one's attention more. But, 'absent friends' it stays . . .

Index of Names